DOCTOR WHO

THE
EIGHTIES

First published in 1996 by
Doctor Who Books
an imprint of Virgin Publishing Ltd
332 Ladbroke Grove
London W10 5AH

ISBN: 1 85227 680 0

Cover and internal layout
designed by Mark Stammers Design, London

Printed and bound in Great Britain by
Jarrold Books Limited, Norfolk

Certain Photographic illustrations

© BBC Photographs, © Colin Lavers, © Rosalind Ebbutt, © Dee Robson, © Ken Trew, Peter Pegrum, © Fiona Cumming, © John Black, © Mike Tucker, © Neal Simpson, © John Rendle, © Pat Godfrey, © Dee Baron, © Tony Masero, © Richard Bignall, © Steve Cook, © Sue Moore.

Acknowledgements

No factual book of this nature is produced in complete isolation, and over the years we have been indebted to a large number of people who have given their time to speak to us and to share their knowledge of *Doctor Who*. We would like to thank in particular the following:

Anthony Ainley, Sophie Aldred, Robert Allsopp, Mark Ayres, Colin Baker, Dee Baron, Keith Barnfather and Reeltime Pictures, Richard Bignell, David Brunt and the DWAS Reference Department, Nicola Bryant, Stephen Collins, Chris Crouch, *DWB*, Chris DeLuca, Michael J. Doran, Rosalind Ebbutt, David Gibbes-Auger, Pat Godfrey, Kay Green and everyone at the BBC Records Management Centre, Simeon Hearn, Richard Hollis and Alex Lindsay at BBC Licensing, Antony Howe, Rosemary Howe, Jean-Marc Lofficier, Stephen Mansfield, Sylvester McCoy and Paul Casey of Silvester Management, Susan Moore, Sydney Newman, Phil Newman, Andrew Pixley, Marc Platt, Steve Preston, Tim Robins, Nigel Robinson, Gary Russell, David Saunders, Eric Saward, Paul Scoones of New Zealand's *Time Space Visualiser* (especially David Bishop for the original interview with Andrew Cartmel), Andrew Skilleter, Joan Stribling, Mike Teague, Ken Trew, Mike Tucker, Doug Vermes, Alan Wareing, Gary Gillatt and *Doctor Who Magazine*, Martin Wiggins, Graeme Wood.

Especial thanks to Paula Moore for speaking to us about *Attack of the Cybermen* and to anyone else we may have inadvertently missed. All your help and enthusiasm is greatly appreciated.

As with our previous books that have looked at *Doctor Who* in the eighties, we approached John Nathan-Turner, who was producer during that decade, to request his personal recollections. Unfortunately he was ultimately unable to give them.

Continued thanks to Peter and Bex, without whom.

David J. Howe
Mark Stammers
Stephen James Walker

For Claire Chaubert – SJW

For Sunita Rastogi with love and thanks – DJH

For Kiri with love – MS

Introduction

By the close of the seventies, *Doctor Who* had been in continuous production for some seventeen seasons, making it the longest-running science fiction series in the world – and one of the longest-running television dramas of any description. It had achieved the status of a well-loved national institution in its home territory of the UK, where many families continued to follow a happy weekly ritual of gathering around the TV set at teatime on a Saturday evening to witness the latest exploits of the good Doctor and his friends in their battles against the evils of the universe. Overseas, too, it continued to entertain audiences in a large number of different countries – perhaps most notably the USA, where since 1978 it had enjoyed a considerable upsurge in popularity.

The Doctor himself had now appeared in four different incarnations, portrayed first by William Hartnell as a kind-hearted but sometimes tetchy grandfather figure with flowing white hair and Edwardian clothes; secondly by Patrick Troughton as an impish, dark-haired character, scruffily dressed in an old frock coat and baggy checked trousers; thirdly by Jon Pertwee as a dashing man of action with silver hair and a deeply-lined face, elegantly attired in frilly shirt and velvet jacket; and lastly by Tom Baker as a wild-eyed bohemian with dark, curly hair and a toothy grin, sporting a battered felt hat and a long, multicoloured scarf. He had been joined by numerous companions on his journeys around the universe in his time and space vessel the TARDIS – 'borrowed' from his fellow Time Lords of the planet Gallifrey – and come up against a whole host of adversaries, ranging from the villainous to the downright monstrous.

The series had also given rise to a whole host of spin-off merchandise, much of it featuring the

The first Doctor (William Hartnell).

The second Doctor (Patrick Troughton).

PRODUCTION TEAMS

BBC production teams in the eighties generally consisted of a producer and a script editor, supported by a production associate (known as production unit manager until 1980) and a secretary. The producer would have overall artistic and financial responsibility for the show, liaising with the various service departments and overseeing the work of individual directors and crews brought in to handle particular episodes or stories, while the subordinate script editor would find and work with writers to provide the scripts. The production associate would look after the programme's finances on a day-to-day basis, while the secretary would carry out normal secretarial functions, including dealing with mail received from members of the public.

COMMISSIONING SCRIPTS

In a number of places in this book, reference is made to script editors commissioning scripts, storylines or other material from writers. This is a simplification of the BBC's procedures. Having asked a writer to carry out a particular assignment, the script editor would in fact brief the Copyright Department formally to commission the work. Where commissioning dates are given in the text, these refer to the dates when the script editor briefed the Copyright Department.

SEASONS

*When discussing **Doctor Who's** history, fans and media researchers generally divide it up into a number of separate seasons, each corresponding to a regular run of episodes in the original UK transmission sequence. This book follows the standard convention.*

LOCATIONS

*In the eighties, location work for **Doctor Who** was relatively common. There is unfortunately insufficient room in a book of this scope to list in detail all the locations used. For each story we have therefore generally indicated just the main location areas visited. Up to and including season twenty-two, location shooting was normally done – as in the past – on 16mm film. From season twenty-three onwards, however, it was invariably done on videotape using lightweight OB (Outside Broadcast) cameras.*

PRODUCTION BASE

*Throughout the 1980s the **Doctor Who** production office remained in Union House, a BBC-owned building overlooking Shepherd's Bush Green in west London. It moved from Room 505 to Rooms 203 and 204 at the close of the 1970s and then to Rooms 303 and 304 at the end of 1984. The making of the series continued to be based around the BBC's various premises and facilities in the west London area. All studio recording was done at Television Centre, a large, torus-shaped complex of administrative offices and production studios in White City. Film inserts continued to be shot at the BBC's Television Film Studios in Ealing until their use was abandoned in 1983, while model work and other visual effects sequences were carried out in a variety of places, including Visual Effects Department premises and outside facilities such as Peerless Studios. Rehearsals almost invariably took place at the BBC's Rehearsal Block in North Acton.*

The third Doctor (Jon Pertwee).

The fourth Doctor (Tom Baker).

ever-popular Daleks; spawned a number of different fan organisations, including in 1976 the *Doctor Who* Appreciation Society; been the focus of several exhibitions, including two permanent displays at Longleat and Blackpool respectively; and even inspired two cinema feature films – *Dr Who and the Daleks* (1965) and *Daleks' Invasion Earth 2150 A.D.* (1966), both starring Peter Cushing as the Doctor – and two West End stage productions – *The Curse of the Daleks* (1965) and, with Trevor Martin in the lead role, *Doctor Who and the Daleks in Seven Keys to Doomsday* (1974).

As its seventeenth season drew to a close, however, *Doctor Who* stood on the verge of a new era. Perhaps most significantly, it was about to acquire a new producer, who would remain in that post throughout the whole of the following decade, giving him an unprecedented degree of influence over the series' content and development. The eighties would also see *Doctor Who* facing unparalleled external pressures, including some formidable opposition from the rival ITV network in the increasingly important competition for high ratings and, at times, a considerable degree of hostility from within the upper echelons of the BBC itself.

The story of *Doctor Who's* first six seasons is covered in *Doctor Who – The Sixties* and that of the following eleven in *Doctor Who – The Seventies*. In this volume, we recount what happened during the years 1980 to 1989, when the Doctor concluded his fourth incarnation and then appeared in relatively rapid succession as a youthful, fair-haired man dressed in period cricketing attire; an unpredictable, tousle-mopped maverick with twinkling eyes and a garish, multicoloured coat; and a lively fellow with dark hair and a faint Scots accent, sporting a paisley-patterned scarf and a question-mark pullover and brolly.

We look at the changes in format, production style and transmission slot that saw *Doctor Who* attaining some new highs and lows of popularity; recall the variety of behind-the-scenes storms that beset the series before its eventual cancellation as a traditional BBC production at the end of the decade; detail the careers of the actors who portrayed the Doctor in his fifth, sixth and seventh incarnations; examine the wealth of *Doctor Who*-related merchandise produced during this decade; describe the third stage play inspired by the series; and chronicle the continued growth of fan interest.

Join us on another trip back in time, to relive, remember and, above all, enjoy a little slice of TV history.

DJH, MS and SJW

CHAPTER ONE

Dawn of a New Era

octor Who had been beset by numerous problems during the late seventies, and its then producer Graham Williams had repeatedly requested the appointment of an associate producer to take some of the workload off his shoulders. It had seemed to him that this would be an ideal promotion for production unit manager John Nathan-Turner, who during his stint on the series had shown considerable skill in managing the budget and been involved in many important decisions. These requests had all been turned down, however, and Williams had eventually decided that it was time to move on and let someone else take over. Script editor Douglas Adams had already made known his intention to depart at the conclusion of work on the series' seventeenth season, so it would be a completely new production team that would take *Doctor Who* into the eighties.

Around August 1979, the month in which he finally made his decision to leave, Williams suggested to Head of Serials Graeme McDonald – his immediate superior – that Nathan-Turner would be the obvious choice to succeed him. McDonald agreed with the principle of appointing a PUM as producer, but decided to offer the job to Nathan-Turner's predecessor George Gallaccio, who had already gained a year's experience as a producer on the BBC Scotland supernatural thriller series *The Ωmega Factor*. Gallaccio, however, declined. 'When Graeme McDonald offered me the job of producing *Doctor Who* in 1979 I had to say no,' he explained in 1990. 'I felt I wanted to work more on the artistic than the technical side of

TERRANCE DICKS
WRITER

*Born in East Ham, London, in 1935, Terrance Dicks was educated at the local grammar school and went on to read English at Downing College, Cambridge. After two years' national service in the army, he got a job as an advertising copywriter. This lasted for five years, during which time he started writing radio scripts as a sideline. Eventually he switched to full-time freelance writing, first on plays and comedy series for radio and then in television on programmes including **The Avengers** and **Crossroads**. Following some five years as script editor on **Doctor Who**, during which period he also co-created and script edited **Moonbase 3**, he returned in 1974 to a freelance writing career. Later he produced some of the BBC's classic serials. Aside from his contributions to the **Doctor Who** TV series, including the eighties stories **State of Decay** and **The Five Doctors**, he has written two spin-off plays – **Doctor Who and the Daleks in Seven Keys to Doomsday** in 1974 and **Doctor Who – The Ultimate Adventure** in 1989 – and well over fifty novelizations. He has also written several original **Doctor Who** novels for Virgin's **The New Adventures** range. Today he is, amongst his other writing projects, one of the UK's most prolific authors of children's fiction.*

Out-going producer Graham Williams.

New producer John Nathan-Turner.

JOHN NATHAN-TURNER
PRODUCER

*John Nathan-Turner was born and brought up in the Midlands. As a boy he acted in numerous school plays and revues and appeared as an extra in several TV series, including **The Newcomers** and **United!** for the BBC and **Crossroads** for ATV. By the time he reached the sixth form his interests had widened to encompass producing, directing and writing. On leaving school he turned down the offer of a university place in order to pursue a theatrical career. A short spell as stage manager in a nightclub led to a post as assistant stage manager at Birmingham's Alexandra Theatre. Later, during a period of unemployment as an actor, he filled in for a couple of months with a job in the Costume Department at the BBC's Gosta Green studios, where he gained an interest in television production. He was working as a senior stage manager and actor at the Everyman Theatre in Chelmsford when an acquaintance suggested that he apply to the BBC in London for a general exploratory interview. He did so, and shortly afterwards was taken on as a floor assistant. It was in this capacity that he first worked on **Doctor Who**, being assigned to **The Space Pirates** in season six, **The Ambassadors of Death** in season seven and **Colony in Space** in season eight. He remained at the BBC throughout the 1970s, gaining successive promotions to assistant floor manager, production assistant and production unit manager. It was in the latter capacity that he was again assigned to **Doctor Who**, handling the series' budget during seasons fifteen, sixteen and seventeen. He took over as producer from season eighteen in 1979 and remained in that post until the BBC discontinued making the series a decade later. Since 1990 he has maintained contact with the **Doctor Who** world, producing some special releases for BBC Video in 1991 and 1992 and **Dimensions in Time** for the BBC's **Children in Need** telethon in 1993, while also pursuing a variety of other projects.*

Tom Baker in his re-designed costume.

television.' Nathan-Turner was therefore invited to become producer. He accepted, and formally took over the reins around the beginning of November 1979. Williams and Adams subsequently marked their departure with a farewell party held on 14 December 1979 in one of the basement conference rooms at the BBC's Television Centre.

McDonald himself was in the process of changing jobs during the latter part of 1979. The Serials Department had been merged with the Series Department in the first major reorganisation of the BBC's Drama Group to have taken place since 1963, and he had been appointed to head the new, larger Department thus created. Realising that his increased responsibilities would leave him less time than in the past to devote to individual series, and mindful also of Nathan-Turner's inexperience in his new post, he decided to appoint former *Doctor Who* producer Barry Letts as executive producer for season eighteen. This in essence simply formalised and expanded an arrangement that had been operating informally since part-way through production of season sixteen, when – initially to help out while Williams was incapacitated for a time with a broken leg – Letts had been given a 'watching brief' over the series.

Letts's executive producer role, which would not officially begin until around the second week of June 1980, basically entailed his offering comments on scripts, giving advice and approving major production decisions – in short, taking over the supervisory function normally performed by the head of department.

An early priority for Nathan-Turner and Letts at the end of 1979 was to find a new script editor to replace Adams. Their first choice was writer and poet Johnny Byrne, whom Nathan-Turner knew from his work on *All Creatures Great and Small*, but Byrne declined the offer, partly because he was disinclined to relocate from Norfolk to London. Also considered was writer Ted Rhodes, but this too came to nothing. Nathan-Turner had meanwhile sought the advice of a number of colleagues at the BBC, and former *Doctor Who* writer Robert Banks Stewart, now working as producer of the detective series *Shoestring*, suggested journalist and scriptwriter Christopher H. Bidmead as a promising candidate. Bidmead too was initially reluctant to accept the job, considering that *Doctor Who* had abandoned its factual science roots and become 'very silly'. He was persuaded, however, after discovering that Nathan-Turner and Letts shared his concerns and wanted to return to the more serious style of earlier eras.

Bidmead began working on the series in December 1979 and formally took up post at the beginning of the following month. With all members of the new production team then in place, preparations began in earnest for the forthcoming season.

One problem requiring urgent attention was a dearth of scripts ready for production. A number of four-part stories lined up by Williams and Adams for possible use in season seventeen or, after further development, in season eighteen had ultimately come to nothing. These included a Pennant Roberts-written science fantasy tale known first as *Dragons of Fear* and then as *Erinella*, the scripts for which had been commissioned on 10 January 1979; a John Lloyd idea with the working titles *Shylock* and *The Doomsday Contract*, the scripts for which had been commissioned on 7 February 1979 from a different writer, Allan Prior, after Lloyd's continued involvement had been vetoed by the BBC's Light Entertainment Department due to his existing commitments on their *Not the Nine O'Clock News* show; and an Alan Drury submission entitled *The Tearing of the Veil*, the scripts for which had been commissioned on 2 April 1979. Other, more tentative ideas, including *Valley of the Lost* by former producer Philip Hinchcliffe and *The Secret of Cassius* by Andrew Smith, had also failed to bear fruit. As Bidmead recalled in 1986, there was in fact only one script still in reserve at the point when he arrived:

'I read this script with great care, which you had to do because it was typed in single spacing right across the page like a novel. I gather it was written by a professional writer, but that didn't show. It was a kind of whimsical Victorian story, but it was quite unworkable as a script.

'We did also have a David Fisher story, which had been commissioned by John before I joined, and that was the only one on the shelf that we were committed to doing. But it had been commissioned before we hammered out the new principles of scientific integrity and it did contain a lot of silliness. This wasn't David's fault – he was picking up on the previous season. So he had to do a great deal of rewriting.'

Fisher's story had been commissioned on 20 December 1979 under the working title *Avalon* and was based on a scenario supplied by Nathan-Turner himself. Of the other extant material, only one idea was thought by Nathan-Turner and Bidmead to be suitable for use. This was a Terrance Dicks-written vampire tale known first as *The Witch Lords* and then as *The Vampire Mutation*, which would have been produced as the opening story of season fifteen had it not been vetoed at the last minute by BBC management to avoid it clashing with a prestigious adaptation of *Dracula* that was then in the works. A revised storyline had been commissioned by Nathan-Turner on 13 December 1979, and Dicks was given the go-ahead to write the full scripts early in 1980. These were subsequently developed under the new working title *The Wasting*.

Seasons of *Doctor Who* had for some years been generally subdivided into five four-part stories and one six-part story, but Nathan-Turner was now keen to dispense with the six-parters as he felt that they rarely held up over their full length. He managed to persuade his superiors to give season eighteen an extra two slots so that it could instead be subdivided evenly into seven four-parters. With Fisher and Dicks commissioned to provide one apiece, a further five stories would therefore be required in order to make up the season's full complement. This requirement would be by no means easy to meet, as Bidmead quickly realised:

'I turned to the production heads and said, "Please can we have the file index on all our writers and I'll get busy ringing them up and talking to them." They turned round and said, "What file index?" The horrific thing was that we'd inherited no list of writers at all. Nobody had collected any views on the work available, we didn't know who was around and all we had to go on were the

Executive producer Barry Letts.

existing scripts. And of course I didn't actually want to use the writers from the previous season.

'I first approached writers of the calibre of Nigel Kneale, but the last thing they wanted to do was our show – partly because it was so old, and high-calibre writers are really interested only in first-series stuff, and partly because of the reputation the show had achieved in previous seasons for input and rewriting from the actors. So I then scraped around in the back of my memory.'

Bidmead sent to all prospective contributors a copy of a document that he had prepared under the heading *Doctor Who: Notes for New Writers*. Building on an earlier note by Adams, this summarised the basic format of the series but emphasised its new, more serious direction. Submissions soon began to arrive on Bidmead's desk, and those that he considered promising were pursued further during the early months of 1980.

These submissions included: *Sealed Orders* by Christopher Priest (scene breakdown (SB) commissioned 27 February, scripts (S) 24 March); *Meglos* by John Flanagan and Andrew McCulloch (SB 29 February, S approximately a week later); *The Planet that Slept* by Andrew Smith (exact commissioning dates currently unknown); *Mark of Lumos* by Keith Miles (story outline commissioned 14 March); *The Dream Time* by Steve Gallagher (SB 17 March, S 14 April); *Mouth of Grath* by Malcolm Edwards and Leroy Kettle (SB 18 March); *Farer Nohan* by Andrew Stephenson (SB 18 March); *The Keeper of*

BARRY LETTS
EXECUTIVE PRODUCER

*Barry Letts started his career as an actor. He began in repertory in York whilst also working for a local radio station in Leeds. After a chance meeting with BBC producer/director Rex Tucker, he started working with him first on radio and then on television. His first television appearance was in a 1950 production of **Gunpowder Guy**, about Guy Fawkes. He eventually decided he wanted to go into directing and in 1967 attended the BBC directors' course. He worked on episodes of **Z Cars** and **The Newcomers** before directing the six-part **Doctor Who** story **The Enemy of the World** in 1967. He became producer of **Doctor Who** in 1969 and remained in that post until 1974. During this period he also co-created and produced the six-part BBC science-fiction drama series **Moonbase 3**, transmitted in 1973. After leaving **Doctor Who** he marked time for a while by acting as an assistant of sorts to department head Ronnie Marsh. He then decided to make a return to directing and approached various producers for work. One of the assignments he landed was **The Android Invasion** for **Doctor Who** in 1975. Straight after that came a production of **The Prince and the Pauper** for John McCrae. However, McCrae was promoted to Head of Drama for a New Zealand TV station, so Letts was asked to take over as producer of the classic serials on BBC1. Amongst those for which he was responsible were **Rebecca of Sunnybrook Farm** (1978), **The Mill on the Floss** (1979) and **The Old Curiosity Shop** (1980). Following his stint as **Doctor Who**'s executive producer at the beginning of the eighties he continued to work as a director, particularly on the classic serials. More recently he has written and novelised two **Doctor Who** radio serials, **The Paradise of Death** and **Doctor Who and the Ghosts of N-Space**, both starring Jon Pertwee.*

CHRISTOPHER H. BIDMEAD
SCRIPT EDITOR

Christopher Hamilton Bidmead was born in 1941. He trained as an actor at the Royal Academy of Dramatic Arts (RADA) and pursued this career for a number of years, winning many roles on stage, television (he was a regular in **Emergency Ward 10**) *and radio (including numerous episodes of the BBC's* **Waggoner's Walk**). *Gradually however he turned to scriptwriting, including in the early seventies on two Thames TV shows,* **Harriet's Back in Town** *and* **Rooms**. *He then worked successfully as a journalist, specialising in scientific and technical subjects, until late 1979 when he was recommended by Robert Banks Stewart for the post of script editor on* **Doctor Who**. *Having remained in this post for a year, and having also written two stories in the form of* **Logopolis** *and* **Castrovalva**, *Bidmead returned to freelance projects – including a third* **Doctor Who** *story,* **Frontios**, *and novelisations of all three for Target books. He continues to work as a scientific and technical journalist, including on the magazine* **Wired**.

DAVID FISHER
WRITER

David Fisher was already a very experienced television writer by the time he came to work on **Doctor Who**. *Series to which he had contributed included* **Orlando** *(1967),* **Dixon of Dock Green** *(1969),* **The Troubleshooters** *(1969-71),* **Sutherland's Law** *(1973) and* **General Hospital** *(1977). Following* **Doctor Who**, *for which he wrote four stories, he contributed some scripts to* **Hammer House of Horror** *(1980). He has in more recent years been collaborating with Anthony Read on a number of historical books dealing with subjects including World War Two espionage, the Nazi persecution of the Jews and the Nazi/Soviet pact of the early 1940s. He lives with his second wife in a 16th-century house in Suffolk.*

Traken by Johnny Byrne (exact commissioning dates currently unknown); *The Dogs of Darkness* by Jack Gardner (SB 29 March, S 11 August – by which time it was being considered for season nineteen rather than for season eighteen); and *Soldar and the Plastoids* by John Bennett (SB 10 April – and possibly considered from the outset for season nineteen rather than for season eighteen).

The scripts by Flanagan and McCulloch, Smith, Gallagher and Byrne eventually progressed to production, but all the others fell by the wayside; and a further Fisher submission, thought to have had the working title *Psychonauts*, also proved unsuitable. Other writers with whom Bidmead had discussions between May and August 1980 included John Gribbin, Richard Sparks, Christopher Bailey, Ian Marter (who as an actor had earlier played the Doctor's companion Harry Sullivan), Jim Follett (who came up with a storyline called *Into the Comet* about the discovery of a monster-threatened civilisation within Halley's Comet), Terence Greer, David Tebbet, Geoff Lowe (who submitted a storyline entitled *Romanoids*) and Eric Saward, but by this time he was looking ahead to future years rather than seeking further scripts for season eighteen.

'We had two types of writer on the season,' recalled Bidmead. 'We had those with no experience but with super ideas and bursting with enthusiasm – Andrew Smith being one. They were people I was very keen to work with, but they needed a great deal of help from that old hack, Chris Bidmead! On the other hand we had old hacks like Chris Bidmead who knew how to put a script together but hadn't got enough ideas. Andrew McCulloch was a guy I'd known as an actor and he was writing with a partner, so we had them in. I found Johnny Byrne by going back to an old telephone list of mine from the early seventies. I'd met him in a pub, where he claimed to be a poet. When I did track him down, I found I wasn't getting somebody new to TV but someone who at that stage had considerably more experience than I did.'

While Bidmead concentrated on the scripting of the forthcoming season, Nathan-Turner focused his attention on other aspects of the production. He was keen to make his mark and give *Doctor Who* a new, much more glossy, expensive and up-to-date look. The phenomenally popular cinema film *Star Wars* and its imitators had dramatically increased the public's expectations of science fiction in the media, and he wanted to counter the commonly

held perception of *Doctor Who* as a cheap series with relatively low production values and substandard visual effects.

One specific innovation that the producer wanted to make was to change the style of the series' incidental music. As early as 25 September 1979, even before his appointment as producer had been confirmed, he had sent McDonald two records by rock musician Jean Michel Jarre as an indication of the sort of synthesizer-based music that he had in mind. McDonald had initially misunderstood him to mean that he actually wanted to use Jarre's own music, rather than simply something in a similar style, and had replied three days later noting: 'I wonder…if it isn't too ethereal/floating/romantic /drug-oriented for our purposes.' Once this confusion had been cleared up, however, McDonald was content to go along with Nathan-Turner's idea.

The producer approached the BBC's Radiophonic Workshop and around January 1980 reached agreement with them that they would in future be responsible for providing all *Doctor Who*'s incidental music. Workshop composers Peter Howell and Paddy Kingsland were each given a videotape of an undubbed season seventeen episode for them to add music to as a 'dummy run' for the forthcoming season. Nathan-Turner meanwhile had a lunch meeting with Dudley Simpson, who had been the series' regular composer throughout the seventies and had first contributed to it as far back as 1964, and informed him that his services were no longer required.

'With all due respect to Dudley Simpson,' explained Nathan-Turner in 1982, 'he was restricted financially in the number of musicians he could use. Consequently, he would go for certain instruments that the musicians could double with. There was a sameness, whether the story was set on Earth or on another planet. Now, that wasn't *his* fault, but that of the financial restrictions imposed upon him. With electronic music, there are so many different sounds and musical noises that can be made. There's a distinct alien feel. If there's an Earth-based story, we can augment with a piano or drums which gives us a more Earthly sound. But on the whole, when we're on alien planets, we get a whole variety of sounds, which helps to set up different civilizations. I think it makes the whole thing more acceptable.'

Another factor in the producer's thinking was that a radiophonic score would help to distinguish *Doctor Who* from the BBC's other ongoing science fiction series, *Blake's 7*, for which Simpson also composed.

Not only did Nathan-Turner want the Radiophonic Workshop to take charge of *Doctor Who*'s incidental music, he additionally requested that they provide a completely revamped version of the series' famous theme music. Howell was the composer assigned this task.

'I realised how dangerous an area I was entering,' noted Howell in 1983, 'because the tune was so very well established and in a way had helped make the Workshop's name for all of us I didn't want to throw out the baby with the bath water; didn't want to do something so ridiculously new that nobody would know it was the same tune. As far as I was concerned, I was trying to prove that you could use all the techniques that we have learned over the years and still make something fresh with all this new equipment.'

To accompany Howell's revamped theme music, Nathan-Turner commissioned a completely new set of opening and closing titles; and on this occasion the task fell not to Bernard Lodge, who had been responsible for all the series' previous sequences, but to BBC graphic designer Sid Sutton.

'Bernard Lodge's titles were always considered – and were – very innovative,' recalled Sutton. 'They were held up as a sort of milestone, you know. Well, the assistant head of department, John Aston, just walked in one day and said, "We need a new set of *Doctor Who* titles – do you fancy doing it?" It was a rather unenviable decision, because it was really a case of "Follow that!"

'John Nathan-Turner wanted something different, something new. When the news got around that I was getting to do the titles, everyone was saying, "Poor old Sid! Dear, dear. Fancy having to try to do something after Bernard's. Rather you than me!" So it was with a bit of trepidation that I actually tackled it.

'Peter Howell was working on the music and I was working on my ideas. I can't remember the exact sequence of events but at some stage we got together and discussed various things. Then there came a point while we were both finalising our work when we met up again and he added some extra bits into the music to emphasise bits of the film so that the two married together.

'I thought that Bernard's titles were smashing –

Sid Sutton's re-designed title sequence.

LALLA WARD
ROMANA

*Lalla Ward, born Lady Sarah Ward, daughter of Lord Bangor – Edward Ward – and his writer wife Marjorie Banks, always wanted to act, paint and draw, and so joined the Central School of Speech and Drama in 1967. When she left in 1970, it was straight into a part in the Hammer film **Vampire Circus**, released in 1971. Following this she worked extensively on stage, in films – including **Matushka, England Made Me** (1972), **Rosebud** (1974) and **The Prince and the Pauper** (1977) – and on television – including appearances in **Quiller** (1975), **Hazell** (1979), **Who Pays the Ferryman?** (1977) and **The Duchess of Duke Street** (1977). She also appeared in a film called **Got it Made** in 1974, which was later reissued as **Sweet Virgin** with sex scenes added featuring other actors. This led to her winning a libel action against **Club International** magazine, which ran a selection of nude photographs from the film purporting to be of her. Her guest appearance in the **Doctor Who** story **The Armageddon Factor** in 1979 led to her being chosen to play Romana when the original actress, Mary Tamm, left after one season. Ward quit **Doctor Who** in 1980, and in December of that year married Tom Baker. The marriage lasted 16 months. Ward continued to act, with roles in **Schoolgirl Chums** (1982) and **Hamlet, Prince of Denmark** (1980) for the BBC and **The Jeweller's Shop** and **The Rehearsal** on stage. She also developed her love of painting and wrote and illustrated several books. In 1992 she married eminent biologist Dr. Richard Dawkins, author of such books as **The Selfish Gene** and **The Blind Watchmaker**, and gave up acting to concentrate on writing and on her family.*

Graphic designer Sid Sutton created the new title sequence for season eighteen.

Lalla Ward and Tom ▶
Baker on their wedding day
in December 1980. The
marriage was short-lived,
lasting only sixteen months.

JOHN LEESON
VOICE OF K-9

*After leaving school John Leeson
worked in a bookshop, and then as
a porter in the Leicester Royal
Infirmary Hospital. He joined the
Leicester Dramatic Society and
ultimately applied for and won a
place at RADA. On leaving RADA
he worked in repertory and
pantomimes, including **Toad of
Toad Hall**, in which he met his
future wife. His first work on
television was as a walk-on in a
BBC play, **The Wedding Feast**.
The Spanish Farm (1968),
Dad's Army and numerous
situation comedies followed. He
played the original Bungle the bear
in the children's series **Rainbow**
(1972), set questions for
Mastermind and did a lot of
freelance voice work for the BBC.
The part of K-9's voice came his
way after he bumped into the
director, with whom he had worked
previously, in a pub. Since his time
in **Doctor Who**, Leeson has
continued to act and provide voice-
over services for the BBC and
many other companies. In 1995 he
appeared in the **Doctor Who**
spin-off video drama **Downtime**,
playing a disc jockey.*

John Leeson returned ▲
to voice K-9 for the whole
of season eighteen.

Romana and the Doctor ▶
find themselves in
E-space. *State of Decay.*

the way he developed them over the years from the
original idea – but the one thing about them that
kind of bugged me was that the tunnelling effect
they had gave me a sort of "enclosed" feeling.
What I wanted to do was to open them up. The
idea really was that Doctor Who is a mysterious
figure who came from the galaxy somewhere, and
that was the kind of image I wanted to portray. So,
in the sequence I came up with, there was a galaxy
that we were travelling through, with stars
rushing past. Then some of them stopped, then a
few more stopped, until eventually they made up
the face of the Doctor, like a being literally
coming from outer space. That basically was the
idea – a very simple idea really.

'Every bit of the sequence was done on a
rostrum camera as a series of overlapping tracks.
We had something like forty overlapping tracks
on one piece of film, so each frame had about half

a dozen exposures on it, to produce a multi-
image effect.

'The new logo was my idea too. I think the
previous logo was very "Edwardian" looking, and
I think I'm right in saying that John wanted it
slightly more modern looking. Well, I didn't
want to use chrome because everyone was
starting to use chrome at that time, so I tried to
make it look like glass.'

So determined was Nathan-Turner to
transform and update the style of *Doctor Who* that
he even considered changing the image of Tom
Baker's Doctor by having him dressed in a
completely different costume, without the
famous hat and scarf. Costume designer June
Hudson was effectively given *carte blanche* to
come up with something new, but in the end
persuaded the producer that it would be sensible
to retain at least the basic silhouette of the
established outfit.

'John Nathan-Turner wanted to change the
image,' explained Hudson in a 1992 interview,
'but Tom's personality was so enmeshed with the
coat, hat and scarf that I felt they should remain.
However, I did change the colour, texture and
shape.

'The new overcoat came from a 1918 Russian
officer design, with matching scarf in richer
Chenille wool. The jacket and breeches came
from an Edwardian Norfolk suit, which suited
Tom Baker's style. Prince Charles's sock-makers,
Corgi Knitwear, provided diamond patterned
socks – I couldn't find them anywhere else.

'John also requested a shirt that could be
marketed, but basic shirt design couldn't be
bettered. I suggested a big collar incorporating
question marks.'

A pair of brown leather brogues completed the
ensemble, but Baker greatly disliked wearing
these and they were later dropped in favour of his
familiar buccaneer boots. In fact, although
generally very appreciative of Hudson's work, the
actor was altogether less than happy with the
new costume, which – partly due to Nathan-
Turner's desire to create a readily marketable
image – had a much more stylised, uniform look
than those he had worn previously.

The cumulative effect of all the changes
instituted by Nathan-Turner was that *Doctor Who*
would enter the eighties as a very different series
from the one that had seen out the seventies.

CHAPTER TWO

Season Eighteen: Into Another Dimension

The first story of season eighteen to go into production was David Fisher's *Avalon*, which is reported to have had the working title *The Argolins* at the script stage and which eventually became *The Leisure Hive*. Shooting got under way on 20 March 1980 with the first of two days' location work on Brighton beach – although very little was actually accomplished on this first day, owing to the fact that Tom Baker and certain members of the behind-the-scenes team were indisposed.

These location scenes marked the debut of a new TARDIS exterior prop. This was made of fibreglass rather than of wood and was consequently somewhat lighter and easier to assemble than had been the previous version constructed at the start of season fifteen. It was in addition somewhat truer to the design of a genuine police box, having a stacked roof arrangement.

Also intended to make its debut in the Brighton beach scenes was a rebuilt version of the Doctor's robot dog K-9, its operator Nigel Brackley having recently fitted it with new mechanics and radio control equipment. In the end however a hollow, non-functional K-9 prop had to be used instead, pulled along the beach on a piece of invisible thread, as the rebuilt model failed to work as required. This subsequently led to a heated exchange of correspondence between the BBC and Slough Radio Control Models, the outside contractors by whom Brackley was employed.

The first interior recording session for the season took place less than a fortnight later, from 2 April to 4 April 1980 in Studio TC1.

Director Lovett Bickford chose to record many scenes using a single camera technique – repeating the action several times with the camera in

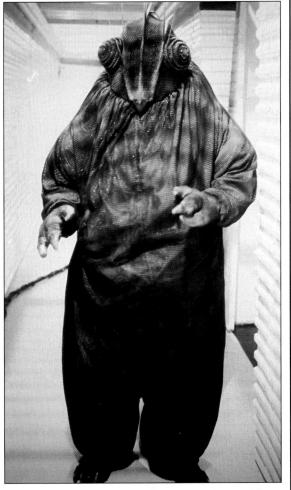

A Foamasi stalks the corridors of *The Leisure Hive*.

SEASON EIGHTEEN	
CODE	**TITLE**
5N	*The Leisure Hive*
5Q	*Meglos*
5R	*Full Circle*
5P	*State of Decay*
5S	*Warriors' Gate*
5T	*The Keeper of Traken*
5V	*Logopolis*

RATINGS

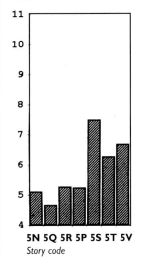

Story code

*Paddy Kingsland composed the music for the first episode of **Meglos** as Peter Howell, who had been due to handle the whole story, was ill. Howell recovered in time to complete the music for episodes two to four.*

*A one-minute excerpt from Schubert's 'Unfinished' symphony No 8 was used in part 4 of **Logopolis**. The piece was conducted by Karl Munchinger with the Vienna Philharmonic Orchestra.*

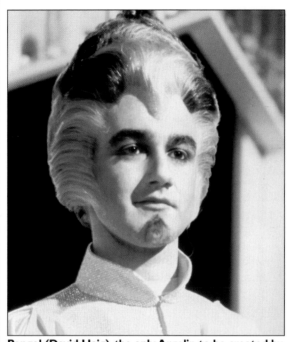

Pangol (David Haig), the only Argolin to be created by the Tachyon Recreation Generator. *The Leisure Hive*.

different positions, as in film work – rather than the more usual multi-camera technique – capturing the action from several different angles simultaneously. This helped to lend the story a very distinctive visual style. It also meant that recording progressed relatively slowly and went a whole day over schedule, putting the production over budget. This earned Nathan-Turner a reprimand from his superiors.

The Leisure Hive was not only the first of the season's stories to be made but also the first to be transmitted, its opening episode going out at 6.15 pm on Saturday 30 August 1980. It sees the TARDIS visiting the Leisure Hive on the planet

The Doctor is greatly aged when he attempts to inspect the Tachyon Recreation Generator. *The Leisure Hive*.

Argolis, the surface of which is uninhabitable following a nuclear war between the Argolins and their enemies the Foamasi. The Argolins themselves are now sterile. Pangol, the youngest, was actually created by the Tachyon Recreation Generator, a machine that runs games in the Hive. He now secretly plans to use the Generator to re-create himself many times over, forming an army of duplicates to destroy the Foamasi. The Doctor however reconfigures the equipment using components from a randomiser device previously linked to the TARDIS's navigation circuits, and Pangol's plan is foiled as he rejuvenates into a babe in arms.

Next to be transmitted, although third to be made, was the story from John Flanagan and Andrew McCulloch, which had gone through the working titles *The Golden Star*, *The Golden Pentangle* and *The Last Zolfa-Thuran* before reverting to its original *Meglos*. This concerns an attempt by the megalomaniacal xerophyte Meglos, last survivor of the planet Zolfa-Thura, to steal from the inhabitants of the neighbouring Tigella a phenomenally powerful device known as the dodecahedron. The Doctor has been summoned to Tigella by Zastor, an impartial leader who mediates between the scientist Savants and the deist Deons. He ultimately brings about Meglos's destruction by tampering with the dodecahedron's controlling computers when the creature absconds with it to Zolfa-Thura and attempts to use it as a weapon.

Meglos made use of a new effects technique referred to as Scene-Sync. This was a development of the established Colour Separation Overlay (CSO) process whereby a composite image could be formed from the output of two or more different cameras – in this case, overlaying live-action shots of actors onto a model set representing the surface of Zolfa-Thura. Scene-Sync involved two cameras being electronically synchronised to follow identical movements so that they could be made to track in unison and maintain the composite image, whereas previously CSO shots had almost invariably been static. The company that developed the technique was so keen to show it off that they made it available for use on *Meglos* for only a fraction of their normal charge. CSO itself would fall gradually into disuse during the eighties as it became superseded by more sophisticated electronic effects techniques such as the digital Quantel Image Processing system, which had made its *Doctor Who* debut on *The Leisure Hive*.

Following transmission of *Meglos*'s second episode, the series was moved to a new regular time slot starting at 5.40 pm – over half an hour earlier

Lalla Ward poses with one of the series's original cast members, Jacqueline Hill, who returned to the programme as high-priestess Lexa. *Meglos*.

Meglos, the last Zolpha-Thuran (Tom Baker) impersonates the Doctor in order to steal the Dodechahedron from the planet Tigella.

than in the recent past.

On 24 October 1980, the Friday of the week following transmission of the story's final episode, the BBC held a press conference – hastily arranged, to pre-empt a leaked report in the *Daily Mirror* – to make a momentous announcement: after some seven years in the lead role, Baker would be leaving *Doctor Who* at the end of this season.

John Nathan-Turner had never been particularly enamoured of Baker's portrayal of the Doctor, considering that his increasingly assured and flippant interpretation made the character seem too dominant and invulnerable, detracting from the series' dramatic potential. He also greatly disliked the general air of jokiness that Baker now tended to inject into the proceedings. He had indeed taken steps to address these concerns right from the outset of production on season eighteen, prevailing upon his directors to keep a far tighter rein on their leading man – a policy that, at least initially, had created considerable friction between himself and Baker.

'We had to persuade Tom Baker that the adlibbing that he felt was so necessary to fill in the script was no longer needed,' recalled Christopher H. Bidmead, 'which was something he didn't take to.'

Nathan-Turner's preferences could ultimately be met only by the casting of his own, completely new

Doctor, and so it was that he reached a mutual agreement with Baker that the actor would bow out upon the expiry of his current contract.

The scripting of the season had been further complicated by the fact that, around the end of January 1980, Nathan-Turner and Bidmead had decided to have three of the stories linked by a running theme – an idea that had been tried once before, over six stories, with the quest for the Key to Time in season sixteen.

The stories initially intended to form this loose trilogy were Andrew Smith's *The Planet that Slept*, Terrance Dicks's *The Wasting* and Christopher Priest's *Sealed Orders*, but the latter (which would have involved the Doctor receiving orders from Gallifrey to obliterate Romana) was dropped at a relatively late stage in favour of Steve Gallagher's *The Dream Time*.

The linking theme, devised by Bidmead, concerned the dangers encountered by the Doctor and his companions after being accidentally transported by the TARDIS to a completely different universe, known as E-Space. Bidmead set out his ideas in detail in the following note dated 12 June 1980:

The DOCTOR's Adventures in E-Space

Distinguish between the Charged Vacuum Emboitment

ADRIC

The production team's original character outline for Adric reads as follows:

ADRIC is fifteen, small for his age, wiry and strong, with short straight black hair. His dominating elder brother, AFRUS, is the leader of a juvenile street gang on a planet we'll call YERFILLAG, and under his tuition ADRIC has learnt to lie and steal, activities which are the dark side of his natural optimistic brashness and enormous intellectual curiosity.

ADRIC never fitted into the gang he was pressed into by his brother, partly because of his superior education, and partly because he is a born non-conformist, even among outlaws. When he meets the DOCTOR his strong sense of self-preservation prompts him to assume an air of subdued innocence and false naivety. Though a disguise, this impersonation reminds us of ADRIC's very real vulnerability as a young mortal (as opposed to the Time Lords and their all-capable K-9) – vulnerability that is going to play an important part in future adventures.

At the end of the story that introduces Adric, his brother AFRUS has given up his life to save the DOCTOR and ROMANA. With the last of his family ties broken, ADRIC stows away in the TARDIS, where he remains undiscovered until the opening of the next story.

The DOCTOR subsequently shoulders the responsibility for returning ADRIC to YERFILLAG, but what with one thing and another… Meanwhile, ADRIC's true character is emerging – enquiring, intelligent, but definitely and irritatingly a mendacious magpie. The DOCTOR's view of his responsibility towards the boy shifts: rather than return him to a planet where he will resume life as a criminal orphan, wouldn't a certain amount of education, reform and expansion of his moral horizon be appropriate…?

A number of these details were altered in the transmitted stories, including the name of Adric's brother – which was changed from Afrus to Varsh – and that of his home planet – which was changed from Yerfillag (Gallifrey spelt backwards) to Alzarius.

NYSSA

The character outline for Nyssa, credited to Johnny Byrne, John Nathan-Turner and Christopher H. Bidmead and dated 30 October 1980, reads as follows:

Nyssa is the daughter of Tremas, First Scientist and Consul of the Empire of Traken. Tremas is now dead at the hand of the Master, who has commandeered his cadaver by way of a thirteenth regeneration.

She is eighteen, of noble birth; an attractive young girl with values and skills deeply rooted in her Traken past. Tutored by her father in the advanced sciences, she is already a skilled apprentice in bioelectronics, a discipline in which her people excelled.

Nyssa is an open young woman. Idealistic and pragmatic by turn, she has an abiding belief in the essential goodness of all things, which sometimes blinds her to the less overt manifestations of evil. For example, on meeting the Master for the first time in his new guise she has mistaken him for her father, only being rescued from his clutches by the intervention of Adric and the Doctor. A threat once visible, however, brings out all that is best in Nyssa: calm assessment, lightning judgement, and nicely judged action.

Nyssa's aristocratic background sometimes leaves her oblivious to the simpler needs of others, and occasionally prevents her from seeing the funny side of situations. Adric, an orphan like her, is very fond of Nyssa, but at times her innocence, seriousness and inability to compromise seem to him like deliberate stubbornness.

The Doctor feels, irrationally, a sense of responsibility for the death of her father, but has too much respect for her individuality to see himself as any kind of substitute. He appears, in his offhand way, to enjoy having her around and being in some small part a force in her spiritual development. He would never allow it to be seen that deep, deep down inside the presence of all these young people in the TARDIS is very wearing!

The Doctor succeeds in ▶ driving the Marshmen out of the starliner. *Full Circle.*

A group of Gaztac space raiders capture an Earthling (Christopher Owen) for Meglos. *Meglos.*

through which the TARDIS passes, and E-Space where the adventures take place. Mathematically, perhaps, E-Space is _inside_ the CVE, but for our purposes we had better think of them as the mouth of the bottle and the bottle itself.

THE CHARGED VACUUM EMBOITMENT

Experimental observation shows that matter and anti-matter can be created inside a vacuum subjected to a strong electromagnetic field. Twenty-first century physics has also discovered that in some extremely rare circumstances the same conditions can create a charged vacuum within a charged vacuum, and that theoretically at least an almost infinite (and almost infinitely improbable) regression of charged vacuums can be nested inside each other like Chinese boxes. This 'emboitment' leads through to an independent universe (E-Space) that is in all other respects completely isolated from the one we

know; and the TARDIS has accidentally verified this theoretical finding by falling right into it!

Such Charged Vacuum Emboitments (CVEs) differ from Black Holes in being considerably rarer as space-time events, and also in having absolutely no effect on space in the immediate vicinity. Because they exert no gravitational force it is possible (unlike Black Holes) to pass right by them without even being aware of them. The TARDIS and its crew have been very unlucky indeed!

THE NATURE OF THE OTHER UNIVERSE

The DOCTOR and Co are in E-Space (or more fully, the exo-Space/Time continuum), which lies outside the finite but boundless Space/Time of Einstein (N-Space). The TARDIS has undergone a negation isometry – that is to say the space in which it now finds itself has negative co-ordinates with respect to our familiar universe. The mathematics of the CVE suggest that this new world has an equal probability of being composed of matter or anti-matter, but its nature in this respect is not really an issue: anti-matter itself may be fairly familiar to twenty-first-century physicists. The major problems, in inverse order of importance, are:

(1) Because of the relative smallness of E-Space (there are only two galaxies) the TARDIS behaves with unpredictable _reliability_, especially on short temporal and spacial hops.

(2) The Laws of Physics in this universe tend to operate in familiar ways, but may not be one hundred per cent trustworthy.

(3) Romana and the Doctor are trapped, unless they can find another CVE.

A further function that the production team wanted the E-Space trilogy to fulfil was to provide a vehicle for the writing out of the Doctor's two established companions, Romana and K-9, and the introduction of a new one in their place.

Lalla Ward, who had played Romana since the beginning of season seventeen, was contracted for just the first twenty episodes of season eighteen as she had agreed with Nathan-Turner that it would then be time for her to move on from the series. K-9's exit had been decreed by Nathan-Turner as he disliked the character and felt that it provided too easy a solution to the problems that the Doctor encountered. The producer was however pleased to be able to persuade K-9's original voice artist, John Leeson, to return for its last few stories. (The production team had in fact considered paying off his successor, David Brierley, and inviting him back for *Shada*, the story planned to close the previous season.)

The news that K-9 would soon be leaving the series filtered out in early June 1980 and provoked something of an outcry from many young fans, leading to the launch of a 'Save K-9' campaign in the tabloid press. Nathan-Turner was even asked by his superiors if he would reconsider his decision. He declined to do so, but put forward the suggestion that K-9 should instead be given its own programme. This idea was quickly approved, and a production set in motion (see Chapter Nineteen). Nathan-Turner meanwhile continued to maintain in public statements that there were no immediate plans to write K-9 out of *Doctor Who*. An official announcement to the contrary was not made until early October 1980.

The new companion devised by Nathan-Turner and Bidmead to replace Romana and K-9 was Adric, a young boy whose name was suggested by the script editor as an anagram of that of eminent physicist P.A.M. Dirac (who in 1930 was the first to predict the existence of anti-matter). Conceived as a rough diamond, Artful Dodger type, he was to be introduced in *The Planet that Slept*. The character outline, dated 30 January 1980, was given to writer Andrew Smith to enable him to adapt his story accordingly.

Eventually retitled *Full Circle*, *The Planet that Slept* was the third story of the season to be transmitted and the fourth to be made. The TARDIS falls through a CVE into E-Space and arrives on the planet Alzarius, where the

Decider Draith (Leonard Maguire) is killed shortly before the arrival of mistfall. *Full Circle.*

inhabitants of a crashed Starliner are being terrorised by a race of Marshmen who emerge from the marshes at a time known as Mistfall. The Doctor discovers that the Starliner's inhabitants are not the descendants of its original crew, as has been claimed by their leaders the Deciders, but evolved Marshmen. With his help and encouragement, they are able leave the planet in the repaired Starliner.

Adric was presented – along with his doomed brother Varsh – as one of a group of youthful Outlers rebelling against the Starliner community. No indication was given at the end of the last episode that he was to be joining the Doctor on a regular basis – that revelation was reserved for the following story, in which it would become apparent that he had stowed away on board the

TEGAN JOVANKA

The production team's 1 August 1980 character outline for Tegan reads as follows:

Tegan is twenty-one, an attractive and intelligent Australian trainee air stewardess, whose brash confidence in her own abilities actually conceals inner insecurity, a state of affairs that becomes clear in moments of stress.

On her way to her first real flight she accidentally blunders into the TARDIS and thus finds herself being inadvertently abducted by the DOCTOR. Characteristically her inner bewilderment at the new situation in which she finds herself causes her to assume an attitude of overweening self-assertion, and she begins to take charge of the DOCTOR and ADRIC.

During the course of three stories, TEGAN's superficial self-assurance will build until it becomes a real problem for the other two occupants of the TARDIS, and it will need drastic action on the part of the DOCTOR to put things to rights and show her the error of her ways. She may or may not continue with the DOCTOR thereafter.

MATTHEW WATERHOUSE
ADRIC

*Matthew Waterhouse was born in 1962, the son of a company solicitor. He joined the BBC as a clerk, working in the news and information department, while also pursuing an acting career. His first TV role was as a public schoolboy in **To Serve Them All My Days** (1980). He had not even started working on that programme when he auditioned for and won the role of Adric in **Doctor Who**. Since his departure from the series he has worked mainly in the theatre, appearing as Puck in **A Midsummer Night's Dream**, as Peter Pan in **Peter Pan** and as Edmund in **The Lion, the Witch and the Wardrobe**. He has also starred in a one-man show, **The Adventures of Huckleberry Finn**, adapted by him from Mark Twain's novel.*

SARAH SUTTON
NYSSA

*Sarah Sutton was born on 12 December 1961 and began her acting career at the age of seven when, while attending the Elm Hurst Ballet School, she was picked to play the part of Roo in a Phoenix Theatre production of **Winnie the Pooh**. By the age of eleven she had landed a number of TV roles, including in **Menace: Boys and Girls Come Out to Play** (1973), **Late Call** (1974) and **Oil Strike North** (1975). Her biggest success came when she won the lead in the children's drama serial **The Moon Stallion** (1978). She went back to her acting studies at the Guildhall School of Music and Drama as a part-time student. It was shortly after taking a Caribbean holiday that she was called to audition for the part of Nyssa in **Doctor Who**. Following her stint on the series she returned to theatre work, touring in the play **Policy for Murder** (1986). She subsequently got married and had a baby daughter, Hannah, which contributed to her taking a break from acting. She did however win a small role in the TV play **Unnatural Pursuits**. She hopes to return to full-time acting when her daughter is older.*

JANET FIELDING
TEGAN

*Janet Mahoney – now better known by her stage name Janet Fielding – was born in Brisbane, Australia, in 1957. She gained A Levels in Physics, Chemistry and Maths and joined Queensland University, where she first took up acting. After leaving university she worked with an English writer/director named Albert Hunt, who in 1977 brought her to England in one of his shows. Once in England she joined Ken Campbell at the Science Fiction Theatre of Liverpool and appeared in productions including **The Warp** and **The End is Nigh**. Following this she won a small part in an episode of the 1980 **Hammer House of Horror** series. She was then cast as Tegan in **Doctor Who**. After leaving the series in 1984 she appeared in episodes of **Shelley** and **Minder** on TV and in productions of **The Collector** and the pantomime **Aladdin** in the theatre. In 1991 she gave up acting to work as an administrator in the pressure group Women in Film and Television, where she stayed for three and a half years. She then became a director of Marina Martin Associates, an actor's agency, representing amongst others the eighth Doctor, Paul McGann.*

The three who rule. Zargo (William Lindsay), Aukon (Emrys James) and Camilla (Rachel Davies) are the servants of the Great Vampire. State of Decay.

TARDIS when it left Alzarius.

Chosen by Nathan-Turner to play the new companion was Matthew Waterhouse, a young *Doctor Who* fan who had been working as a BBC clerk. He had been suggested to the production office by Jenny Jenkins of the BBC's internal Casting Advisory Service and been judged by Nathan-Turner, Letts and director Peter Grimwade to be the best of all those who auditioned for the role. His appointment was first made public in a short article in London's *Evening News* on 26 February 1980.

'What we did,' Bidmead later explained, 'which may have been a mistake in practical terms but which I still think is a good idea, was that we invented the character as a whole, rounded entity

K-9 waits in the TARDIS doorway whilst the set's floor is dressed with loose earth. State of Decay.

and then cast it. Other shows often work the other way around. What drew us to Matthew, although he wasn't wholly the character we designed, was his tremendous enthusiasm as a real fan of the show, coupled with his interesting and unusual face.'

The first story on which Waterhouse worked was Dicks's *The Wasting*, which was transmitted as *State of Decay*. It was actually the second of the season to be made, between *The Leisure Hive* and *Meglos* – a production order dictated largely by considerations of script availability. (The remainder of the season's stories were made in the same order as they were transmitted.)

K-9 was required to play a large part in the action, so visual effects designer Mat Irvine (although not officially assigned to this story, the effects for which were handled by Tony Harding) worked with assistant Charlie Lumm to strip out the drive mechanism recently installed by Slough Radio Control Models and replace it with a new one of their own. They also updated the dog's radio control to a more modern FM type, using two six-channel MacGregor JR Series sets. Irvine also operated K-9 for one of the story's two studio sessions, as Brackley was unavailable.

State of Decay begins with the Doctor, Romana, K-9 and Adric arriving on a planet where the natives live in fear of three Lords – Zargo, Camilla and Aukon – who rule from an imposing Tower.

The Lords are soon revealed to be vampire servants of the last of the Great Vampires, a race referred to in Time Lord mythology. The Great Vampire is about to be revived from its resting place beneath the Tower – in truth the spaceship in which the Lords, in their original human forms, came to E-Space – but the Doctor launches one of the ship's three shuttle craft and it pierces the heart of the creature, killing it. The Lords, deprived of their master, crumble to dust.

The last episode of *State of Decay* was transmitted on 13 December 1980. There was then a short break in the season over the Christmas holiday period. It resumed on 3 January 1981 with the first episode of Gallagher's *The Dream Time*, the conclusion to the E-Space trilogy, which had by this point been retitled *Warriors' Gate*. This was actually promoted as the start of a new season in the BBC's listings magazine *Radio Times*. Following the break, the series' regular time slot was changed once more, starting still earlier at 5.10 p.m.

Warriors' Gate centres around the plight of the leonine Tharils (originally to have been called Tharks), who have been enslaved by a humanoid race for their ability to navigate the time lines. One of the Tharils, Biroc, brings the TARDIS to a white void where others of his kind are held prisoner aboard a privateer. The only other thing present in the void is a gateway that leads to N-Space. Rorvik, the commander of the privateer, tries to break through by blasting the gateway with his engines. The blast however is simply reflected back, destroying the ship and freeing its prisoners. Romana and K-9 elect to remain in E-Space to help liberate the remainder of the Tharil race, while the TARDIS – now occupied only by the Doctor and Adric – is flung back into N-Space.

Warriors' Gate proved the most problematic of the season's stories to make. The production team had a number of reservations about Gallagher's scripts and took the unusual step of asking director Paul Joyce to carry out some late rewrites – a task for which in early September 1980 they agreed a fee of £750. Gallagher, although accepting that his original scripts showed a lack of television experience, was less than pleased with some of the changes that had been made. Joyce also found himself coming into conflict with Nathan-Turner, Letts and other members of the behind-the-scenes team over his ambitious and painstaking execution of the story's studio sessions. This resulted in the production assistant, Graeme Harper, playing a rather larger part in the proceedings than would normally have been the case. Nathan-Turner

The Tower in the Visual Effects workshop. *State of Decay*

subsequently sent McDonald a memo dated 8 October 1980 in which he noted that the story could not have been completed without 'massive co-operation…in particular [from] the vision mixers, the camera crew and the production team' and conceded that it had been an error of judgement on his part to engage a director who, although imaginative and highly recommended, had 'so little experience of the speed at which a *Doctor Who* needs to work'.

The imminent change of Doctors had left Nathan-Turner not only with the task of finding a new leading man for the series but also with the problem of trying to retain the loyalty of its regular audience. Baker had built up an enormous following amongst the general viewing public during his unprecedented seven-year stint, and many were no doubt unaware that there had ever been any other actors playing the Doctor. To recast the lead role in a long-running and popular show is

▲ The scout ship crashes into the Great Vampire's pit, striking the monster through the heart. *State of Decay*.

Visual effects assistant Stuart Murdock adds detail to the ▼ Tower. *State of Decay*.

ANTHONY AINLEY
THE MASTER

Anthony Ainley was born on 20 August 1937, the son of famous thespian Henry Ainley. After a short time working as an insurance clerk he joined RADA to train as an actor. His many TV appearances include roles in It's Dark Outside *(Granada 1965, as a regular),* The Avengers: Noon-Doomsday *(ABC 1968),* Doomwatch: No Room for Error *(BBC 1971),* Out of the Unknown: Welcome Home *(BBC 1971),* Elizabeth R: The Marriage Game *(BBC 1971),* Spyder's Web *(ATV 1972, as a regular in the starring role),* Upstairs, Downstairs *(LWT 1973, as a regular),* The Pallisers *(BBC 1974, as a regular),* Warship *(BBC 1975),* Nicholas Nickleby *(BBC 1977),* Secret Army: Lisa – Code-Name Yvette *(BBC 1977) and* Lillie *(LWT 1978). He also has numerous film credits to his name, including* A Man for all Seasons *(1966),* Naked Evil *(1966),* Inspector Clouseau *(1968),* Oh What a Lovely War *(1969),* Blood on Satan's Claw *(1970),* Assault *(1970) and* The Land that Time Forgot *(1974). He continues to act today, whilst also pursuing interests such as watching and playing cricket.*

◄ **Matthew Waterhouse, Lalla Ward and Tom Baker record a scene set in the white void of the CVE. A green CSO cyclorama used to add in the pure white background behind the Gate.** *Warriors' Gate*.

THE FIVE FACES OF *DOCTOR WHO*

One way in which John Nathan-Turner attempted to smooth the transition from the fourth Doctor to the fifth – and also to bridge the longer-than-usual break between seasons eighteen and nineteen – was to request, in addition to the standard summer reruns (which would this year comprise **Full Circle** *and* **The Keeper of Traken***), a season of repeats from earlier eras of* **Doctor Who***'s history, thus reminding viewers that there had been actors other than Baker in the lead role. Despite the trouble and expense involved in renegotiating rights on 'out of time' repeat material – that is, material more than three years old – the powers-that-be acceded to this request. Five stories –* **100,000 BC** *(Hartnell),* **The Krotons** *(Troughton),* **Carnival of Monsters** *(Pertwee),* **The Three Doctors** *(Hartnell, Troughton and Pertwee) and* **Logopolis** *(Baker) – were transmitted in an early evening BBC2 slot in November and December 1981 under the banner title* **The Five Faces of Doctor Who.** *The final scene of* **Carnival of Monsters** *was slightly edited by Nathan-Turner at the request of its original director, former* **Doctor Who** *producer Barry Letts, who was dissatisfied with the bald wig make-up of one of the characters.*

One of two concept ▲ drawings for the gateway. *Warriors' Gate.*

The dying Keeper (Denis ▲ Carey). *The Keeper of Traken.*

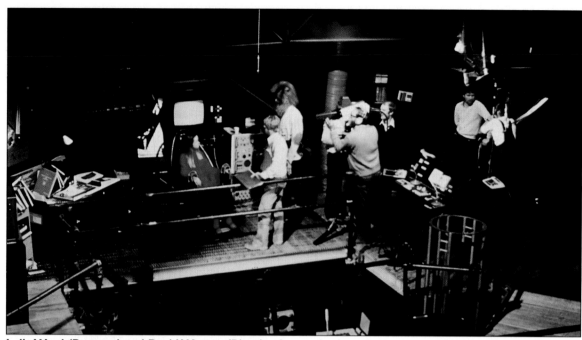

Lalla Ward (Romana) and David Weston (Biroc) rehearse in the privateer spaceship set. *Warriors' Gate.*

always a high-risk endeavour, and Nathan-Turner felt that Baker's successor would be bound to face an uphill struggle to win acceptance from *Doctor Who*'s many regular viewers.

One strategy that the producer developed with a view to alleviating this problem was to make the last two stories of season eighteen and the first story of season nineteen a loosely linked trilogy in which the Doctor's old arch-enemy the Master would be reintroduced in a new physical form. Thus Johnny Byrne was asked to incorporate the Master into his scripts for *The Keeper of Traken*, which would constitute the first part of the trilogy, and two new stories were commissioned to serve as the second and third respectively. These were *Logopolis* by Bidmead, who as script editor was considered ideally suited to the difficult task of writing out the fourth Doctor, and *Project '4G'* by

Lane (David Kincaid), Rorvik (Clifford Rose) and Sagan (Vincent Pickering) find themselves trapped within the CVE. *Warriors' Gate.*

Flanagan and McCulloch.

In *The Keeper of Traken*, the Doctor and Adric learn from the wizened Keeper that a great evil has come to his planet in the form of a Melkur – a calcified statue. The Keeper is nearing the end of his reign and seeks the Doctor's help in preventing the evil from taking control of the bioelectronic Source that is the keystone of the Traken Union's civilisation. The Melkur, via various deceptions, becomes the next Keeper. It is then revealed to be the Master's TARDIS. Its owner, still blackened and emaciated as when last seen (in season fourteen's *The Deadly Assassin*), hopes to use the Source's power to regenerate himself. The Doctor manages to expel him and install a new Keeper in his place, but in a last minute ploy the Master traps one of the Traken Consuls, Tremas, and merges with his body before fleeing the planet.

The Master as seen in his blackened and emaciated form was played by Geoffrey Beevers. Following his transformation at the end of the story, however, he was played by the same actor who had portrayed Tremas. This was Anthony Ainley, who had been chosen as the new, regular Master largely on the strength of his portrayal of the villainous Reverend Emilius in *The Pallisers* – a 1974 BBC classic serial on which Nathan-Turner had worked as production manager.

Nathan-Turner, keen to provide still further incentive for viewers to stick with *Doctor Who* after the forthcoming change-over of Doctors, had initially considered replacing Romana with an already established companion character from the series' past. To this end he had approached both Elisabeth Sladen, who had played Sarah Jane Smith from 1973 to 1976, and Louise Jameson, who had played Leela from 1976 to 1977, to see if they would be interested in reprising their roles. Both actresses had declined, however, so he had then decided instead that two completely new companion characters should be introduced towards the end of season eighteen – the theory being that these would quickly gain their own respective groups of fans who would want to follow their adventures and see how they coped with the new Doctor.

The first of these newcomers to appear on screen was Nyssa, daughter of Tremas. She had originally been created by Byrne as a one-off character for *The Keeper of Traken*, but Nathan-Turner had quickly decided to keep her on for at least a further three stories. Even before rehearsals for *The Keeper of Traken* had begun, actress Sarah Sutton – who had been cast in the role by director John Black – had signed a contract for additional episodes.

Viewers who had missed the public announcement of Nyssa's arrival, which was covered in numerous newspaper articles published on 31 January 1981, would not have guessed from the final episode of *The Keeper of Traken* that she was to become a series regular, as the closing scene sees her left behind on Traken when the TARDIS departs. She was however reintroduced in the following story, *Logopolis*, which has her being brought to join the Doctor and Adric by the Watcher – a wraith-like transitional form of the Time Lord, between his fourth and fifth incarnations.

It was also in *Logopolis* that the second new regular, Tegan Jovanka, made her debut. Created by Nathan-Turner and Bidmead before it was realised that Nyssa would also be a companion, she was originally to have had a three-story 'trial run' but later became thought of as a more long-term regular. Her initial character description, dated 1 August 1980, established her as a bossy, argumentative air hostess from Australia – a country of origin chosen by the producer partly in order to break the precedent of exclusively British human companions.

The actress chosen for the role was Janet Fielding, who had been suggested to Nathan-Turner by the Actors Alliance organisation, of which she was a member, on the basis that she was a genuine bossy Australian! The producer had at first considered her unsuitable, partly because she was two inches shorter than the normal five feet four inches height

Disaster befalls Kassia (Sheila Ruskin) and her new husband Tremas (Anthony Ainley) when the Master attempts to seize the power of the Keeper. The Doctor and Adric (Matthew Waterhouse) are summoned to help Traken by the dying Keeper. *The Keeper of Traken*.

The Melkur, an evil being which is calcified when it lands on Traken, is in reality the Master's TARDIS. *The Keeper of Traken*.

The model landscape of Logopolis is recorded by the BBC's Visual Effects Department.

requirement for an air hostess. She had eventually won him over, however, by convincing him that Qantas and other airlines serving the Far East had a

CASTING IDEAS

Often, directors would have several ideas as to who might play a given part. The following are examples of actors considered for parts in season eighteen but who – because they turned them down, were unavailable or were ultimately considered unsuitable – did not play them. The artiste actually cast in each case is given in square brackets.

The Leisure Hive
Clive Swift (Brock) [John Collin]
Sian Phillips (Mena) [Adrienne Corri]

Full Circle
John Franklyn-Robbins (Garif) [Alan Rowe]

Warriors' Gate
Frank Windsor (Rorvik)
Robert Hardy (Rorvik)
Derek Jacobi (Rorvik) } [Clifford Rose]
Stratford Johns (Rorvik)
John Normington (Rorvik)

The Keeper of Traken
Francesca Annis (Kassia) [Sheila Ruskin]
Mary Morris (Katura)
[Margot van der Burgh]
Philip Locke (Seron) [John Woodnutt]

Logopolis
Hywel Bennett (Monitor) } [John Fraser]
Nigel Stock (Monitor)
Elizabeth McKewen (Aunt Vanessa)
[Dolore Whiteman]

▲ Amy Roberts's costume designs for the Melkur and ▼ Kassia. *The Keeper of Traken*.

NOTES

Edward Underdown
Distinguished actor Edward Underdown, who played Zastor in **Meglos**, *found it difficult to complete his scenes as he was in a poor state of health. Unable to eat normally, he had to feed himself through a tube. This was his last acting role, and he died shortly afterwards.*

Barbara's Back
Cast as the Deons' High Priestess Lexa in **Meglos** *was Jacqueline Hill, who years earlier had played companion Barbara Wright in the series' first sixteen stories.*

New Companion
Barney Lawrence, who played one of the Marshmen in **Full Circle**, *wrote to the production team after completion of the story making the light-hearted suggestion that a Marshman should be discovered on board the TARDIS, change into a citizen and become the Doctor's next companion.*

Ouch!
Matthew Waterhouse suffered a slight injury to his foot when he accidentally dropped a prop dagger on it while recording **State of Decay**.

The Gateway
The design of the gateway in **Warriors' Gate** *was based on two concept paintings commissioned by director Paul Joyce from artist David H. Smith.*

The Doctor regenerates. ▲
Logopolis.

The Watcher (Adrian ▶
Gibbs). *Logopolis.*

Recording a scene from *Logopolis*. The Logopolitans, Nyssa (Sarah Sutton) and Tegan (Janet Fielding) attempt to stabilise the rapidly shrinking TARDIS, caused by the Master's sabotage, whilst the Doctor is trapped inside.

different height requirement — a complete fabrication on her part — and also by claiming that she was three years younger than was actually the case. She signed her initial contract for the series in October 1980 and was presented to the press and public later the same month.

The fourth Doctor's final adventure finds him visiting the planet Logopolis, home to a race of advanced mathematicians whose help he hopes to enlist in reconfiguring the outer shell of the TARDIS. The Watcher warns of impending danger, and this is borne out as the Master arrives and kills a number of the Logopolitans. The Logopolitans' leader, the Monitor, then reveals that the universe passed its normal point of heat death long ago and has been preserved only by his people's calculations, which — by way of a signal beamed from a perfect copy of the Pharos Project radio telescope on Earth — have kept open numerous CVEs through which the excess entropy can drain. This process has now been halted by the Master's interference, and the Doctor is forced to join forces with his arch-enemy in order to save the universe. The two Time Lords hurry to Earth with a copy of the Logopolitan program, intending to use the real Pharos Project to transmit it and thus keep open the CVEs. The Master, seeing an opportunity to seize power, promptly blackmails the peoples of the universe by threatening them with destruction unless they agree to his demands. The Doctor foils this scheme but is thrown from the gantry of the radio telescope. As he lies injured on the ground, his companions — Adric and the newcomers Nyssa and Tegan — rush to join him. The Watcher appears again and merges with the Doctor as he regenerates into a younger form.

Recording of *Logopolis* was completed on 24 January 1981 and the final episode transmitted on 21 March 1981, bringing to an end Baker's stint as the Doctor — and arguably the most successful era in *Doctor Who*'s history. When the series returned, it would have a new leading man in the form of twenty-nine-year-old Peter Davison.

CHAPTER THREE

Who Was Peter Davison

Peter Moffett, now better known by his stage name Peter Davison, was born on 13 April 1951 in the Streatham area of London. In 1961, he and his family – parents Sheila and Claude (an electrical engineer who hailed from British Guiana) and sisters Barbara, Pamela and Shirley – moved to Woking in Surrey, where Davison was educated at the Maphill School. It was here that he first became interested in acting, taking parts in a number of school plays, and this eventually led to him joining an amateur dramatic society, the Byfleet Players. On leaving school at the age of sixteen, having achieved only modest academic success with three O Levels of undistinguished grades, he took a variety of short-lived jobs ranging from hospital porter to Hoffman press operator. He was still keen to pursue an acting career, however, and so applied for a place at drama school.

'Because I'd got the equivalent of only one pass in my exams,' he noted in a 1983 interview, 'I was able to do what I wanted to do rather than be directed towards a certain profession. So I applied to drama school and, very fortunately, got into the Central School of Speech and Drama, where I was for three years.'

Davison's first professional acting work came in 1972 when, after leaving drama school in the July of that year, he secured a small role in a run of *Love's Labour's Lost* at the Nottingham Playhouse. This marked the start of a three-year period in which he worked in a variety of different repertory companies around the UK, often in Shakespearean roles. He then made his television debut, playing a blond-wigged space cowboy character called Elmer in *A Man for Emily*, a three-part story in the Thames TV children's series *The Tomorrow People*, transmitted in April 1975. Appearing alongside him in this production was his future wife,

American-born actress Sandra Dickinson, whom he had first met during a run of *A Midsummer Night's Dream* in Edinburgh. They would marry on 26 December 1978 in Dickinson's home town of Rockville in Maryland, USA.

'I suppose *The Tomorrow People* was ITV's answer to *Doctor Who*, really,' observed Davison in a 1985 interview, 'except they tried to get children to relate to it by having children in it, and children are usually terrible actors.

'The story we did was not terribly popular with children because we sent the whole thing up. I remember we had this terrible talking ceiling, and I reached up and tickled it and it let out this booming "Ho-ho-ho"!'

Peter Davison as Henry Myers in *Anna of the Five Towns* (1985).

THE FILMS OF PETER DAVISON

A Man You Don't Meet Every Day (1994); *Black Beauty* (1995). Films in colour.

SELECTED TV APPEARANCES

Top of the Pops (BBC 1970, as a member of the audience); *The Tomorrow People: A Man for Emily* (Thames 1975); *Love for Lydia* (LWT 1977); *Print Out* (Granada 1977); *All Creatures Great and Small* (BBC 1978-80, 1983, 1985, 1988-1990); *Once Upon a Time* (ITV 1980); *The Gentle Touch: Decoy* (LWT 1980); *Holding the Fort* (LWT 1980-82); *Sink or Swim* (BBC 1980-82); *Nationwide* (BBC 1980, 1983); *Pebble Mill at One* (BBC 1979, 1980); *Boxing Night at the Mill* (BBC 1980); *The Hitch-Hiker's Guide to the Galaxy* (BBC 1981); *Doctor Who* (BBC 1982-84, 1993); *So You Think You Know What's Good for You* (BBC 1982); *This is Your Life* (Thames 1982); *Saturday Superstore* (BBC 1983); *The Late, Late Breakfast Show* (BBC 1984); *L Driver* (BBC 1985); *Breakfast Time* (BBC 1985); *Pebble Mill* (BBC 1985); *Anna of the Five Towns* (BBC 1985); *Miss Marple: A Pocketful of Rye* (BBC 1985); *Jackanory* (BBC 1985, 1990); *Magnum PI: Echoes of the Mind* (CBS/Universal/Bellisarius/Glen Larson Productions 1985); *A Very Peculiar Practice* (BBC 1986, 1988); *Tales of the Unexpected: Wink Three Times* (Anglia 1988); *Campion* (BBC 1989-90); *Going Live* (BBC 1990); *Fiddler's Three* (Yorkshire 1991); *Screen One: A Very Polish Practice* (BBC 1992); *Kinsey* (1992); *Molly* (Children's Channel 1993); *Harnessing Peacocks* (ITV 1993); *Doctor Who: Dimensions in Time* (BBC 1993); *Ain't Misbehavin'* (BBC 1994-95); *The Good Sex Guide* (1994); *Heavenly Bodies* (1995).

Peter Davison as Tristan ▶
Farnon in *All Creatures Great
and Small.*

SELECTED RADIO APPEARANCES

*Ed Stewart Show (BBC 1983);
Gloria Hunniford Show (BBC
1985); King Street Junior (BBC
1985); Globe Theatre: Whatever
Happened with St George (BBC
1992); Dr Who – 30 Years (BBC
1993); Memoirs of Sherlock
Holmes (1993).*

SELECTED THEATRE APPEARANCES

*Love's Labour's Lost (1972-73);
The Shrew (1973); A Midsummer
Night's Dream (1974); The Two
Gentlemen of Verona (1974);
Hamlet (1974); Barefoot in the
Park (1981, 1984); Cinderella
(1982, 1984); Aladdin (1985); The
Owl and the Pussycat (1986);
Arsenic and Old Lace (1991); The
Decorator (1992); The Last Yankee
(1993); An Absolute Turkey (1994);
Mother Goose (1994); Dick
Whittington (1995/1996); Dial M
For Murder (1996).*

COMPOSED MUSIC

*Button Moon theme (1980s);
Mixed Blessings theme (1981);
lyrics to Let the Love In (single).*

ADVERTISEMENTS

*Yorkshire Bitter (1980?); Prestige
Saucepans (1982?); Nescafé
(1984); Pedigree Chum (1995).*

VIDEO APPEARANCES

*Grimes Goes Green (Video Arts
1990); Daleks: The Early Years
(BBC 1992); The Airzone Solution
(BBV 1993), The Zero Imperative
(BBV 1994); The Devil of
Winterborne (BBV 1995); The
Wind In The Willows (Video Films
1995).*

Davison spent the following eighteen months working as a filing clerk at Twickenham tax office. He also took the opportunity to pursue an interest in singing and songwriting, which led him to record several singles with his wife. (He would later provide the theme tunes for a number of TV series, including *Mixed Blessings* and *Button Moon*.)

'Every actor has to have a year and a half out of work,' he joked. 'It teaches him humility – I think. After that I was very, very lucky in that I got two very big television parts following each other. The first was in a thing called *Love for Lydia*. The second was the part of Tristan Farnon in *All Creatures Great and Small*.'

Love for Lydia, a London Weekend Television (LWT) period drama serial transmitted in 1977, saw Davison playing the romantic lead, Tom Holland. It was the BBC's *All Creatures Great and Small*, however, that was really to propel him into the limelight. Based on the books of country vet James Herriot, this highly successful series ran initially for three seasons between 1978 and 1980. Davison, co-starring with Robert Hardy and Christopher Timothy, portrayed an impetuous young vet in Herriot's practice.

Davison's success in *All Creatures Great and Small* brought him many other offers of TV work. Amongst those that he took up were lead roles in two sitcoms: LWT's *Holding the Fort*, in which he played Russell Milburn, and the BBC's *Sink or Swim*, in which he played Brian Webber. Three seasons of each were transmitted between 1980 and

1982, consolidating Davison's position as a well-known and popular television actor.

It was in September 1980 that John Nathan-Turner first telephoned Davison to suggest that he might take on the mantle of the fifth Doctor in *Doctor Who*. The actor's initial reaction was one of considerable scepticism and reluctance, as he considered himself completely unsuitable for the role. He was however sufficiently interested to meet Nathan-Turner for lunch the following week to discuss the idea. This led to a series of further meetings and discussions, in which Nathan-Turner attempted to allay his concerns.

Prominent amongst these concerns was the fact that the producer saw him as a 'personality actor' and wanted him to bring to the part of the Doctor the same boyish charm and enthusiasm as he had to that of Tristan Farnon. Davison himself had not previously thought in these terms, preferring to believe that he was essentially a character actor who just happened to have come to public attention in one particular type of part. He was aware that *Doctor Who* was an established national institution with a large fan following, and was somewhat daunted by the prospect of taking on such a weighty commitment. He also felt that the role of the Doctor was ideally suited to an older actor, and that he was too young for it.

In the end, however, he decided to accept the job, almost on a whim, as he could not bear to think that someone else would be given it instead and that he would then have to remain silent about the fact that he had been offered it first. News of his appointment filtered out to the press on 4 November 1980, and an announcement was even made on the main BBC news bulletin that evening. A hastily arranged press conference was held the following day to give journalists their first opportunity to ask questions of the new Doctor, and this marked the start of an intensive round of interviews and public appearances in which the actor spoke about his new role. These included a guest spot on the BBC's lunchtime magazine programme *Pebble Mill at One* on 3 December 1980, when he discussed with the presenter a number of costume ideas sent in by viewers and was particularly impressed by a suggestion from one of a panel of young fans assembled in the studio that the new Doctor should be 'like Tristan Farnon, but with bravery and intellect'.

It was during this period of publicity activity that Davison made a brief appearance in another science fiction series, when he accepted a cameo role as Dish of the Day – a cow-like alien creature

– in the fifth episode of the BBC's television adaptation of Douglas Adams's cult radio serial *The Hitch-Hiker's Guide to the Galaxy*. He had been suggested for this part by Dickinson, who was playing Trillian – one of the regulars in the series.

Davison's appearance in *The Hitch-Hiker's Guide to the Galaxy* was recorded on 19 December 1980 and transmitted on 2 February 1981, by which time the viewing public were well aware that he would soon be taking over the lead role in *Doctor Who*. There was in fact only a month to go before he would make his on-screen debut in the series – albeit a brief one, in the regeneration sequence at the end of *Logopolis*.

When work subsequently began on Davison's first full season as the Doctor, recording getting under way on 13 April 1981, he found that he was afforded relatively little advice or guidance by Nathan-Turner as to how he should approach the part – perhaps not surprisingly, given the producer's view that he was a personality actor who would bring to the series his own distinctive personal qualities and traits.

'I don't think John had much in mind about what he wanted the part to be,' noted Davison in a 1985 interview, 'except for casting me in it. I mean, he didn't say "I'm offering you the part, and I want you to play it like *this*." The trick of a good producer is to cast someone who is right for the part in the way that they see it, and then let them do it. Which is really what he did. I was very much thrown in and told "You're the Doctor – now do it!"'

To start with, Davison adopted a style of performance that he would later describe as 'bland', his aim being to avoid establishing too firm a precedent before he had fully refined his approach to the role. He had however already formed some quite specific views as to what the fifth Doctor should be like, and these would underpin his interpretation of the character. In common with Nathan-Turner, he wanted to make the Time Lord more heroic and resourceful but at the same time more vulnerable, so as to bring back an element of tension that was felt to have been lacking during the latter stages of the fourth Doctor's era.

'The suspense of "Now how is he going to get out of this tight corner?" has been missing,' he was quoted as saying in an early press interview. 'I want to restore that. My Doctor will be flawed. He will have the best intentions and he will in the end win through, but he will not always act for the best. Sometimes, he will even endanger his companions.

But I want him to have a sort of reckless innocence.'

Davison also drew a certain amount of inspiration for his performance from the earlier Doctors – particularly the first and second, as played by William Hartnell and Patrick Troughton respectively, whose exploits he had followed avidly as a teenager. More recently he had studied a number of stories from all four of his predecessors' eras after borrowing videotape copies from Nathan-Turner.

Davison's debut season, season nineteen, was well received both by the general viewing public and by BBC management, who considered the actor to have made a major contribution to its

▲ Peter Davison played a double role as the Doctor and Omega in *Arc of Infinity*

◄ Davison gives Terry Wogan the Doctor's jacket to auction off for the BBC's charity *Children in Need*.

▲ The Doctor suffers at the hands of Stotz (Maurice Roëves) and his mercenaries. *The Caves of Androzani*.

▲ Peri (Nicola Bryant) and the Doctor Find themselves prisoners of Sharez Jek (Christopher Gable). *The Caves of Androzani*.

▲ Davison and Patricia Hodge indulge in some early 80s role-reversal in the successful ITV comedy series *Holding the Fort*.

◄ The Doctor and Kalid who is revealed to be the Master (Anthony Ainley). *Time Flight*.

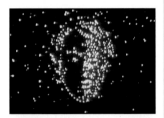

Graphic designer Sid ▲
Sutton reshot his title
sequence design to include
the new Doctor's face.

Davison made the part of ▶
the fifth Doctor his own.

Peter Davison as ▲
presenter of the 1985 BBC
series *L Driver.*

success. Davison, for his part, was very pleased with the way his stint on the series had begun and well satisfied with all aspects of the production. Season twenty, however, was rather less successful in his eyes. In particular, he felt that the character of the Doctor had fallen into something of a rut and that he was being less well served than he should be by the series' scripts. One thing that he was especially keen to do was to inject some elements of flippant humour into his portrayal, but any such suggestions were generally vetoed by Nathan-Turner in what the actor regarded as an over-reaction against the perceived excesses of his predecessor in this regard. Davison was also rather dissatisfied with his own performance during the course of this season.

Quite apart from these concerns about his own role, the actor had a number of misgivings about the general direction in which the series was moving at this point.

'I was actually very unhappy with the second season, script-wise and concept-wise,' he admitted in 1988. 'I just felt that it didn't go anywhere and John couldn't quite decide if he was having old monsters back or bringing in new ones. And I wasn't very happy with me in it.

'It was then – in the second year – that I had to decide if I wanted to do a fourth year, because of the way it works. But I just wasn't sure about the programme.

'John and I have always got on very well, but we

did have a creative difference over the direction in which he wanted *Doctor Who* to go, and the direction in which I thought it should go. We talked it through and I decided I would be better off if I left...

'It wasn't a row at all – indeed, I didn't decide until about two months after our discussion that maybe I should leave. It was kind of frustrating coming to the BBC rehearsal rooms every day as well, and seeing people doing other things.'

Davison was in fact much happier with his third and final season, season twenty-one, than he had been with the previous one. By this point, however, steps had already been taken to write him out and to cast a replacement, so it was too late for a rethink. Thus it was that the fifth Doctor bowed out with the transmission on 16 March 1984 of his final regular episode.

After leaving *Doctor Who*, Davison continued to pursue a very successful acting career. He also became a father when on Christmas day 1984 his wife gave birth to a daughter, Georgia Elizabeth, at Queen Charlotte's Hospital in London. Ten years later, however, his marriage to Dickinson broke down and they separated.

Although he has taken occasional roles in theatre, radio and film, most of the actor's work has been in the medium for which he is best known: television. His credits have included regular stints as Henry Myers in *Anna of the Five Towns*, as Dr Stephen Daker in *A Very Peculiar Practice*, as Albert Campion in *Campion* and as Clive Quigley in *Ain't Misbehavin'*, all for the BBC, and as Ralph in Yorkshire TV's *Fiddler's Three*. In addition, he has reprised his popular role of Tristan Farnon on a number of occasions for one-off specials and revival seasons of *All Creatures Great and Small*. He has also returned several times to the world of *Doctor Who*. In 1993 he appeared as the fifth Doctor in *Dimensions in Time*, a brief two-part skit transmitted as part of the BBC's annual *Children in Need* charity appeal, and in 1985 he narrated an abridged novelisation of the season twenty-one story *Warriors of the Deep* for BBC Worldwide's *Doctor Who* audio book series. In addition, he has appeared in a number of video dramas produced by Bill Baggs Video.

'*Doctor Who* was a lot of fun to do,' he said in 1988. 'We had some terrific guest artists, and I wouldn't have missed it for anything. It was very demanding, and strikes delayed my last story so I was too tired to feel sad when it was all finally over, but, yes, one does suffer the odd pang.'

CHAPTER FOUR

The Fifth Doctor: A Vulnerable Hero

T he Doctor's regenerations always bring about a change not only in his physical appearance but also in his personality – although many underlying aspects of his character remain the same from one incarnation to the next.

The fifth Doctor's debut adventure, *Castrovalva*, sees him making a gradual recovery from a condition of post-regeneration trauma. His behaviour is initially muddled and erratic. In this confused state he mistakes his current companions for some of his earlier ones; seems to think that he is caught up in past adventures; and even speaks with the vocal inflexions of his former selves. Perhaps bearing out the old adage that 'clothes maketh the man', he seems to grow more lucid only after he stumbles upon the period cricketing gear that will become his regular attire. From this point on, as he seeks sanctuary in the neutral environment of the TARDIS's zero room and later in the supposedly healing domain of Castrovalva, he becomes progressively more stable and his true nature starts to emerge.

Even once his regeneration has stabilised, however, aspects of his previous incarnations' personalities can still be discerned. Like the first Doctor he can sometimes be tetchy and irritable; in common with the second he prefers to influence events from the sidelines rather than take centre stage; like the third he shows no reluctance to get

THE DOCTOR'S CHARACTER

The character summary of the Doctor sent out by the BBC to freelance writers in the closing months of 1980, when scripts for season nineteen were being commissioned and prepared, gave a general description of his background but offered little hint as to the new incarnation's personality traits, which were still being worked out by the production team and by actor Peter Davison. It reads as follows:

The Doctor

The DOCTOR comes from the planet Gallifrey, in the constellation of Kasterborus. His relationship with his fellow TIME LORDs has been portrayed in contradictory ways during the programme's long history; but the original premise is worth bearing in mind: the TIME LORDs were aloof super-creatures who watched the workings of the universe objectively, building up their store of knowledge without interfering. One of their number, unable to remain detached, plunged himself into moral involvement by 'borrowing' a TARDIS from the dry-dock where it was undergoing repairs. This fugitive was the DOCTOR. Subsequent adventures have had him revisiting Gallifrey and redeeming himself in the eyes of the TIME LORDs. There is, however, evidence that at least some of these stories may be forgeries!

Like all TIME LORDs the DOCTOR has two hearts and a normal body temperature of 60 degrees Fahrenheit. He's over seven centuries old, and has the capability of regenerating himself into different appearances – his present form being his fourth regeneration.

Incidentally, he's never referred to as 'DOCTOR WHO' either in speech headings or by other characters. His name is the DOCTOR – 'Who?' is the mystery! The fact that he is always

The Doctor realises that there is something very wrong with the history of Castrovalva. *Castrovalva.*

Continued on page 24

Two early photocall ▲ pictures of Peter▶ Davison as the Doctor.

From page 23

'DOCTOR WHO' for the purpose of the closing titles is a historical quirk, reminding us that the format has been shaped more by collective intuition than by centralised logic.

The DOCTOR shouldn't be seen as a sort of Superman. He's fallible and vulnerable and only too conscious that life consists largely of things going wrong for well-intentioned people like himself. Note too, that he's only rarely intentionally funny. If many of his responses and solutions make us laugh with their unexpected appropriateness it's because we lack his agility of mind and breadth of experience, and didn't see them coming.

involved in physical action, whether it be frantically operating computer equipment, racing to prevent a bomb from detonating or rushing to the rescue of one or other of his companions; and like the fourth he exhibits a sense of laconic wit and a tendency to eulogise at times of reflection.

His wisdom and experience are such that he can sometimes seem like an old man in a young man's body, but at the same time he possesses a boyish charm and a quality of naïve enthusiasm and vulnerability that really set him apart from all his former selves. The combined traits of heroism and fallibility can sometimes lead him to behave in a rather headstrong and reckless manner, rushing breathlessly into new situations with an air of innocent curiosity and failing to consider all the risks. Although he always acts with the best of intentions, he sometimes makes mistakes that land him and others in trouble – a trait never more apparent than when he finds himself unable to prevent the death of Adric in a space freighter crash at the end of the story *Earthshock*.

As in his first incarnation, he sometimes needs the aid of a pair of spectacles to read; and in *Four to Doomsday* he reveals that he is short-sighted in his right eye and carries a magnifying glass in his pocket. Also in *Four to Doomsday*, however, he is seen to be able to survive for several minutes in the freezing vacuum of space without the benefit of a pressure suit (although it is possible that the helmet-like apparatus that he is wearing to enable him to breathe is also generating some sort of a protective force field around him).

His improvised use of a cricket ball in the latter incident reinforces the impression given by his clothing that he has something of an affinity for the sport, and this is confirmed in the later story *Black Orchid,* when he actually takes part in a match in 1920s England and gives a good all-round performance. He is a strong swimmer, as demonstrated in *Warriors of the Deep*, but reveals in *The Caves of Androzani* that he is allergic to certain gases 'in the praxsis range of the spectrum' – hence his habit of wearing a stick of celery on his lapel, as this will turn purple if exposed to the gases and so warn him of their presence, after which he will eat the celery.

Like all his predecessors, the fifth Doctor is a resolute champion of the cause of good against evil, invariably standing up for the underdog and combating tyranny and oppression wherever he encounters them. He also has a considerable degree of moral courage, as is well illustrated by the following confrontation from *Earthshock*, when he seeks to prevent the Cyber Leader from harming Tegan:

CYBER LEADER: I see that Time Lords have emotions.

THE DOCTOR: Of sorts.

CYBER LEADER: Surely a great weakness in one so powerful?

THE DOCTOR: Emotions have their uses.

CYBER LEADER: They restrict and curtail the intellect, and logic of the mind.

THE DOCTOR: They also enhance life. When did you last have the pleasure of smelling a

A photograph from a special session arranged for the *Radio Times'* twentieth ▼ anniversary special.

The Doctor finds himself ▶ in trouble again on the planet Androzani Minor. *The Caves of Androzani.*

REPEATS

*Following **The Five Doctors** in 1984, no further **Doctor Who** stories were repeated on terrestrial television in the UK until 1992, when **The Time Meddler** was re-shown.*

The **TARDIS** lands in 1666 on the site of what will be Heathrow Airport. *The Visitation.* ▼

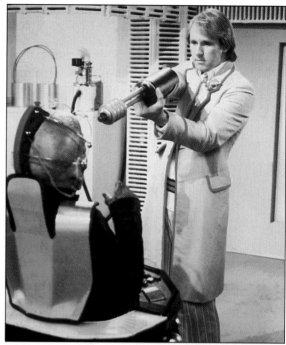

Although given the opportunity, the Doctor finds he is unable to kill Davros (Terry Molloy). *Resurrection of the Daleks.*

flower, watching a sunset, eating a well-prepared meal?

CYBER LEADER: These things are irrelevant.

THE DOCTOR: For some people, small beautiful things is what life is all about!

While his former selves acted as father figures or even grandfather figures to those who travelled with them, the fifth Doctor's relative youthfulness leads him to become almost an older brother figure to his own companions. He certainly has his hands full with the impulsive Tegan, and both Nyssa and Adric are more than capable of holding their own in their respective areas of expertise. At times, on the other hand, their behaviour can be more like that of a bunch of squabbling children, and he has to try to mediate and keep the peace between them. For all the exasperation his companions cause him, however, he clearly holds them in great affection and is invariably sad to see them go when the time comes for a parting of the ways. Even the initially threatening Turlough turns out to be a faithful friend – despite a continuing tendency to follow his own agenda.

The fifth Doctor's final adventure in *The Caves of Androzani* sees his youthful enthusiasm and curiosity undimmed and his heroism and resourcefulness arguably reaching new heights. It is only through sheer determination and physical courage that he is able to secure from the bowels of the planet Androzani Minor the vital antidote needed to cure his companion Peri of a potentially fatal case of spectrox toxaemia. In so doing he makes the ultimate sacrifice, as he too has contracted the disease and there is insufficient antidote for both of them. His fifth incarnation comes to a noble end as he is forced once again to regenerate.

CHAPTER FIVE

Season Nineteen: Unfamiliar Territory

John Nathan-Turner's main requirement for the fifth Doctor was simply that he should be very different from the fourth. In this he was motivated not only by his misgivings about Tom Baker's portrayal but also by the thought that to cast an actor who was at all similar to the outgoing star would be to invite invidious comparisons (a consideration that had weighed similarly heavily with past producers who had overseen the Doctor's previous regenerations). He had no definite preconceptions beyond this basic desire for contrast, and no specific actors initially in mind. He considered numerous candidates – including distinguished character actors Richard Griffiths (who proved to be unavailable) and Iain Cuthbertson – before eventually settling on Peter Davison.

Pinned up on the *Doctor Who* office wall were an array of photographs relating to past productions on which Nathan-Turner had worked, including one of Davison taken at a charity cricket match during his time in *All Creatures Great and Small*. It was this that brought the actor to his mind when he happened to notice it while mulling over his choice of Baker's successor. He put the suggestion to his superiors and they quickly gave their approval.

Davison embodied all Nathan-Turner's ideal characteristics for the fifth Doctor. He was younger and slighter in build than Baker and had straight, fair hair in contrast to his predecessor's dark, curly locks. He was also somewhat more reserved and easy-going in manner, and brought with him a large fan following from *All Creatures Great and Small* – something that the producer considered a great asset, given that Baker had become so closely associated with the role of the Doctor and would

consequently be very difficult to displace in the public's affections.

Christopher H. Bidmead, due largely to dissatisfaction with the amount that he was being paid by the BBC, had relinquished his post as the series' script editor after the completion of work on *Logopolis*. He had however already commissioned most of the stories that would make up the new season. The total number of episodes required had been cut from twenty-eight to twenty-six at Nathan-Turner's instigation as, despite putting forward strong arguments based on the considerable commercial income generated by *Doctor Who*, he had failed to secure a requested budget supplement of £2,000 per episode from BBC Enterprises – the commercial arm of the BBC, who regularly used *Doctor Who*'s props and

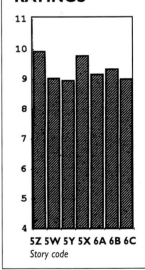

SEASON NINETEEN	
CODE	TITLE
5Z	Castrovalva
5W	Four to Doomsday
5Y	Kinda
5X	The Visitation
6A	Black Orchid
6B	Earthshock
6C	Time Flight

RATINGS

(bar chart, y-axis from 4 to 11)

5Z 5W 5Y 5X 6A 6B 6C
Story code

◀ The newly regenerated Doctor (Peter Davison) climbs out of the TARDIS, piloted to Castrovalva by Tegan. *Castrovalva.*

Tegan (Janet Fielding), and ▲
Nyssa (Sarah Sutton) inside
the zero room. *Castrovalva.*

LOCATIONS

Castrovalva
*Crowborough WT
Station, Duddleswell
(on B2026), nr
Crowborough, East
Sussex; Buckhurst Park,
Withyham, East Sussex;
Harrison's Rocks, Birchden
Wood/Ayttons Wood, nr
Groombridge, Sussex.*

Four to Doomsday
No location work

Kinda *No location work*

The Visitation
*Black Park, nr Iver, Slough;
Tithe Barn, Hurley.*

Black Orchid
*Quainton Railway
Station, Quainton Road,
nr Aylesbury; Quainton
Road between Quainton
and Waddesdon; house and
yard in Quainton Road,
Waddesdon; Buckhurst
Park, Withyham, East
Sussex; Buckhurst
House, Buckhurst Park,
Withyham, East Sussex.*

Earthshock
*Springwell Lock Quarry, off
Springwell Lane,
Rickmansworth, Herts.*

Time-Flight
*Heathrow Airport,
Middlesex.*

The design for the ▶
fifth Doctor's costume by
Colin Lavers.

costumes for display in the permanent exhibitions at Longleat House and at Blackpool (see Chapter Twenty-One). Nathan-Turner's feeling was that as BBC Enterprises gained financially from using these items, then perhaps they could contribute towards their creation in the first place. Without these additional funds, Nathan-Turner felt that he had insufficient resources to maintain acceptable production standards over twenty-eight episodes' worth of screen time. The season would consequently consist of six four-part stories and one two-part story (a pattern that would be followed throughout the fifth Doctor's era, even though in later years Nathan-Turner would succeed in

Beige frockcoat with
scarlet neat trim
Knitted waistcoat
Striped trousers
Lace-up boots dyed beige

obtaining a BBC Enterprises input towards the series' budget).

The original intention was that the season should open with the John Flanagan and Andrew McCulloch four-parter *Project '4G'*, commissioned on 7 October 1980 and now retitled *Project Zeta-Sigma*, and that this should be followed, both on transmission and in production, by another four-parter, *Day of Wrath*, commissioned around the turn of the year from Terence Dudley.

Bidmead's successor as script editor was Antony Root, who took up the post in January 1981 on a temporary basis. He had begun his BBC career as an assistant floor manager but was now trying to break into production by completing an in-house script editor's training course. This involved spending around three months on attachment to the BBC's Television Drama Script Unit followed by a period as a trainee back in the Series and Serials Department.

'At the end of my time at the Script Unit,' recalled Root in 1992, 'Chris Bidmead decided to leave *Doctor Who* and they needed someone to plug the script editor job for a limited period while they found a replacement. I arrived back with perfect timing and was asked if I would do it – which, of course, I did.'

A major change of plan occurred around the end of February 1981 when, even though pre-production had already begun, Nathan-Turner decided to drop *Project Zeta-Sigma* from the season's schedule, possibly with a view to moving it back to a later slot (although ultimately it was abandoned altogether). This created an urgent need for a replacement first story, and Nathan-Turner decided that the ideal person to provide it would be Bidmead, who had returned to freelance writing following his departure from the production team. Bidmead was approached and readily agreed. His story was commissioned in outline form on 9 March 1981 under the working title *The Visitor* and in full script form on 8 April 1981 as *Castrovalva*. Like *Project Zeta-Sigma*, it featured the Master as its principal villain, thus preserving the original idea of a loose trilogy of stories revolving around that character.

One consequence of the late abandonment of *Project Zeta-Sigma* was that Davison's first transmitted story could no longer be the first made, for the simple reason that recording was due to start in mid-April and the scripts for *Castrovalva* could not be completed in time. *Day of Wrath*, which in late February had been retitled *Four to*

Enlightenment (Annie Lambert), Monarch (Stratford Johns) and Persuasion (Paul Shelley). *Four to Doomsday.*

Doomsday, was therefore moved forward to fill the production slot previously held by *Project Zeta-Sigma*. *Castrovalva* was meanwhile scheduled to be made fourth in line, after *Four to Doomsday* and two other stories, *The Visitation* and *Kinda*, which would be transmitted fourth and third respectively. Making a virtue of this necessity, Nathan-Turner considered it a positive advantage that Davison would now have a little time to settle into the role before having to record the story that would introduce his Doctor to the public.

Season nineteen began its on-air run when the first episode of *Castrovalva* went out on 4 January 1982, heralded in the *Radio Times* with a colour photo-feature. The series was to be found not in its traditional Saturday teatime slot, but in an unfamiliar weekday evening slot, transmitted at the rate of two episodes per week in the manner of contemporary soap operas. This was the first major change of scheduling that *Doctor Who* had ever undergone, and was effectively imposed on the production team by Alan Hart, the Controller of BBC1. It is believed to have been motivated in part by a wish to see an improvement in the series' ratings – which had slumped during season eighteen as many viewers abandoned *Doctor Who* in favour of the glossy American sci-fi series *Buck Rogers in the 25th Century*, scheduled in direct competition on the ITV network – and in part by a desire to test the viability of running a twice-weekly drama serial on prime-time BBC1 (an idea later carried forward with the phenomenally successful soap opera *EastEnders*).

Adric (Matthew Waterhouse) and Nyssa (Sarah Sutton) wear oxygen helmets due to the low oxygen levels on the Urbankan ship. *Four to Doomsday.*

MUSIC

Story	Composer
Castrovalva	Paddy Kingsland
Four to Doomsday	Roger Limb
Kinda	Peter Howell
The Visitation	Paddy Kingsland
Black Orchid	Roger Limb
Earthshock	Malcolm Clarke
Time-Flight	Roger Limb

Castrovalva featured several stock sound effects. There was a siren, an ambulance siren, rushing wind (as atmosphere), footsteps and a bump, a head bump, a door crashing down, the sounds of a jungle in Sri Lanka at dawn in January 1945, a canary singing, swimming and diving noises, a Tibetan ceremonial horn, an open fireplace, some wind and finally the sound of glass crashing.

To give an authentic feel to the recreationals performed by the different human cultural groups in **Four to Doomsday** an excerpt from **Flutes of the Andes** was used, as was the signature tune to a BBC programme called **Quest Under Capricorn**, which featured a didgeridoo, and finally a piece taken from a National Theatre production of **The Royal Hunt of the Sun**.

Peter Davison hummed a few bars of the popular song 'London's Burning' in the closing moments of **The Visitation**.

Black Orchid featured the following period tracks: 'Lazy' by Irving Berlin, 'Show Me The Way To Go Home' by Irving King, 'Pasadena' by Warren, 'Charleston' by Mack-Johnson, 'Gentlemen Prefer Blondes' by Irving Berlin, 'I Want To Be Happy' by Irving Caesar/Vincent Youmans, 'Dinah' by Feldman, '5'2" Eyes Of Blue' by Henderson and 'When Erastus Plays His Old Kazoo' by Coslow-Fain-Spier.

WELSH VARIATIONS

The episodes which comprised season nineteen had a different transmission slot in Wales than in the rest of the UK. They were transmitted on Mondays and Wednesdays at around 7.45 p.m.

◀ The Doctor meets the android, Bigon (Philip Locke). *Four to Doomsday.*

Karuna (Sarah Prince) ▶
and Panna (Mary Morris).
Kinda.

Four drawings from the ▲
storyboard for a scene
where the Doctor walks in
space. *Four to Doomsday.*

The scene as recorded, ▲
using CSO and a flying
harness. *Four to Doomsday.*

After reprising the closing scene of *Logopolis* in the form of a pre-credits sequence – the first time such a device had ever been used in *Doctor Who* – *Castrovalva* involves the Doctor suffering from post-regeneration trauma, in which state he only narrowly manages to save the TARDIS from destruction as it plunges back to Event One, the hydrogen in-rush that preceded the creation of the universe. He seeks sanctuary in the peaceful domain of Castrovalva, only to discover that it is an illusory, dimensionally paradoxical trap set for him by the Master with the unwilling aid of a kidnapped Adric. He eventually wins the day by enlisting the help of the Castrovalvan people who, although also part of the Master's creation, are nevertheless able to exercise free will.

Karuna (Sarah Prince) offers Sanders (Richard Todd) the Box of Jhana. *Kinda.*

Part of Bidmead's inspiration for the domain of Castrovalva (including its name) was provided by the works of Dutch artist M. C. Escher – something that was also reflected in the set and costume designs for the story. He got this idea when he saw some prints of Escher's work hanging in the office of Graeme McDonald (who around this time was promoted within the BBC from Head of Series and Serials to Head of Drama).

Protracted behind-the-scenes discussions took place regarding the choice of the new Doctor's costume, which would be seen for the first time (publicity appearances excepted) in the opening episode of *Castrovalva*. Nathan-Turner and Davison both felt that it should have, in keeping with the series' established traditions, an air of old-fashioned and slightly eccentric Englishness about it. A sporting motif was also thought to be a good idea. Polo jodhpurs were at one point considered but, in the end, period cricketing attire – a suggestion made by Davison and possibly again inspired partly by the photograph of him on the *Doctor Who* office wall – was decided upon as being a better choice. Nathan-Turner recorded these ideas in a memo dated 10 February 1981 to costume designer Colin Lavers, who then proceeded to refine and develop them. The final result, like the redesigned version of the fourth Doctor's costume seen during the previous season, had a highly stylised, uniform look very much in keeping with Nathan-Turner's preferences. The finishing touch was a prop stick of celery affixed to the coat lapel – another idea hit upon by Nathan-Turner.

The change of Doctor demanded as usual a change in the series' title sequence. Graphic designer Sid Sutton was again assigned this task, and came up with a sequence very similar to the one he had created just a year earlier for season eighteen.

'It was similar for that very reason,' he said in a 1992 interview. 'We didn't particularly want to change the titles very much after just a year. There were less stars and things, but only because Peter Davison's head was less interesting in shape than Tom Baker's. Tom had this rather large face and lots of hair, so it gave us a nice, interesting shape to work with, while Peter's was a lot smoother with less hair and so on, so the sequence seemed less "full up" on screen.'

Four to Doomsday, the story that followed *Castrovalva* on air, had got the season's recording under way when its first studio session took place over 13 to 15 April 1981. Set almost entirely on board a huge spaceship, it introduces the frog-like

The Terileptil leader (Michael Melia) plots to release plague infested rats in London and wipe out mankind. *The Visitation.*

Urbankans and tells of a complicated scheme by their leader Monarch (played by Stratford Johns, star of the BBC police series *Z Cars* and its *Softly, Softly* spin-offs) to travel back in time and thereby confirm his belief in his own divinity.

One of the most notable aspects of *Four to Doomsday* was that it featured a series of elaborate dance sequences, termed 'recreationals', staged by the android population of Monarch's ship. The production team engaged a choreographer, Sue Lefton, to help with these sequences. The androids were divided into four different ethnic groups – Greek, Chinese, Mayan and Aboriginal Australian – and an advert seeking ethnic minority actors to play them was published in the 12 March 1981 edition of *The Stage* newspaper.

A number of other stories initiated by Bidmead during 1980 for possible inclusion in season nineteen met the same fate as *Project Zeta-Sigma*, although most of them were rejected at a much earlier stage of their development. These included: *Psychrons* by Terence Greer (scene breakdown (SB) commissioned 13 June); *The Torsan Triumvirate* by Andrew Smith (SB 25 November); *Hebos* by Rod Beacham (SB 5 December); and *The Enemy Within* by Christopher Priest (SB 5 December, scripts 6 February 1981).

Kinda, which had the working title *The Kinda*, was commissioned in scene breakdown form on 10 April 1980 and in full script form on 25

September 1980. It was charged with Buddhist and other religious symbolism reflecting the interests of its writer, sometime polytechnic lecturer Christopher Bailey. The TARDIS visits the planet Deva Loka, where Tegan becomes possessed by an evil force called the Mara. The Doctor ultimately succeeds in banishing this creature, which manifests itself in the form of a snake, with the help of the outwardly primitive but telepathically-gifted native people, the Kinda.

Janet Fielding was given an opportunity to take centre stage in *Kinda*, due partly to the nature of

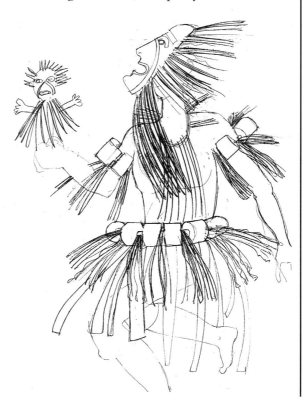

▲ The android (Peter Van Dissel) adopts the disguise of the grim reaper. *The Visitation.*

▲ Out-of-work actor Richard Mace (Michael Robbins) helps the Doctor to defeat the Terileptils' plan. *The Visitation.*

◀ Costume designer Barbara Kidd's initial sketch for the Trickster. *Kinda.*

Lieutenant Scott (James ▶ Warwick) accuses the Doctor and his friends of being responsible for the deaths of a group of geologists. *Earthshock.*

THE MONSTERS

The large amount of press coverage and appreciative comment generated by the return of the Cybermen in **Earthshock** *led John Nathan-Turner to suspect that further reappearances by popular monster races from* **Doctor Who**'s *past would be welcomed not only by the series' fans but also by the general viewing public. Partly in order to test this hypothesis, he gained agreement to the transmission during the summer months of 1982 of a season of repeats under the banner heading* **Doctor Who and the Monsters.** *The positive feedback and good ratings won by these repeats – edited compilation versions of season nine's* **The Curse of Peladon**, *season twelve's* **Genesis of the Daleks** *(the extensive editing on which was carried out by veteran BBC director David Sullivan Proudfoot, assisted by Nathan-Turner) and* **Earthshock** *itself, transmitted on BBC1 rather than on BBC2 as the previous year's* **The Five Faces of Doctor Who** *had been – convinced the producer that he was on the right track. Subsequent seasons would consequently feature many other return visits by popular foes.*

Costume designer Ros ▲ Ebbutt's design sketch for Tegan's party costume. *Black Orchid.*

Tegan's plight and partly to the fact that Nyssa played no part in the main action. The younger girl's absence was explained to viewers as the result of an illness forcing her to remain behind in the TARDIS. The true reason was – as Nathan-Turner recalls – that the scripts for the story had been prepared before it was realised that Nyssa would become a regular character, and it was considered impracticable to amend them to give her a significant part in the action. Sarah Sutton was contracted to appear in only sixteen of the season's last eighteen episodes (originally sixteen of the last twenty when the season was envisaged as twenty-eight episodes long), so it presented no contractual difficulties for her to be briefly written out.

The Visitation was the first *Doctor Who* story for some years to have a historical setting. The scripts were commissioned by Bidmead on 20 November 1980 from a writer named Eric Saward, who had previously had some success with work for BBC radio. Saward's original outline for the story had been written some months earlier, around March 1980, under a working title that he would later recall as having been something like *The Invasion of the Plague Men*. This had at first failed to find favour with Nathan-Turner owing mainly to the fact that it featured a semi-humorous actor-manager character – a device that the producer disliked. However, a shortage of suitable ideas from other writers had caused a rethink and Saward had been commissioned on 23 September 1980 to write a full scene breakdown. This had borne the revised working title *The Plague Rats* and been much more to Nathan-Turner's liking.

In *The Visitation*, the Doctor and his three companions arrive in England in the year 1666 to discover that the Terileptil occupants of a crashed space capsule are planning to compound the effects of the plague and wipe out all indigenous life on Earth. Aided by itinerant thespian Richard Mace (a character of which Saward had used variations before in three of his radio plays), the time travellers win the day when the Terileptils are consumed in an explosion that initiates the Great Fire of London.

The Terileptil leader's mask was the first example in *Doctor Who* of an effect achieved with animatronics – the use of mechanically controlled components to achieve lifelike movement. It was constructed by Peter Wragg of the BBC's Visual Effects Department.

The Visitation was notable also for marking the final appearance of the Doctor's sonic screwdriver, which had been a feature of the series for some fourteen years. Nathan-Turner felt that, like K-9, this device provided too easy a solution to the problems encountered by the Doctor, and he therefore arranged to have it written out – destroyed in a blast from the Terileptil leader's gun.

As production of the season progressed, some significant behind-the-scenes changes took place. Saward, on the strength of his work on *The Visitation*, was invited to become the permanent successor to Bidmead as the series' script editor. He took up the post in mid-April 1981 and worked alongside Root on the K-9 spin-off programme and on a number of season nineteen stories before assuming full responsibility around mid-way through the season's production. *Castrovalva* had in fact been the only new story commissioned during Root's short stint on the series; his involvement had been confined essentially to suggesting and performing rewrites and ensuring that scripts were ready in time for production.

'I went there originally for three months,' noted Saward in 1993. 'Antony Root had been working on the series, but unfortunately knew very little about putting scripts together. That's not deriding him; he was just inexperienced. Even after he had done three months on *Doctor Who*, the powers-that-be still wanted him to do something else before they would offer him a staff script editor post – this was how the BBC viewed *Doctor Who*, which in my own view was the most difficult assignment anyone could be given. So Antony went to work on *Juliet Bravo* and then on *The Chinese Detective.*

'Anyway, there was a lot of humming and

Lord Cranleigh (Michael Cochrane), Ann (Sarah Sutton), Lady Cranleigh (Barbara Murray), the Doctor and Adric (Matthew Waterhouse) return from the funeral of George Cranleigh. *Black Orchid*.

hawing, and they kept extending my contract by a month at a time as they didn't know if Antony was going to be coming back to *Doctor Who* or what was going to be happening. We had this messing around for about three months, which was really very aggravating... Eventually they decided that I would be staying, and I was then given a nine-

month contract.'

Another important behind-the-scenes change was the discontinuation of Barry Letts' role as the series' executive producer. This was confirmed in the following memo sent to Nathan-Turner on 19 August 1981 by new Head of Series and Serials

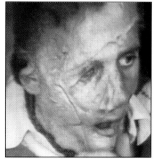

▲ The disfigured George Cranleigh (Gareth Milne). *Black Orchid*.

STOCK FOOTAGE

*A transparency of a forest was provided by Barnaby's Picture Library for **Kinda**. The photographer was Keith N. Radford.*

*Stock footage of fireworks was used for where lights are seen in the sky as the Tereptil ship crashes to Earth in **The Visitation**.*

*The shots of a train arriving in part one of **Black Orchid** were taken from a programme called **God's Wonderful Railway**.*

***Earthshock** featured a stock shot of a hillside in part one.*

*The sequence in **Earthshock** when the Cybermen view past encounters with the Doctor featured clips from the following: **The Tenth Planet** episode two, **The Wheel In Space** episode six and **Revenge of the Cybermen** episode three. All clips were seen in monochrome.*

*Episode four of **Time-Flight** featured some specially shot 16mm film sequences of the Concorde landing and taking off. These were completed by film cameraman Peter Chapman, film sound recordist John Gatland and edited by Mike Houghton.*

▲ Details are added to the freighter spaceship model. *Earthshock*.

▲ The finished ship against a starfield background. *Earthshock*.

Briggs (Beryl Reid), the captain of a freighter ship en-route to Earth unknowingly carrying an invasion force of Cybermen. *Earthshock*.

NOTES

Sink or Swim

John Nathan-Turner was obliged to release Peter Davison for six weeks between the completion of recording on **The Visitation** *and the start of rehearsals for* **Kinda**. *This was so that the actor could work on the second season of* **Sink or Swim**.

Kinda Additions

The first studio session for **Earthshock** *was used to record some additional material for* **Kinda**, *the final episode of which had been discovered to run badly under time.*

ANTONY ROOT
SCRIPT EDITOR

After leaving university Antony Root worked in the theatre for five years, initially as a theatre manager and then as a publicist. At the age of 25 he took a three-month holiday relief job as an assistant floor manager at the BBC, working on the season seventeen **Doctor Who** *story* **Destiny of the Daleks**. *This led on to a permanent AFM post, which lasted for around two years. He then secured a training attachment as a script editor, in the course of which he joined* **Doctor Who**, *having impressed the departing script editor Christopher H. Bidmead with a Script Unit critique that he had written of an unsolicited submission for the series. He left the production team when his training attachment came to an end but, having no desire to go back to being an AFM, managed to gain further script editor postings, including on* **Juliet Bravo** *(as an assistant) and* **The Chinese Detective** *(1982). He left the BBC in 1984 and moved to Euston Films, where he worked initially as a script editor and then as script executive on a number of programmes, including a five-part gangster series called* **Fear**, *which he also co-produced. Later he moved to a company called Working Title, where he continued to serve as a producer on such projects as* **Newshounds** *(a co-production with the BBC),* **Lorna Doone** *(a co-production with Thames) and the acclaimed Derek Jarman film* **Edward II**. *More recent projects have included the award-winning TV adaptation of* **Tales of the City**. *He continues to pursue a career in film and television production and in 1995 became Head of Drama at Thames Television.*

The Cybermen take ▶ control of the freighter as it nears Earth. *Earthshock.*

The Cyberleader (David Banks) and his lieutenant (Mark Hardy) discuss the Doctor's interference in their plan to destroy the Earth. *Earthshock.*

David Reid:

Although I have asked Barry Letts to read and comment on the two sets of scripts he presently has, we are both of the view that following your appointment as a substantive producer and indeed your own confidence in your abilities, the role of executive producer on Doctor Who *is no longer relevant. In future, will you deal direct with me on any problems/advice.*

The season's fifth story, both in production and on transmission, was Dudley's two-parter *Black Orchid*, which had the earlier working title *The Beast*. Like *The Visitation*, it featured a historical setting – in this case, England in the 1920s. It was the first *bona fide* historical story since season four's *The Highlanders*, in that it featured no alien monsters or other science-fiction trappings, and was thought of by Nathan-Turner as something of an experiment to see how this approach would be received by a modern audience. The producer initially contemplated directing the story himself, but his other commitments eventually ruled this out and the job went instead to newcomer Ron Jones.

Picking up on the motif of the Doctor's costume, *Black Orchid* sees the Doctor participating in a cricket match. Events soon take on a more sinister tone as a number of murders are perpetrated at the country home of the travellers' host, Lord Cranleigh. These crimes are eventually revealed to be the work of Cranleigh's deranged and disfigured brother George, who has been kept locked up in the house and who, despite the Doctor's attempts to save him, ultimately falls to his death from the roof.

Sarah Sutton was given a chance to shine in this story as she was required to play not only Nyssa but also her physical double, Ann Talbot. Some scenes in which Nyssa and Ann were required to be seen together in the same shot were achieved partly through the use of a double, actress Vanessa Paine.

The historical setting of the story offered costume designer Rosalind Ebbutt an opportunity to create some impressive period clothes, of which viewers were given a sneak preview in a December 1981 edition of *Blue Peter* as part of an item on the work of the BBC Costume Department.

'We hired in most of the standard 1920s clothes,' said Ebbutt in 1989, 'and others came from stock. It was the fancy dress for the party scenes that caused a bit of a problem. Every period has its own interpretation of the past and what people wore then. In the twenties, fancy dress parties were very popular, but there was a definite twenties interpretation of what period costume was – particularly if it was meant to be fancy dress. I tried to get that sort of look to it.

'I used a lot of things for reference: pictures of people in fancy dress at the time; some things of my grandmother's; and also pictures from that time of people in plays. The plays were set in the 1800s but the interpretation of them was very much 1920s. All those things helped. Basically, the conclusion I drew was that everything was very stylised, and that was the sort of thing they went for in the fancy dress – very stylised interpretations.'

The next story, *Earthshock*, was scripted by Saward. It had been commissioned on 24 July 1981 under the working title *Sentinel*. One of its most notable aspects was that it marked the long-awaited return of some of the Doctor's most formidable and popular adversaries, the Cybermen, who had last appeared some seven years earlier in the season twelve story *Revenge of the Cybermen*. The creatures' costumes were heavily redesigned for this latest reappearance. Their new look was devised by costume designer Dinah Collin in collaboration with Richard Gregory of Imagineering, a group of freelance visual effects contractors who had been commissioned to make the costumes – just one of a number of *Doctor Who* assignments that they would pick up during this period of the series' history.

Nathan-Turner was determined to keep the Cybermen's involvement in *Earthshock* a secret and went to great lengths to achieve this, even turning down the offer of a *Radio Times* front cover and article. The creatures' return therefore came as a complete surprise to most viewers – although shortly afterwards it formed the basis of a presentation by Gavin Scott on the BBC's television review programme *Did You See?*, which also covered some of the series' other monster races.

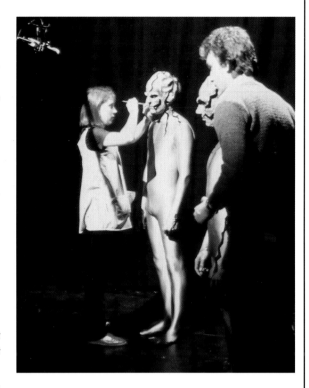

The Cybermen's scheme in *Earthshock* is to attack a twenty-sixth-century Earth using both a bomb and an invasion force hidden on board a space freighter under the command of Captain Briggs – a guest role for noted actress and comedienne Beryl Reid. When the Doctor intervenes, the freighter is sent millions of years into the past, where it explodes and causes the extinction of the dinosaurs – and also the death of Adric. The Doctor destroys the Cyber Leader by forcing into its chest unit some

◄**Preparing to record a scene with the Xeraphin. *Time-Flight*.**

ERIC SAWARD
WRITER/SCRIPT EDITOR

*Eric Saward was born in December 1944 and attended grammar school until the age of 18. After working for a short time as an estate agent he moved to Holland, where he lived for three years and was briefly married. On his return to England he took a succession of jobs, including as a publisher's proof editor and as a bookshop sales assistant. He then trained and worked for a while as an English teacher. He also started to write and found some success with drama scripts for radio, the first he had accepted being a play entitled **The Fall and Fall of David Moore**. At around the age of 30 he gave up teaching in order to pursue a full-time writing career. To supplement his income he also filled in with some odd jobs, including a stint in the theatre as a self-taught electrician working on productions such as **Hair** and **The Canterbury Tales** at the Phoenix in Shaftesbury Avenue. He was then approached by **Doctor Who** script editor Christopher H. Bidmead to submit some ideas to the series, having been recommended to him by the senior drama script editor at BBC radio. This led to a commission to write the season nineteen story **The Visitation**, on the strength of which he was subsequently appointed as Bidmead's successor. Since his acrimonious and controversial departure from the series some five years later he has continued to pursue a career as a freelance writer, including for German radio (his scripts being translated into German for production).*

CHRISTOPHER BAILEY
WRITER

*Writer and academic Christopher Bailey was resident in the Farringdon area of London during the period of his association with **Doctor Who**. Strongly interested in aspects of religion and philosophy, particularly Buddhism, he drew inspiration from these for his scripts for the series. His later work included lecturing at Brighton Polytechnic.*

◄**The TARDIS is loaded aboard Concorde. *Time-Flight*.**

The Doctor discovers that ▶
the Master (Anthony Ainley)
is behind the disapearance of
Concorde. *Time-Flight.*

FIONA CUMMING
DIRECTOR

Fiona Cumming began her career as an actress. She started out at the Royal Scottish Academy and went on to a variety of theatre and television work, including a spell at Border Television in the dual role of announcer and features interviewer. Then, deciding that she would prefer production work, she moved to London and in 1964 gained a post as an assistant floor manager at the BBC. It was as such that she first worked on **Doctor Who**, *on the season three story* **The Massacre of St Bartholomew's Eve**. *Following her promotion to production assistant she gained two further credits on the series, on season four's* **The Highlanders** *and on season nine's* **The Mutants**. *Shortly after this she completed the BBC's internal director's course, and in 1974 she was taken on as a staff director. Amongst the productions on which she worked in this capacity were* **Z Cars**, **Angels** *and* **The Ωmega Factor** *(1979). In 1979 she left the BBC and went freelance, early projects including* **God's Wonderful Railway**, **Square Mile of Murder** *and* **Blake's 7**, *all in 1980, and four* **Doctor Who** *stories between 1981 and 1983. She has since remained active as a freelance director while also pursuing a number of other projects, including some with John Nathan-Turner in their Teynham Productions organisation.*

RON JONES
DIRECTOR

Ron Jones was born in Bristol in August 1945. Straight after leaving university he joined the BBC as a studio manager in local radio. At the end of October 1968 he transferred to television and became an assistant floor manager, in which capacity he subsequently worked on a wide range of programmes. Next came a two-year stint as a researcher, writer and occasional film insert director on **Blue Peter**. *His preference was for drama, however, and after gaining promotion to production manager he secured assignments on a number of productions including the popular series* **Bergerac** *and* **Secret Army**. *He had by this time also completed the BBC's internal director's course, and this led to him gaining his first credits as a bona fide director on the season nineteen* **Doctor Who** *stories* **Black Orchid** *and* **Time-Flight**. *He died in 1995.*

gold fragments from a badge previously worn by Adric to signify his mathematical excellence (gold being fatal to Cybermen if introduced into their respiratory system).

Adric was the first regular to be killed off since Sara Kingdom in season three. The production team's hope was that this dramatic end – the emotional nature of which was heightened by having the closing credits rolled in silence over a shot of Adric's shattered badge against a black background – would leave a lasting impression on viewers. Matthew Waterhouse was less than happy to make his exit in this way, partly because he thought it would preclude any possibility of a return appearance in later years.

Nathan-Turner had always intended to have one of the Doctor's companions written out during the course of the season but had originally thought that it should be Nyssa, whom he had envisaged making her exit in *Four to Doomsday*. He had changed his mind, however, after Davison raised strong objections to this plan. The actor, although sympathising with the producer's desire to reduce the number of companions and thus make life easier for the series' writers, had been keen that the one to go should not be Nyssa, whose pleasant, refined character he considered made her the most suited of the three to accompany his Doctor. It was in the light of this that Nathan-Turner had decided to have Adric written out instead – an arrangement with which Davison was content.

The young Alzarian's final story was originally to have been Priest's *The Enemy Within*, the plot of which would have involved the Doctor coming into conflict with a fearsome entity revealed to be

living at the heart of the TARDIS and supplying it with its power. This had fallen through at the end of June 1981, when Nathan-Turner had rejected the second draft of the scripts. *Earthshock* had then been commissioned from Saward as a direct replacement. Priest – an established and respected science fiction author – was displeased with the way that he had been treated, and a dispute subsequently arose between him and the BBC over payment for the work that he had carried out. Matters were resolved at the end of September when the BBC agreed to pay him what he and his agents maintained that he was owed, albeit without admitting liability. Root was given the script editor credit on Saward's story but had no real involvement with it; this was done simply to avoid Saward being acknowledged as the editor of his own scripts – a practice normally forbidden under BBC rules.

The season's finale was Peter Grimwade's *Time-Flight*, which came about after Nathan-Turner gained agreement from British Airways to feature their Concorde aircraft in the series and obtained permission from the airport authorities to carry out filming at London Heathrow. The story had initially been considered for possible inclusion in season eighteen, and had been commissioned on 19 March 1980. It was developed under the working titles *Zanadin* and, later, *Xeraphin*.

Time-Flight tells of an intricate scheme by the Master, in his latest guise as a genie-like figure named Kalid, to gain control over a powerful alien race, the Xeraphin. During the course of the action, two Concordes are seen to be transported through a time rift to the Xeraphin's location on prehistoric Earth – sequences that stretched to the limit the ingenuity of the series' design and visual effects teams. Recording was hampered by industrial action but eventually concluded on schedule on 3 February 1982 – the last studio day for the season.

At the end of the story's last episode – which brought season nineteen to a close when transmitted on 30 March 1982 – the Doctor and Nyssa depart together in the TARDIS, apparently abandoning Tegan at Heathrow. However, there was never any serious possibility that this would be Fielding's last appearance in *Doctor Who*; the aim was simply to create a cliff-hanger ending and thus help to maintain viewers' interest over the long between-seasons break – an idea also prompted in part by the use of a similar device in *Blake's 7*. Tegan would therefore return in the first story of the following year's run.

CHAPTER SIX

Season Twenty: Moving Forward, Looking Back

During the course of 1981 and 1982 the production team set about assembling a package of stories to make up the season that would mark *Doctor Who*'s twentieth anniversary on air.

As had been the case for the previous two seasons, a considerable number of ideas that were accorded serious consideration were ultimately dropped. These included a four-parter, title unknown, by Tanith Lee (scripts (S) commissioned 6 February 1981); *Way Down Yonder* by Lesley Elizabeth Thomas (scene breakdown (SB) commissioned 23 April 1981); *Space-Whale* (also known as *Song of the Space Whale*) by Patrick Mills and John Wagner (SB 7 September 1981, S 2 December 1981); and *Parasites* (also known as *The Parasites*) by Bill Lyons (SB 22 September 1981, S 16 February and 23 April 1982).

There were however seven stories – six four-parters and one two-parter – that were eventually judged suitable for inclusion in the season. One of these was Johnny Byrne's *Arc of Infinity*, the scripts for which were commissioned on 13 January 1982

SEASON TWENTY

CODE	TITLE
6E	Arc of Infinity
6D	Snakedance
6F	Mawdryn Undead
6G	Terminus
6H	Enlightenment
6J	The King's Demons

RATINGS

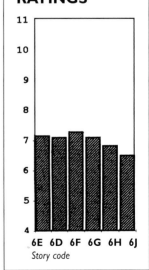

Story code

◄ The Doctor is threatened by Omega's accomplice, Councillor Hedin (Michael Gough). *Arc of Infinity.*

MUSIC

Story	Composer
Arc of Infinity	Roger Limb
Snakedance	Peter Howell
Mawdryn Undead	Paddy Kingsland
Terminus	Roger Limb
Enlightenment	Malcolm Clarke
The King's Demons	Jonathan Gibbs

Arc of Infinity featured two tracks used during the sequences in Amsterdam. The first was 'Tulips From Amsterdam' played by a street organ and the other was 'Canal Song' played by a barrel organ. Both were recorded live on location.

Arc of Infinity also featured ambient music composed by Dick Mills for the sequences set inside the Matrix.

Peter Howell re-used many musical cues and stings from Kinda in his score for Snakedance.

Mawdryn Undead featured the stock track 'Lilliburlero' arranged by Edrich Siebart.

Malcolm Clarke's score for Enlightenment featured a track called 'The Milonga' from The Borges at 80 for the scenes at Captain Wrack's party.

Peter Howell was originally to have composed all the incidental music for The King's Demons, but, due to commitments on the BBC's radiophonic drama Inferno Revisited, he was in the end able to complete only the lute music, which was played in studio by Jakob Lindberg. The rest of the story's incidental music was composed by Jonathan Gibbs. A musician named Tim Barry was hired to play the drums for this.

STOCK FOOTAGE

The flashback sequence seen by the Brigadier in part two of Mawdryn Undead featured clips from the following episodes: The Three Doctors part two (Brigadier), The Web of Fear part one (Yeti), The Invasion part five (Cyberman), The Claws of Axos part four (Axon), Day of the Daleks part four (Daleks), Spearhead from Space part three (The Doctor), Robot part two (Robot), Terror of the Zygons part two (Zygon) and Terror of the Zygons part four (the Doctor).

The design for Omega's ▶ costume by costume designer Dee Robson. *Arc of Infinity.*

under the working title *The Time of Omega* on the strength of an original outline dated 15 December 1981 and entitled *The Time of Neman*.

In this original outline, the TARDIS arrives on Earth in the near future in the Dutch city of Amsterdam. The Doctor is suffering nightmares involving his recent regeneration, and Nyssa's Traken sensitivity to evil is aroused. In the city they encounter the Anarchs (barbaric individuals wearing punk clothes and make-up), the Sweepers (heavily armed and blank faced automata guards) and the Resisters (organised Old City dwellers). The Doctor learns that history has been drastically altered and Earth is now in the grip of an all-powerful leader called Neman (with no connection to the similarly-named minor character in Byrne's earlier story *The Keeper of Traken*).

Neman is in truth the Avatar – an extra-dimensional being who can obtain carnate existence only during a Time Lord's regenerative process and who has now taken on the Doctor's exact appearance. The Doctor and Nyssa travel

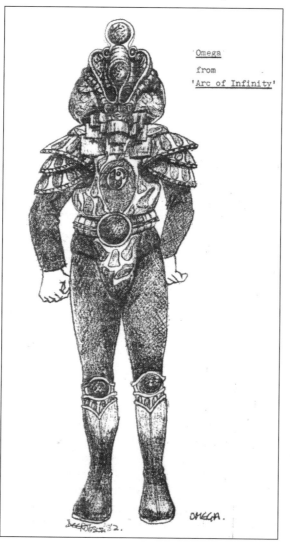

Omega
from
'Arc of Infinity'

OMEGA.

back in time to the present day to try to return history to its proper course. There they meet up with Tegan, who has spotted the Avatar during a visit to Amsterdam and mistaken him for the Doctor. The Avatar, under cover of an organisation called Neman Industries, is using industrial, political and military contacts to carry out a systematic alteration of people's minds to do his bidding. His ultimate aim is to cull the mental and genetic resources of humankind and create a living vessel through which he can find imperishable carnate existence. The Doctor defeats him by the dangerous ploy of reliving his own regeneration.

Few of these early ideas from *The Time of Neman* were apparent in the final version of *Arc of Infinity*. In fact the only major elements to be retained were the villain's replication of the Doctor's physical appearance and the Amsterdam setting. The latter had been requested by the production team (the basic story requirements having been confirmed to Byrne by Saward in a letter dated 1 October 1981) as Nathan-Turner was keen to feature an overseas location following the success of the season seventeen story *City of Death*, some of which had been shot in Paris. Amsterdam was chosen as the venue on this occasion as it could be reached relatively quickly and easily by air and – partly because of contacts the BBC had built up there

Omega's finished costume. *Arc of Infinity.*

during production of the soap opera *Triangle* – economical deals could be made for flight and hotel reservations.

In the story as transmitted, a traitor from the High Council on Gallifrey purloins the Doctor's bio data extract from the Matrix – the computer repository of all Time Lord knowledge – and transmits it to an alien composed of anti-matter who has managed to cross into normal space by way of a collapsed Q-star known as the Arc of Infinity. The alien must bond physically with a Time Lord in order to remain in this dimension, and the Doctor has been chosen as the victim. The High Council, headed by President Borusa, decides that the Doctor's life must be terminated in order to sever the bond and thereby remove the danger.

Tegan meanwhile arrives in Amsterdam to visit her cousin, Colin Frazer, only to learn from his friend Robin Stewart that he has disappeared. She enters an old crypt where he was last seen and is captured by a hideous creature, the Ergon. On Gallifrey, the Doctor escapes termination. The traitor is exposed as Councillor Hedin and his master is revealed as Omega, one of the founders of Time Lord society, who has been trapped for centuries in the universe of anti-matter (as seen in the season ten story *The Three Doctors*). Omega seizes control of the Matrix, but the Doctor is able to trace him to Amsterdam thanks to clues received from Tegan – who, along with Colin and Robin, has been taken to Omega's TARDIS by the Ergon. Omega's body is turning into a replica of the Doctor's, but the bonding is incomplete and there will soon be a massive explosion as he reverts to anti-matter. The Doctor, Nyssa and Tegan chase Omega through the streets of Amsterdam and eventually corner him at some lock gates. Omega wills his own destruction, but the Doctor fires the Ergon's matter converter weapon at him and he fades harmlessly away.

Commander Maxil (Colin Baker) and the Castellan (Paul Jericho) discover that the Doctor's bio data extract has been stolen. *Arc of Infinity.*

It was the production team's idea to substitute Omega for Byrne's character of Neman. This was inspired partly by a perceived similarity between the two characters and partly by a feeling that it would be fitting for the twentieth anniversary season to feature a villain from the story that had celebrated the series' tenth anniversary. It was later pointed out to Nathan-Turner by prominent fan Ian Levine – who sometimes informally advised the production team on continuity matters – that all the other stories of the twentieth season also featured at least one element from the Doctor's past. This fact was subsequently highlighted by the producer when promoting the season. To preserve the initial mystery surrounding Omega's identity in *Arc of Infinity*, the character was credited as 'the Renegade' in *Radio Times*.

As Nathan-Turner had hoped, the use of an overseas location attracted much interest from the British press. Five newspapers sent journalists to cover the filming, as did the Press Association. Much of the subsequent coverage focused on the new regular costumes that had been created for Janet Fielding and Sarah Sutton to wear this season (although in *Arc of Infinity* itself Sutton would still be seen in her old costume).

The Amsterdam location also featured prominently in the finished episodes, and particularly in the climactic chase through the city, much of the action in these scenes having been worked out by director Ron Jones during the shooting itself.

Omega takes on the Doctor's physical form as he attempts to enter the universe of matter. *Arc of Infinity.*

NOTES

Infinity Casting

The following shows those artistes considered for parts in **Arc of Infinity**. *The artiste actually cast in each case is given in square brackets.*

Castellan
Colin Baker, Bernard Hepton, Derek Godfrey, Patrick Stewart, Francis Matthews, Morris Perry, Keith Michell, Terence Hardiman, Anton Rogers, Peter Vaughan, Edward Woodwood, Charles Kay, Peter Gilmore, Sean Arnold. **[Paul Jerricho]**

Lord President
Robin Bailey, Geoffrey Bayldon, Andrew Cruikshank, John Horsley, Bernard Archard (2nd choice), Richard Vernon, Terence Alexander, David Langton, Michael Lees, Peter Cushing. **[Leonard Sachs]**

Hedin
Alan McNaughton, William Fox, Donald Bisset, Glyn Owen, Richard Leech, William Lucas, Jonathan Newth, Jeffrey Dench, Maurice Denham, Conrad Phillips. **[Michael Gough]**

Robin
[Following seen by director Ron Jones on 6 April 1982]
Matthew Ryan, Ian Michie, Bernadus Voorpostel, Steven Firth, Ian McCurrach, Gary Love, Neil Nisbet, Darren Hatch, Nigel Carrivick, David Wilkinson, Julian Ronnie. *[Also considered]:* Robin Hayter and Jason Carter **[Andrew Boxer]**

Damon	Daniel Hill [Neil Dagleish]
Talor	Nigel Lambert, David Rolfe [John D. Collins]
Zorac	Robert Swann [Max Harvey]
Omega	Stephen Riddle, Jonathan Newth, Malcolm Stoddard [Ian Collier]
Ergon	Gareth Milne [Malcolm Harvey]
Thalia	Honor Blackman, Jennie Linden, Linda Bellingham [Elspet Gray]
Maxil	Pierce Brosnan, Tim Woodward [Colin Baker]

Nyssa and the Doctor ▶
search the market place for
the missing Tegan.
Snakedance.

Lon (Martin Clunes) in ▲
ceremonial robes. *Snakedance.*

Dojjen (Preston Lockwood).
Snakedance. ▼

The Doctor defeats the Mara
at the climax to the ceremony.
Snakedance. ▼

The people of Manussa celebrate the defeat of the
Mara 500 years before. *Snakedance.*

'With a week's filming we wanted to get some
sort of value out of it,' noted Jones in 1985, 'and a
chase on foot has to be very carefully constructed to
make it exciting. I added things like a bridge
being pulled up just as they wanted to cross it, as a
way not only of prolonging the suspense but also of
saying, "Look everybody, this is the locale at its
most dramatic." My locating of the final moments
on the lock gates was another change from the
original script. I thought it pointed out rather
nicely that Omega had nowhere to run any more.'

Byrne was well pleased with the final result. 'I
think *Arc of Infinity* falls into the mainstream of
Doctor Who stories,' he said in 1991, 'and I liked it.
I was concerned to bring back Omega as someone
who was not so terribly black and white and
ranting as before. I saw the first story he was in and
although he was good he was completely over the
top. I tried to convey that an injustice had been
done. I also wanted to involve the characters on
Gallifrey, rather than simply using the place as a
setting. The final playout in Amsterdam was
decently shot and it did have a few moments of the
almost Frankenstein idea of returning to life.'

Arc of Infinity launched season twenty on air. Its
first two episodes went out on the evenings of
Monday 3 January and Wednesday 5 January 1983
respectively, although the regular transmission
pattern was then changed from the planned
Mondays and Wednesdays to Tuesdays and
Wednesdays for the remainder of the season.

The next story to air was Christopher Bailey's
Snakedance (referred to as *Snake Dance* on some early
BBC documentation). A sequel to the previous
season's *Kinda*, it was commissioned in scene
breakdown form on 28 September 1981 and in
script form on 9 November 1981.

Tegan falls once more under the influence of the
Mara and directs the TARDIS to Manussa, part of
the Federation of Three Worlds. Also present on
the planet are Lon, the Federator's son, and his
mother Tanha. Preparations are in hand for a
ceremony to celebrate the banishment of the Mara
five hundred years earlier. Tanha and Lon go with
Ambril, the planet's Director of Historical
Research, to see a cave system where the history of
the Manussan empire and the earlier Sumaran
empire is told in a series of pictograms on the
walls. This is where the climax of the forthcoming
ceremony is to take place. The Mara takes control
of Lon and uses him and Tegan to obtain from
Ambril the 'great crystal' – the large blue stone
that originally brought it into being by focusing
the energy from the living minds of the planet's
one-time inhabitants. The Mara now plans to use
the crystal during the ceremony to bring about its
return to corporeal existence.

The Doctor and Nyssa, aided by Ambril's
assistant Chela, locate Ambril's aged predecessor
Dojjen, who predicted the Mara's rebirth before
wandering off into the wilderness and
disappearing. The Doctor allows himself to be
bitten by a snake in order to enter a state of mental

commune with Dojjen, who tells him that fear is the only true venom and that in order to defeat the Mara he must find the still point within himself. The Doctor and his friends then return to the caves, where the ceremony is in progress. The Doctor, by concentrating his thoughts with the aid of a small replica of the great crystal, is able to find the still point and repel the Mara. As the Manussans recover, the Doctor tells a tearful Tegan that she is now free of the Mara forever.

Jan Spoczynski, the designer assigned to *Snakedance*, wanted to have the studio settings made by an outside contractor but was initially refused permission. Then, at a very late date, it was decided that half the work should go outside after all. This resulted in a rushed job, with which Spoczynski was dissatisfied. Part of the set for Lon's chambers was reused from a *Song for Europe* broadcast.

Although transmitted second, *Snakedance* was the first story of the season to be made. Film inserts were shot on 31 March 1982 at Ealing and studio recording got under way with a three-day session from 12 to 14 April 1982 in studio TC6. *Arc of Infinity* was next to go before the cameras, having been assigned this production slot mainly in order to increase the chances of getting good weather for the location filming in Amsterdam. After a break of around two months – during which Peter Davison was working on a new season of the *Sink or Swim* comedy series in which he starred – the remainder of the season's stories were then scheduled to be made in the same order as they would ultimately be transmitted.

The next three stories were conceived as a trilogy reintroducing the awesomely powerful Black Guardian and his opposite number the White Guardian – characters originally devised by former producer Graham Williams as part of his concept for the Doctor's quest for the Key to Time, as seen in season sixteen. They would be played, as before, by Valentine Dyall and Cyril Luckham respectively.

The first story in the trilogy was Peter Grimwade's *Mawdryn Undead*, the scene breakdown and scripts for which were commissioned simultaneously on 27 May 1982.

The TARDIS, its instruments jammed, materialises on board an apparently deserted spaceship. The Doctor discovers that the nearby Earth is the source of the jamming signal – a radio beam to guide the ship's transmat capsule. He travels to Earth in the capsule, leaving Nyssa and Tegan in the TARDIS with the co-ordinates pre-set to follow once he has deactivated the signal.

Things go wrong, however, as the Doctor arrives on Earth in 1983 but the TARDIS materialises in 1977. The Black Guardian has meanwhile recruited a young man, Turlough, to assassinate the Doctor. Although outwardly an ordinary pupil at a boys' private boarding school – a school at which, coincidentally, the Doctor's old friend Brigadier

◄ **Nyssa's new costume design by Ken Trew.** *Snakedance.*

INCOMPREHENSIBLE?

*David Reid, the Head of Series/Serials, Drama, Television, wrote to John Nathan-Turner on 22 February 1982 after having seen the scripts for **Snakedance**. He commented:*

I think you are making a mistake pursuing this line of story telling. I genuinely believe it is far too abstract and obscure. I really haven't got a clue what actually happens in the last episode.

To help – is it not possible to spell out (in Ep. 1) far more clearly what the Mara is – 'an evil force that takes people over via their dreams and can then break out to become a physical reality (presumably a snake?)'.

I think the various shots of Dojjen throughout the story will be simply confusing. I have the benefit of the stage directions; the audience does not. I think you would be better to drop any visualisation of Dojjen until they go off to find him in the mountains.

I suspect the end of Episode 3 could be a little weak.

3/56 and 4/41 [episode and scene numbers from the script] I suspect this was meant to be the answer to everything – to me I'm afraid it made very little sense. Sorry!

Nathan-Turner and Eric Saward responded on 24 February, taking each of the points in turn. They said that the Mara's image was explained and set up in the script for episode one and that the shots of Dojjen were intended to heighten uncertainty about the character's motivations. On the ending of episode three, they commented: 'More than enough has been set up to convey the importance of the Doctor escaping. The fact he is prevented is bad enough; the possibility of his being sliced to pieces by two bodyguards is made even worse.'

On the subject of overall explanations, Nathan-Turner and Saward felt that the story worked and that the audience learnt all that was necessary to know. 'The style of the story may be a little eccentric,' they noted, 'but is original, and, we feel, works very well indeed.'

They finished by suggesting a meeting to discuss the script further, if Reid so wished, and noted that the remainder of the stories in the season were 'more conventional sci-fi adventures'.

◄ **Tegan's new costume design by Ken Trew.** *Snakedance.*

MARK STRICKSON
TURLOUGH

Born in Stratford-on-Avon in 1961, Mark Strickson was brought up in the small village of Ilmington. His father was a professional musician and Strickson had learnt to play several instruments – as well as singing in the Trinity Church choir – by the time he went to grammar school, where he continued his musical training. After finishing school, Strickson went to RADA, where he studied music and acting. His first acting job was as part of the Mikron Theatre Company, who travelled the canals of Britain on a narrow boat performing up and down the country. Strickson wrote and composed many of the plays performed by the company over the two years he worked with them. Leaving the theatre for a while, Strickson gained his first television roles in **Celebration** *and* **Strangers**, *both for Granada television. For the BBC he appeared in* **Angels** *and* **Juliet Bravo** *before being auditioned for the role of Turlough. Strickson found himself in the enviable position of having to choose between the role of Turlough and the part of an ambulance driver in* **Angels**, *which he had also been offered. After leaving* **Doctor Who**, *Strickson played the young Scrooge in a remake of Dickens'* **A Christmas Carol** *(1985). In 1988 he emigrated to Australia with his wife, actress Julie Brennan, where he took a break from acting to study for a degree in zoology. He returned to the UK in 1995, and in 1996 he produced a number of wildlife films for television.*

The Doctor travels to ▶ Earth to find the source of the signal, and there meets Turlough (Mark Strickson). *Mawdryn Undead.*

Lethbridge-Stewart is working as a maths teacher following his retirement from the military – Turlough is in fact an alien who believes that the Black Guardian will return him to his home planet if he succeeds in his assignment.

Tegan and Nyssa encounter a man with a badly burned body. Not yet aware that they are in 1977, they think this may be a regenerated Doctor. Tegan goes for medical aid and runs into the Brigadier. They rejoin Nyssa in the TARDIS and, at the mysterious stranger's urging, return it to the spaceship. The stranger is actually Mawdryn, one of a group of alien mutants travelling endlessly through space in a state of perpetual regeneration brought upon themselves through the use of a stolen Time Lord device. The Doctor meets Turlough and the 1983 version of the Brigadier and takes them to the ship in the transmat capsule. He reluctantly agrees to supply from his own body the energy needed to end the mutants' ordeal, even though this will mean the loss of his remaining regenerations. In the event, however, the energy comes not from the Doctor but from an explosion caused when the two Brigadiers meet. The Time Lord returns the Brigadiers to their respective time zones and agrees

Mawdryn (David Collings), an alien scientist caught in an un-ending loop of regenerations, longs to die but needs the Doctor to achieve this end. *Mawdryn Undead.*

to allow Turlough to travel with him, seemingly unaware of the boy's murderous intentions.

As originally envisaged, the school teacher character featured in *Mawdryn Undead* was to have been the first Doctor's companion Ian Chesterton. Actor William Russell turned out to be unavailable, however, and so – after consideration was briefly given to using Harry Sullivan from the fourth Doctor's era – Grimwade decided to substitute Brigadier Lethbridge-Stewart instead. Nicholas Courtney again reprised the role.

'The return of the Brigadier was entirely my idea,' confirmed Grimwade in 1985. 'The nature of the plot meant that it had to be someone who had known the Doctor; the only brief was to include the Black Guardian and Turlough. I'd had the idea of a schoolboy character already and so, when Turlough was given to me, certain characteristics that I had in mind were amalgamated.'

Turlough had been devised as a new companion character by the production team. The original character outline, written by Nathan-Turner and dated 15 May 1981, described him as a 'twenty-year-old blond skinny youth, whom the Doctor first meets on a planet, on which he has lived as long as he can remember'. This tied in with the plot of the ultimately unmade story *Space-Whale*, in which it was originally intended that he should be introduced.

Writers Mills and Wagner, best known for their work in comics such as *2000 AD* (for which Wagner had created the popular Judge Dredd character), had first conceived of *Space-Whale* as a strip adventure for Marvel's *Doctor Who Monthly* but had submitted it to the production office at the suggestion of Mills's wife. Wagner had been somewhat reluctant to continue working on it after this point and had eventually agreed that Mills should take it over as a solo project. The plot involved the TARDIS bringing the Doctor, Tegan and Nyssa to an intergalactic whaling ship hunting the Ghaleen – a huge space whale inside which lives a whole community of castaways, including Turlough (substituted for another young man named John in the original story idea).

From an early stage, disagreements arose between Mills and Saward about the tone and content of the story, which was developed under the new title *Song of the Space Whale*.

'The original story featured this captain of the factory spaceship,' commented Mills in 1995. 'Now I didn't want a typical, neat captain. They bore the pants off me! So I had a captain who was rather a gross character, based on the captain of a Dutch dredger. But for Eric, this was inconceivable. He said that you could not have a working-class captain of a spaceship, even within the fantasy context of *Doctor Who*. He insisted that he had to be the perfect gentleman type. Tense, tough, a Biggles. The problem is, what on Earth do you do with a Biggles character? All they can do is shout orders.

'I also originally had the inhabitants inside the whale as a bunch of demented priest-like characters, but I was told that they wanted to get away from the "flowing robe" types. So I came up with something else and that was okayed, but ultimately rejected.'

Mawdryn Undead was substituted for Mills's story, which nevertheless continued to be considered for production for several years afterwards, going through numerous rewrites and revisions until it was eventually abandoned altogether in the autumn of 1985.

The actor chosen by Nathan-Turner to play Turlough after extensive auditions for the role was Mark Strickson, who accepted it in preference to an alternative offer of a regular part in the BBC's hospital-based drama serial *Angels*. His fair hair was died red for the part as Nathan-Turner thought that he would otherwise look too similar to Davison in long-shot.

The second story of the Guardian trilogy was

Terminus by Steve Gallagher, from whom the script for the first episode was commissioned on 15 October 1981 and those for the remaining three on 3 December. This was to be Nyssa's swansong as, notwithstanding Davison's fondness for the character, Nathan-Turner had decided that she could be developed no further and should now be written out.

Turlough – still under the Black Guardian's influence – damages the TARDIS's control console. The ship begins to disintegrate but, due to the operation of a fail-safe device, attaches itself to a nearby space liner. Nyssa is forced to board the liner, and the Doctor follows. Two space pirates, Kari and Olvir, have also come on board in search of plunder, only to discover that the ship is apparently deserted. Tegan and Turlough leave the TARDIS to look for the Doctor and Nyssa but get lost. The Doctor and Nyssa are meanwhile taken prisoner by Kari and Olvir just before the liner docks with what appears to be a hulk floating in space. This is Terminus, which claims to offer a cure to the leprosy-like lazar disease. It is crewed by a group of armoured slave workers, the Vanir, while the cure itself is administered by a huge dog-like creature known as the Garm.

Nyssa, who has contracted the lazar disease from other sufferers transported to Terminus in sealed units aboard the liner, discovers that the cure – involving exposure to a massive dose of radiation – does actually work. The Doctor and Kari meanwhile find their way to Terminus's control

MARY RIDGE
DIRECTOR

*Mary Ridge started her career in television working on **Theatre 625** from 1964 to 1967. Since then she has worked on numerous shows including **The Newcomers** (1967-1968), **The Doctors** (1970-1971), **Z Cars** (1971, 1972, 1974), **Dixon of Dock Green** (1972–1974), **The Brothers** (1973, 1976), **Owen MD** (1973). She was instructor to directors at Staff Training in 1969 in the build-up to the launch of **The Open University**. In 1977 she was associate producer on the second season of **The Duchess of Duke Street** and, as director, she worked on, amongst others, **Angels** (1978–1980, 1982-1983), **Blake's 7** (1980, 1981) and **The District Nurse** (1983–1984).*

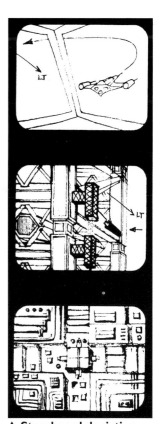

▲ Storyboard depicting the scene of the lazar ship docking at Terminus. *Terminus*.

◀ The Garm (R. J. Bell) cures Nyssa's lazar disease with a dose of radiation from Terminus's engines. *Terminus*.

GERALD FLOOD
VOICE OF KAMELION

Gerald Flood was born in Portsmouth, son of a Naval family. He was a wireless operator during the War and worked as a filing clerk after the War ended until he landed a job with the Farnham Repertory Company. It was there that he met his future wife, Anne. He toured in rep, and appeared in productions including **Hamlet**, **Power and Glory** *and* **Charley's Aunt**. *In 1960 he performed in* **The Complaisant Lover** *at the Globe Theatre and went on to appear in* **The Formation Dancers**, **Children's Day** *and* **There's A Girl In My Soup**. *In the 1960s he appeared in a science fiction series called* **Pathfinders in Space** *(1960), and its sequels* **Pathfinders to Mars** *(1960-1961) and* **Pathfinders to Venus** *(1961). Other television roles followed, including* **The Ratcatchers** *(1966/67),* **A Sharp Intake of Breath**, **Third Time Lucky** *and* **Bleak House**. *He also guested on shows like* **Randall and Hopkirk (Deceased): A Disturbing Case** *(1969),* **Strange Report** *(1969),* **Steptoe and Son: What Prejudice** *(1970) and* **Return of the Saint** *(1979). His films included* **Black Beauty** *(1946),* **Patton** *(1970),* **Smokescreen** *and* **Frightmare** *(1974). He died in April 1989.*

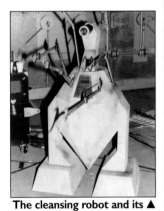

The cleansing robot and its ▲ control box. *Terminus.*

The Black Guardian (Valentine Dyall). *Terminus.* ▼

Recording scenes in the Terminus corridor sets. *Terminus.*

Marriner (Christopher Brown), Tegan and the Doctor attend a social gathering on the *Buccaneer*, captained by Wrack (Linda Baron) ship. *Enlightenment.*

room and learn that the ship was once capable of time travel and, moreover, was directly responsible for the creation of the universe when an ejection of fuel from one of its engines caused the 'big bang'. With the aid of Kari and the Garm, the Doctor is able to disconnect a still active engine that is on the point of exploding – something that could result in the universe's destruction. Nyssa decides to remain with the Vanir and help them run Terminus as a proper hospital. Tegan and Turlough are reunited with the Doctor, but the Black Guardian's wish to see the Time Lord dead is still unfulfilled.

'The misery of the lazars was based very much on medieval iconography of death and suffering,' recalled Gallagher in 1988. 'The costumes that the sufferers wore were all based on shrouds that were used around the time of the Black Death. The costume designer, Dee Robson, went into that quite deeply, and the costumes of the Vanir, the guardians of Terminus, were based on *memento mori* sculpture of the Middle Ages, which you get in Westminster Cathedral. The Garm is from Scandinavian mythology, just as are the Vanir, but they have a medieval image. A wonderful kind of stirred-up mixture of stew in there!'

Industrial action by BBC electricians flared up in October 1982 and disrupted *Terminus*'s studio sessions. At the end of the five days' recording (curtailed from the six originally scheduled) there were still some twenty-five shots left to be done, and a one-day remount was consequently required. This was initially planned for November and eventually took place on 18 December.

The concluding part of the Guardian trilogy was Barbara Clegg's *Enlightenment* (working title: *The Enlighteners*), commissioned in scene breakdown form on 22 September 1981 and in script form on 22 October 1981 (episode one) and 6 January 1982 (episodes two to four).

The White Guardian warns the Doctor of

impending danger and directs the TARDIS to what at first sight appears to be an Edwardian sailing yacht but is later revealed to be one of a number of spaceships taking part in a race through the solar system, the prize being Enlightenment. The yacht's Captain Striker and his fellow officers are telepathic Eternals who feed off the thoughts and emotions of their kidnapped human crew – Ephemerals – in order to fill their own empty existences. Turlough attempts to escape the Black Guardian's influence by jumping into space but is rescued and taken on board the ship of Captain Wrack – another of the Eternals. Two of the other ships involved in the race are destroyed and Turlough discovers that, far from being accidental, this has been brought about by Wrack using a concentrated beam of mental energy with the aid of the Black Guardian. The Doctor boards Wrack's ship, finds her source of power and, with Turlough's help, ejects her and her number two, Mansell, into space. The Doctor and Turlough then pilot the ship into port – a glowing crystalline structure hanging in space – and, in doing so, win the race.

The Doctor turns down Enlightenment, saying that none should have it. The White Guardian agrees, and returns the Eternals to the void. The White Guardian then offers a portion of Enlightenment to Turlough, while the Black Guardian demands that the boy give the Doctor over to him in exchange for the huge diamond within the glowing artifact. Turlough makes his choice: he sweeps the crystal from the table to the Black Guardian, who vanishes in flames. The boy is now free, as Enlightenment was not the crystal but the choice. Even so, the White Guardian cautions continued vigilance; while he still exists, so too does his Black counterpart, until they are no longer needed.

Production of *Enlightenment*, like that of

Turlough (Mark Strickson) must choose whether to aid Wrack (Linda Barron) and her first officer (Leee John) and complete his deal with the Black Guardian, or help the Doctor. *Enlightenment.*

Terminus, was hit by the ongoing industrial action within the BBC. The shooting of film inserts went ahead as intended between 3 and 5 November 1982 on Stage 3B at Ealing, but the two studio sessions planned for 16 and 17 November and 30 November to 2 December had to be cancelled. They were eventually rescheduled for 17 and 18 January and 30 January to 1 February 1983 respectively. One consequence of this was that some members of the guest cast, including Peter Sallis and David Rhule, had to drop out – even though they had already started rehearsals – as they were otherwise engaged on the new dates. Keith Barron was brought in at short notice to take over from Sallis as Striker, while Leee John – lead singer of the pop group Imagination – replaced Rhule as Mansell. Neither Sallis nor Rhule had appeared in the film inserts, so no continuity difficulties were created in this regard.

'In rehearsal we had the most difficulty with the scenes in the hold of the yacht,' recalled director Fiona Cumming in 1992. 'The perimeter of the set was marked out, but we knew that the shape would be determined by the boxes and ropes stowed, and that the pools of darkness that lighting director Fred Wright was planning would create the right atmosphere. Even so it was difficult to stop the giggling setting in when the cast were all negotiating non-existent hurdles at non-existent levels in broad daylight!'

The next story was the season's two-parter, *The*

King's Demons, the scripts for which had been commissioned from Terence Dudley on 22 February 1982 under the working title *The Android*. (Other working titles are reported to have been *A Knight's Tale* and *The Demons*, but these are unsubstantiated.)

The TARDIS materialises in thirteenth-century England during a joust held in the presence of King John. The King welcomes the Doctor, Tegan and Turlough as his 'demons', but his actions towards the family of his host Ranulf Fitzwilliam are decidedly hostile. The Doctor discovers that what appears to be the King is, in reality, a shape-changing android called Kamelion whom the Master found on Xeriphas (following the events of the previous season's *Time-Flight*). The Master has disguised himself as the King's Champion, Sir Gilles Estram, and is using Kamelion in a plot to discredit the King and prevent the signing of the Magna Carta, thereby changing the course of history. The Doctor manages to wrest control of Kamelion away from the Master, exposing his arch enemy's scheme. To Turlough's surprise and Tegan's dismay, the Doctor then accepts Kamelion as a new travelling companion aboard the TARDIS.

To conceal the fact that the Master was making his latest return appearance in *The King's Demons*, Nathan-Turner had the *Radio Times* credit the part of Sir Gilles Estram – whose surname was itself an anagram of 'Master' – as being played by 'James Stoker' – an anagram of 'Master's Joke'.

Kamelion was a computer controlled, sound activated, animated robot created by software designer Mike Power and computer hardware expert Chris Padmore of a firm called CP Cybernetics. Padmore was a colleague of

◀Tegan dresses in Edwardian costume at Marriner's bidding. *Enlightenment.*

▲ Storyboards showing the Eternals' ships in space. *Enlightenment.*

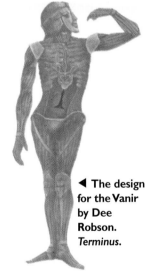

◀ The design for the Vanir by Dee Robson. *Terminus.*

TONY VIRGO
DIRECTOR

*In 1986 Tony Virgo took over as producer on the BBC soap opera **EastEnders**. He had worked as a PA on **Blake's 7** in 1978 and his first directing job was on the series **The Bill**. He became head of TV Drama at BBC Pebble Mill in 1995.*

Hugh (Christopher Villiers) ▶ takes Turlough to the dungeon of the castle. *The King's Demons.*

Recording the fight-scene ▲ between the Doctor and the Master. *The King's Demons.*

Sir Gilles Estram, alias the ▲ Master (Anthony Ainley). *The King's Demons.*

SARAH HELLINGS
DIRECTOR

Sarah Hellings joined the BBC as a film editor before moving on to make documentaries for the BBC children's magazine programme **Blue Peter**. *She worked on many* **Blue Peter Special Assignments** *before leaving the BBC to work as a freelance director on shows including* **Juliet Bravo** *(1982–1983). After* **The Mark of the Rani** *for* **Doctor Who** *she continued to work as a freelance director on many shows, including episodes of* **Howard's Way** *(c.1985).*

The Master (Anthony Ainley) uses the android Kamelion to prevent the signing of the Magna Carta. *The King's Demons.* ▼

Imagineering's Richard Gregory, who had approached Nathan-Turner on his behalf during recording of the previous season's *Earthshock* to see if he would be interested in featuring the robot in the series. Nathan-Turner had agreed, and Dudley had subsequently been briefed to include it in his story. The robot's operation proved by no means straightforward, however. Its speech reportedly took nearly two weeks to program for each episode; it was unable to walk; and it became the subject of numerous BBC union demarcation disputes. A further complication arose when Power, the only person who possessed a detailed knowledge of its software, was killed in a boating accident shortly after the decision was taken to feature it in the series. As a result of all these problems, Nathan-Turner quickly decided to have Kamelion written out in one of the following season's stories and its appearances kept to a minimum until then.

The voice of Kamelion was supplied by veteran actor Gerald Flood, who also portrayed King John in *The King's Demons.* Other notable members of the guest cast for this story included *Z Cars'* Frank Windsor as Ranulf and Isla Blair as his wife, Isabella.

One problem faced by cast and crew alike was the unfavourable weather encountered during the story's location filming, which took place in Bodiam, East Sussex, from 5 to 7 December 1982.

Studio recording of *The King's Demons* was originally scheduled for 18, 19 and 20 December 1982, but, as the first of these dates was now required for the remount on *Terminus*, it eventually took place on 19 and 20 December and 16 January 1983 instead.

The production team had originally intended that the season should close with a climactic four-part anniversary story featuring the Daleks and Davros. They had approached the characters' creator Terry Nation to write this, and although he had

been too busy to do so he had agreed that Saward could take on the task instead provided that he had script approval. A storyline entitled *The Return* was subsequently prepared and sent to Nation at his home in the USA. Nothing was heard in reply for several months, so Saward went to work on the scripts. Then, around the start of November 1982, Nation finally contacted the production office to say that he was happy with the basic storyline but would like several changes made. Nathan-Turner wrote back on 12 November agreeing to his requests:

I note your points regarding the realisation of this story and will ensure that your fears are allayed. The points being namely:

(1)   The Daleks should appear less vulnerable – more ingenuity being required to defeat them rather than firing into the top of their casings.

(2)   That their first appearance in the warehouse should be more spectacular.

(3)   Davros reviving the Daleks should be more heavily science fiction – e.g. mechanical injection into the casing.

(4)   We should leave Davros with a stronger hint of escape.

I enclose a copy of episodes one and two and the first draft of episode three which, I'm sure you will agree, work very well indeed. You may even find that some of your fears are allayed by the full text rather than the initial story breakdown.

The location filming for *The Return* had been due to take place on 4 and 5 January 1983 and the studio recording sessions had been scheduled for 16 to 18 January and 30 January to 1 February respectively. All these studio dates were now taken up with remounts on *The King's Demons* and *Enlightenment*, however, and – as no others could be found for it by the BBC's planners – the story had to be temporarily shelved. Director Peter Grimwade, designer Malcolm Thornton and the other chosen crew and cast members (including Michael Wisher as Davros, a character he had first brought to life in season twelve's *Genesis of the Daleks*) were all released to move onto other projects.

The season thus ended prematurely with *The King's Demons*, the closing episode of which was transmitted on 16 March 1983. This was not quite the end of *Doctor Who*'s twentieth anniversary celebrations on air, however, as later in the year it would be back again for a unique, one-off special.

CHAPTER SEVEN

Anniversary Special: The Five Doctors

It was John Nathan-Turner who had the idea of celebrating *Doctor Who*'s twentieth anniversary with a special story. He started thinking about this as early as the summer of 1981, and on 3 August that year sent Head of Series and Serials David Reid a memo requesting that transmission of season twenty be moved forward to the autumn of 1982 so that transmission of season twenty-one could similarly be moved forward to the autumn of 1983 and the special slotted into its running order so as to coincide with the anniversary date. Reid consulted Controller of BBC1 Alan Hart, who was unwilling to agree to this change but suggested instead that a one-off ninety-minute programme might be produced to mark the anniversary.

As plans for the special developed, Nathan-Turner and Eric Saward decided that they wanted a story that would feature all five television Doctors to date as well as numerous companions and monsters. Nathan-Turner was particularly keen that the Cybermen should appear. One early consideration was how to include the first Doctor, in view of the fact that William Hartnell had died in 1975. It was concluded that the best option was to cast another actor to play the part.

To script the story Saward and Nathan-Turner first approached Robert Holmes, who had extensive experience of working on *Doctor Who* both as a writer and as a script editor. Holmes had grave misgivings about the assignment in view of the large number of predetermined elements and characters that would have to be worked into the story, but agreed to see what he could come up with. In an undated letter to the production office,

TWENTIETH ANNIVERSARY SPECIAL

CODE	TITLE
6C	*The Five Doctors*

RATINGS

Story code (90–minute special)

◀ Tom Baker's waxwork from Madame Tussaud's, Peter Davison, Jon Pertwee, Patrick Troughton and Richard Hurndall pose for publicity photos in Bessie for *The Five Doctors*.

▲ Richard Hurndall took the part of the first Doctor.

MUSIC

Story	Composer
The Five Doctors	
	Peter Howell

NOTES

Casting Ideas

Charles Grey was considered for the part of Rassilon [Played by Richard Mathews] and Denis Quilley was considered for Borusa [Played by Philip Latham]

Hieroglyphics Explained

The hieroglyphics used on the obelisk in Rassilon's tomb were the same as those denoting the Doctor's name in the book **The Making of Doctor Who** *published in 1972 by Piccolo Books. The reason for this is that the designer of* **The Five Doctors,** *Malcolm Thornton, obtained a copy of the book to use as reference.*

LOCATIONS

The Five Doctors
Plasbrondanw, Llanfrothen, Penrhyndeudraeth, Gwynedd; Carreg Y Foel Gron, off B4407, nr Ffestiniog; Manod Quarry, Cwt Y Bugail, Ffestiniog; Cwm Bychan, nr Llanbedr, Gwynedd; Tilehouse Lane, Upper Denham, Bucks; MOD/YMCA Hostel, Hayling Lane, off Tilehouse Lane, Upper Denham, Bucks; West Common Road, Uxbridge, Middlesex.

The Tower of Rassilon in ▲ the Death Zone on Gallifrey, in actuality a model set on the Visual Effects Department's stage. *The Five Doctors*.

The Cyber Leader (David ▶ Banks) sees his patrol wiped out by the deadly chessboard floor. *The Five Doctors*.

he outlined for discussion three possible scenarios, the most detailed of which had all the Doctors and their respective companions being drawn to the planet Maladoom, where the Cybermen, aided by the Master, plan to dissect them in order to discover the genetic secret that separates the Time Lords from other beings.

On 4 August 1982, Holmes was formally commissioned to provide a scene breakdown for the special. It now had the working title *The Six Doctors*, reflecting the idea that the first Doctor seen in the story would turn out to be a cyborg replica constructed as a trap by the Cybermen – thus explaining why he looked somewhat different from Hartnell. However, as Holmes remained very uncertain as to whether or not he would be able to come up with a workable scene breakdown by the delivery date of 23 August, the production team decided to ask another writer to 'stand by' to take over. This was Terrance Dicks, another former *Doctor Who* script editor with numerous credits to his name.

On 1 September, with his scene breakdown still unfinished, Holmes attended a meeting at the production office to discuss progress to date. Saward subsequently wrote to Dicks on 2 September saying that Holmes had decided to try to script the first twenty minutes of the special, despite the fact that he still had huge reservations as to whether or not he could make it work.

Holmes delivered his scene breakdown on 13 October. Dicks was then commissioned on 18

October to provide an alternative, and Holmes's version was subsequently dropped. Dicks delivered his breakdown on 1 November, at which point the story had been renamed *The Five Doctors*, and was commissioned on 16 November to write a full script.

'I knew from the beginning that the job was going to be appallingly difficult and complicated and full of the most enormous hassles, as indeed it was,' explained Dicks in a later interview. 'Since I was prepared for that, nothing actually threw me. I knew it was going to be like jumping into a combine harvester from the very beginning … My standing joke about it was that it was like that game where you make up a story about objects that come out of a box. This particular box had an awful lot of objects in it!'

As *The Five Doctors* was produced as an addition to the standard pattern of *Doctor Who* seasons, the money with which to finance it had to be found from outside the series' normal budget. The BBC, realising that the story had great overseas sales potential, approached the Australian Broadcasting Commission (ABC) with a view to obtaining co-production funding. After numerous discussions, an agreement was signed on 7 April 1983 by the BBC and on 16 May 1983 by the ABC which brought in $60,000 in Australian currency. This meant that *The Five Doctors* was effectively pre-sold to the ABC, although under the terms of the agreement no credit to the co-producer would appear on screen. The series' production team had not been involved in this deal, and were unaware of it at the time.

The casting of a *Doctor Who* story would normally be carried out by the director in collaboration with the producer, but in this instance, as many of the cast were returning characters from the series' history, the question was usually simply a case of whether or not the required actor was available and willing to take part.

One of the exceptions to this rule was the first Doctor. Consideration was apparently given around July 1982 to casting Geoffrey Bayldon, who had appeared in the season seventeen story *The Creature from the Pit*, but the part was eventually offered to Richard Hurndall, whom Nathan-Turner had seen in an episode of *Blake's 7* and considered to resemble Hartnell. Hurndall accepted the offer on 6 October 1982. As Nathan-Turner wanted to have something of the original first Doctor in the story, he decided to use a clip from *Flashpoint*, the final episode of the season two story *The Dalek Invasion of Earth*, as a short sequence preceding the opening titles.

Second Doctor Patrick Troughton presented a scheduling problem as he was tied up working on Granada TV's *Foxy Lady* series on the April 1983 dates originally proposed for the story's location filming. Nathan-Turner, recognising that the story relied on the participation of as many of the surviving Doctors as possible, consequently moved the dates forward to March so that Troughton could appear.

Third Doctor Jon Pertwee was less of a problem as the actor was available on the required dates and happy to reprise his role.

By far the greatest challenge to the production team was presented by fourth Doctor Tom Baker.

'I think I first approached Tom in April 1982,' recalled Nathan-Turner. 'Initially he said that he was interested but would like to see a script. Then our first writer fell through, so although we had hoped to have a script within three months we didn't, and the time was going on. Eventually in the December we were filming *The King's Demons* somewhere down south and I knew that Tom was appearing at the Theatre Royal in Brighton, so I sent him the first seventy pages of the script, which was all we had. I met him after one of his shows to talk about it and at that time he agreed to do it. We were then able to contact Terrance and tell him that Tom was to be included. Within about ten days or so, he pulled out and changed his mind.

'That was an extremely big hurdle to overcome, because we were saying up front that it was the *five* Doctors, when really it was four and a bit, and one of those was a re-cast, so suddenly it started to look as though it was falling round my ears.'

To ensure that the fourth Doctor was represented in the show, Nathan-Turner had the idea of incorporating some scenes from the season seventeen story *Shada*, which had been abandoned part-completed due to industrial action and never transmitted. To this end on 10 January 1983 he wrote both to Baker and to Lalla Ward, who had played the Doctor's assistant Romana in that story, requesting permission to use appropriate clips of them. Both agreed.

'My feeling is that it all worked better the way it ended up,' noted Dicks. 'Five Doctors were just too many to handle but four worked very neatly, and you did at least *see* Tom. The other thing that I found quite amazing was how well the footage from *Shada* fitted in. I'll swear that if you didn't

know, you would think it was written for the special.'

Nathan-Turner was keen to have each Doctor accompanied by at least one of his original companions from the series. The initial intention was to team Susan (Carole Ann Ford) with the first Doctor, Victoria (Deborah Watling) with the second, Jo (Katy Manning) with the third, Sarah (Elisabeth Sladen) with the fourth and, naturally enough, Tegan (Janet Fielding) and Turlough (Mark Strickson) with the fifth. Watling and Manning ultimately proved to be unavailable, so Sarah was paired with the third Doctor and the Brigadier (Nicholas Courtney) with the second. Dicks also wrote in 'cameo appearances' by four other companions, who were confirmed only at a very late stage. These were Liz (Caroline John),

◀ K-9 warns Sarah Jane Smith (Elisabeth Sladen) of impending danger, shortly before she is grabbed by the time scoop. *The Five Doctors*.

▲ The third Doctor (Jon Pertwee). *The Five Doctors*.

▲ The first Doctor (Richard Hurndall) meets his grand-daughter Susan (Carole Ann Ford) and a Dalek in the Death Zone. *The Five Doctors*.

The Brigadier (Nicholas Courtney) and the second Doctor (Patrick Troughton) enter the Tower from the caves ▼ below. *The Five Doctors*.

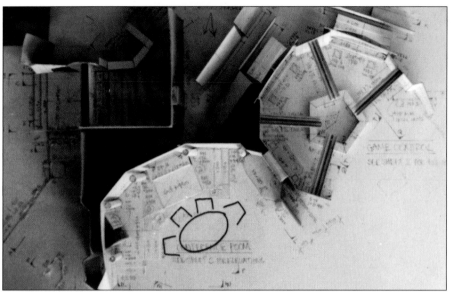

The design model for the sets of the Capitol, including the High Council chamber and the game control room. The Five Doctors.

Captain Yates (Richard Franklin), Jamie (Frazer Hines) and Zoe (Wendy Padbury).

Nathan-Turner's initial choice of director for *The Five Doctors* was Waris Hussein, who had handled the series' very first story, *100,000 BC*, back in 1963. On 20 December 1982, however, Hussein turned the offer down. The assignment eventually went to one of Nathan-Turner's regular directors, Peter Moffatt.

Dicks's story sees the fifth Doctor and his past incarnations being taken out of time by a forbidden time scoop device. They find themselves, together with a number of their old companions, in the Death Zone on their home planet Gallifrey, facing a Dalek, a Yeti, a deadly Raston Warrior Robot and a force of Cybermen. Also present is the Master, who has been summoned by the High Council of Time Lords to help the Doctor. It turns out that President Borusa is the mysterious operator of the time scoop. He aims to use the Doctors to breach the defences of the Dark Tower – Rassilon's tomb – so that he can enter the place and claim immortality. When he does so, however, he is condemned by Rassilon to eternal existence in the form of a living statue.

Moffatt, after briefly considering Scotland, chose Wales as the location for filming of the scenes representing the bleak Gallifreyan landscape. The filming at this location – hampered by bad weather – was carried out between 5 and 15 March 1983. The crew then moved back to London, and filming continued on 17 March at Tilehouse Lane in Upper Denham, Buckinghamshire, for the sequences

where the third Doctor is snatched by the time scoop; at a Ministry of Defence/YMCA Hostel in the adjacent Hayling Lane that represented the exterior of UNIT HQ (as it had done in the season ten story *The Three Doctors*); and outside a house at 2 West Common Road in Uxbridge, Middlesex, for the scenes where Sarah bids farewell to K-9 – tying in with the *K-9 and Company* special (see Chapter Nineteen) – and is snatched by the scoop. At the Hayling Lane location a photo-call was held for the story, with Baker represented by his waxwork model from Madame Tussaud's (see Chapter Twenty-One). The final day's filming took place on 18 March at Ealing, where sets had been erected for the interior of UNIT HQ and for the top of the Dark Tower.

Once all these scenes had been completed, final preparations were made for the studio recordings, which took place between 29 and 31 March in studio TC6.

Nathan-Turner had commissioned the Visual Effects Department to construct a new, updated TARDIS control console for *The Five Doctors*, and scenic designer Malcolm Thornton convinced him that a new TARDIS interior set should also be built. Although this was a requirement additional to those originally envisaged in the costings for the special, the producer agreed to it in the knowledge that it could then be reused for many future stories.

The incidental music for the production was scored by Peter Howell, who, with Nathan-Turner's agreement, also provided a new, one-off version of the closing theme music mixing together the original Delia Derbyshire arrangement of the sixties and his own current arrangement of the eighties.

Nathan-Turner had hoped that the special would be transmitted in the UK on the actual anniversary date, 23 November. This was not to be, however, as scheduling problems caused the Controller of BBC1 to move it back to Friday 25 November, when it went out at 7.20 pm as a part of the annual *Children In Need* appeal fronted by popular television and radio presenter Terry Wogan. As the appeal was geared towards raising money via telephone pledges, in some regions captions were run across the bottom of the screen during the transmission giving updates on the amounts pledged.

The Five Doctors was premièred in Chicago, USA, on 23 November, making it the first *Doctor Who* story ever to receive its initial screening outside the UK.

CHAPTER EIGHT

Season Twenty-One: Time of Change

The story chosen to open *Doctor Who*'s twenty-first season was Johnny Byrne's *Warriors of the Deep*, the scripts for which were commissioned on 10 September 1982 and recording of which commenced on 23 June 1983. The intention was to create a sequel to the two third Doctor stories *Doctor Who and the Silurians* and *The Sea Devils* by bringing both species of Earth's original reptilian inhabitants together in a battle for supremacy over humanity.

The Doctor, Tegan and Turlough arrive at an underwater Sea Base on which a group of humans led by Commander Vorshak are monitoring a rival power bloc. The humans undergo regular missile launch test sequences to ensure that they are ready at all times to combat an attack. Three Silurians led by Icthar – the surviving member of a Silurian triad – revive a colony of Sea Devil Warriors in order to invade the base and use its weapons to attack the humans' opposing power bloc, thus provoking a global war that will allow the reptiles to conquer the Earth. The Doctor uses ultraviolet light to destroy the reptiles' giant electrified sea-beast, the Myrka, and suggests using hexachromite gas to kill the remaining invaders. He then links his own brain into the base's computer to prevent the firing of the missiles.

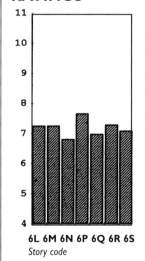

Icthar (Norman Comer) leads the Silurians attempt to recapture the Earth from mankind. *Warriors of the Deep.*

SEASON TWENTY-ONE

CODE	TITLE
6L	**Warriors of the Deep**
6M	**The Awakening**
6N	**Frontios**
6P	**Ressurection of the Daleks**
6Q	**Planet of Fire**
6R	**The Caves of Androzani**
6S	**The Twin Dilemma**

RATINGS

Story code: 6L 6M 6N 6P 6Q 6R 6S

◀ Tegan and the Doctor encounter the Myrka (William Perrie, John Asquith). *Warriors of the Deep.*

Part one of **Planet of Fire** features some stock music composed by J. Leach and produced by Alan Howe. This is from an LP called 'From Other Lands No. 12' published by Music de Wolfe Ltd, and the track used is band seven, 'Zapateado', from side one, 'Spain'.

Sauvix (Christopher ▲ Farries) the leader of the Sea Devils. *Warriors of the Deep.*

Solow (Ingrid Pitt), an enemy spy who attempts to sabotage the nuclear base. *Warriors of the Deep.* ▼

The Myrka sea creature under construction in the visual effects workshop. The creature was operated by two actors in the same manner as a pantomime horse. *Warriors of the Deep.*

Production of *Warriors of the Deep* was not at all smooth. Many of the problems were due to a lack of time – a constraint caused largely by the fact that Prime Minister Margaret Thatcher had decided to call a General Election and that a lot of the BBC's resources had consequently been diverted to cover that event.

'John Nathan-Turner was quite strong on having an underwater sequence,' recalled director Pennant Roberts in 1987, 'and we were all poised to shoot it on film at the BBC's Ealing Studios. The Election meant that Planning came back and said "Can you think in terms of doing a studio session, then your location work and then another studio session? Or else you'll have to lose the show." Obviously, we said

Recording scenes featuring the Silurians submarine at the Visual Effects Department's film stage. *Warriors of the Deep.*

we'd try to cope. Ealing wasn't available any more, so we had to go to Shepperton, which had a vast tank.

'The other factor you have to put down to Mrs Thatcher is that, because we had changed the production order, what was to have been recorded in, say, week four, was shunted forward to week two. On top of that, Mat Irvine, the visual effects designer, was delayed on a previous job that was shooting up in Scotland. His preparation time for all the effects work was slashed from maybe ten weeks to three or four.'

To play the Myrka, Roberts hired the two operators of a phantom pantomime horse from the children's series *Rentaghost*. This was partly on the assumption that they would be experienced in working in that type of costume and partly in the knowledge that – as they were at the BBC anyway, making *Rentaghost* – they would be prepared to accept a lower-than-usual fee. The original intention was that they should be given a week in rehearsal to get used to the Myrka, with Irvine close at hand to ensure that all went satisfactorily. As things transpired, the change in schedule meant that the costume was unavailable until the last few hours of the studio day itself. The two actors found that they could hardly stand up inside it and, to make matters worse, the fluorescent green paint with which it was coated was still wet.

The Malus is revealed behind the church wall by the Doctor, Jane Hampden (Polly James) and Will Chandler (Keith Jayne). *The Awakening.*

'Everything that was shown on screen was unrehearsed,' Roberts later recalled. 'We went straight in and did a maximum of two takes on each scene.'

After the production had been completed, Irvine echoed Roberts' dissatisfaction in a memo dated 10 August 1983 to Michealjohn Harris, the head of the Visual Effects Department. He pointed out that it had been known in advance that he would be delayed by three weeks in joining the production, and yet the Department had apparently done nothing about it. He also noted that, because of his work in Scotland, he had been unable to have the usual pre-production meetings with the director and other relevant people. Another problem had been that the Myrka had taken up a major part of the initial preparation time as it had been required for the first studio session. Irvine praised the efforts of his assistants, and particularly Stuart Murdoch, who had worked all hours in order to get the creature finished in time.

Byrne was not best pleased with the final results. 'I felt very disappointed and let down and I wasn't very happy about the idea of writing further for the programme,' he later said. He was also unhappy that Eric Saward and Roberts had 'massively' rewritten his scripts without any reference to him, as he had been out of the country at the time. 'If I had been involved,' he commented, 'the end result might have done justice to a story that merited enhancing, not the crude thrashing that ultimately showed up on screen. I certainly couldn't have done worse.'

Points in the script noted by Byrne as being not his work included the depiction of the Myrka ('I remember the Myrka as menacing, unstoppable and well-nigh indestructible – nowhere did I describe it as a four-legged beast on loan from Panto-Horses-Are-Us'); the deaths of both Vorshak and Icthar at the conclusion; the inclusion of a female drop-kicking Germanic scientist; and the general look of the Sea Base. ('I was very specific in my description of the base – rusting, leaking, virtually forgotten by all except those on board – the atmosphere and look was something like in *Alien* with the Myrka essentially a lurking deadly presence waiting to reveal itself.')

As Irvine noted at the close of his memo, 'When you have a situation as we have at present with productions being serviced with effects that have had no research and development done, probably not enough preparation time and definitely not enough testing, standards will suffer, people will become disillusioned and the programmes are not going to get the results that the Visual Effects Department is quite capable of producing.'

STOCK FOOTAGE

Part three of **Planet of Fire** featured a transparency of the Kouros Acropolis from the Sheridan Photo Library, while part four featured stock footage of erupting volcanoes and lava from Movietone (33.5 seconds) and Visnews (5 seconds).

NOTES

Doctor's Dive

Stuntman Gareth Milne doubled for the Doctor when he falls headlong into the watertank at the climax to episode one of **Warriors of the Deep**. The scenes were mixed shots from a tank at Shepperton Studios – for the sequences where the Doctor falls in – and a facility at the Royal Engineers Diving Establishment – for the sequences where the Doctor operates an underwater airlock and escapes.

Casting Ideas

Anthony Valentine was originally offered the part of Sir John (later changed to Sir George) in **The Awakening**. The role was then offered to Charles Kay, whom the director knew from HTV's **Fall of Eagles** and finally to Clifford Rose, who turned it down as he couldn't ride a horse. The part was finally taken by Denis Lill. Maurice Denham was originally offered the role of Andrew Verney. The part was taken by Frederick Hall.

▲ Underwater nuclear missile base Sea Base Four. *Warriors of the Deep.*

Will Chandler (Keith Jayne) is transported to the present day from the 17th century. ▼ *The Awakening.*

A Change of Designer

Visual effects designer John Horton was originally assigned to **The Awakening,** *but on 3 June 1983 John Nathan-Turner wrote to Michealjohn Harris at the Visual Effects Department requesting that Horton be removed, as the director, Michael Owen Morris, had worked with him on a previous production and there had been 'a clash of personalities'. The visual effects were eventually handled by Tony Harding.*

Helmet Reuse

The guards' helmets in **Frontios** *had originally been created for the Federation Guards in* **Blake's 7.**

Pump It Up

During studio recording breaks, the actors playing the Tractators in **Frontios** *had air pumped into their costumes from underneath. The cast would otherwise have collapsed as the costumes were insufficiently ventilated for the hot studio conditions.*

Flashback

As the Doctor regenerates in **The Caves of Androzani** *he sees the faces and hears the voices of his previous five assistants in his most recent incarnation; Tegan, Nyssa, Adric, Turlough and Kamelion. He also sees and hears the Master urging him to die. Rather than utilise clips from past episodes John Nathan-Turner decided to bring in the artistes concerned and specially record the sequence.*

The people of Little Hodcombe capture the Doctor. *The Awakening.* ▼

The Malus – a living machine sent to Earth as a precursor to an invasion. *The Awakening.*

The opening episode of *Warriors of the Deep* was transmitted on 5 January 1984, the series having been allocated Thursday and Friday evening slots for this season.

The production team continued during this period to commission a large number of stories that ultimately failed to make it to the screen. Those under consideration for season twenty-one included: Rod Beacham's *Poison* (scene breakdown (SB) commissioned 27 April 1982, scripts (S) 27 May 1982); Colin Davis's *The Place Where All Times Meet* (SB 10 June 1982); Andrew Stephenson's *The House That Ur-Cjak Built* (SB 10 June 1982); Christopher Bailey's *May Time* (SB 24 August 1982), later retitled *Man-Watch* (S 16 September 1982); Robin Squire's *Ghost Planet* (SB 5 January 1983, S 20 May 1983); and Ben Steed's two-parter *Circus of Destiny* (S 1983, exact dates unknown). Also discussed but not commissioned in any form were two ideas from William Emms entitled *The Zeldan* and *The SCI* and a proposal from Marc Platt and Charles M. Stevens

(pseudonym for fan historian Jeremy Bentham) for a story called *Warmongers*, set in England during the Second World War and featuring the Sontarans.

Eric Pringle had submitted two story ideas, *War Game* and *The Darkness*, in August 1981 via his agent Peter Bryant – who had been *Doctor Who's* producer at the end of the second Doctor's era but who was now working as a literary agent. Bryant chased the production office for a reply in November 1981 and Pringle was eventually commissioned on 1 March 1982 to write a four-episode scene breakdown for *War Game*.

'My inspiration stemmed partly from an interest in the English Civil War and partly from a desire to set a *Doctor Who* on Earth and to create a different kind of monster,' explained Pringle in 1991. 'I wanted to see what could be done by "shifting" time and, if possible, actually merging two time periods.'

It wasn't until 1 September 1982 that Saward got in touch with Pringle to say that the production team liked the scene breakdown but felt that it would be expensive to realise. A meeting was convened to discuss the idea, and Saward then commissioned Pringle around the end of 1982 to write one episode only, to see how it went. Commissions for the other three episodes followed.

The production team subsequently decided that the story should be condensed from a four-parter into a two-parter. This reworking was done by Pringle around March 1983, although he would later assert that no major changes had been made as a result. Saward then carried out a major re-write of the second episode and also amended the first for continuity. He sent Pringle the final scripts on 27 April 1983 along with a note apologising for the fact that a heavy edit had been performed to tighten and clarify the story – now entitled *The Awakening*.

The story involves an alien war machine, the Malus, affecting the inhabitants of the English country village of Little Hodcombe so that a re-enactment of a Civil War battle turns into the real thing. The Malus's aim is to gather sufficient psychic energy to activate itself fully. The TARDIS travellers arrive to meet Tegan's grandfather – one of the villagers – but become involved in the machinations of Sir George Hutchinson, who is in thrall to the Malus. The battle in 1643 becomes linked through time to 1984 and Will Chandler, a youth from the earlier time, finds himself in the present day. The Malus is defeated when Will pushes Sir George to his death.

An out-take from the location filming of *The*

Brazen (Peter Gilmore) attempts to cover up the mysterious disappearance of Captain Revere (John Beardmore) from the colonists on Frontios. *Frontios.*

The Doctor tricks the Gravis (John Gillett) into re-assembling the TARDIS. *Frontios.*

Awakening was later made famous by its exposure on several television blooper programmes. For a scene in episode two, a horse-drawn cart carrying several members of the cast was required to stop by a prop lich-gate leading to the village church. The horse was then supposed to remain outside the gate while the cast got off and went through, but in the event it decided to follow them – and pulled the whole thing down! According to Nathan-Turner, the horse had initially been reluctant to approach the gate owing to the presence of its mare in an adjacent field; the crew had attempted to solve this problem by bringing the mare round to stand in the church grounds, but had failed to anticipate the final result.

The scenic designer assigned to *The Awakening* was Barry Newbery, who had been working on *Doctor Who*, on and off, since the very first story back in 1963.

'The largest set in *The Awakening* was the main church interior,' he recalled in 1992. 'It took up the entire length of the studio. It was quite a tall set too; the three stained glass windows above the altar were about twenty-five feet from the studio floor, as I recall. Some of the walls were designed to swing open so that the camera could move into the set to get the required shots. Some were simply painted cloths. The pulpit was a stock one, but I had a carving of the Malus added to the side of it as referred to in the script.'

Newbery retired from the BBC following completion of *The Awakening*, making this his final production as a designer.

In post-production it was discovered that the story was running over length, so a few scenes from episode one were edited out. In the missing scenes, Kamelion – last seen in *The King's Demons* – imitated both Turlough and the Doctor and was discovered by Tegan in a TARDIS corridor with its hand inserted into a roundel socket, ostensibly learning

more about the Doctor's ship. The loss of these scenes meant that Kamelion was completely absent from the story.

The third story of the season was Christopher H. Bidmead's *Frontios*. This had been commissioned in scene breakdown form on 4 August 1982 as *The Wanderer* and in script form on 26 November 1982 under the titles *Frontious* and *Frotious* – although it is likely that these were simply mis-spellings of *Frontios* rather than alternatives.

The plot follows the fortunes of a colony of humans stranded on the far-flung planet Frontios. The TARDIS is dragged down to the surface during a bombardment of meteorites and apparently destroyed. The Doctor is forced to help the colonists and eventually discovers that their problems stem from an infestation of Tractators – burrowing insect-

◄ The Doctor and Norna (Lesley Dunlop) discover the Tractators. *Frontios.*

The Doctor pushes a ▶
Dalek out of a warehouse
loading bay. *Resurrection of*
the Daleks.

PENNANT ROBERTS
DIRECTOR

Pennant Roberts graduated from
reading Physics at Bristol University
and joined a new ITV station called
West and Wales North as a floor
manager. He eventually moved to
work at BBC Cymru as an assistant
floor manager. In 1969 he moved to
the BBC in London as a production
manager and worked on shows
including **Softly, Softly** *and* **The**
Expert. *His first directing experience*
was with **Doomwatch,** *followed by*
episodes of **Softly, Softly: Task**
Force *and* **The Regiment.** *In 1973*
he turned freelance and worked on
programmes including **Sutherland's**
Law, Survivors *and* **The Double**
Dealers, *although some of the latter*
was lost due to internal strikes at the
BBC. He directed several **Doctor**
Who *stories:* **The Face of Evil, The**
Pirate Planet, The Sun Makers,
Shada *(also lost due to strikes),*
Warriors of the Deep *and*
Timelash. *Since his last* **Doctor**
Who *work, Roberts has been*
directing and producing a wide variety
of shows, including **Juliet Bravo,**
Tenko, Howard's Way, The Snow
Spider, The Sherman Plays
(1994,TV), **The Bristol Old Vic**
Plays *(1994,TV) and* **Sport** *(1995,*
theatre). In 1994 he became
chairman of the Directors' and
Producers' Rights Society.

The Doctor and Brazen
(Peter Gilmore) discover
that Plantagenet (Jeff Rawle)
has become part of the
Tractators' tunneling
machine. *Frontios.* ▼

like creatures led by the intelligent Gravis. The Tractators have been causing meteorite bombardments in order to keep the colonists weak so that they can prey on their bodies and use them as components in their mining machines. Turlough knows of the creatures through a deep-seated racial memory from his own planet. He recalls that they can be rendered harmless by separating the Gravis from the rest of the colony. The Doctor achieves this by tricking the Gravis into re-assembling the TARDIS around itself.

One of Bidmead's original ideas for the story had been to make the Doctor as vulnerable as everyone else, and it was for this reason that he engineered the removal of the TARDIS. The plight of the colonists as they were subjected to constant bombardment from unknown enemies was inspired by images of the war being fought in Beirut, while the Tractators were based on the common woodlouse that the writer recalled infesting his old flat.

Production of *Frontios* was hit by two deaths. First Barrie Dobbins, the original designer assigned to the story, committed suicide shortly after work commenced, leaving his assistant David Buckingham to take over at short notice around the start of July 1983. Then actor Peter Arne, who had been cast to play the colonists' scientific officer Mr Range, was murdered at his Kensington flat on 2 August 1983, just hours after attending his costume fitting for the part. The role was hastily recast, going to William Lucas instead.

'I was in something else, and I saw that sad headline [about Arne's death] in the paper,' said Lucas in 1994. 'It's the sort of thing that happens to actors as a black joke. You say, "Oh, my best friend's dead! I wonder if I can play the part?" The very next day I was phoned and asked if I would be in *Doctor Who*. It didn't click until I got there and they said it was the part that Peter Arne was going to play.'

Peter Davison had decided around May 1983 that this season would be his last as the Doctor, and Janet Fielding and Mark Strickson had also both expressed a desire to leave the series. Realising that this would mean a complete change of regular cast over the course of the season, Nathan-Turner and Saward determined to spread the departures and arrivals over as many stories as was practicably possible.

This process was started with the writing out of Fielding in the Saward-scripted *Resurrection of the Daleks* – a new version of *The Return*, the story that had been due to close the previous season until industrial action intervened. Final approval for the scripts was received from Terry Nation around the end of June 1983.

On leaving Frontios the TARDIS becomes caught in a time corridor. The Doctor manages to free it, and it then materialises in present-day London within sight of Tower Bridge. Investigating some nearby warehouses, the Doctor and his friends stumble into a trap set for them by the Daleks. The Daleks also attack a space station orbiting Earth in the future. Their aim is to rescue their creator, Davros, who has been held there in suspended animation since his capture by humanity (as seen at the conclusion of season seventeen's *Destiny of the Daleks*). They want him to help them find an antidote to an anti-Dalek virus created by their enemies the Movellans (also from *Destiny of the Daleks*).

The Daleks have also constructed android duplicates and installed some of them in key positions in Earth government. They now intend to send duplicates of the Doctor and his assistants to Gallifrey in order to assassinate the High Council of the Time Lords. Their plans ultimately fail, however, as one of their duplicate humans, Stien, rebels and destroys the space station. Davros is unable to find a cure for the virus, but has an escape pod ready in case of problems. Commander Lytton, an alien mercenary used by the Daleks, escapes to Earth. Tegan, sickened by all the killing she has seen, decides to leave the TARDIS and remain on her home planet.

The cast of *Resurrection of the Daleks* included Rodney Bewes (well known from his starring role in *The Likely Lads*), Chloe Ashcroft (*Play School*) and

Davros (Terry Molloy) uses the Movellan virus to attempt to seize control of the Daleks. *Resurrection of the Daleks.*

Recording the Daleks' attack on Davros's prison. *Resurrection of the Daleks.*

Rula Lenska (*Rock Follies*). Also featured – as Davros's assistant Kiston – was Leslie Grantham, who would go on to find fame playing 'dirty' Den Watts in the BBC soap opera *EastEnders*.

'I met Leslie when he took the lead in a small theatre play that I'd written about television,' explained director Matthew Robinson in 1995. 'I actually offered him the choice of playing either Kiston or Galloway, a man who gets bumped off right at the start of *Resurrection of the Daleks*. Leslie, being the canny person he is, realised he'd be on screen for far longer if he did Kiston. That was his first television.'

For Fielding, her exit was a tearful one.

'I had a major problem,' she later recalled, 'in that stories were commissioned quite a long way ahead. Peter Davison had decided not to renew his contract, therefore they had this situation where I was leaving, Peter was leaving and Mark was leaving and there would be no continuity in the TARDIS at all. I ended up leaving two stories earlier than I might otherwise have done.

'Tegan's exit was a bit abrupt – there was no sort of lead in to it – but I was quite happy about how it was written.'

Before recording her final scene, Fielding stalked the studio occasionally kicking a prop packing case or two. Tegan's tears as she hurried from the TARDIS and exchanged a brief farewell with the Doctor were real.

Although written and made as a four-part story, *Resurrection of the Daleks* was ultimately edited into two roughly forty-five-minute episodes and transmitted on successive Wednesday evenings – a change of scheduling necessitated by the BBC's

coverage of the Winter Olympics. (This foreshadowed a change of episode format already decided upon for the following season.)

The fifth story of the season was Peter Grimwade's *Planet of Fire* (working title: *Planet of Fear*), commissioned in scene breakdown form on 29 March 1983 and in full script form on 20 April 1983. The need to provide for further changes of regular cast meant that Grimwade had a complex set of requirements to meet. Not only did he have to write out Turlough and introduce a new companion to take his place, but he also had to dispose of Kamelion, as the production team had decided it was time it went.

A character outline for the new companion – a young botanist named Perpugilliam Brown, or Peri for short – was finalised by Saward and Nathan-Turner, with input from Grimwade, in February 1983. Auditions for the part were held during May and June, and Nicola Bryant, a young actress just out of stage school, was chosen.

On holiday in Lanzarote, Peri narrowly escapes drowning when she is rescued from the sea by Turlough and taken into the TARDIS to recover. The Doctor is on the island because the TARDIS has detected a mysterious signal being transmitted from an unknown artefact retrieved from the sea bed by Peri's stepfather, Howard Foster. The Master reasserts his control over Kamelion and gets it to bring the TARDIS, along with the Doctor, Turlough and Peri, to the planet Sarn, where he is hoping to use that world's supply of revitalising numismaton gas to restore his body – accidentally shrunken in an experiment with his tissue compression eliminator weapon – to its correct dimensions. It transpires that Sarn is a prison planet, populated by political prisoners from Trion – Turlough's home world. Turlough too is revealed to be a political refugee. He meets his brother and later discovers that Trion has

ERIC PRINGLE
WRITER

*Eric Pringle was born and bred in Morpeth, Northumberland, and took a degree in English and American Literature at Nottingham University. After spending several years working in insurance, he ended up writing and editing various publications, including staff newspapers. After deciding to take up writing as a career, Pringle wrote plays and one-off episodes for series on HTV, Yorkshire TV and BBC 2, including **The Carnforth Practice** in 1974. His play, **Jogger**, was made by Radio 4 in 1983 and a play in the series **The Ten Commandments** was transmitted by the BBC's World Service. Other radio work has included a five-part comedy thriller called **A Change in the Weather**, a ghost story entitled **Is Anybody There?**, The Voyage of the Swallow, Ways of Escape: Sarah (1994), **The Wolves of Willoghby Chase** (1995), **Ways of Escape: Elisabeth** (1995), **It's Cold Outside** (1995), **Goodbye, Simple Girl** (1995) and **Parson Harding's Daughter** (1995). Before writing **The Awakening**, Pringle had a **Doctor Who** submission entitled **The Angurth** rejected in 1975.*

▲ Stein (Rodney Bewes). *Resurrection of the Daleks.*

Lytton (Maurice Colbourne), the leader of the Daleks' duplicate human force. ▼ *Resurrection of the Daleks.*

MICHAEL OWEN MORRIS
DIRECTOR

The Awakening was Michael Owen Morris's first directorial job at the BBC. He had previously worked as a production assistant on the **Doctor Who** story **The Pirate Planet** amongst other productions. He is the cousin of **Casualty** producer Geraint Morris. After directing **The Awakening** for **Doctor Who** he went on to direct episodes of other BBC drama series, including **Juliet Bravo**, **Campion** and **Tenko** and episodes of ITV series such as **Medics** and **Coronation Street**.

MATTHEW ROBINSON
DIRECTOR

Matthew Robinson left college in 1966 and started work immediately as a researcher for ATV. After working on a show called **Braden's Beat** *he moved across to BBC Current Affairs and worked on* **Nationwide** *and* **The Money Programme** *for about five years. Following this he was taken on as a director and worked on several productions of* **Play for Today**, **Tropic**, **Crown Court**, **Emmerdale Farm**, **Wilde Alliance**, **Softly, Softly: Task Force**, **Z Cars** *and* **Angels**. *He directed two stories for* **Doctor Who**, **Resurrection of the Daleks** *and* **Attack of the Cybermen**, *and was asked to direct an ultimately abandoned story for the twenty-third season,* **The Nightmare Fair**. *In 1984 he became the lead director for the setting up of* **EastEnders**, *as well as directing shows including* **Bergerac**, **Howard's Way**, **The District Nurse** *and* **Shadow of the Noose**. *In 1989 he created and was executive producer of the children's series* **Byker Grove**.

The Master (Anthony Ainley) is reduced to a few inches in height whilst experimenting with his tissue compression eliminator. Planet of Fire. ▼

The Doctor, Malkon (Edward Highmore), the Master (Anthony Ainley) and Timanov (Peter Wyngarde). *Planet of Fire.*

granted an amnesty to all political prisoners, enabling them to return home. The Master is apparently killed when a stream of numismaton gas in which he is bathing turns to a normal hot flame. The Doctor destroys Kamelion at the robot's own bidding as it has become completely unstable. Peri decides to stay with the Doctor when he leaves the planet.

Lanzarote had been earmarked by Nathan-Turner as a potential *Doctor Who* location after one of the series' regular directors, Fiona Cumming, sent him a holiday postcard from there. He considered that the combination of volcanic rock formations, mountainous terrain, picturesque beaches and coastal scenery made it ideal to represent both an alien planet and Earth; and, on checking the costings, he found that it was an affordable prospect. Cumming was hired as director for the story and two reconnaissance trips were made to the island prior to the actual filming, which took place from 14 to 19 October.

The robot Kamelion could not be taken on location as this would have entailed the cost of an additional three people travelling with the team to operate it. The scripts were therefore structured so that when Kamelion was seen it was either in the form of the Master or of Howard. Dallas Adams, the actor playing Howard, also appeared with his face painted silver to represent the robot in a third, mid-transformation state.

Nathan-Turner had decided that, in a departure from recent precedent, the fifth Doctor should be written out not in the final story of the season but in the penultimate one, the aim being to give viewers an opportunity to become acquainted with his successor before the between-seasons break.

The writer chosen to script Davison's swansong was Robert Holmes, who had been invited by Saward to contribute some further ideas after his twentieth anniversary story, *The Six Doctors*, had

fallen through. A scene breakdown was commissioned on 6 May 1983 as *Chain Reaction* and the scripts on 28 July under the final title *The Caves of Androzani*.

The Doctor and Peri arrive on Androzani Minor, where they become involved in the political manoeuvrings of several different parties. The planet is the source of spectrox, a life-prolonging drug when refined from its raw state. Production of the drug is controlled by Sharaz Jek, a facially deformed madman who blames Morgus, a powerful industrialist on Androzani Major, for his disfigurement and self-imposed exile. Jek is fighting government troops sent to liberate the drug, and Jek's weaponry is being supplied by gun-runners secretly employed by Morgus, who receives payment from Jek in refined spectrox. This gives Morgus a monopoly of the drug on Major.

The arrival of the Doctor and Peri causes these fragile relationships to fall apart. Jek becomes infatuated with Peri and saves her and the Doctor from being executed by government troops on Morgus's orders. The two travellers escape after learning that they have contracted spectrox toxaemia, a fatal condition to which there is only one antidote – the milk from a queen bat, which the Doctor must obtain from the deep caves on Minor. Morgus, seeing his power base slipping away, travels to Minor. In a climactic battle, Morgus, Jek and all the soldiers are killed. With moments to spare, the Doctor carries Peri back to the TARDIS, where he gives her all the milk that he has managed to collect. She recovers, but the Doctor has to regenerate to save his own life.

Holmes had decided to use the Gaston Leroux novel *The Phantom of the Opera* as his springboard for the story.

'I always tried to look for a strand that was familiar to the viewer,' he said in 1985. 'If you have straight SF with aliens and without parallels people can pick up on, to my mind it doesn't work too well. I agreed to write *The Caves of Androzani* firstly because I'd not written for Peter Davison and secondly because everyone knows this is the last story and so you can have that kind of in-built drama.'

Saward was pleased with the story, citing it as his favourite in the season:

'Originally, *The Caves of Androzani* was mainly about the two gun-running elements of the plot, but as we went on the use of spectrox toxaemia to cause the regeneration seemed like a good idea, and so it was used.'

Now free to return to his homeworld of Trion having been pardoned, Turlough bids farewell to the Doctor. *Planet of Fire.*

Peter Davison, new companion Nicola Bryant and Mark Strickson enjoy the sunshine in Lanzarote. *Planet of Fire.*

GRAEME HARPER
DIRECTOR

*Graeme Harper was originally a child actor, appearing in adaptations of **The Silver Sword** and **The Pickwick Papers** amongst other productions, before becoming a floor assistant at the BBC in 1965 and then an assistant floor manager in 1969. He worked on the **Doctor Who** adventures **Colony In Space**, **Planet of the Daleks** and **Planet of the Spiders** during the Jon Pertwee years, and **The Seeds of Doom** and **Warriors' Gate** in the Tom Baker era. In 1980 Harper started on the BBC's director's course. **The Caves of Androzani** was the first job he got as a freelance director after working on **Angels** for Julia Smith. Harper went on to direct one further **Doctor Who** story, **Revelation of the Daleks**, and was also to have directed the third story in the abandoned season twenty-three which would have been either Philip Martin's **Mission to Magnus** or Robert Holmes's **Yellow Fever and How To Cure It**. Harper went on to work on shows such as **District Nurse**, **Hope and Glory**, **Star Cops**, **Boon**, **The House of Windsor**, **The Bill**, **The House of Elliot** and **September Song** and is one of the industry's most sought after directors. In 1993 he was scheduled to direct **The Dark Dimension**, an ultimately un-made thirtieth anniversary **Doctor Who** story.*

The Caves of Androzani was directed by Graeme Harper, whose previous work on the series had been as a production assistant.

'It was terrifying!' said Harper in 1992. 'My approach was to play it dead straight all the way through, even though there were moments of black comedy. I allowed the actors to know and develop their own characters and told them to play straight down the line. I wanted to allow the evil and black humour to come out of the story rather than the way the actors played it.'

To play the critical role of Sharaz Jek, Harper wanted someone with a powerful and rich voice. He also knew that, as he was to be wearing a full face mask, the actor would have to have grace and elegance in the way that he moved. Those he considered included Tim Curry and Oliver Tobias. He had initially approached distinguished ex-ballet dancer Christopher Gable with a view to him playing another character named Salateen, assuming that he would be unwilling to consider a part where his face would be hidden throughout. Gable however turned out to be more interested in Jek, and Harper persuaded Nathan-Turner that he would be the ideal person to take the part.

'I was very honoured and very lucky to get him,' commented Harper in a later interview.

The actor chosen by Nathan-Turner to play the sixth Doctor was forty-one-year-old Colin Baker, whom he had first met when he was cast in the relatively minor role of Maxil, Commander of the Chancellery Guard on Gallifrey, in the previous season's opening story *Arc of Infinity*. Following the completion of production on that story, Nathan-Turner, along with several members of the cast and crew, had attended the wedding of Lynn Richards,

one of the BBC's assistant floor managers, where Baker had proved to be the life of the party.

'He came out with an endless stream of funny anecdotes, wickedly accurate impressions and acid comments,' the producer later recalled. 'I remember thinking that if Peter decided to leave, I already had a strong contender for the most sought-after part in British TV.'

When Davison decided to bow out of *Doctor Who*, Nathan-Turner telephoned Baker and arranged a meeting on 10 June 1983 at which he asked him if he would be interested in playing the part if it were offered him – to which Baker replied with an enthusiastic 'Yes!'

The character of the new Doctor required, as always, a degree of consideration.

'I thought it would be quite nice if sometimes he didn't behave in the way we would expect him to

Timanov (Peter Wyngarde), Perpugilliam [Peri] Brown (Nicola Bryant) and the Master (Anthony Ainley).
▼ *Planet of Fire.*

NICOLA BRYANT
PERI

*Nicola Bryant was born in Surrey. The daughter of a central heating engineer, she attended drama school at Webber Douglas and her final production there was the musical **No, No, Nanette** in which she played the lead. She was spotted by an agent and asked to audition for the part of Peri in **Doctor Who**, which she got. It was while at drama school that she was married to American Broadway singer Scott Kennedy, although they later separated. After leaving **Doctor Who**, she worked mainly in the theatre, appearing in productions of **So Long on Lonely Street, Jeeves, Twelfth Night, Killing Jessica** and **Who's Afraid of Virginia Woolf**. She has also appeared on television in **Blackadder's Christmas Carol** and in the 1993 Doctor Who skit, **Dimensions in Time**. In 1992 she lived in Los Angeles for several months before returning to the UK. In 1994 she toured with **Thank You For Having Me**, and in 1994 she appeared as a regular character in the children's television series **The Biz**.*

Anthony Ainley supplies ▲ the Master's screams off-camera at the climax to *Planet of Fire*.

Nicola Bryant, Dallas Adams and Peter Davison record Kamelion's death scenes. *Planet of Fire*. ▼

The Doctor is held prisoner in Stotz's ship. *The Caves of Androzani*.

behave,' explained Baker in 1990. 'So, on one day, if a person was mown down in front of him he might just step over them and ask somebody the time; another day, he might go into terrible paroxysms of grief about a sparrow falling out of a tree.'

Other character traits suggested by Baker included the Doctor being a little unapproachable and exploding in rage for obscure reasons; coming out with really terrible jokes and puns; and using a very rich vocabulary.

Saward also wanted something rather different from what had gone before.

'Because the Doctor has always been slightly seedy after regenerating and because we wanted to make the sixth Doctor different,' he said in 1984, 'we decided to make the regeneration so extreme it would resemble madness.'

To script the new Doctor's debut story Saward wanted someone who could make this sort of situation believable and write convincing dialogue. He decided to approach Anthony Steven, an experienced and successful writer who had previously worked with Nathan-Turner on *All Creatures Great and Small*. Steven had some preliminary discussions with the production team and was then commissioned on 19 July 1983 to provide a story idea under the title *A Stitch In Time*. On 2 August he was commissioned to write the first episode script, the story's title having by this point been changed to *A Switch In Time*, and finally on 24 August he was commissioned to write the remaining three scripts, the title eventually having been settled as *The Twin Dilemma*.

Although a great deal of work had to be done on the scripts to prepare them for recording, including a major re-write by Saward of the final episode in order to bring events to a greater climax than in the original version, Steven was more than happy with

Krelper (Roy Holder), Stotz (Maurice Roëves) and a fellow gunrunner. *The Caves of Androzani*.

his experiences on the production. In a letter of 19 March 1984 to the production office he described Saward as an excellent and innovative script editor and commented that working on *Doctor Who*, which was outside his normal field, was challenging and enjoyable.

The plot of *The Twin Dilemma* involves the intrigues of a giant gastropod called Mestor, who with other members of his race has taken over the planet Joconda. Mestor intends to cause an enormous explosion in order to spread his eggs throughout the galaxy, and he kidnaps two juvenile geniuses to work out the necessary mathematical equations. The Doctor and Peri become involved and help the elderly Time Lord Azmael, the former ruler of Joconda, to defeat Mestor and free the planet's indigenous people from the gastropods' reign of terror.

The BBC was again hit by industrial action at the end of 1983 and the start of 1984, and this time the stories to suffer were *The Caves of Androzani* and *The Twin Dilemma*. The former eventually had to take over the first two filming days scheduled for the

Krau Timmin (Barbara Kinghorn) seizes control of Morgus's company while her former employer is on Androzani Minor. *The Caves of Androzani*.

Sharez Jek (Christopher Gable) with his androids (Keith Harvey, Andrew Smith and Stephen Smith). *The Caves of Androzani*.

latter so that all the necessary scenes could be completed. The time was later recovered however. In another unusual move resulting from the industrial action, the story's location work was carried out between its two studio sessions rather than before them (as had earlier happened, for

different reasons, on *Warriors of the Deep*).

The gastropods were designed by BBC costume designer Pat Godfrey and created by the Imagineering effects house. Their appearance was based on that of a giant slug, and three costumes were constructed in all.

Mestor (Edwin Richfield), the leader of the gastropods and the tyrant of Joconda. *The Twin Dilemma*.

ROBERT HOLMES
WRITER

Robert Colin Holmes was the youngest ever commissioned officer in the Queen's Own Cameron Highlanders, serving in Burma. After demob he joined the police and passed out top of his year at Hendon Police College. He eventually moved to court work, and left the force to become a court reporter and journalist. His work as a sports reporter took him to the Midlands, where he became the final editor of **John Bull Magazine**, *at the same time submitting material to Granada TV for* **Knight Errant***. Other early TV work included* **Emergency Ward 10, Ghost Squad, Public Eye, Undermind** *(his first science fiction) and* **Intrigue***. His first work for* **Doctor Who** *was a commission to write* **The Space Trap***, later retitled* **The Krotons***. Subsequently he went on to become one of the series' most popular writers, responsible for more than a dozen televised stories. He also had a successful period as* **Doctor Who***'s script editor between 1974 and 1977. He scripted much TV drama during the seventies and eighties, including a* **Wednesday Play** *(***The Brilliant New Testament***) and episodes of* **Doomwatch, Dr. Finlay's Casebook, Dead of Night, The Regiment, Warship, Spy Trap** *and* **Dixon of Dock Green***, and he adapted the BBC's 1981 science-fiction thriller serial* **The Nightmare Man** *from David Wiltshire's novel. He was working on further* **Doctor Who** *episodes when he died, after a short illness, on 24 May 1986.*

▲ Morgus (John Normington), Chairman of Sirius Conglomerates. *The Caves of Androzani*.

◄ The Doctor (Colin Baker) meets the two child geniuses Romulus (Gavin Conrad) and Remus (Andrew Conrad). *The Twin Dilemma*.

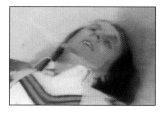

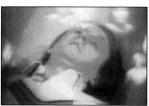

Poisoned by spectrox ▲ toxaemia, the fifth Doctor regenerates. During the process he sees visions of his recent companions and the Master. *The Caves of Androzani.*

PERI

The following is the BBC character outline created for Peri:

Perpugilliam (Peri for short) Brown is a wealthy 18-year-old American student studying Botany. She has long blonde hair which complements her attractive looks. She does not suffer fools gladly and her most charming attribute is an acute sense of humour.

We meet Peri for the first time while she is on holiday in whichever country we decide to film next season's foreign story.

Peri's mother, Janine, has remarried a man Peri dislikes – Howard. Peri still treasures the memory of her father, who died when Peri was 13, particularly as her mother appears to care more for Howard's three children than for Peri herself. It is because of her respect for her father that Peri thinks so highly of the Doctor – to some extent the Doctor replaces the gap in Peri's life. When he died he was the same age as the Doctor appears now. This never develops further than admiration and close friendship. Peri is the kind of girl who is popular – not just because of her looks, but because her warmth and sense of fun make her appeal to people of all ages.

The freighter ship touches down with the twins and Azmael on board. *The Twin Dilemma.*

'The body was a cross between a bag and a sack,' explained Godfrey in 1991. 'It consisted of three layers of material mounted on calico, the top layer being organza to give it a shiny look. The back was covered in a textured latex, with a fibreglass carapace which was also covered in textured latex.'

Godfrey was also responsible for designing the new Doctor's costume.

'I talked to John Nathan-Turner about his ideas. John very much wanted to achieve a development from one Doctor to another. He wanted to get the feel of the previous costumes by going back to a more Victorian shape, but he also wanted to make the new one look very bizarre, rather fairground and clown-like. His own words

Designer Pat Godfrey's sketch for the new Doctor's costume. *The Twin Dilemma.*

Azmael (Maurice Denham), Peri (Nicola Bryant) and the Doctor (Colin Baker) discuss their plan to defeat Mestor. *The Twin Dilemma.*

were "a totally tasteless costume".'

Godfrey eventually developed the multi-coloured patchwork coat, yellow and black striped trousers and patchwork waistcoat that were to become the recognisable image of the sixth Doctor.

'I think John himself was very happy with the final costume,' said Godfrey. 'Most people's reaction when they first saw it was that it knocked them out, although I know that there were a lot who didn't like it.'

The series' title sequence also needed updating to show Baker's face rather than Davison's. The new version was again created by Sid Sutton, this time with assistant Terry Handley. Sutton re-shot the original artwork through a prism to create additional coloured dilations, but otherwise the only difference was in the image of the Doctor's face. To ease the transition between Doctors, a special version of the end title sequence was used for the final episode of *The Caves of Androzani*, showing the new Doctor's face receding into the distance.

Recording of *The Twin Dilemma* was completed on 16 February 1984, bringing to a close the studio work for the twenty-first season (the stories of which had, unusually, been made in the same order as they were eventually seen).

By the end of the season, the final episode of which was transmitted on 30 March, *Doctor Who* had again undergone a transformation. A new Doctor and a new companion were in place ready to launch the series into its twenty-second year – and into the greatest controversy it had ever encountered.

CHAPTER NINE

Who Was Colin Baker

olin Baker was born in 1943 in the Royal Waterloo Lying-In Hospital in London during an air raid. He spent his earliest years in London with his mother, while his father served in the armed forces. He narrowly avoided an early death during the wartime blitz when a piece of flying shrapnel just missed him, embedding itself in the side of his cot.

After the war, Baker's father took a job as managing director of an asbestos company in Manchester. The family moved north to live in Rochdale, although Baker attended school in Manchester. It was during his early schooling that

– through the mother of one of his fellow pupils, who was a casting director at Granada TV – he had his first experience of acting.

'They wanted three kids,' he recalled in 1987, 'and they asked who was good at French. "Oh, Colin is," came the reply. That set me on the slippery slope.

'This was around 1954. It was for a series called *My Wife's Sister*, starring Eleanor Summerfield, Martin Wyldeck and Helen Christie.

'In this particular story, Eleanor Summerfield has met a Frenchman who is very good looking,

THE FILMS OF COLIN BAKER

Zandorra; Clockwork(1989).
Films in colour.

SELECTED TV APPEARANCES

My Wife's Sister (Granada c.1954); *Roads to Freedom* (BBC 1970); *The Silver Sword* (BBC 1970); *The Adventures of Don Quick: People Isn't Everything* (LWT 1970); *Happy Ever After: The Ambassador* (ATV 1970); *The Ronnie Corbett Show* (BBC 1970); *Hamlet* (BBC/Open University 1970); *The Mind of J. G. Reader* (Thames 1971); *Cousin Bette* (BBC 1971); *Public Eye* (ATV 1971); *War and Peace* (BBC 1971–2); *The Moonstone* (BBC 1972); *Baker's Dozen* (BBC 1972); *Villians* (LWT 1972); *The Edwardians: Daisy* (BBC 1972); *Horizon* (BBC 1973 narration); *Harriet's Back in Town* (BBC 1973); *A Matter of Honour* (BBC 1973); *Orsen Welles Playhouse: A Terribly Strange Bed* (Anglia 1973); *Within These Walls* (LWT 1973); *The Carnforth Practice* (BBC 1974); *The Brothers* (BBC 1974–7); *Fall of Eagles* (BBC 1974); *She and Me* (LWT 1977); *Blake's 7: City at the Edge of the World* (BBC 1980); *For Maddie With Love* (ATV 1980); *Dangerous Davies: The Last Detective* (ATV 1981); *Doctor Who: Arc of Infinity* (BBC 1983); *The Citadel* (BBC 1983); *Juliet Bravo* (BBC 1983); *Swallows and Amazons Forever* (BBC 1984); *Harty* (BBC 1984); *Doctor Who* (BBC 1984–6); *Saturday Superstore* (BBC 1984); *Crosswits* (ITV 1988); *The Pyramid Game* (ITV 1989); *Cuckoo* (The Children's Channel 1989); *Casualty* (BBC 1989).

◄Another man's clothes. Colin Baker takes over the role of the Doctor from Peter Davison. *The Twin Dilemma*.

Colin Baker at the press call ▶
to announce that he had been
chosen to portray the sixth
Doctor.

SELECTED THEATRE APPEARANCES

*Plaintiff in a Pretty Hat (1969);
The Other House (1969);
Shakespeare Cabbages and
Kings (1970); 1956 and All That
(1970); The Wizard of Oz (1970);
Green Julia (1970); Everyman
(1970); The Long Christmas
Dinner (1970); New Lamps for
Old (1970); Reunion in Vienna
(1971); Caesar and Cleopatra
(1971); The Price of Justice
(1971); Conduct Unbecoming
(1972); Vivat Vivat Regina (1972);
Christie in Love (1972); A Game
Called Arthur (1972); A
Christmas Carol (1972); The Lion
in Winter (1973); Guys and Dolls
(1973); Journey's End (1973);
Hamlet (1973); French Without
Tears (1974); Move Over Mrs
Markham (1974); September
Tide (1975); Let's Do It Your Way
(1977); Underground (1977); The
Flip Side (1977); Trap for a
Lonely Man (1978); Macbeth
(1978); Odd Man In (1979);
Doctor in the House (1979);
Dick Whittington (1980); Traitors
(1980); Private Lives (1981); The
Norman Conquests (1981);
Stagestruck (1981); Goldilocks
(1982); The Mousetrap (1982
Swedish tour); Relatively Speaking
(1982); Suddenly at Home
(1984); Cinderella (1985); Alladin
(1986); Cinderella (1986); Corpse
(1987); Robinson Crusoe (1988);
Deathtrap (1988); Run For Your
Wife (1989); Bazaar and
Rummage (1989); Doctor Who:
The Ultimate Adventure (1989);
Private Lives (1989); Peter Pan
(1990); Born in the Garden
(1990); Spider's Web (1990); Jack
and the Beanstalk (1991); Great
Expectations (1996 musical); Fear
of Frying (1996).*

with a moustache and everything. She then has a
dream that she is married to him, and has three
little boys gathered around a Christmas tree. They
all turn around, and they all have moustaches
pencilled on. The middle one, which was me, then
says *"Jolie Noël Papa".'*

Colin Baker shortly after ▶
being announced as the
Doctor.

Baker went on to attend St Bede's College in
Manchester, where he was invited to take part in
their annual productions of Gilbert and Sullivan
operettas. The twelve-year-old Baker appeared in
the chorus for a production of *Yeoman of the Guard*,
and a year later landed a more major part – playing
the female lead, Phyllis – in *Iolanthe*.

'I got a review in the school magazine which
read "Colin Baker threw himself with verve into
the part of Phyllis and rarely strayed more than half
an octave from the notes." At the time I thought
that was a good review!'

After completing his schooling Baker went on
to study law. One day during this period, he and
his mother went to see an amateur production of
The King and I at the Palace Theatre, Manchester.
Inspired by the performance and encouraged by the
president of the company that had staged the
production, he joined the North Manchester
Amateur Dramatic Society and quickly became
hooked on acting.

Baker took a job as a solicitor, but as time went
on became less and less interested in this career.
Finally, at the age of twenty-three, he decided to
become a full-time actor.

'After five years I thought "Blow this for a game
of soldiers. I'll have a go at doing what I want to
do. I've only got one life, so I'll have a try." So I
went to drama school and started acting.'

His transition from solicitor to actor was not a
smooth one. His fellow amateur thespians were less
than supportive of his application to gain a place at
RADA, and their lack of faith in his chances
seemed to be borne out when he was rejected.
Undeterred, Baker reapplied the following year
and also applied for the first time to all the other
major acting schools. To his delight, they were all
willing to accept him.

Baker joined the London Academy of Music and
Dramatic Art (LAMDA), where he trained for
three years. At the end of this he was summoned
with two of his fellow students to see the head of
drama, who gave them rather gloomy predictions
for their future prospects as actors and suggested
that they seek alternative careers. These predictions
proved somewhat wide of the mark as not only did
Baker go on to great success but so too did his
fellow students – David Suchet (who amongst
many other achievements starred in LWT's award
winning productions of Agatha Christie's *Poirot*)
and Mel Martin (whose numerous credits include
the series *Love for Lydia*, also for LWT).

After leaving LAMDA, Baker took a temporary job driving a taxi in Minehead in order to be near his then girlfriend. He then received a call to come to London to audition for a part in a BBC2 drama series called *The Roads to Freedom* (1970), which he won. This led to further TV roles, including two more for BBC2: Count Wenceslas Steinbock in Balzac's *Cousin Bette* (1971) and Prince Anatol Kuragin in an ambitious twenty-part serialisation of Tolstoy's *War and Peace* (1972-73). He also took on a wide range of theatre work, including several Shakespeare festivals, appearing in productions of *Macbeth* and *Hamlet*.

In the mid-seventies, Baker landed the role that would make him 'the man viewers love to hate'. This was Paul Merroney in the BBC1 series *The Brothers*.

'It was a series that was on ... from about 1972 until 1976,' he recalled in a 1984 interview. 'Halfway through the run I came into it. It was about a haulage company – truck driving – run by three brothers. And the three brothers all had their own problems. It was a bit like the *Dallas* set-up only it was set in London and they didn't sit by the pool freezing to death pretending it was hot. Halfway through the series the company had to expand so they had to borrow from the bank, and the bank put in a chairman at the company. This young guy was Paul Merroney, a whiz-kid banker. He was totally ruthless, totally unscrupulous but totally honest, unlike J.R. He never did anything anyone could send him up for, he just ruined people's lives.

'He was a very interesting character and he made my name what it was ... so much so that when the programme ended in 1976 I was out in the cold a bit.'

After *The Brothers* ended, Baker married actress Liza Goddard, who had played his on-screen wife in the series, but the marriage eventually ended in divorce. Baker later remarried, to actress Marion Wyatt.

Baker found that his success as Paul Merroney had strongly typecast him as a bad guy on TV. However, there was still a wide variety of work available to him in the theatre.

'That's the good thing about England; there's a very vital theatre network, and they're very anxious to get people they've seen on television out into the theatres. So you can earn a very good living working in the theatre.'

Theatre work kept Baker almost constantly busy

for the next five years. He made numerous appearances in everything from comedies to thrillers, as well as more Shakespeare. He also had a few further TV roles, including one as Bayban in *Blake's 7: City at the Edge of the World* (BBC, 1980) and one opposite Nyree Dawn Porter and Ian Hendry in the drama series *For Maddie with Love* (ATV, 1980).

'Bayban was the second most dangerous man in the galaxy,' he recalled in a 1989 interview, 'which caused him great annoyance because he wanted to be the most dangerous man. It was a great part, an over-the-top role.'

Baker's next TV role after *For Maddie with Love* was as Maxil in the *Doctor Who* story *Arc of Infinity*.

'I've never been one to regard a small part as a small part. So this guy Maxil struck me as the most important person on the show. I was doing a fair few things during the producer's run, and at the

▲ Baker returned to the role of the Doctor in 1989, taking over from Jon Pertwee in the *Doctor Who* stage play *The Ultimate Adventure*.

Baker appeared with his ▲ first wife Liza Goddard, when he took the role Paul Merroney, in the BBC drama series *The Brothers*.

SELECTED RADIO APPERANCES

All BBC productions unless stated
Titus Andronicus (1973); Anatol (1973); Vivat Rex (1977); Freedom Farewell (1977); Chesterton (197?); Amelia (1980); Time for Verse (1980); In Silver Mist (1982); Doctor Who: Slipback (1985); Our Father (ILR 1990).

Colin Baker as Bayban ▲ in *Blake's 7*.

Colin Baker makes an ▶ appearance at the PanoptiCon VII convention held at Imperial College, London in 1986.

end of it John Nathan-Turner said to me, "Yes that's fine, but … This isn't about Maxil the guard it's about the Doctor." And I replied, "Is it really? Good Heavens, I didn't realise that. I thought it was called *The Maxil Show*." He said "Could you tone down the reactions, please, and the acting in the background." Ha ha! But because of that, when Peter Davison said a few months later he was going to leave, John thought of me for the part of the Doctor. So it paid off in the end!'

Baker was introduced to the press as the sixth Doctor on 20 August 1983. Reflecting public

interest in *Doctor Who*, the announcement even made the BBC's early evening news, which featured a clip of the actor's appearance as Maxil, in a scene where he shoots and stuns the fifth Doctor. In a brief interview, Baker confirmed that he intended to stay with the series for some considerable time, even suggesting an intention to outdo the fourth Doctor's record seven-year stint.

Shortly before Baker took up the role of the Doctor, he and his wife suffered the loss of their baby son Jack to cot death syndrome. Baker subsequently became a passionate fund raiser for the Foundation for the Study of Infant Deaths, with many of his personal appearance fees being donated to the charity.

Baker's time as the sixth Doctor was cut unexpectedly short, initially by the hiatus between the series' twenty-second and twenty-third seasons and then by the decision by BBC executives to oust him from the role.

After his departure from *Doctor Who*, the actor returned to the theatre, appearing in highly successful runs of *Corpse* and *Deathtrap* and having a four-month stint in the West End farce *Run for Your Wife* with Terry Scott. TV work included a guest appearance in the BBC's *Casualty* and presenting assignments on programmes for the Children's Channel.

After directing a play called *Bazaar and Rummage*, Baker was asked to play the Doctor once again – this time on stage, taking over from Jon Pertwee in the Mark Furness Ltd production *The Ultimate Adventure* (see Chapter Twenty). This tour proved to him that, despite the brevity of his time as the Doctor on TV, he had amassed a loyal following amongst younger viewers:

'I've had young kids hugging me in tears, saying, "Why can't you come back on TV? You will always be our Doctor." That's probably just because I just happened to be the one who was in it when they started watching, I realise that. But its nice to know that there are people out there who feel that way.'

In the 1990s Baker has continued to pursue a successful career, mainly in the theatre. He has made regular appearances in pantomime, and recent stage work has included roles in the musical adaptation of Dickens' *Great Expectations* and in a comedy entitled *Fear of Frying*. He has also starred in the *Stranger* series of videos made by Bill Baggs Video, alongside a number of other actors known for their work in *Doctor Who*.

CHAPTER TEN

The Sixth Doctor: Larger-Than-Life Adventurer

The Doctor's physical transformation from his fifth incarnation to his sixth seems to be a rather more traumatic event than any of his previous regenerations. Lying prostrate on the TARDIS floor at the conclusion of *The Caves of Androzani*, he is heard to comment that the process 'feels different this time'.

After regaining consciousness, the Time Lord suffers a number of violent fits, at one point actually attempting to strangle Peri. Even during his more lucid periods he is seen to experience a rapid succession of different moods, ranging from disconsolate self-pity through cringing cowardice to narcissistic bravado; and it is initially unclear whether these bewildering switches of temperament are to be confined to his immediate post-regeneration recovery period or whether they are to remain a lasting feature of his character.

One fact that does very quickly become apparent is that the sixth Doctor is distinctly lacking in taste – at least where sartorial matters are concerned. The garish, multicoloured attire that he chooses for himself after rummaging through the abundance of clothing in the TARDIS wardrobe room inevitably makes him the centre of attention wherever he goes. Not for him the role of a passive observer, staying quietly in the background until forced into action; on the contrary, he seems actively to court attention, displaying a brash, ostentatious, self-important personality.

This is a Doctor who positively relishes the use of language. He generally expresses himself in a

◀ The sixth Doctor (Colin Baker), a flamboyant character with a questionable taste in clothes.

The sixth Doctor comes to ▲ the rescue of his former self, the second Doctor (Patrick Troughton). *The Two Doctors.*

IN A FIX WITH SONTARANS

This was a eight minute 46 second segment from the popular BBC Children's series Jim'll Fix It in which celebrity Jimmy Savile OBE made the dreams of those who wrote in come true. Recorded on 20 Feburary and transmitted on 23 February 1985, the production starred Colin Baker as the Doctor, with Gareth Jenkins as himself, Janet Fielding as Tegan, Clinton Greyn as Group Marshal Nathan and Tim Raynham as Nathan's aide. The Doctor learns that two Sontarans are on board the TARDIS along with a vitrox bomb. The TARDIS' matter transporter brings Tegan and a young boy called Gareth Jenkins to help. With Gareth's assistance the Doctor destroys the Sontarans and saves the TARDIS. Then Jimmy Savile OBE appears on the TARDIS' scanner screen and moments later he enters the TARDIS, asking the Doctor to present Gareth with a Jim'll Fix It medallion. Jenkins was also given one of the Sontaran's mezon-guns.

The script for this short adventure was written by Eric Saward and was transmitted as a short episode, complete with opening title sequence. Saward had originally written the piece for the character of Peri, but Nicola Bryant was not available, therefore it was re-written for Tegan. Another change was in the name of the lead Sontaran which was changed from the scripted Stern, to Nathan by Clinton Greyn during recording. The second Sontaran, Turner, was not named on screen.

The Doctor arrives on ▶ Joconda. *The Twin Dilemma*

grand, oratorical manner, employing an unusually rich vocabulary, making frequently excruciating puns and liberally quoting (or sometimes misquoting) from the literature of Earth or other planets. He likes nothing better than to engage in debate or argument – although he frequently pontificates and interrupts opponents with petulant outbursts or childish insults. In short, in keeping with the egotistical aspects of his nature, he positively loves the sound of his own loud, booming voice.

The mood-swings that he first experienced immediately after his regeneration do become less extreme and erratic as time goes by, but never abate entirely. This makes the sixth Doctor a highly volatile and unpredictable character. Theatrical,

pretentious, arrogant, rude, impatient, irascible; all these adjectives could be reasonably used to describe typical aspects of his behaviour. He is certainly more inclined than his immediate predecessor to resort to physical violence, as evidenced for example when he shoots down some Cybermen with a gun in *Attack of the Cybermen* and when he causes a number of people to die by contact with poisonous vines in *Vengeance on Varos*. He also has a wicked streak of black humour, as demonstrated on a number of occasions when he makes jokes at the expense of defeated or injured opponents – such as when he goes to shake Davros's hand at the conclusion of *Revelation of the Daleks*, after Davros has just had his fingers shot off.

While these traits might perhaps suggest that he is in some respects unpleasant or even unlikeable, their presence should not be allowed to overshadow the fact that on many occasions he also displays the Doctor's more traditional virtues of kindness, compassion, humour and courage. After the events of *The Two Doctors*, in which he encounters the resolutely carnivorous – and decidedly gluttonous – Androgums, he even resolves to become a vegetarian!

He possesses a crusading spirit, with a clear desire both to relieve oppression and to deal with the oppressor, and exhibits strong moral outrage at many of the injustices he encounters. This is never more forcefully illustrated than when he rails against the corruption of his own people, the Time Lords, in *The Trial of a Time Lord*:

DOCTOR: In all my travellings throughout the universe, I have battled against evil, against power-mad conspirators. I should have stayed here! The oldest civilisation, decadent, degenerate and rotten to the core! Power-mad conspirators, Daleks, Sontarans, Cybermen – they're still in the nursery compared to us! Ten million years of absolute power – that's what it takes to be really corrupt!

The sixth Doctor is however no more likely than any of his predecessors to want to remain on Gallifrey, or to settle down in any other particular place or time; he remains a restless wanderer in eternity, intent on experiencing for himself the many wonders of the universe. He continues to travel with a human companion, but is always conscious of the great differences between them. This is well illustrated by his reaction in *Vengeance on Varos* on learning that the TARDIS is apparently permanently stranded in space and time:

DOCTOR: Oh, it's all right for you, Peri.

◄Peri (Nicola Bryant). *The Two Doctors.*

▲ Nicola Bryant played Peri for the majority of the sixth Doctor's era.

RECALL UNIT

Recall UNIT was the title of a play presented at the 1984 Edinburgh Festival Fringe, written and directed by Richard Franklin who had appeared in **Doctor Who** playing Captain Mike Yates during the era of the third Doctor.

The play was conceived by Franklin while witnessing the camaraderie between the actors who appeared as the UNIT regulars in **Doctor Who** during a convention appearance. He wanted to try and recapture that feeling on stage. In the writing, Franklin was assisted by George Cairns, and the plot brought together many aspects of **Doctor Who** continuity as well as some topical material featuring a satire on Margaret Thatcher and the Falklands War. Originally Nicholas Courtney was to have appeared as the Brigadier, but he was forced to drop out due to other work commitments and so contributed a pre-recorded voice-over instead while another actor, Roger Kettles, appeared as a substitute character on stage.

The cast and credits for the show were as follows: Graham Smith (Alistair), Lene Lindewell (Miss Bergo), Paul Holness (Silent Stephen), Richard Franklin (Mike Yates), David Roylance (Hamish), Liam Rudden (Jimmy), Kevin Philpotts (Tim), Glynn Dack (Stallion), John Levene (Sergeant Benton), Richard Kettles (Major Molesworth MC), Nicholas Courtney (voice of the Brigadier), John Scott Martin (Supreme Dalek). The designer was James Helps, costumes by Jennifer, Technical ASM by Stephen Charles and with thanks to John Nathan-Turner, Christopher Crouch, Roger Hancock and Brian Codd.

The Doctor finds himself on trial for his life during the whole of season twenty-three, *The Trial of a Time Lord*.

▲ Patrick Troughton and Colin Baker appear together in *The Two Doctors*.

The Doctor and his companion Mel (Bonnie Langford). *The Trial of a Time Lord*. ▼

PERI: Me? Why's it OK for me?

DOCTOR: You've only got one life. You'll age here in the TARDIS and then die. Me, I shall go on regenerating until all my lives are spent.

The sixth Doctor, like the previous five, demonstrates intellectual powers and mental abilities far superior to those of a human being. In *The Two Doctors* he is seen to suffer a psychic trauma when his second incarnation is apparently put to death, and later he communicates with his other persona telepathically across space. He is inclined to take a cerebral approach to problems and finds it unnecessary always to display his true feelings. In consequence he sometimes appears rather cold and unfeeling; but this is just a front, masking a gentler and more concerned nature that comes to the fore on other occasions. The distinction between his superficial image as perceived by others and his true underlying qualities is apparent in other ways, too. He often introduces himself with the words 'I am known as the Doctor,' for instance, whereas his predecessors were content to say simply 'I am the Doctor'.

The gentler side of the sixth Doctor's nature is perhaps most readily apparent in *The Trial of a Time Lord* (a story that also, by contrast, presents a distillation of all the Doctor's darker aspects in the form of the Valeyard). To the casual observer he might still appear to be little more than a rather egotistical, larger-than-life adventurer with a poor taste in clothes and a tendency towards over-reaction and brash theatricality. Beneath this façade, however, he has mellowed and become generally more agreeable. Whilst continuing outwardly to appear offhand and detached, as illustrated by his habit of offering allusive quotations rather than making direct statements, he is now more clearly capable of feeling sympathy and affection.

This progressive softening of the sixth Doctor's demeanour is particularly evident in his relationship with Peri. Whereas previously their conversations were characterised by ill-tempered bickering and petty point-scoring, by the time of *The Trial of a Time Lord* the two travellers have clearly developed a much easier rapport and are far more comfortable in each other's company. This development is carried forward to the Doctor's relationship with his next companion, Mel, which is equally caring and harmonious – despite the fact that, as a fitness fanatic, she sometimes subjects him to light-hearted nagging over his unhealthy diet and lack of exercise!

All in all, the sixth Doctor is undoubtedly the most impulsive, erratic and surprising of them all.

CHAPTER ELEVEN

Season Twenty-Two: Video Nasty?

Doctor *Who*'s twenty-second season would not only show the new Doctor becoming noticeably more stable after his rather manic debut in *The Twin Dilemma*, but would also see some important changes being made to the style and pacing of the stories themselves. These came about largely as a consequence of a decision – reportedly taken by Controller of BBC1 Alan Hart – to double the length of each episode, with a concomitant halving from twenty-six to thirteen of the number of episodes per season. The new episode length was originally to have been fifty minutes but was eventually fixed at forty-five minutes after John Nathan-Turner pointed out that, with fewer title sequences required, a fifty-minute episode would actually have demanded *more* than twice the usual programme content, increasing the strain on the series' budget and resources.

The extended episode length was publicly welcomed by Nathan-Turner. 'I feel that the show lends itself more easily to that formula,' he commented in 1984. 'I know that's a kind of outrageous thing to say after twenty-one years of the old format, but it provides an opportunity for us as programme makers to examine the relationship between the Doctor and his companion … and to find out more about the guest characters, to flesh them out more.'

Notwithstanding this potential advantage, Nathan-Turner and Eric Saward both realised that the transition from the old format to the new would require careful handling.

'It involved, from my point of view,' recalled Saward, 'an attempt to talk to our writers about a format of which I had no experience, although obviously I'd written fifty-minute things myself for other programmes. While rethinking the

format, we were very careful to keep the essence of the show, which is a fantasy/SF adventure story. We couldn't just cobble together two twenty-five-minute episodes, because a compilation of two fast-running parts is very off-putting – it jars. We had time to stop and think a bit more, although we did have to keep on hammering away with the action.'

As usual during Saward's tenure as script editor, a considerable number of commissioned story ideas ultimately failed to reach production. These

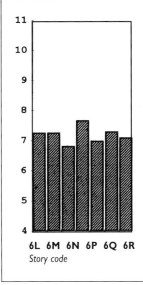

◀ The Doctor attempts to rescue Lytton (Maurice Colbourne) from the Cybermen, but discovers that the mercenary has already been partially converted. *Attack of the Cybermen.*

SEASON TWENTY-TWO

CODE	TITLE
6T	Attack of the Cybermen
6V	Vengeance on Varos
6X	The Mark of the Rani
6W	The Two Doctors
6Y	Timelash
6Z	Revelation of the Daleks

RATINGS

Story code: 6L 6M 6N 6P 6Q 6R

MUSIC

Story	Composer
Attack of the Cybermen	
	Malcolm Clarke
Vengeance on Varos	
	Jonathan Gibbs
The Mark of the Rani	
	Jonathan Gibbs
The Two Doctors	
	Peter Howell
Timelash	
	Elizabeth Parker
Revelation of the Daleks	
	Roger Limb

A version of part of Ron Grainer's **Steptoe and Son** theme is used when the TARDIS arrives in the junkyard in **Attack of the Cybermen**. When the TARDIS converts into its pipe organ form, an arrangement of Bach's 'Toccata and Fugue' is heard.

The incidental music for **The Mark of the Rani** was originally to have been provided by freelance composer John Lewis, but he died while working on it. He had completed 32.5 minutes' worth of music for the first two episodes but none was eventually used in the transmitted story.

Les Thatcher played Spanish guitar in Peter Howell's score for **The Two Doctors**.

The following tracks were played by the DJ of Tranquil Repose in **Revelation of the Daleks**: 'Good Vibrations' by Wilson/Love performed by The Surfers; 'Whiter Shade of Pale' by Reid Brooker, performed by Procul Harem; 'Hound Dog' by Leiber – Stoller from 'Smash Hits – Presley Style'; 'Blue Suede Shoes' by Carl Davis from 'Smash Hits – Presley Style'; 'In The Mood' by Garland Razaf performed by the Ted Heath Orchestra; 'Moonlight Serenade' by Miller; Parish performed by the Ted Heath Orchestra; 'Fire' by Jimi Hendrix performed by the Jimi Hendrix Experience.

Episode two of **Revelation of the Daleks** featured five tracks of 'Death Music' composed by Dick Mills at the BBC's Radiophonic Workshop.

Peri is taken prisoner by ▶ Varne (Sarah Greene) a Cryon who cannot live in temperatures above freezing. Attack of the Cybermen.

Two partially cybernized humans, Stratton (Jonathan David) and Bates (Michael Attwell), escape from a forced labour gang on the surface of the planet Telos. Attack of the Cybermen.

included *Hex* by Peter Ling and Hazel Adair (scene breakdown (SB) commissioned 12 July 1983); *Children of Seth* by Christopher Bailey (scripts (S) commissioned 14 July 1983); *Livanthian* by Brian Finch (S 14 August 1983); *The First Sontarans* by Andrew Smith (SB 10 January 1984); *The Macro Men* (later retitled *The Macros*) by Ingrid Pitt and Tony Rudlin (S (episode one only) 19 January 1984); *Volvok* by Ian Marter (SB 2 February 1984 under the working title *Strange Encounter*, S (episode one only) 1984, exact date unknown); and one, title unknown, by Chris Boucher (SB 7 February 1984). All script commissions were for episodes in the new forty-five-minute format.

Ling and Adair had created the popular soap operas *Compact* and *Crossroads* in the sixties, and it was this rather than Ling's contribution of the season six story *The Mind Robber* to *Doctor Who* that brought them into contact with Nathan-Turner.

'At the time he was casting around to produce another programme,' recalled Ling in 1994. 'His idea was that Hazel Adair and I should revive *Compact*. We had lots of discussions with him about bringing it back as a twice-weekly serial, renamed *Impact*. The discussions went quite a long way – even as far as writing the first three or four scripts.'

He was very happy about all this until, right at the last moment, somebody much higher up decided that they didn't want to revive an old serial and wanted to do a new one instead.'

Nathan-Turner invited Ling and Adair, by way of a consolation, to submit a story to *Doctor Who*. As Peter Davison was still the Doctor at this point and was regarded by the writers as a 'juvenile lead', they came up with an idea for a story (in four twenty-five-minute episodes) that would see him having something akin to a love affair with the villainous Queen Zafia of Hexagora, a planet where society runs along the same lines as in a bee hive (an idea inspired by the sight of a number of such hives kept in Adair's garden). Nathan-Turner and Saward both liked the first draft of the storyline, although Saward had some reservations and detailed suggestions. Ling and Adair did a number of rewrites, adapting the storyline to fit two forty-five-minute episodes, but it was ultimately rejected by Saward.

The Macro Men was one of a number of ideas submitted by horror film star Ingrid Pitt and her husband Tony Rudlin after she appeared in the role of scientist Solow in season twenty-one's *Warriors of the Deep*. Like *Hex*, it was initially thought of as a fifth Doctor story and later adapted to suit the sixth. The plot concerned events surrounding the Philadelphia Project – a US military experiment during the Second World War to try to make the naval destroyer USS *Eldridge* invisible to radar – about which Pitt and Rudlin had read in a book entitled *The Philadelphia Experiment* by leading paranormal investigator Charles Berlitz. It involved the Doctor and Peri arriving on board the USS *Eldridge* in Philadelphia harbour in 1943 and becoming involved in a battle against microscopic humanoid creatures native to Earth but previously unknown to humankind. The writers had several meetings with Saward and carried out numerous revisions, but the story progressed no further than the preparation of a draft first episode script under the new title *The Macros*.

Ian Marter's *Volvok* was reputedly a story with the unusual theme of hospital overcrowding, but this too ultimately met with rejection.

An idea that failed to make it even as far as being commissioned was Johnny Byrne's *The Guardians of Prophecy* (also known as *The Place of Serenity*). This came about when the production team asked Byrne if he could devise a sequel to his season eighteen story *The Keeper of Traken*. He submitted in July 1983 a plot outline concerning the planet Serenity, which like Traken is part of the

Benign Union. The Doctor and Peri encounter an immortal tomb-robber named Malador who plans to steal the power of a sophisticated computer called Prophecy and thereby animate his creations the Melkurs to enable him to conquer the inhabited planets they have already seeded. Nathan-Turner and Saward reacted unenthusiastically to this idea and it stalled in the very early planning stages.

The first story actually to go into production for season twenty-two was a Cyberman tale written by a friend of Saward's who adopted the pseudonym Paula Moore. It had the working title *The Cold War*, and the scripts for its two episodes were commissioned on 10 January and 21 February 1984 respectively. Moore had no previous professional writing experience, so Saward himself made a large contribution to the story, which became a sequel of sorts to season four's *The Tenth Planet* and season five's *The Tomb of the Cybermen*.

The story was eventually made as *Attack of the Cybermen*. Its location filming took place from 29 May to 1 June 1984, the first of its two studio sessions on 21 and 22 June and the second from 5 to 7 July. It later launched the season on air when its opening episode went out at 5.23 pm on 5 January 1985 – marking *Doctor Who*'s return to a traditional Saturday teatime slot for the first time since season eighteen.

The TARDIS is lured to Earth in 1985 by a distress call sent by Lytton – the alien mercenary first encountered in the previous season's *Resurrection of the Daleks* – who has made contact with a group of Cybermen based in London's sewers. The Doctor and Peri are then captured and forced to take them in the TARDIS to the Cybermen's home planet, Telos. The Cybermen have stolen a time vessel from another race and plan to change history by crashing Halley's Comet into Earth and obliterating it before it can bring about the demise of their original home world, Mondas, in 1986. Lytton is in truth a double agent employed by the Cryons – a female species native to Telos. His mission is to capture the stolen time vessel, but he fails and is partially converted into a Cyberman. The Doctor is unable to save him, but manages to kill the Cyber Controller. A Cryon sacrifices her own life to cause a huge explosion that completely destroys the tombs.

'The Cryons being a female race was entirely my idea,' explained director Matthew Robinson in a 1995 interview. 'I remember persuading Eric Saward, and then him going off to see if he could persuade John Nathan-Turner. I was waiting

somewhat nervously to hear the great man's views, but it came back relatively positively. I think that was because I suggested a couple of people to be the Cryons, and John liked big names to flesh out even the smallest parts. Faith Brown, Sarah Greene and Sarah Berger were three quite good names to get as *masked*, please note, monsters. Esther Freud, the little Cryon, was the sister of Emma, the radio

The Doctor and Peri search the area around Totter's Lane to find the alien distress signal. *Attack of the Cybermen.*

▲ The model of the Cybermen's base on Telos is rigged to explode at the climax of *Attack of the Cybermen.*

▲ Flast (Faith Brown), the leader of the Cryons. *Attack of the Cybermen.*

◄ The Cybermen patrol the tombs of Telos. *Attack of the Cybermen.*

Nicola Bryant (Peri) and ▶
Geraldine Alexander (Areta) lie
still on set as the make-up team
complete their transformations.
Vengeance on Varos.

Areta (Geraldine Alexander) is ▲
transformed into a reptile by
Quillam's transmogrification
device. *Vengeance on Varos.*

Peri is partially transformed ▲
into a bird. *Vengeance on Varos.*

The sadistic Quillam (Nicholas ▲
Chagrin). *Vengeance on Varos.*

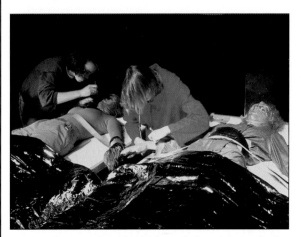

The Doctor and Jondar (Jason Connery) are forced to take part
in a mock execution. *Vengeance on Varos.*

personality, and indeed grand-daughter of the famous Sigmund Freud.

'My idea was always to have a mask over their heads through which the face could be recognised, but it would have cost loads of money. I developed the Cryon movements with Faith Brown. She came in for rehearsals with me, and we worked on the finger movements and the slow-motion style of walking, as if through treacle. She got that the way I wanted it to be, and then the others copied Faith's movements.'

The next story to be made and transmitted was Philip Martin's *Vengeance on Varos*. This had been in preparation for over two years, and had originally been considered for inclusion in season twenty under the working title *Domain*. The scene breakdown had been commissioned on 13 April 1982 and the original draft scripts (in the old twenty-five-minute-episode format and featuring the fifth Doctor) on 14 October 1982 (episode 1) and 27 January 1983 (episodes 2 – 4). It had then been reworked during the early part of 1983 under the new working title *Planet of Fear*, which was later changed to avoid possible confusion with season twenty-one's *Planet of Fire* (coincidentally also known as *Planet of Fear* at one point during its development).

Martin delivered revised draft scripts in the new forty-five-minute format on 11 August 1983 and eventually discussed them with the production team at a meeting on 9 February 1984. He subsequently recorded the production team's requirements for the series' current direction in a file note dated 11 February, which read in part as follows:

What is required now by Eric Saward and John Nathan-Turner is a 'departure from the style of "predictable" stories and "linear" exposition' of previous seasons so that meaningful complexity and more refined development of story and character can take place with, in

the case of my scripts, some contemporary relevance to 'snuff' movies, video 'nasties' etc.

I am delighted to do this but must stress that it is now a different brief to that previously given and will necessitate thought and effort throughout the scripts to bring forth the changes they are now asking for. When I wrote the draft delivered on 11 August 1983 neither the new Doctor Who nor his companion, Peri, had been cast [in fact, both characters had been cast by this date, but Martin was unaware of this at the time]. *Now, some six months later, when actors are fleshing out roles and scripts featuring them exist, I have been asked to read scripts and watch episodes with a view to incorporating their characteristics and foibles into the next draft of Planet of Fear.*

While carrying out the requested rewrites, Martin also wrote outline proposals for three further stories. *Doomwraiths* revealed that the human race is an amalgam of coded genetic information sent from space by the eponymous beings, who decide that something has gone wrong with this experiment and plan to bring it to an end by way of a deadly plague; *Space Sargasso* had the TARDIS being pulled to a 'ship's graveyard' in space, where a goblin-like creature called the Engineer is constructing a super warship at the bidding of the Master; and *Valley of Shadows* found the Doctor and Peri travelling back to Ancient Egypt to investigate an alien landing and its effects on the Pharaoh Akhenaton and his people. The writer submitted these outlines to Saward, who replied on 9 March 1984 indicating that they were too vague to judge in their present form and suggesting a discussion after completion of the current project. (In the event, nothing came of the ideas.)

Martin submitted his final scripts for *Vengeance on Varos* shortly after this and the story was

The Governor (Martin Jarvis) and Sil (Nabil Shaban) discuss the Doctor's approaching death in the Punishment Dome, whilst Peri is forced to watch by the Chief Officer (Forbes Collins). *Vengeance on Varos.*

assigned the second slot in the season's running order as a replacement for Patrick Mills' *Song of the Space Whale* (first considered for production in season twenty and still being reworked for possible use).

In the story as transmitted, the Doctor visits the planet Varos to obtain supplies of a rare ore called zeiton 7, vital to the functioning of the TARDIS. Varos was once a colony for the criminally insane. The descendants of the original guards still rule, while the poverty-stricken people are kept entertained by screenings of public torture from the Punishment Dome. Their Governor has been trying to negotiate a better export price for zeiton ore from Sil, an envoy of the Galatron Mining Corporation, whose reptilian body is supported and kept cool by a mobile water tank. The Doctor and Peri meet two rebels, Jondar and Areta. Peri and Areta are almost reshaped into beast-like creatures by Quillam, the Dome's sadistic commandant, but the Doctor saves them and tells the Governor the true value of zeiton 7. Quillam and Varos's Chief Officer, who are in the pay of the Galatron Mining Corporation, try to kill the Doctor and the Governor but are themselves despatched. Sil plans an invasion of Varos by a force from his home world, Thoros-Beta, but the Corporation veto this and instruct him to buy the zeiton ore at any price.

The director originally sought by the production team to handle *Vengeance on Varos* – an

all studio-recorded story – was Michael Owen Morris, who had made his debut on the series with the previous season's *The Awakening*. Eventually however the assignment went to Ron Jones.

'I read the script,' recalled Jones in 1985, 'and thought at once "This is very exciting." If you remember Philip Martin's *Gangsters*, it was in the same way a mix of toughness and humour. *Vengeance on Varos* fitted quite comfortably in the studio and I was quite happy for it to be that way. I thought the sets were most effective, and they were fairly flexible.

'We were very lucky in our cast. Jason Connery, who played Jondar, is very up-and-coming, for instance, and Nabil Shaban was exactly right as Sil. I wanted him to appear as slimy as possible, and Nabil gave a lovely performance of the right kind of eye-rolling evil. The voice was designed to be quite sinister as well.'

Shaban was cast as Sil after Jones had interviewed a number of dwarves and midgets for the role. Shaban suffers from a disease called osteogenesis imperfecta, as a result of which his legs are underdeveloped and he has to use a wheelchair. It was originally intended that Sil should be partly submerged in his water tank, but this proved too difficult to realise in the studio and so instead he was perched on a platform above it. His costume was designed and made by visual

STOCK FOOTAGE

Vengeance on Varos featured 45 seconds of colour film of a desert from the EMI Picture Library in part one, and 16 seconds of colour film of a bluebottle fly from Oxford Scientific Films in part two.

Revelation of the Daleks part one featured a ten-second shot of factory complexes from World Backgrounds.

NOTES

Casting One

The following artistes were considered for roles in **Attack of the Cybermen**. The artiste actually cast in each case is given in square brackets.

Rost: Jenny Hanley, Angela Down [Sarah Berger]

Flast: Maureen Lipman [Faith Brown]

Varne: Angela Pleasance, Georgina Hale [Sarah Greene]

Russell: Brian Glover, Bob Peck, Francis Matthews [Terry Molloy]

Payne and Griffiths: Stephen Bill, Terry Molloy, David Foxxe, Hilary Minster, Terry Mendlicott [James Beckett and Brian Glover]

Trevor Raymond was actually cast as Stratton. However he broke his wrist prior to the show being made and the role was given to Jonathan David instead. Other artistes considered for parts in the story included Brian Blessed, James Bolam, Michael Elphick, Bernard Hill, Bob Hoskins, Anton Rodgers, Jack Shepherd, Edward Woodward, Dave Allen, Ralph Bates and Lance Percival.

▲ Arak (Stephen Yardley) and Etta (Sheila Reid), two ordinary Varosians who watch the events in the Punishment Dome as entertainment. *Vengeance on Varos.*

Black and White
The opening shots of **The Two Doctors**, with the second Doctor and Jamie in the TARDIS, were transmitted in black and white.

Casting Change
The role of Chessene in **The Two Doctors** was originally to have been played by Elisabeth Spriggs, but she had to pull out shortly before production. The part then went to Jacqueline Pearce.

Painting
The image of the third Doctor seen on the wall behind the smashed panelling in **Timelash** was painted by American fan artist Gail Bennett.

Casting Two
The following artistes were considered for roles in **Revelation of the Daleks**. The artiste actually cast in each case is given in square brackets. (* indicates they were free.)

DJ:
Kenny Everett, Rik Mayall, Ringo Starr, David Bowie, Roger Daltrey*, Sting, Rowan Atkinson, Adam Faith*, Tim Curry, Bob Geldoff, Paul McCartney, Robert Lindsey, Gary Glitter*, Jasper Carrott*, David Essex, Nicky Henson*, Paul Nicholas, Richard O'Sullivan, Dennis Waterman, Christopher Timothy, Jim Dale, Lenny Henry, Bryan Ferry, Phil Collins, Kenneth Cranham, Robert Powell, Freddie Starr, Jim Davidson, Rod Stewart, Gary Hatton, Billy Connolly and Shakin' Stevens.

[Alexei Sayle]

All the following artistes were sent scripts:

Jobel: Denholm Elliott, Ronald Lacey [Clive Swift]
Kara: Nerys Hughes, Anna Carteret [Eleanor Bron]
Orcini: Ray Brooks [William Gaunt]
Takis: Robbie Coltrane [Trevor Cooper]

effects designer Charles Jeanes.

The next story to be transmitted, although the fourth of the season to be made, was *The Mark of the Rani* by husband and wife writing team Pip and Jane Baker. This had been commissioned in scene breakdown form on 30 September 1983 as *Too Clever By Far* and in draft script form on 7 November 1983 as *Enter the Rani*.

The TARDIS's latest arrival point is Killingworth in nineteenth-century England, where the Master is plotting to alter history by killing some of the key figures of the industrial revolution. Also present is the Rani, a brilliant Time Lord biochemist who was cast out from Gallifrey because of her cruel and dangerous experiments and is now dictator of the planet Miasimia Goria. The Rani has altered the metabolism of Miasimia Goria's populace to heighten their awareness, but in the process has inadvertently lowered their ability to sleep. In order to correct this she has been drawing a fluid from the brains of humans at various points in Earth's history, unconcerned that this leaves them aggressive and unable to sleep themselves. She is adding to the unrest caused in England by the Luddites. She also plants some land mines that turn people into trees. The Doctor sabotages the Rani's TARDIS and she and the Master are sent spinning into the vortex at the mercy of a rapidly growing Tyrannosaurus Rex embryo – a specimen collected on one of her earlier visits to Earth.

The Rani (Kate O'Mara) and ▶ the Master (Anthony Ainley) in the Rani's TARDIS. The Mark of the Rani.

The director of *The Mark of the Rani* was newcomer Sarah Hellings, who had asked Nathan-Turner around November 1983 if she could be considered for any forthcoming stories with a period setting. One unexpected advantage she had on the production was that, due to a glitch in the BBC's planning, it was allowed an unusually large amount of location filming. The main venue chosen for this was Blists Hill Open Air Museum in Ironbridge Gorge, Shropshire.

'I wouldn't say it was a planning *error* exactly,' observed Hellings in 1985, 'because it worked in our favour, but there was some kind of hiccup in the regular planned facilities so that John found himself with a story into which he could slip a bit more film than normal. I was absolutely thrilled, because I prefer film to studio work. I suppose because I'm trained as a film editor, I feel very much at home with film and I find it more exciting. I enjoyed *The Mark of the Rani* not just as a *Doctor Who* story but as a good drama, and I feel that the film went a long way to help that feeling.

'We started shooting in October and the days were very short. So it was a very tight schedule, and I think what came as a great blow to everybody was the fact that the last day was rained off. It rained so hard that we got in only three shots, which in the end proved unusable. We had to do a re-shoot a little way outside London in an area called Queen Elizabeth Woods, which looked very similar to Blists Hill. It is very unusual to do a re-shoot because it involves a lot of time and money, but it was an element – a scene where the Doctor is tied up and carried off by the miners, who are then turned into trees – that was very filmic and just would not have worked in the studio.'

The Mark of the Rani was followed on transmission by the story that had preceded it into production. This was Robert Holmes's *The Two Doctors* – the season's only three-parter, the others all being two-parters. The scripts were commissioned on 13 February 1984 (episode one) and 9 March 1984 (episodes two and three) under the title *The Kraalon Inheritance*, which was later revised to *The Androgum Inheritance*. (The story is also referred to in some BBC documentation as *The Kraglon Inheritance*, but this is probably a misprint. Three other rumoured working titles, *Parallax*, *The Seventh Augmentation* and *Creation*, are unsubstantiated.) The final title was chosen in early June 1984.

Nathan-Turner had intended from the outset that *The Two Doctors* should be the latest story to feature overseas location filming. The location he

Peri and the Doctor uncover the Rani's scheme to steal a chemical from the brains of the local miners. *The Mark of the Rani.*

favoured was New Orleans, USA, and production associate June Collins calculated that this would cost around £150,000 more than filming in the UK, so on 15 February 1984 he formally requested this additional funding from BBC Enterprises (who had by now agreed to contribute £4,000 per episode – £52,000 for the season as a whole – to the series' budget). On 16 April, the Head of Drama's special assistant Ronald Marsh replied that no additional money was available. Undaunted, Nathan-Turner then suggested Venice, Italy, as a possible location. This too was ruled out, however, partly as it was felt that there would be too many tourists who would disrupt filming. Eventually Seville, Spain, was chosen – although in order to make this financially viable the producer still had to prevail upon the cast and crew to accept only two-fifths of the normal daily allowance for Spain (which worked out at around £22) and pay for their own dinners.

The second Doctor and Jamie visit Dastari, head of a scientific group based on space station Camera, to investigate on the Time Lords' behalf some unauthorised time travel experiments. Dastari has been biologically augmenting Androgums, a race of voracious gourmands, including the chatelaine Chessene. Chessene has secretly allied herself with Group Marshal Stike of the ninth Sontaran Battle Group. The Sontarans raid the station, killing almost all aboard. They capture the second Doctor and take him to Seville, where Dastari, also in league with them, plans to dissect him in order to find the Rassilon Imprimature – the symbiotic nuclei within a Time Lord's genes that are the key to time travel. The sixth Doctor and Peri rescue Jamie from the station and then follow the trail to Spain. The second Doctor is imprinted by Dastari with genes taken from the Androgum station chef, Shockeye. The sixth Doctor rescues his second incarnation and kills Shockeye. Chessene destroys the Sontarans and, reverting to base instincts, kills

Colin Baker's make-up is touched up in a break during filming at the pit head. *The Mark of the Rani.*

Dastari. She herself then dies through molecular disintegration when she attempts to time travel without the Imprimature.

Interviewed in 1985, Holmes explained the genesis of his story:

▲ The Rani (Kate O'Mara) disguised as an old bathhouse keeper. *The Mark of the Rani.*

◀ Colin Baker and Patrick Troughton on location for *The Two Doctors.*

PAULA MOORE
WRITER

Paula Moore is the pseudonym for a friend of script editor Eric Saward, who was asked by Saward to contribute a story idea involving the Cybermen in late 1983 or early 1984. The initial outline was called **The Cold War** *and this was developed, with help and guidance from Saward, into the scripts for* **Attack of the Cybermen***. Paula Moore has had no other professional writing experience either before or since the* **Doctor Who** *commission.*

PHILIP MARTIN
WRITER

Philip Martin was born in Liverpool in 1938 and started his career as an actor, training at RADA in the early sixties. He made many television and stage appearances, including in the film **The Loneliness of the Long Distance Runner***. In the late sixties he was writing for series such as* **Z Cars** *and in 1974 he wrote the series* **Gangsters** *for the BBC. In 1977 he was resident dramatist at the Liverpool Playhouse and his work there included the plays* **Dead Soldiers***,* **A Tide in the Affairs of Women** *and* **Sambo***. Also in 1977 he won the Imperial Tobbaco prize for best original radio play. He has written extensively for television and radio, including several* **Play for Today** *contributions and episodes of* **Star Cops***,* **Shoestring** *and* **Tandoori Nights***. For* **Doctor Who** *he wrote* **Vengeance on Varos** *for the twenty-second season and* **The Trial of a Time Lord** *parts five to eight for the twenty-third. He was also scheduled to write a story called* **Mission to Magnus** *involving Sil and the Ice Warriors for the abandoned twenty-third season. He continues to work in radio drama and on television and was the Senior Radio Drama Producer at BBC Pebble Mill at the end of the eighties. More recently he wrote for the series* **Virtual Murder** *(1992) and was involved in* **Thirty Minute Theatre: A Scent of Myrrh** *(1995).*

▶ Green gunge is added to the costume of the Sontaran Stike (Clinton Greyn). *The Two Doctors.*

Chessene (Jacqueline Pearce) is an Androgum, a normally unintelligent race, who has been augmented by Dastari (Laurence Payne). *The Two Doctors.*

'Apparently Patrick Troughton and Frazer Hines so enjoyed *The Five Doctors* that they asked if they could come back and do another one. We were moving to the forty-five-minute time slot and this was going to be the season 'biggie'. Eric Saward wanted someone with experience of writing what was virtually an old six-parter and asked if I'd

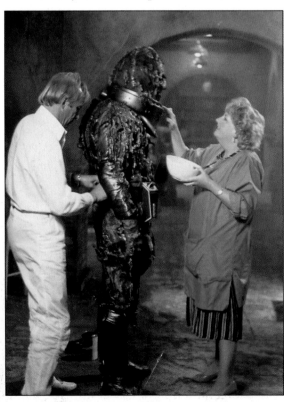

mind writing it. Then they said "Can we have Sontarans?" I don't really like bringing back old monsters, but I didn't think the Sontarans had really been well used in their previous appearances so I was glad to redress the balance.

'I had written the story to be set in New Orleans, not Seville. I couldn't think of any reason why aliens should visit New Orleans. I recalled it was a jazz place, but not even I could envisage a race of aliens obsessed with jazz. Then I remembered that New Orleans is the culinary centre of America, with lots of restaurants. So I invented the Androgums, who are obsessed with food – an anagram of gourmand. They went to New Orleans for the food. They stayed in the script however when it shifted to Seville because I couldn't think of anything else!'

Holmes also incorporated into the story some ideas from his original storyline for *The Six Doctors*.

The season's penultimate story was *Timelash* by Glen McCoy, who when not writing worked as an ambulance driver. The scene breakdown was commissioned on 11 May 1983 and the scripts on 24 June (episode one) and 23 November (episode two).

The TARDIS arrives on the planet Karfel, where, through threats to Peri's safety, the Doctor is blackmailed into going to Earth and bringing back a young girl called Vena who, while holding a precious amulet, accidentally fell into the Timelash – a time tunnel through which the planet's hideous tyrannical ruler the Borad banishes all rebels. The Doctor also inadvertently brings back Herbert, a man from the nineteenth century, who stows away aboard the TARDIS. The Borad was once a Karfelon scientist who accidentally sprayed himself with an unstable compound called mustakozene 80 while experimenting on a Morlox – a savage underground reptilian creature – and thus became half-Karfelon, half-Morlox. The Borad plans to bring about the deaths of all the Karfelons by provoking a war with their neighbours, the Bandrils, and repopulate the planet with creatures such as himself, starting with Peri. The Doctor uses a kontron time crystal to defeat a Borad clone, and makes peace with the Bandrils. He then defeats the real Borad by banishing him through the Timelash to twelfth-century Scotland. Herbert turns out to be the famous science fiction novelist H. G. Wells.

The director engaged to handle *Timelash* was Pennant Roberts, who was less than fully satisfied with the end result.

Vena (Jeananne Crowley), Herbert (David Chandler) and Katz (Tracy Louise Ward) watch as the Doctor tranforms one of the kronton crystals from the Timelash into a device to aid him in defeating the Borad. *Timelash.*

'I was a bit disappointed when I read the script,' he said in 1985. 'I remember Eric Saward was a bit defensive about it. He said "It's really quite good – Glen McCoy is quite a good writer." I disagreed and persuaded Eric to do a complete rewrite on it, to make it more lucid.

'Our original set designs kept getting sent back and pared down because of lack of money, and that scaling down was, in itself, time-consuming. We'd taken the time on the first draft, so the last one – which the viewers saw – was a bit slapdash.

'We were short of material for the second episode, so we had to go into one of the next story's studio sessions and record an extra scene in the TARDIS to fill it out. This was written by Eric as padding, a complete deviation from the story. I don't think *Doctor Who* was built for forty-five-minute episodes, with its emphasis on a kind of adventure shorthand, and rapid pace.'

The season concluded with *Revelation of the*

The Doctor and Peri arrive on Necros, wearing the official mourning colour of blue, so that the Doctor can pay his repects to the late Arthur Stengos. *Revelation of the Daleks.*

The Doctor and Peri meet the ambitous Tekker (Paul Darrow). *Timelash.*

Daleks, a story written by Saward. Although Saward has no recollection of this, BBC documentation shows that it had the original working title *The End of the Road* when the scene breakdown was commissioned on 27 March 1984 and the two scripts on 20 November. The final studio session for the season took place from 30 January to 1 February 1985 in studio TC8.

The Doctor and Peri arrive on the planet Necros, where, in a facility called Tranquil Repose presided over by Mr Jobel and his assistant Tasambeker, the wealthy can have their newly deceased bodies cryogenically frozen until such time as medical science can cure whatever killed them. The Doctor wishes to pay his last respects to his friend Professor Arthur Stengos, and also to assuage some nagging suspicions about the man's death. His suspicions prove justified, as it turns out that this is just a ruse to lure him into a trap. The Great Healer who masterminds Tranquil Repose is none other than Davros, who is using the organic material in the cryogenic storage units both as the raw material for the synthetic food that is Necros's biggest export and also to create a whole new army of Daleks with which to take control of the

Peri, Orcini (William Gaunt) and the Doctor discover that Davros (Terry Molloy) has been building a new army of Daleks in the crypts of Tranquil Repose, using the bodies of the dead. *Revelation of the Daleks.*

PIP AND JANE BAKER
WRITERS

*Husband and wife writing team Pip and Jane Baker have enjoyed an extensive career as novelists, playwrights and film and television writers since the early sixties. According to Pip, they met when very young: 'Jane was secretary of the Hanger Lane Labour Party and her friend was the chairman. They shared a flat together and her friend was standing for a marginal seat in an election. I came from a different constituency to act as their agent.' The first film they worked on was **The Third Alibi** (1961) and from there they wrote episodes of a British-based American series called **The Pursuers** (1961-1962). Other films they worked on included **The Break** (1962), **The Painted Smile** (1962), **Night of the Big Heat** (1967) and **Captain Nemo and the Underwater City** (1970). On television they have written for **The Expert** (1976), **Z Cars, Detective** (1968) and **Space: 1999** (1976) as well as three stories for **Doctor Who**. More recently they worked on **Watt On Earth** (1991-1992) and a German production called **Ruby**.*

▲ The Androgum chef Shockeye (John Stratton). *The Two Doctors.*

A new Dalek begins to form. ▼ *Revelation of the Daleks.*

GLEN McCOY
WRITER

*Glen McCoy started writing when he was only nine years old. His first work was for a school play in 1965. In 1975 McCoy wrote and produced his own Super-8mm film. This ran for eighty minutes and had an original score by Peter Vernon Carrol, one of the original members of the rock group The Who. He then turned to writing books and has continued to write ever since. At the time of his sole **Doctor Who** submission he was working on the BBC's hospital drama series **Angels**, which was his first television work. Since then he has continued to write for television, including episodes of the BBC soap opera **EastEnders**.*

The Bandril ambassador ▲ (voiced by Martin Gower) was a hand operated puppet. *Timelash*.

The android (Dean Hollingsworth). *Timelash*.

The DJ of Tranquil ▶ Repose (Alexei Sayle). *Revelation of the Daleks*.

The assassin Orcini (William Gaunt) and his squire Bostok (John Ogwen) are hired to kill Davros by Kara (Eleanor Bron). *Revelation of the Daleks*.

universe. Davros's plans are foiled when Daleks loyal to the Dalek Supreme arrive on Necros and take him prisoner. The Doctor suggests to the planet's inhabitants a new basis for their economy.

'I actually went off contract for six weeks to write *Revelation of the Daleks*,' recalled Saward in 1993. 'I went away to Rhodes for three weeks round about June or July 1984, had a nice holiday, enjoyed myself, and wrote the scripts.

'I wanted to do something about a planet that specialised in dealing with the dead. I worked out a rough storyline – and it was *very* rough – and went through it with John, and he said "Okay".'

Saward's initial inspiration for the story came from an Evelyn Waugh novel.

'When I was on holiday I re-read *The Loved One*,

which is Waugh's skit on how the Americans view the dead. I had first read it many years before, and I remembered that there is a character in it called Joyboy, who is a make-up artist for the dead. He is a very sad character. He is in his thirties, still living with his mother, and is pursued in the novel by an even more lonely and sad woman. I took the idea of Mr Joyboy and made him Mr Jobel, and the poor infatuated woman became Tasambeker.'

Revelation of the Daleks was one of a number of season twenty-two stories to provoke criticism regarding the level of violence and horror in the series. Some commentators even suggested that this season marked a departure from the strong moral standpoint that had previously been one of *Doctor Who*'s most distinctive and popular features. Even the Doctor's actions did not entirely escape reproach, attention being drawn to his shooting down of some Cybermen in *Attack of the Cybermen*, his engineering of the killing of Quillam and the Varosian Chief Officer with poisonous vines in *Vengeance on Varos* and his asphyxiation of Shockeye in *The Two Doctors*. The stories, it was said, dealt with some unusually heavy themes, including video nasties, genetic experimentation and cannibalism, and also featured gory and disturbing scenes of torture, dismemberment and suffering.

Eric Saward saw these criticisms as naive. 'I've always felt,' he said in 1993, 'that if you're going to show violence, you should also show the horrific effects of it. If you hit somebody, it hurts; it hurts your hand for one thing, and it certainly hurts the person you hit. If you hit them in the face, they're going to get a black eye or a bloody nose. Similarly, if you shoot at somebody's hand, they're going to lose fingers, as Davros did in *Revelation of the Daleks*. That's a terrible thing to happen, but if you present an action-adventure story in which there's no apparent consequence to the violence then I think you're cheating the audience.'

Another significant factor was that season twenty-two had been planned on the basis that the episodes would be going out at around 6.20 pm, and not in the 5.20 pm slot to which they were eventually consigned. Nevertheless, it was not only viewers who had concerns about aspects of the season's content; some senior members of the BBC hierarchy also had serious reservations. As written and recorded, *Revelation of the Daleks* should have ended with the Doctor promising to take Peri to Blackpool. By the time its closing episode came to be transmitted on 30 March 1985, however, the series' very continuation was in doubt, and a freeze-frame ending was substituted with the word 'Blackpool' left unspoken on the Doctor's lips.

CHAPTER TWELVE

The Unmade Season

Over the weekend of 23 and 24 February 1985 rumours began to circulate amongst the series' fans that *Doctor Who*'s twenty-third season had been cancelled by the BBC. John Nathan-Turner received official confirmation the following day, when the decision was conveyed to him in a short meeting with Head of Series and Serials Jonathan Powell. The news was first broken to the general public on 26 February through a report in the London evening newspaper, the *Standard*, which indicated that the cancellation had been decreed by Controller of BBC1 Michael Grade as a cost-cutting measure and that the fans were launching a letter-writing campaign to try to get it reversed.

This marked the start of a whirlwind of press coverage and fan activity the like of which *Doctor Who* had never seen before. The first national report came just a few hours later courtesy of the BBC itself on the children's news magazine programme *Newsround*, and this was quickly followed by brief items on BBC1's main evening news bulletins. Further developments then occurred virtually daily over the following few weeks, and media interest in the story remained strong for several months.

It has been suggested by some sources that Grade's initial intention had been not just to cancel the twenty-third season but to take *Doctor Who* off the air altogether. Colin Baker, speaking in a 1989 interview, asserted:

'Originally it was the axe; it was coming off! Grade back-tracked very swiftly when he found out the reaction was as strong as it was, and it turned into a suspension, which was the only way he could get it back without losing too much face I suppose.'

Nathan-Turner however has denied that outright cancellation was ever a real possibility. Certainly it

'Of course I care about the *Dr Who* fans, but I'm only thinking about British viewers. Do you know how many watched *Dr Who* last week? Six million. Very low indeed. Two or three years ago it was getting 10 to 11 million viewers.

'But there's no reason for anyone to make waves. It's not as if I'm cancelling the series. We've got a lot of work to do on it but the show *will* be back. That's a promise. And it will be better than ever.

'The BBC is *not* broke. It's just a question of priorities. A lot of drama shows are reaching their natural end. The writers don't want to write. The actors don't want to act. We need new material.

'The policy has been for short-run series in the last couple of years. We hope these new ones will run for more than a year or two.

'Taking *Doctor Who* off the air is a piece of professional judgement. It is nothing to do with the license fee coming up. We take a million of these decisions every day of the week.

'It's just an extraordinary storm in a teacup. Anyway, we've just had our best week in a long time on BBC1 and 2 – over 51 per cent of the total TV audience from 6 pm to closedown every day.'
Michael Grade quoted by Corinna Honan in the Daily Mail (2 March 1985)

◀ The Sensationalist front page headline of the *Sun* that greeted *Doctor Who* fans on 28 February 1985.

Three of the stories ▶ originally planned for season twenty-three were eventually novelised by their respective writers – Graham Williams, Philip Martin and Wally K. Daly – for W H Allen.

became clear within days of the controversy erupting that the hiatus was to be only a temporary one, and that *Doctor Who* would eventually be back for a further season. This was confirmed by the BBC in a press release issued on 1 March 1985, which read:

More Doctor Who *in 1986 – Another Miraculous Escape for Fiction Favourite*

As every follower of Doctor Who *knows … You can't kill a Time Lord. Today Bill Cotton, Managing Director of BBC Television, phoned David Saunders, Co-ordinator of the* Doctor Who *Appreciation Society, to explain the BBC plans.*

He said: 'Doctor Who will be on the air in 1986, as it is in 1985, and as it has been for each of the past 22 years.

'Instead of running in January 1986 we shall wait until the start of the Autumn schedule, and then Doctor Who *will be a strong item in the mix.*

'We are also going to go back to the old tradition and have 25-minute programmes rather than the 45-minute version running at the moment. We think that is what the public wants. So does the producer, and his team.

'The 45-minute series has been a good experiment, but we need to get back to basics, and to established ways. It also means that with a 25-minute length we can run the series for a greater number of weeks.'

Mr Cotton added: 'We appreciate the passionate support of the fan club in this country, and of fans around the world. We ask them to be a little patient while we get the Doctor back onto familiar rails. I am confident that Doctor Who *has a great future on BBC1.'*

The initial furore over the cancellation – reportedly fuelled in

part by Nathan-Turner leaking information to the press via fan campaigner Ian Levine – caused considerable consternation amongst the BBC's Board of Governors, who saw themselves being drawn into an unexpected and embarrassing controversy. They regarded it as just the latest in a succession of poor management decisions – less than a month earlier, for example, Grade had dropped the popular soap opera *Dallas* and then been forced to reinstate it following a public outcry – and they apparently took the matter up in forceful terms with Director-General Alasdair Milne. Milne's own view was that Grade, in underestimating the strength of the public's affection for *Doctor Who*, had made a serious error of judgement. On the other hand, he admired the way in which his subordinate had coped with the ensuing media circus.

In responding to the many enquiries that they received during the course of 1985 from journalists and members of the public, Grade and Powell offered a number of different – and often conflicting – justifications for the cancellation decision. They asserted that *Doctor Who* had become too violent; that it had lost its popular appeal; that the production team had grown complacent; and that – as suggested in the 1 March press notice – the forty-five-minute episode format had proved unsuccessful, necessitating a return to the old twenty-five-minute length. Their true motivation, however, appears to have been – as indicated in some of the earliest press reports – to help alleviate a financial crisis within the BBC. Two factors were particularly significant in this regard.

First, there was an enormous commitment involved in producing 104 episodes per year of the new soap opera *EastEnders*, which made its on-air debut in the week beginning 18 February 1985 – the very same week that the cancellation decision was taken. The need to finance and support this show, which would soon become the BBC's most successful in the ratings, placed a very considerable strain on the budget and other resources of the Series and Serials Department and resulted in a permanent reduction in the number of other programmes that it was able to make.

Secondly, and even more significantly, there was a substantial financial shortfall in the 1985/86 accounting year due to a decision taken by top-level management to bring forward by several months the launch of the BBC's daytime TV service, so as to get it up and running in advance of ITV's rival effort. This rescheduling meant that several million pounds had suddenly to be clawed back from the previously allocated departmental budgets, with

Several papers launched campaigns to save *Doctor Who*, including the *Daily Star*, who issued stickers in support of the series.

cuts being made right across the board. *Doctor Who* was just one of the programmes to suffer, along with others such as *Mike Read's Pop Quiz*, *Come Dancing*, *The Hot Shoe Show* and *Crackerjack*.

At the beginning of April 1985, further rumours began to circulate among the series' fans, this time to the effect that season twenty-three, when it did eventually appear, might be only twenty episodes long rather than the standard twenty-six. Then, on 8 June, a report in the *Sun* suggested that Grade, along with Powell and BBC Director of Programmes Brian Wenham, had decided to reduce the season to only fourteen episodes and subsequently to cancel *Doctor Who* altogether if its ratings failed to improve. The BBC Press Office were quick to deny that any such steps were being contemplated, but in fact this report was entirely accurate: the production team had been informed at the beginning of June of the season's reduction to fourteen episodes, and had already begun to adjust their plans accordingly.

The cancellation of the original season twenty-three had naturally come as a severe blow to the morale of the production team and of the regular cast. Speaking in 1985, Nathan-Turner described their reaction to the news:

'It's a horrid thing to happen, to be told that the season you've prepared is kind of pulled from under your feet. I think my feeling was that of the rest of my team and of all the actors concerned, and indeed of all the directors who had been engaged. It's all very well to get your money at the end of the week,

but it's far, far better actually to earn it. So I think we all felt fairly devastated.'

At the point when the cancellation decision was taken the scripts for the season's first story, *The Nightmare Fair* by former producer Graham Williams, had already been distributed to the regular cast and to key members of the production crew, including director Matthew Robinson. This serial, in two forty-five-minute episodes, had been commissioned on 17 November 1984 on the basis of a scene breakdown under the title *Arcade*, which had itself been commissioned on 25 September 1984. It would have seen the Doctor and Peri arriving on Blackpool's famous Pleasure Beach (a setting decided upon by Nathan-Turner after he and Baker made a promotional visit there in 1984 to open a new ride). There they would have discovered that one of the amusement arcades was in fact a deadly trap set by the sinister Celestial Toymaker – a character who had first appeared in an eponymous story in *Doctor Who*'s third season of adventures, back in 1966.

The second two-parter was to have been *The Ultimate Evil*, written by Wally K. Daly and directed by Fiona Cumming. This would have involved the Doctor and Peri arriving in the peace-loving domain of Tranquela with the intention of taking a holiday, only to get caught up in the devious schemes of an unscrupulous arms dealer, the evil Dwarf Mordant, who hopes to provoke a

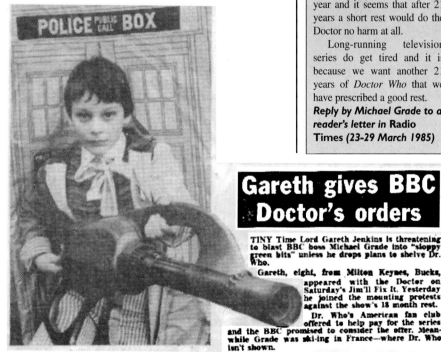

Gareth gives BBC Doctor's orders

TINY Time Lord Gareth Jenkins is threatening to blast BBC boss Michael Grade into "sloppy green bits" unless he drops plans to shelve Dr. Who.

Gareth, eight, from Milton Keynes, Bucks, appeared with the Doctor on Saturday's Jim'll Fix It. Yesterday he joined the mounting protests against the show's 18 month rest.

Dr. Who's American fan club offered to help pay for the series and the BBC promised to consider the offer. Meanwhile Grade was ski-ing in France—where Dr. Who isn't shown.

The *Daily Mirror* featured the reaction of Gareth Jenkins, a boy whose wish to appear with the Doctor in an adventure had been granted on the BBC TV programme *Jim'll Fix It* a few days before the cancellation announcement.

SLIPBACK

*One indirect consequence of the cancellation of the original twenty-third season was the commissioning from series script editor Eric Saward of an original **Doctor Who** radio serial, **Slipback**. Its six stereo episodes, each approximately ten minutes long, were recorded on 10 June 1985 in Studio B11 at Broadcasting House. They were subsequently broadcast on BBC Radio 4 at the rate of two episodes per week between 25 July and 8 August as part of a new children's Thursday morning magazine programme, **Pirate Radio Four**. The producer and director of the **Doctor Who** segment was Paul Spencer. Saward's story, which had the working title **The Doomsday Project**, told of the dangers encountered by the sixth Doctor and Peri (played as usual by Colin Baker and Nicola Bryant) on board a spaceship called the Vipod Mor, where the alien Captain Slarn (Valentine Dyall) threatens in a fit of pique to unleash a deadly psychosomatic virus. It was subsequently novelised by Saward for Target Books and released in an edited compilation version on cassette by the BBC Audio Collection.*

THE JIMMY YOUNG SHOW

*The latest in a succession of different explanations for the cancellation decision was given by Michael Grade in a September 1985 interview on BBC Radio 2's popular **Jimmy Young Show**:*
*'The people who make [**Doctor Who**] have got rather complacent. The show got rather violent and lost a lot of its imagination, a lot of its wit, and was relying far too much on straightforward on-the-nose violence and had failed really to capture a new audience.*
*'There's no question of it being killed off. There is going to be another series next year. The problem with the programme was that it had been losing its appeal. I decided that it was time to take stock, to look at the show, to rethink the scripts, to rethink the shape of the programme, to think how we might revitalise **Doctor Who** so that it's going to last another 20 years.'*

war between the Tranquelans and their neighbouring race, the Amelierons, by causing them to suffer sporadic fits of extreme violence.

Another two-parter for which draft scripts had already been prepared was Philip Martin's *Mission to Magnus*, previously entitled *Planet of Storms*. This was set on the female-dominated planet Magnus and would have featured the return of both Sil – the villain from the previous season's *Vengeance on Varos* – and the Ice Warriors – a celebrated monster race from the series' past – as well as a new Time Lord villain named Anzor, a childhood nemesis of the Doctor.

The season's longest story, a three-parter, had the working title *Yellow Fever and How to Cure It* (shortened in some later documentation to *Yellow Fever*). Written by Robert Holmes, it was to have been set in Singapore and included return appearances by the Autons, the Rani and possibly also the Master. The production team initially took steps to commission the script for the first episode on 26 October 1984, but this was put on hold at Holmes's request as the location and the rights to the use of the Rani had still to be agreed at that point. Scripts for all three episodes were subsequently commissioned on 6 February 1985.

One of the two remaining two-part slots would

Colin Baker and Nicola Bryant pose for a photo call outside Broadcasting House in London, to publicise the special radio serial Slipback.

probably have been filled by a Christopher H. Bidmead story entitled *In the Hollows of Time*, commissioned on 21 November 1984. The other would probably have gone either to a story, title unknown, by Bill Pritchard or to one called *The Children of January*, commissioned on 6 February 1985 from Michael Feeney Callan. A two-parter entitled *League of the Tandreds* by Peter Grimwade had at one point been considered, but had been abandoned at around the end of 1984 after completion of the scene breakdown. Also under consideration had been a Gary Hopkins story, title unknown, set in and around a nuclear power station, but this too had fallen by the wayside after just the first episode had been commissioned in script form. Another writer commissioned at around the same time was Jonathan Wolfman, but again nothing came of his idea.

Following the cancellation decision, Holmes, Bidmead and Callan were all asked to continue working on their stories, but in the new twenty-five-minute-episode format rather than the old forty-five-minute one – a request to which all three writers immediately acceded. Pip and Jane Baker were also commissioned as early as 11 March 1985 – less than three weeks after the cancellation decision was taken – to write a story, in four twenty-five-minute episodes, with the working title *Gallifrey*. This is rumoured to have involved the destruction of the Doctor's home planet. In the end, however, these stories were all abandoned – in Holmes's case, because the writer himself asked at the end of May 1985 to withdraw from the project – and so were those by Williams, Martin, Daly and Pritchard. The cancellation was ultimately seen by the production team as an indication that they had to make a fresh start, with new writers and new ideas.

On 16 July 1985 Terence Dudley wrote to BBC management offering to take over production of *Doctor Who*. This offer was declined, and – despite the public criticism levelled at them by Grade and Powell – the possibility of Nathan-Turner and Eric Saward being replaced seems never to have been seriously contemplated.

The reduction of the season to only fourteen episodes prompted a completely new approach to its development. Saward suggested having a single, season-spanning story in which the Doctor would be seen to be on trial, reflecting the fact that the series itself was still in this situation. Nathan-Turner readily agreed, and the two men then set about devising a workable format for what would ultimately become *The Trial of a Time Lord*.

CHAPTER THIRTEEN

Season Twenty-Three: The Trial of a Time Lord

T he basic premise of the story devised by Eric Saward and John Nathan-Turner to form the basis of the revised twenty-third season was that the Doctor would be brought back to his home planet Gallifrey to stand trial for his interference in the affairs of other worlds – an expansion of an idea used previously in the final episode of *The War Games* at the conclusion of *Doctor Who*'s sixth season in 1969. The main action would take the form of audio-visual evidence considered by the Time Lord court; and, in a conscious allusion to the structure of Charles Dickens's *A Christmas Carol*, this would be presented in three segments – the first concerning an incident in the Doctor's recent past, the second an incident in his present and the third an incident in his future – before the story was eventually wrapped up in a fourth and final segment.

Two pivotal figures in the proceedings would be the prosecuting counsel – the Valeyard – and the judge – otherwise known as the Inquisitor – for whom Nathan-Turner and Saward worked out character notes dated 5 July 1985. The intention was that, somewhere around the story's twelfth episode, the Valeyard would be revealed to be a corrupt future incarnation of the Doctor who had manipulated the whole trial simply in order to destroy his own former persona. Peri was to be killed off at the end of the eighth episode, becoming trapped in a situation from which the Time Lords were unable to extricate her, and a new companion called Mel – for whom Nathan-Turner wrote the character outline, also dated 5 July – introduced in the ninth. It was also decided at the outset that the Master should put in an appearance

The Valeyard (Michael Jayston) attempts to prosecute the Doctor, but hides an incredible secret from the court. *The Trial of a Time Lord.*

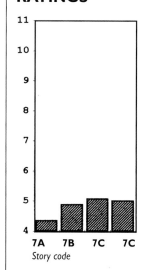

SEASON TWENTY-THREE
The Trial of a Time Lord

CODE	PARTS	WORKING TITLE
7A	1-4	**The Mysterious Planet**
7B	5-8	**Mindwarp**
7C	9-12	**The Ultimate Foe**
7C	13-14	**Time Inc.**

*The above story titles were used during production of season 23, but the season was broadcast as one 14-part story entitled **The Trial of a Time Lord**.*

RATINGS

Story code

LOCATIONS

Parts One to Four
Butser Ancient Farm Project, Pidham Hill, Hants; Queen Elizabeth Country Park, Gravel Hill, Horndean, Hants.

Parts Five to Eight
Telscombe Cliffs, East Sussex.

Parts Nine to Twelve
No location work

Parts Thirteen to Fourteen
Gladstone Pottery Museum, Stoke on Trent, Staffs; Camber Sands, East Sussex.

MUSIC

Episodes	Composer
Parts One to Four	Dominic Glynn
Parts Five to Eight	Richard Hartley
Parts Nine to Twelve	Malcolm Clarke
Parts Thirteen to Fourteen	Dominic Glynn

Parts thirteen and fourteen featured some stock barrel organ music called 'Can You Handle This?' by Ken Jones/Keith Grant.

Malcolm Clarke was originally due to provide the music for parts five to eight but at a relatively late stage was replaced by Richard Hartley.

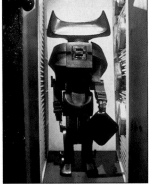

Drathro (voiced by Roger ▲ Brierley) holds the stolen secrets from the Matrix. *The Trial of a Time Lord: Parts 1 – 4.*

Sabalom Glitz (Tony Selby) ▶ meets Katryca (Joan Sims), Queen of the Tribe of the Free. *The Trial of the Time Lord: Part 1 – 4.*

The Inquisitor (Lynda Bellingham) presides over the Doctor's trial. *The Trial of a Time Lord.*

as one of the witnesses in the later stages of the proceedings.

The original writers chosen to provide the scripts for the season were Robert Holmes, Philip Martin, award winning playwright David Halliwell and novelist Jack Trevor Story. The idea was that Holmes and Martin would contribute the first two segments of evidence, each in four episodes; that Halliwell and Story would then write two episodes apiece of the third four-part segment, liaising closely to ensure that their ideas dovetailed and could be realised using the same sets; and that Holmes would then provide the final two episodes

to form the concluding segment. The story would have the sole overall title *The Trial of a Time Lord* on screen, but each segment would have its own separate working title for production purposes.

On 9 July 1985, all four writers travelled to the BBC's Threshold House offices for an initial discussion with Nathan-Turner and Saward, who explained the format to them and briefed them on their respective contributions.

Michael Grade, despite having made great play in his public comments of the need for *Doctor Who* to be revamped, had apparently taken no active interest in the formulation of the trial idea. The only advice he had given Nathan-Turner was that the new season should contain less violence and more humour than the previous one. The production team therefore instructed the four writers along these lines, stressing the need to avoid any graphic violence and to make the stories fun and entertaining, albeit with humour arising organically out of the drama rather than grafted on artificially.

The season's first OB recording (the use of film for *Doctor Who*'s location work having now been completely discontinued) took place between 8 and 11 April 1986. This was for Holmes's four-part opening segment, which had been commissioned on 2 September 1985 and developed under the working titles *Wasteland* and *The Mysterious Planet*. Shooting was carried out in part at Butser Ancient Farm Project, a faithful re-creation of an Iron Age village in Pidham Hill, Hampshire, where a press photocall was held to help generate publicity for the new season. Studio recording subsequently commenced with a two-day session on 24 and 25 April.

This opening segment sees the TARDIS drawn to a Time Lord space station where the Doctor is forced to stand trial before the Inquisitor. The Valeyard presents the first piece of his evidence, which consists of a recording played back on a screen linked to the Matrix – the repository of all Time Lord knowledge. It concerns a visit by the Doctor and Peri to the desolate planet Ravolox, which turns out to be a future Earth, shifted light-years through space. The court watches as the pair get caught up in a conflict between the surface-dwelling Tribe of the Free and the planet's other inhabitants, a group of subterranean technocrats and their robotic ruler Drathro, whilst two shady off-worlders, Glitz and Dibber, attempt to appropriate some mysterious 'secrets' – details of which are censored from the Matrix record.

These episodes marked the debut of another new arrangement of the series' famous theme music.

The Doctor finds himself in a court room on a Time Lord space station, with little knowledge of events immediately prior to his arrival. *The Trial of a Time Lord.*

This was commissioned by Nathan-Turner from Dominic Glynn, a freelance composer and long-time fan of the series who had sent the production team some sample recordings of his work.

'I just gulped when he said "We need it in five days",' recalled Glynn in 1993. 'The thing was, I hadn't got my equipment at the time. I had my keyboard but I hadn't sorted out my studio equipment, so I was a bit taken aback. I didn't want to lose the opportunity to do it, but I thought "How am I going to do this?" I'd just bought my eight-track recorder and didn't know how to use it. I had to whiz into my studio, plug everything in

The Doctor becomes the victim of a stoning in the UK Habitat, but is rescued by Merdeen (Tom Chadbon). *The Trial of a Time Lord: Parts 1 – 4.*

Drathro (voiced by Roger Brierley) is a robot that rules the UK Habitat and protects the Andromedan sleepers and their stolen secrets. *The Trial of a Time Lord: Parts 1 – 4.*

STOCK FOOTAGE

Part fourteen featured a clip from part eight, showing Peri and Yrcanos held in a cell. This was used to indicate that Peri was alive and well.

THE VALEYARD AND THE INQUISITOR

The following were the character notes for the Valeyard and the Inquisitor prepared by John Nathan-Turner and Eric Saward and dated 5 July 1985:

The Doctor is not very popular on his home planet of Gallifrey. Over the years, his independence of mind has made him many enemies who would like to see him dead.

So when the Doctor is summoned home to stand trial for crimes that could cost him his life, it is decided, by the High Council, that a judge and a prosecuting counsel must be found who are seen to be both above suspicion and free of prejudice concerning the Doctor.

After close consultation with the KEEPER OF THE MATRIX, the High Council decide to find suitable candidates from their own future.

To avoid any form of prejudicial selection, the Matrix itself is ordered to draw up a list of qualified candidates. To make the selection even more random, the Matrix gives each candidate a code number, and it is from this list that the High Council choose their INQUISITOR (Judge) and VALEYARD (Prosecuting Counsel). This way only the Matrix knows the identity of the candidates concerned.

THE INQUISITOR is female, middle fifties and very learned. She is also a friendly, agreeable soul with a strong sense of humour. (Although it is tempting to parody contemporary judges, I think it would be more interesting and more fun to play against the accepted stereotype.)

THE VALEYARD, on the other hand, is far less agreeable. He is tall and lean with strong angular features, giving him the manner and appearance of a powerful, predatory bird, whose talons are a sharpness of mind and a verbal dexterity capable of dismembering the strongest and most considered of arguments.

As the trial continues, evidence comes to light suggesting that the Matrix has been tampered with and that the list of jurists it produced was far from unprejudiced.

But who has manipulated the Matrix? And who of the two jurists is involved in the deception?

The Doctor has to find out, while at the same time fighting for his own existence.

BONNIE LANGFORD
MEL

*Bonita Melody Lysette Langford was born on 22 July 1964 in Hampton Court, Surrey. By the age of six she had won Hughie Green's **Opportunity Knocks** TV talent contest and gained membership of Equity. Later she trained at the Arts Educational and Italia Conti stage schools in London. By her early teens she had starred on New York's Broadway (**Gypsy**), on London's West End (**Gone With the Wind**) and in television shows (including the **Bonnie and Lena** variety spectaculars). Her biggest success of the mid-seventies came when she played Violet Elizabeth Bott in seven out of the twenty-seven episodes of the children's drama series **Just William**. It was this that helped fix her in the minds of the British public as a precocious 'child star' – an image she found it hard to shed in later years, despite amassing an impressive list of credits as a dancer, singer and actress on stage (**Peter Pan: The Musical, Cats, The Pirates of Penzance**) and TV (**Saturday Starship, The Hot Shoe Show**). Shortly after her stint as Mel in **Doctor Who**, this typecasting brought about an emotional crisis that caused her to take almost a year's break from her career. By the close of the eighties she had recovered her health and resumed a hectic schedule of work, which has continued to date. In 1995 she was in the news again when she was married to actor Paul Grunert in Mauritius on 27 September.*

Katryca (Joan Sims) and Broken Tooth (David Rodigan) meet a grisly end. The blood-like make up was cut from the broadcast version of the story. *The Trial of a Time Lord: Parts 1 – 4.*

Affected by Crozier's ▶ mind experiments, the Doctor helps Matrona Kani (Alibe Parsons) with the preparations for Kiv's brain transplantation. *The Trial of a Time Lord: Parts 5 – 8.*

Sil (Nabil Shaban) aids Crozier (Patrick Ryecart) in his search to find a new body for Lord Kiv. *The Trial of a Time Lord: Parts 5 – 8.*

King Yrcarnos of Krontep (Brian Blessed), Peri and the Lukoser (Thomas Branch) hide from the Mentors. *The Trial of a Time Lord: Parts 5 – 8.*

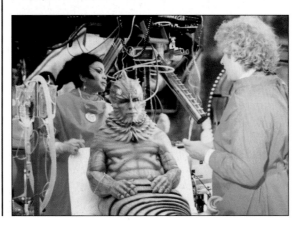

and work out how to use it, and record the theme, in five days! I knew it was going to be quite a job because it was such a popular show.

'I was pleased with the results in relation to the time that I put into it. I would have liked to have been given longer to do it. I feel that it would have been better given more time.'

The shot immediately following the opening titles of the season's first episode consisted of an elaborate model sequence of the Time Lord space station. The model was constructed in six segments by the Visual Effects Department and filmed at Peerless Studios using the latest techniques in computer-controlled camera work. The sequence proved expensive to realise, but elements of it would later be reused – for example to provide establishing shots – in other episodes.

Production of the season continued in mid-May 1986 with the Martin-scripted segment, episodes four to eight, which had been conceived as a sequel to the previous season's *Vengeance on Varos* and developed under the working titles *The Planet of Sil* and *Mindwarp*.

This time, the Valeyard's evidence concerns the planet Thoros-Beta. Here the Doctor and Peri encounter their old adversary Sil and others of his

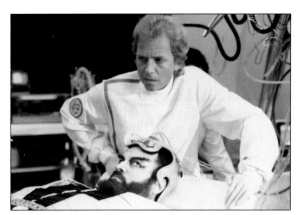

Crozier (Patrick Ryecart) performs an experiment on King Yrcarnos (Brian Blessed). *The Trial of the Time Lord: Parts 5 – 8.*

With the Doctor taken out of time by the Time Lords, Crozier succeeds in transfering Kiv's conciousness into Peri's body. *The Trial of a Time Lord: Mindwarp.*

COURT TV

*The making of episodes five to eight of **The Trial of a Time Lord** was covered by a TV crew from a French science fiction magazine show called **Temps X**. The presenters of this show, Igor and Grichka Bogdanoff, were also featured on the covers of the French translations of some of the Target novelisations.*

▲ **Director Nicholas Mallett (far right) guides a group of actors through a scene during the OB recording of** *The Trial of a Time Lord: Parts 5 – 8.*

Costume design sketch for King Yrcarnos. *The Trial of a* ▼ *Time Lord: Parts 5 – 8.*

Mentor race, whose leader Kiv is awaiting an operation from a human scientist named Crozier to transplant his brain into another body. Peri is eventually chosen as the recipient of Kiv's consciousness, and is apparently killed in an ensuing mêlée contrived by the Time Lords to prevent Crozier's work from disturbing the balance of nature.

Episode eight was the last on which Nicola Bryant worked, as she had reached a mutual agreement with the production team to leave the series at this point. A brief clip of Peri would however be seen at the story's conclusion, when it would be revealed that she had not in fact been killed but had escaped to become the consort of an alien warrior, King Yrcanos.

Mindwarp was notable for being the first *Doctor Who* production to employ the HARRY digital image manipulation process. This was used to add colour tints to the sky and sea of Thoros-Beta and to place in the sky an image of its twin planet Thoros-Alpha.

While production progressed relatively smoothly on the two four-part story segments commissioned from Holmes and Martin, the same could not be said of the two two-part segments sought from Story and Halliwell.

Little headway at all was made on Story's contribution. 'He came up with an idea for his section of the trial,' recalled Saward. 'He said, "I've got an idea of a man sitting in an empty gasometer playing a saxophone." I told him "That sounds wonderful, but I don't think we can use it in *Doctor Who*!"'

Halliwell's segment – which had the working title *Attack from the Mind* – progressed a little further. Set on a planet called Penelope, it would have told of an incident in the Doctor's future in

NO CREDIT FOR NEWMAN

*In 1985 Sydney Newman approached the BBC via his agent to enquire about the possibility of them making him an ex gratia payment in recognition of his role in creating **Doctor Who**. This met with a negative response, so on 16 July 1986 he wrote to John Nathan-Turner to ask if it would be possible for him to receive an on-screen credit at the end of each episode. This request was also turned down. Acting Head of Series and Serials Ken Riddington, to whom Nathan-Turner had referred Newman's letter, replied on 3 September noting: 'This is not in any way to gainsay that the series owed its birth to you, but merely reflects the fact that Heads of Department who originate programmes have to be satisfied with the other rewards that flow from doing so.'*

HOLMES UNDER FIRE

*On 24 February 1986, Head of Series and Serials Jonathan Powell sent John Nathan-Turner and Eric Saward a memo of comment on the draft scripts for the first seven episodes of **The Trial of a Time Lord**. He considered that the Philip Martin-written segment had, on the evidence of episodes five to seven, 'a lot going for it, with a good narrative, involving characters and a sufficiently strong connection with the trial to make this device work'. The Robert Holmes-written episodes one to four, on the other hand, he felt represented 'a substantial problem'. His overall objections were that: the 'tone' was 'very lightweight and silly', undercutting the dramatic potential; the central premise was not 'properly or convincingly set up', so that it was unclear what was at stake for the civilisation on Ravolox; it was difficult to grasp the relationship of this segment to the trial and uncertain what evidence it offered 'as to the Doctor's culpability for any particular transgression of the Time Lords' codes'; and it was never really made clear what the Doctor was on trial for. The memo concluded with a page and a half of specific notes and suggestions on Holmes's scripts. The production team, according to Saward's later recollection, considered these comments largely misconceived – particularly the criticism of the tone, given that Michael Grade had instructed them to give the series more humour and less violence – and Holmes, who had long been widely regarded as one of the series' finest writers, found them highly discouraging.*

In an adventure from the Doctor's near future, he and Mel (Bonnie Langford) find themselves involved in a deadly murder mystery aboard the space liner *Hyperion III*. The Trial of a Time Lord: Parts 9 – 12.

A Vervoid. An intelligent plant species created by professor Laskey, the Vervoids prove to be uncontrollable and begin to kill the crew and passengers when hatched from their pods. The Trial of a Time Lord: Parts 9 – 12.

which he and his then companion Mel got drawn into a conflict between the beautiful, lemur-like Penelopeans and the ugly, rodent-like Freds. At first it would have seemed that the Freds were trying to destroy the Penelopeans – who in their quest for perfection had retreated from physical existence to live in their own imaginations. Later it would have emerged that the Penelopeans were the true aggressors, using their 'supra-imagination' to cause the Freds to suffer hallucinations. The second of the two episodes would have ended with scenes of the Freds and the Penelopeans slaughtering each other – and the Valeyard asserting that the Doctor, with his meddling, was to blame. The scripts went through a number of drafts (the Freds being renamed Trikes in the later ones) but were eventually rejected, Saward informing Halliwell in a letter dated 18 October 1985 that they lacked the sort of energy and humour that he and Nathan-Turner were seeking.

Following this, the production team decided that the four-part gap in the season should now be filled by just a single writer. A submission was commissioned from Christopher H. Bidmead on 29 October 1985 under the working title *The Last Adventure*, although this would later be changed to *Pinacotheca*. By 9 January 1986 Bidmead had delivered second draft scripts of all four episodes. On 7 February, however, Saward wrote to tell him that his story segment was being dropped. The script editor later explained that he had found the scripts dull and lacking in substance.

With the situation becoming ever more urgent, another writer was approached to provide episodes nine to twelve of the story. This was P. J. Hammond, creator of the popular ATV science fiction series *Sapphire & Steel*, whose attempt was commissioned on 10 February 1986 and had the working titles *End of Term* and, later, *Paradise Five*.

A fantasy-orientated piece, *Paradise Five* would have seen the Doctor masquerading as a businessman and Mel as a hostess in order to discover the sinister secrets of a planet supposedly designated as a holiday haven for overworked executives, both human and alien. At first sight the Paradise would have seemed idyllic, being run by two seemingly friendly characters called Michael and Gabriel with the assistance of a host of beautiful girls with names such as Stella and Bella and, to perform the menial tasks, a race of creatures known as Cherubs. However, it would ultimately have been exposed as a brash, artificial front for murderous money-making schemes. The Doctor's task would have been further complicated throughout the plot by the fact that the planet was plagued by a race of

The Mogarians Atza (Sam Howard) and Ortezo (Leon Davies). *The Trial of a Time Lord: Parts 13 –14.*

evil, ghost-like entities called Angels.

According to Hammond, Saward liked this idea but Nathan-Turner did not, and it was consequently rejected after he had completed just the first episode in draft.

On 6 March 1986, yet another four-parter was commissioned to fill the gap in the season. This was by Pip and Jane Baker and had the working title *The Ultimate Foe*. In discussion with Nathan-Turner and Saward, the writers agreed to make their plot a 'whodunit in space', paying homage to the works of Agatha Christie. The scripts were completed to tight deadlines and subsequently accepted by Nathan-Turner for production.

The Ultimate Foe sees the Doctor giving the court his evidence for the defence. He chooses an incident from his own future, in which he and Mel arrive on the space liner *Hyperion III* in response to a distress call. There they battle against and ultimately destroy a hostile race of alien plants, the Vervoids, while also helping to thwart a mutiny by the ship's security officer, Rudge.

This was the last of the story's four segments to be made. The final studio session took place over 12 to 14 August 1986, bringing recording of the season to an end.

Meanwhile, on 4 February 1986, Holmes had been commissioned as planned to write the final two episodes of the Trial, under the working title *Time Inc.*. He had subsequently fallen ill, however, and found it increasingly difficult to work.

A further, even more serious complication arose at around the same time when Saward – who had been growing increasingly unhappy working alongside Nathan-Turner, rarely seeing eye to eye with him

over production decisions – unexpectedly quit the production team to return to freelance writing, leaving the series temporarily without a script editor.

Holmes's illness proved fatal. He died on 24 May 1986 having completed only a rough draft of the first episode of *Time Inc.* and nothing at all beyond an initial outline of the second. Saward was then persuaded by Nathan-Turner to return to the project to take over the writing of the missing episode. In order to facilitate this Saward also reworked completely the latter scenes of Holmes's script, introducing a new character named Mr. Popplewick. Subsequently he had a major disagreement with Nathan-Turner over the story's ending. The original idea had been to close on a cliff-hanger, with the Doctor and the Valeyard locked in mortal combat in the time vortex, but the producer vetoed this on the grounds that it was too down-beat and would end the series on an inconclusive note if BBC management should then decide to cancel it permanently. Saward, incensed by Nathan-Turner's decision, withdrew permission for his script to be used.

The producer, now effectively acting also as script editor, turned to the Bakers to write a completely new final episode for the story.

'Jane had a rather strange conversation with John just after Eric had left,' recalled Pip Baker in 1988. 'He said, "There's a taxi on its way to you with a script

◀ Director Chris Clough (second from right) oversees the OB recording of a scene where the Doctor is dragged under the earth by pairs of hands whilst in the Matrix. *The Trial of a Time Lord: Parts 13 – 14.*

SAWARD'S LAST EPISODE

The unused Eric Saward-written script for episode fourteen of **The Trial of a Time Lord** *begins with the Doctor being rescued by the Master from an illusory quicksand trap created by the Valeyard within the Matrix. The Master soon vanishes, however, as he finds it difficult to sustain his presence in the face of the Valeyard's enormous power, drawn direct from the Matrix itself. In the court room, the Inquisitor tells the Keeper that the Time Lord High Council have resigned, leaving Gallifrey in turmoil. She is anxious that the public should not learn that the Matrix has been violated, as this could lead to civil war. Mel argues that if they help the Doctor to find the Valeyard no one need ever know. The Doctor, watched by the Valeyard and Glitz from the Valeyard's TARDIS, again encounters Popplewick, who leads him to a circular walkway. This turns out to be another trap, complete with an illusory image of Mel to lure him into it, but it vanishes once he has realised its true nature. Glitz taunts the Valeyard, pointing out that he cannot kill the Doctor in case the High Council have reneged on their agreement to let him have his former self's remaining lives. The Valeyard, however, asserts that there is still a chance. The Master, via the screen in the court room, tells the Inquisitor and the Keeper that the Valeyard has managed to secrete his TARDIS in the Matrix and materialise it around a time vent. The Keeper realises that if the door to the vent is opened for more than seventy-two seconds the universe will suffer irrevocable damage. It appears they may have little choice but to meet the Valeyard's demands. The Doctor confronts the Valeyard within the Fantasy Factory – the Valeyard's TARDIS. The Valeyard throws open the time vent door, but the Doctor struggles with him and they both fall through into the vent itself. Glitz, at the Master's urging, manages to close the door and escape. The Inquisitor agrees to return Mel to her own time and planet. Mel is delighted to learn that the Doctor is still alive within the vent, and confident that he will manage to escape. The Keeper reflects that if he doesn't, it will remain his prison for eternity. The final image is of the Doctor and the Valeyard tumbling in freefall through the vent.*

**The Doctor and the ▶
Valeyard (Michael Jayston)
struggle with each other in the
Matrix.** *The Trial of a Time Lord:
Parts 13 – 14.*

NICHOLAS MALLETT
DIRECTOR

*Nick Mallett originally trained as a
dancer but wanted to work in
television. He therefore joined the
BBC as a studio manager in radio
and then moved to television as an
assistant floor manager. He eventually
became a production manager and
then moved to the Special Features
unit. His first directorial duties came
on the drama/documentary series
Oppenheimer and after completing
the BBC's director's course he worked
on **Late Starter** for the BBC in
1985 as well as Central TV's
Crossroads. He had been working
on a 1985 series called **Black Silk**,
had made some video training films
for Video Arts and was working on
Spitting Image when he was
contacted about working on **Doctor
Who**. After completing work on
Paradise Towers, Mallett went to
America to work for the arts channel
W.N.E.T. in New York and later
returned to **Doctor Who** to direct
The Curse of Fenric. More recently
he has worked on **EastEnders**, **The
Bill**, **Boon**, **Lovejoy** and several
series for Sky TV, including **Ghoul-
Lashed!***

CHRIS CLOUGH
DIRECTOR

*Chris Clough was born in the Yorkshire
town of Harrogate in 1951. He initially
trained and worked in accountancy but
then decided on a change of career and
took a degree in English Literature at
Leeds University, where he also staged a
number of student plays. In 1974 he
joined Granada TV as a researcher for
current affairs programmes. His real
interest lay in drama, however, and he
subsequently gained work as a director
on Channel 4's **Brookside** and on the
BBC's **EastEnders**. It was on the
strength of the latter that John Nathan-
Turner invited him to direct for **Doctor
Who**. He has since continued to work
extensively as a freelance director.*

**Anthony Ainley (the ▶
Master) and Michael Jayston
(the Valeyard) chat during
the recording of** *The Trial of
a Time Lord: Parts 13 – 14.*

in it. Read it tonight and come in in the morning."
And he wouldn't say any more. So the taxi came, and
we discovered it was script thirteen. We went in the
following morning and the first ten minutes was just
the usual coffee and gossip. But there was another
person there as a witness to ensure that John didn't
tell us anything that was in script fourteen, because of
copyright difficulties. Obviously he wanted us to
provide a replacement, but he couldn't tell us how the
season was supposed to end! There were thirteen
episodes leading up to a conclusion that wasn't there.
We said we'd think about it, and then John said he
wanted it within the week!'

The Bakers wrote their version of the episode
very quickly and delivered it just days before its
recording was due to begin.

Time Inc., made between *Mindwarp* and *The
Ultimate Foe*, was the first *Doctor Who* assignment
for the actress cast by Nathan-Turner to play Mel.
This was well-known entertainer Bonnie Langford,
whose popularity with youngsters he saw as having
the potential to boost the series' viewing figures. He
has since stated that he initially floated this casting
idea during a meeting with Colin Baker's agent,
Barry Burnett, who also represented Langford.
Saward however has asserted that the producer had
Langford in mind all along, and that his initial
justification for the choice was that he envisaged a

companion character with red hair.

Langford accepted the job after a short meeting
with Nathan-Turner in December 1985 in which
she had an opportunity to read the character
outline. She saw this as a chance to break away from
her popular image as a song-and-dance performer,
and found the prospect of a straight dramatic role
not at all limiting.

'It's a change for me,' she recalled in 1987, 'and
it's great fun to be doing something that's different.
I don't feel as if I'm in a strait-jacket. I probably
have *more* freedom, in fact, as I've managed to
discover a lot more in me without having to kick
my legs in the air! I can run if I want to! I can stand
still if I want to!'

The plot of *Time Inc.* sees the Doctor enlisting the
aid of the Keeper of the Matrix in order to enter the
Matrix itself. There he confronts the Master, who
has gained illicit access in his TARDIS. Glitz is now
revealed to be an associate of the Master, and the
'secrets' to be information stolen from the Matrix.
The Valeyard admits his identity as the dark side of
the Doctor's nature, out to take control over his
remaining incarnations. With the help of Mel, who
has been brought to the space station by the Master,
the Doctor defeats his future self – although, as they
leave in the TARDIS with all charges in the trial
having been dropped, it appears that the Valeyard
has taken over the body of the Keeper of the Matrix
and may not have been as completely vanquished as
they had thought …

When editing of episode fourteen was
completed, it was discovered that it had
considerably overrun. Nathan-Turner consequently
requested, and was granted, permission for *Doctor
Who*'s slot to be extended by five minutes for the
week of its transmission so that most of the
recorded material could be retained.

The season made its on-air debut on 6 September
1986 and received a considerable amount of
promotion. In addition to press and *Radio Times*
articles, there was a guest spot for Colin Baker and
Lynda Bellingham on the *Wogan* chat show and a
visit by Baker and a number of the season's
monsters to *Blue Peter*. Baker even made a brief
appearance on an edition of *Roland Rat – The Series*
broadcast immediately before the second episode.
Despite all this, the ratings were very indifferent
throughout the season, the final episode of which
was transmitted on 6 December.

Grade meanwhile remained less than satisfied
with the current state of *Doctor Who*. During the

early part of the season's on-air run he had a meeting with the series' creator and former Head of Drama Sydney Newman – a near-legendary figure within the TV industry, whose many achievements included introducing 'kitchen sink' drama to British screens in ABC TV's *Armchair Theatre* plays of the early 1960s – and asked if he would be willing to come up with some ideas for revamping it. Newman was subsequently offered a fee of £1,000 for this work. He wrote to Grade on 6 October setting out his proposals and suggesting that if they were judged acceptable he should, in lieu of the fee, be taken on as executive producer to ensure that they were properly executed. He went on to outline what he would do with the series:

STORY SITUATIONS

(1) The out-in-space, other-planet adventures are now somewhat old hat. Their simple good guy vs outer space monsters too rarely go beyond sheer escapism. The best sci-fi always has a mythic, parable element that touches our own lives, and it is this that should make up the outer space stories in the future, which I would limit to 50% of the total.

(2) Our Earth, both present and past, is just as exciting as outer space, when creatively explored. The wonders of technology, science, medicine, the green Earth movement etc are hot subjects today. Doctor Who and his Earthlings should find themselves: inside a human body (child), involved in a war between her life and cancer cells (preferably a war between something medically less frightening, but that's something left up to the research to come); inside a NASA shuttle, a polaris submarine etc, in which of course something dreadful happens; they return to Earth the size of ants while human ecologists are trying to stop farmers from using DDT; they return to the past getting involved in a mutiny on one of Christopher Columbus's ships, which sinks at the right time, allowing Columbus to discover America; and so on.

In the above, containing the standard, do-or-die, life-in-peril approach, at least our central characters will be experiencing adventures which, despite their peripheral educational values, engage the concerns, fears and curiosity of today's audiences of all ages. Don't you agree that this is considerably more worthy of the BBC than Doctor Who's *present largely socially valueless escapist schlock!*

THE CHARACTERS

(3) Doctor Who himself *should see the return of Patrick Troughton – still the not-quite-there tramp from outer-space. It's important that he be innocent, almost child-like, to enable us to see him figure things out in his flashes of incredible intelligence. The important thing is that the audience should see the traps he and the Earthlings will*

fall into, but then Doctor Who, and/or the Earthlings with him, will find a way to avoid the pitfalls the audience cannot foresee. The important fact is that Doctor Who does not *know how to control his time-space machine!*

(4) At a later stage, Doctor Who should be metamorphosed into a woman. This requires some considerable thought – mainly because I want to avoid a flashy Hollywood 'Wonder Woman' because this kind of hero(ine) with no flaws is a bore. Given more time than I have now, I can create such a character.

THE EARTHLINGS

(5) Just as Doctor Who doesn't want to go wandering through space and time and just wants to go home, the same must apply *to the Earthlings with him. I suggest they be:*

(6) A homesick girl of 12 *wearing John Lennon-type Dickensian spectacles (she's stylish). On Earth she played a trumpet in the school orchestra. Sometimes, when nervous, she plays it badly, and at other times gives a virtuoso performance. It's the one possession she values most; sometimes it gets her into trouble when it is taken from her. Her high notes can smash glass, and sometimes it signals the advance to battle or retreat from danger. Sometimes it irritates Doctor Who when he's trying to think. 'Hush child! You're addlepating me!'*

(7) It also irritates her yobbo, over self-confident brother of 18, *who with his aerosol can graffitis the heavens. He's headstrong, often thinks his little sister a pest, but is also protective of her, knowing that if any harm*

The Doctor gains a new ▶ health conscious companion, Mel (Bonnie Langford). *The Trial of a Time Lord: Parts 9 – 12*.

MEL

The following was the character outline for Mel prepared by John Nathan-Turner and dated 5 July 1985:

MELANIE is scintillating, fascinating and irritating. She has a mane of red hair, fierce blue eyes and freckles. She is twenty-one years old and a computer programmer from Pease Pottage, Sussex.

In 1986, when the Master attempted a massive computer fraud, involving all the banking houses in the world, Melanie joined forces with the Doctor, helping to defeat the Master's dastardly plan, and has now been with him for some three months (in Earth time).

Melanie is one of those annoying young ladies, who is a 'women's libber' at all times, except at moments of great stress, when she relies heavily on playing the hard-done-by, down-trodden, crocodile-teared female.

She is heavily into aerobics and health food. She considers the Doctor overweight and in need of regular Jane Fonda-type movement lessons, although the Doctor insists he gets quite enough exercise dashing round the galaxy, defeating evil. She often attempts to force health-giving vitamin-enriched food on the Doctor (muesli, raw carrots, etc.), which may provide useful comedy relief.

Despite her women's liberation attitudes, she appears to attempt to stabilise the Doctor's hitherto, in her opinion, unhealthy and irrational way of life.

She has a strong sense of humour and is often heard singing in the TARDIS, much to the annoyance of the Doctor.

Although the Doctor is ferociously fond of Melanie, who prefers to be known as Mel (well, she would, wouldn't she?), he resists all attempts to stabilise his existence.

Melanie is the first Earth-UK companion for twelve years. We shall soon see why.

Mel screams well and runs down corridors with élan. (Despite being a computer programmer, Melanie cannot operate the TARDIS. On the odd occasion that she tries, disaster ensues.)

befalls her his parents (unseen) would 'kill him' when, oh yes when, they were to get back to Earth. Clearly he thinks Doctor Who *is 'way past it'!*

Very, very briefly, there's my 'way forward' for the Doctor Who *series, which I think is what you want.*

Grade subsequently suggested that Newman meet Powell to talk over his ideas – which, although not included in the letter, included a new outer form for the TARDIS to replace the familiar police box. The two men met for lunch, but Newman failed to hit it off with Powell and found the experience an uncomfortable one. He heard nothing more about the matter, and none of his ideas was ever taken up.

Grade however did eventually give the go-ahead for a further season of *Doctor Who* to be produced – but only on condition that a different actor was given the lead role. Speaking in a 1987 interview, Baker recalled the circumstances of his departure from the series:

'When the time came for the option on my contract to be taken up by the BBC, which was the end of October, John Nathan-Turner rang up and said, "I don't even know if we're doing the programme. They haven't even told me if I'm producing it next year, so I can't take up the option at the moment." So the option lapsed. Then, at the

beginning of November, he rang me up and said, "Look, I've got a bit of bad news. The programme is going ahead but Michael Grade has instructed me to replace the Doctor."

'John said he had told them that he thought it was a dreadful mistake and he wanted me to play the Doctor, but they were adamant. "Grade says three years is quite enough. He's said nothing derogatory about your performance, he thinks you are fine, but he thinks a new Doctor will give the programme a boost. I have pointed out that you have not done three years, that you have done only one and a half seasons, but he remains adamant that that is long enough and it's time for a change." So there was nothing much I could do about it.

'It went against what I was asked to do, when I started the show, by David Reid – Powell's predecessor. He'd asked me if I was prepared to commit myself to the programme for *four* years. Having said yes in 1983 to four years of twenty-six episodes a year, I actually did one year of twenty-six episodes (or the equivalent), nothing at all the next year, and just fourteen episodes the next. Then I was unceremoniously bundled out. So I felt fairly aggrieved.'

Baker was in fact offered the chance to appear in the first four episodes of the twenty-fourth season in a story to explain the Doctor's regeneration, but he declined to do so.

'That was actually a concession won by John,' he recalled in 1989, 'but I said, "Quite honestly, if I've got to leave, I want to leave now and start making a career." The analogy I've always used is that it's like your girlfriend giving you the push and saying, "But you can come back and spend a night with me next year!" It's just not on.'

The news that Baker would not be returning as the Doctor was broken to the general public in early December 1986. The press once again took an interest in the series, the *Sun*'s Charles Catchpole interviewing the actor for a three-part run of articles published in January 1987. Many of the series' fans were incensed by the treatment that Baker had received from the BBC. There was however clearly no prospect of Grade reversing his decision, so another new Doctor would have to be cast to take *Doctor Who* into the late eighties. Nathan-Turner had acceded to his superiors' request to inform Baker of his ousting from the series only on the understanding that he himself would finally be allowed to move on to something different, so it seemed that season twenty-four would find newcomers both in front of and behind the cameras.

CHAPTER FOURTEEN

Who Was Sylvester McCoy

Sylvester McCoy was born James Kent-Smith on 20 August 1943, the son of Molly Sheridan and Percy James Kent-Smith, an Irish couple living in Dunoon, Scotland. His father was killed in the Second World War a couple of months before he was born, and he was brought up by his mother, his grandmother – Mary Sheridan – and aunts.

He attended St Mun's, a local Dunoon school. The headmistress, Rosie O'Grady, was keen that her young charges obtain decent jobs upon leaving the school and so organised regular talks from people in all manner of professions. McCoy expressed an interest in every job, and as a result eventually found himself given an afternoon off school to go to see a local priest about entering the priesthood.

He left school, joined Blair's College, a seminary in Aberdeen, and between the ages of twelve and sixteen trained to be a priest. It was while at Blair's College that he realised that there was more to life than could be found in Dunoon and discovered classical music and history, which fascinated him.

Looking back in later years, he considered that this was the best theatrical training that he could have had. 'I think my interest in the priesthood was always more theatrical than religious,' he noted.

He eventually decided to become a monk and applied to join a Dominican order, but his application was rejected as he was too young. He went instead to Dunoon grammar school, where he discovered the delights of his female fellow pupils and quickly decided that he didn't want to be a priest or a monk after all. On finishing his education he took a holiday down to London, from which he never returned.

Realising that he needed some money on which to live, McCoy approached a youth employment centre looking for a job. Impressed by the fact that he had attended a grammar school, they instantly found him a job in the City working for an insurance company. He trained in this job and stayed there until he was twenty-seven before deciding that it wasn't really for him.

The pop music and theatre industries were booming at this time, and McCoy decided that entertainment was an area he wanted to get into.

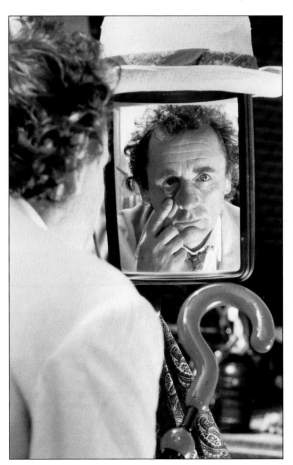

THE FILMS OF SYLVESTER McCOY

Dracula (1979) *appearing as Sylveste McCoy;* **The Secret Policeman's Ball** *(1980);* **Teenie Weenies Parts 1 and 2** *(1994)*

▲ Sylvester McCoy in his first story as the Doctor *Time and the Rani.*

◀ Sylvester McCoy as the Doctor. *Delta and the Bannermen.*

Sylvester McCoy in a ▶
casual pose.

SELECTED TV APPEARANCES

Star Strider (Granada 1985);
Tiswas (BBC 1974 –1984; Dates of
McCoy's appearances unknown);
Vision-On (1964 –1976; dates of
McCoy's appearances unknown); ***Big***
***Jim and the Figaro Club** (pilot)*
(BBC 1979); ***Big Jim and the***
***Figaro Club** (series) (BBC 1981);*
Jigsaw** (BBC 1980–82);* ***Eureka
(BBC 1984/5/6); ***The Last Place***
***on Earth** (Central 1985);*
Dramarama** (TVS);* ***Number 73
(TVS); ***Doctor Who** (BBC 1987 –*
1989); ***Tomorrow's World***
Christmas** (BBC 1987);* ***Comic
Relief** (BBC 1988);* ***Noel
Edmonds' Saturday Roadshow
(BBC 1989); ***What's Your Story***
(BBC 1989/1990); ***Search Out***
***Science/Space** (BBC 1992);*
Jackanory** (BBC 1993);* ***10X10: St
Ann's Big Boy** (1993);* ***Doctor
***Who: Dimensions in Time** (BBC*
1993); ***Thirty Years in the TARDIS***
(BBC 1993); ***Frank Stubbs***
Promotes** (1994);* ***Ghoul-Lashed!
(Sky TV 1995–1996); ***Rab C.***
Nesbit** (BBC 1995);* ***Doctor Who
(BBC/Universal 1996).

RADIO APPEARANCES

Big Jim and the Figaro Club
(1987); ***The Real McCoy** (cassette*
tape interview) (1990); ***The***
Cabinet of Doctor Caligari
(1992); ***Jack the Ripper***
(audiocassette) (1994); ***Prince***
Caspian** (1995);* ***The Voyage of
***the Dawn Treader** (1995).*

He knew the cook at London's Roundhouse Theatre and she helped him to gain a job there selling tickets and keeping the books in the box office.

It was at the Roundhouse that he became friends with an actor called Brian Murphy (now well known for his starring role in the seventies sitcom *George and Mildred*), who was collecting the tickets that he sold. The two friends used to improvise various 'entertainments' for those queuing. For example, Murphy would pretend to be a queue jumper and McCoy would pretend to tackle him. In this way Murphy assumed that, like himself, McCoy was simply another actor earning a living while times were hard. A director named Ken Campbell who was working at the Roundhouse asked Murphy if there were any actors who might be interested in joining him in a new venture called the Ken Campbell Roadshow, and Murphy

Sophie Aldred and ▶
Sylvester McCoy sign
autographs on location for
Silver Nemesis.

suggested that he talk to McCoy.

McCoy readily agreed to join Campbell's show – even though he had no acting experience and knew nothing about the business. He travelled up to Manchester, where he met the rest of Campbell's team – Bob Hoskins, Jane Wood and Dave Hill – and together they started performing a range of plays with the umbrella theme of 'modern myths'. McCoy found himself in a double-act with Hoskins.

Eventually Hoskins left and Campbell booked the team to go and play at a circus. When they arrived, however, they discovered that no one else was there. Consequently they were forced to learn and improvise a circus-based act and to do all the stunts and tricks themselves.

Campbell subsequently devised a show about a fictitious stuntman called Sylvester McCoy and thought it would be amusing if the programme stated that this character was played by 'Sylvester McCoy'. When they staged the show at the Royal Court Theatre, one of the critics missed the joke and assumed that Sylvester McCoy was a real person. McCoy liked the irony of this, and adopted the name as his stage identity.

The stunts McCoy undertook in the Royal Court Theatre show included setting light to his head, shoving ferrets down his trousers, exploding bombs on his chest, mentally combusting cotton wool and hammering nails up his nose. The show was a great success and went on to tour all over Europe.

During one of their UK engagements, the Roadshow team started to go and busk outside other theatres to entertain the patrons as they queued to go in. On one occasion Joan Littlewood, who was directing a production of *The Hostage*, came out to see them busk and eventually invited them in, onto the stage before the performance of her play. This started McCoy in *bona fide* theatre, and he was subsequently invited to appear in numerous plays and musicals.

It was while starring at the National Theatre in *The Pied Piper*, a play written especially for him, that McCoy heard that the BBC were looking for a new lead actor to replace Colin Baker in *Doctor Who*. He had applied for the job once before, when Peter Davison had relinquished the role, but had discovered that Baker had already been cast. Undaunted, he telephoned John Nathan-Turner to put himself forward once more. By an incredible coincidence, moments after they had finished

SELECTED THEATRE APPEARANCES

The Ken Campbell Road Show; A Midsummer Night's Dream; Servant of Two Masters; The Soldier's Tale; Starlight Express; Satie Day Night; Buster's Last Stand; Caucasian Chalk Circle; Androcles and the Lion; The Tempest; Can't Pay? Won't Pay!; Abbacadabra; Gone With Hardy; The Pirates of Penzance; Twelfth Night; Dracula; The Fosdyke Saga (director) *(1981–198?); School for Clowns* (director) *(1981–198?); The Taming of the Shrew (1986); Anthony and Cleopatra (1986); The Pied Piper (1987); The Zoo Of Tranquillity (1988); I Miss My War (1989); Aladdin (1989/1990); Temptation (1990); Babes in the Wood (1990/1991); Having A Ball (1991); Marriage of Figaro (1991); Cinderella (1991/1992); Children's Royal Variety Performance (1992); As You Like It (1992); An Evening With Sylvester McCoy (1992); The Government Inspector (1993/1994); The Invisible Man (1993–1994); Zorro: The Musical (1995); Mother Goose (1994/1995); Dick Whittington (1995/1996).*

▲ Sylvester McCoy takes a break during the recording of scenes for *Silver Nemesis*.

◄ Sylvester McCoy and Bonnie Langford take posession of the **TARDIS** at the press call to introduce McCoy as the seventh Doctor.

VIDEO APPEARANCES

Fireworks (198?); Three Kinds Of Heat (1988); The Hartnell Years (BBC 1991); The Making of Silver Nemesis (BBC 1993); The Airzone Solution (BBV 1993); The Zero Imperative (BBV 1994); Myth Makers 28: Sylvester McCoy (Reeltime Pictures 1994); More Than Thirty Years in the TARDIS (BBC 1995); The Doctors (MasterVision 1995); I Was A Doctor Who Monster (Reeltime Pictures 1996); Bidding Adieu (BBV 1996).

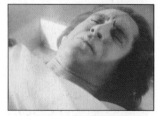

The seventh Doctor ▲ regenerates. Doctor Who.

speaking, a BBC producer named Clive Doig, with whom McCoy had once worked, also telephoned Nathan-Turner to suggest that he would make a good Doctor. Nathan-Turner, although initially suspecting collusion, was sufficiently intrigued to go and see McCoy in *The Pied Piper* on 6 January 1987.

'It was a very good audition piece for *Doctor Who*,' the actor explained. 'I wore an extraordinary, wonderful, multicoloured coat, which I think, visually, must have tingled something in John's mind when he came to see the play.'

McCoy's performance in the play greatly impressed Nathan-Turner, and eventually led to him being offered the role of the Doctor.

McCoy is married to Agnes and has two sons, Joe and Sam. He values his private life and consequently had some concerns in agreeing to take on a role that demanded and guaranteed a lot of public exposure.

'We have never been a particularly showbiz family, which is why I didn't really enjoy the hype that came with the job. It was difficult for us to have fun together, publicly, without being mobbed wherever we went.

'Suddenly there I was, a lunatic actor, thrown into this extraordinary world, which for the most part I enjoyed enormously.'

McCoy was at first not unduly concerned about the characterisation of the seventh Doctor.

'It might sound arrogant,' he said shortly after recording started for his first season, 'but I haven't really worried about that side of it. There's been no time – the only time there's been is to learn the lines and try not to bump into the space furniture. I discussed it with John in the interviews and then I got the scripts, but they weren't written for me, so there's a transition period – I'm trying to fit to the scripts and they're trying to fit to me.'

As his three seasons in the role progressed, McCoy gradually toned down the more humorous elements of his portrayal and brought in a darker and more sinister image.

'I definitely started off playing it for laughs,' he admitted in 1992. 'I hadn't watched *Doctor Who* for years, but had memories of Patrick Troughton, Jon Pertwee and early Tom Baker. I remembered it as being humorous and so started out doing it like that. As it developed, my Doctor became very serious, but still with the comic element there. I

McCoy finds a comfortable spot to take a break from recording.

was moving towards that in the end.'

To emphasise this shift in the character, the Doctor's costume was changed for McCoy's final season from a fawn jacket and paisley scarf, to a dark brown jacket and an altogether more muted and subdued image. This reflected the desire of the production team as a whole to inject more mystery into the Doctor's origins and motivations. If McCoy had played the Doctor for a fourth season, as had been planned, the darkness of the character would have become ever more evident.

Since leaving *Doctor Who*, McCoy has worked extensively in theatre and on television. In theatre he appeared in *The Government Inspector* twice in tours during 1993 and 1994, and in between these he starred as the Narrator, Thomas Marvel, in the stage version of H. G. Wells's *The Invisible Man*. In 1995 he starred in *Zorro: The Musical*. On television his credits include *Frank Stubbs Promotes* and *Rab C. Nesbitt*. More recently he has created the character of Crud in the cult television series *Ghoul-Lashed* for Sky TV. In 1996 he was contracted to reprise the role of the Doctor in a new *Doctor Who* TV movie (see Chapter Twenty-Four), handing over to an eighth incarnation of the Time Lord in the earthly form of his friend Paul McGann. Also in 1996, McCoy devised and presented Reeltime Pictures' *I Was A Doctor Who Monster* – a special video tribute to the men and women who had played the monsters in *Doctor Who*.

CHAPTER FIFTEEN

The Seventh Doctor: Time's Champion

I f his fifth regeneration at the end of *The Caves of Androzani* saw the Doctor plunging into the dark realms of mental instability, his sixth is far less traumatic – although the circumstances surrounding it are the most bizarre of all his transformations.

His previous changes of appearance were all triggered by major calamities or life-threatening injuries: mental and physical exhaustion; enforced regeneration by the Time Lords; a deadly dose of radiation; a fall from the gantry of the Pharos Project's radio telescope; and a fatal case of spectrox toxaemia. By contrast, this latest regeneration is apparently induced by a tumble from an exercise bike when the TARDIS is attacked in flight by his old enemy the Rani.

When the new Doctor regains consciousness he seems quite fit and mentally alert, although for a time he is unable to recall his own identity. After the Rani injects him with an amnesia-inducing drug, however, he starts to act extremely erratically, appearing light-headed and rather comical in nature. He is certainly confused enough to be taken in when the Rani masquerades as Mel, and then to consider some very strange alternatives when selecting a new outfit from the TARDIS wardrobe – although the one he ultimately chooses, while undeniably still eccentric, is positively subdued by comparison with his predecessor's preferred attire!

Although he eventually overcomes the effects of the Rani's drug, he continues to act in a quirky, somewhat clownish manner over the course of his next few adventures. His mental processes also appear a little confused, as he frequently comes out with scrambled adages and mixed metaphors.

By the time he and Mel arrive on Svartos in

Dragonfire, the last story of his first season, there are signs that his character is becoming more stable. His judgement still seems to be impaired, however, as at one point he decides to climb over the edge of an icy precipice and hang by his umbrella for no readily apparent reason.

This umbrella, with its distinctive question-mark handle, is clearly a prized possession to the seventh Doctor as – regardless of the weather – he is rarely seen without it after this point. Occasionally he even presses it into service as a tool or a weapon, in much the same way that the fourth Doctor sometimes made use of his trademark scarf.

When the TARDIS brings the Doctor and his new companion Ace to sixties London in the

The seventh Doctor as he appeared in season twenty-six's *The Curse of Fenric*.

▲ The Doctor tries on a possible new outfit. *Time and the Rani.*

◄ The seventh Doctor was adept at manipulating his friends and enemies. *Survival.*

The Doctor is captured ▲ by a cleaning robot. *Paradise Towers.*

The seventh Doctor ▲ tries on the second Doctor's fur coat. *Time and the Rani.*

The seventh Doctor finds the fourth Doctor's coat a little on the large side. *Time and the Rani.* ▼

following story, *Remembrance of the Daleks*, it appears that some time has elapsed since they first met on Iceworld. They are now clearly close friends, and the Doctor can be seen to have adopted the role of a mentor, or even a teacher, to Ace. It later becomes apparent that he is helping her to come to terms with her own personal demons, which in part contributed to her having a turbulent time as a teenager and acquiring an enduring fascination with fire and explosives. In *Ghost Light*, by showing her events that happened a hundred years earlier, he forces her to confront the reasons why she once burned down a derelict Victorian house; and in *The Curse of Fenric* he brings about a situation in which she sees her previously hated mother as a young baby and has to re-evaluate her feelings towards her. The fruits of these traumatic incidents become apparent as Ace gradually matures from a girl into a young woman.

The Doctor himself has by this point mellowed and become far less manic. He also appears more able than in any of his earlier incarnations to influence and control events taking place around him. Whereas previously he acted for the most part as an aimless traveller, doing his best to help the underdog and to fight injustice whenever he encountered it, now he starts to use carefully-laid plans and near-Machiavellian strategies in order to achieve his objectives. He is content to allow Ace to handle the more physical aspects of his battles while he merely directs from the background, stepping in only where necessary to keep events on track.

Amongst the schemes he brings to fruition – having apparently laid the groundwork for them many years before – are ruses designed to cause the destruction of his old enemies the Daleks in

Remembrance of the Daleks and the Cybermen in *Silver Nemesis*. Such is his adeptness at manipulating events that in *The Happiness Patrol* he is even able to topple an oppressive regime in the course of just a single night. He encounters once again a number of powerful foes from his distant past – including (previously unseen in his televised adventures) the Gods of Ragnarok in *The Greatest Show in the Galaxy* and Fenric in *The Curse of Fenric* – but always seems able to keep one step ahead of them. He reveals that in a previous meeting with Fenric he defeated the evil entity at chess, and the mantle of a chess player seems to fit the seventh Doctor particularly well as he manoeuvres his allies like pieces on a chessboard to counter and defeat his enemies' pawns.

This is not to say that he no longer has a lighter side to his nature. He occasionally amuses himself by playing the spoons, and one of the tactics he adopts to defeat the Gods of Ragnarok in *The Greatest Show in the Galaxy* is to distract them with a dazzling display of extraordinary conjuring tricks and acrobatics.

Other previously hidden talents displayed by the seventh Doctor include the gift of instant hypnosis, as demonstrated in *Battlefield*, and the ability to disable someone simply by placing a finger against their forehead, as seen in *Survival*.

Also in *Battlefield* the Doctor gains a glimpse of events to come, when he learns that in a future incarnation he will be known to some as Merlin. This is only one of a number of revelations that lead viewers to suspect that there is a great deal more to the character than has hitherto been thought. Even things that previously appeared certain, such as the Doctor's Time Lord origins, are now called into question.

Remembrance of the Daleks contains suggestions that, contrary to previous indications, the Doctor might somehow be a contemporary of Rassilon and Omega – the legendary founders of Time Lord society – and therefore presumably a good deal older than the 953 years he claims in *Time and the Rani* (itself a rather greater age than usually indicated by his earlier incarnations). Then, in *Silver Nemesis*, the seventeenth-century sorceress Lady Peinforte claims to be in possession of some momentous secrets about the Doctor's past 'from the dark time', although in the event she never has an opportunity to reveal what these are. There are even hints that some aspects of the Doctor's established history might be a deliberate fabrication on his part.

In summary, the Doctor's seventh incarnation is undoubtedly one of the most complex, intriguing and mysterious.

CHAPTER SIXTEEN

Season Twenty-Four:
A Shaky Start

After informing Colin Baker on 29 October 1986 that his contract as the Doctor was not to be renewed, John Nathan-Turner went on extended leave over the winter. He was under the impression that this would mark the end of his time as producer of *Doctor Who*. On his return, however, he was told that he was to remain in the job for the following season. Despite his stated reluctance to do so, he had no choice but to comply if he was to remain a staff producer at the BBC.

A serious problem requiring immediate attention was the lack of any suitable scripts lined up for production. Nathan-Turner therefore set about as a matter of urgency finding a new script editor to succeed Eric Saward.

Andrew Cartmel had been working for a computer company in Cambridge but had also attended some workshops at the BBC's Television Drama Script Unit and had got an agent on the strength of some unproduced scripts. When his agent, who knew Nathan-Turner, heard that a new script editor was required for *Doctor Who*, Cartmel travelled to London for an interview and was offered the job.

'The reason John gave me the job was that we got along,' explained Cartmel in 1994, 'and I didn't impress him as being an idiot. He'd read a script of mine, and obviously saw qualities in there demonstrating that I knew what a good TV script should be.'

Meanwhile, recognising that time was running very short to get production of the new season under way, Nathan-Turner had contacted Pip and Jane Baker and asked if they would consider writing the new Doctor's introductory story. They agreed, and on 22 December 1986 were commissioned to provide the scripts for a four-parter entitled *Strange Matter*

(adapted from an earlier unused storyline). Nathan-Turner had yet to decide at this point who was to play the new Doctor, but he knew that he wanted him to be behaving 'semi-normally' the first time viewers saw him.

The fact that a new Doctor was required for the series had not gone unnoticed amongst actors and actors' agents, who were eager to put forward suggestions. On 18 December 1986 Nathan-Turner was contacted by Sylvester McCoy (whose agent subsequently sent in a photograph and information about his client) and on 8 January 1987 he received a similar approach from an agent representing Ken Campbell (in whose company McCoy had begun his acting career). This was in fact the second time that

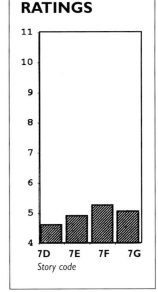

SEASON TWENTY-FOUR	
CODE	TITLE
7D	Time and the Rani
7E	Paradise Towers
7F	Delta and the Bannermen
7G	Dragonfire

RATINGS

◀ The new Doctor and Mel find themselves at a holiday camp in Wales. *Delta and the Bannermen.*

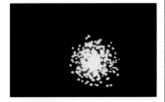

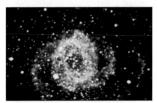

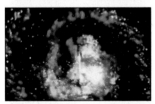

The new title sequence ▲ for season twenty-four, design by Oliver Elmes and realised by CAL Video.

Sylvester McCoy dons the sixth Doctor's colourful costume. *Time and the Rani*.

Campbell had put his name forward for the part of the Doctor – the first had been back on 18 October 1985, when he had done so on the off-chance that the BBC's plans for revamping *Doctor Who* following the cancellation of the original twenty-third season might include a change of lead actor.

Nathan-Turner was keen from the outset to give the part to McCoy, having gone to see him in *The Pied Piper* and been very impressed with his performance. Head of Series and Serials Jonathan Powell, however, asked him to cast his net a little wider and to carry out some screen tests. Nathan-Turner and director Andrew Morgan, who had been assigned to handle *Strange Matter*, eventually came up with a short-list of names, including McCoy, Campbell, Hugh Futcher, Dermot Crowley and David Fielder. McCoy, Campbell, Fielder and

Bonnie Langford keeps warm during a break in recording *Time and the Rani* in Frome, Somerset.

The entrance façade of the Rani's citadel on Lakertya under construction. *Time and the Rani*.

Crowley were invited to audition on 18 February 1987 as Powell had requested. The format of the audition involved them being recorded on the TARDIS set performing a section of script written by Cartmel and directed by Morgan. Former companion actress Janet Fielding was contracted to act opposite them. The final decision to go for McCoy was made by Nathan-Turner in consultation with both Powell and Controller of BBC 1 Michael Grade. The actor's accession to the role was officially announced on Monday 2 March, although news of it had leaked to the press over the previous weekend.

'We were well into writing the story when we were shown a video of Sylvester McCoy,' revealed Pip and Jane Baker in 1988. 'We had to find a) a way of regenerating the Doctor and b) a character for him. John asked for a pre-credit teaser. All of us felt that we couldn't go straight into the story. If we had to regenerate in this way we needed to start with it, then have a full stop and then start the story. It would have been impossible to open with Sylvester's title sequence otherwise; it would have looked silly.'

The new title sequence was designed by Oliver Elmes, one of the BBC's senior graphic designers. Nathan-Turner had in fact been in contact with him the previous year about the possibility of introducing a new sequence for the twenty-third season, but had eventually told him in a memo dated 28 February 1986 that he had decided not to proceed with the idea, although he liked the proposed new logo very much. It seems that a shortage of money had been the reason for that decision. With a new Doctor now cast, however, there was no choice but to change the sequence, so Nathan-Turner got back in touch with Elmes.

The new sequence was to be the first created for the series using computer technology. Elmes had contacted an outside contractor called CAL Video, and Gareth Edwards from that company was given the task of realising his ideas.

The basic concept devised by Elmes and developed by Edwards was of an array of stars exploding from nothing to represent the beginning of the universe. Using computer-generated graphics, they could then move the point of view around the starfield and create a feeling of space. They then wanted a bubble to cross the screen and viewers to feel as though they were on a fairground ride, going up and down very quickly. This latter aspect was simplified and ended up with the point of view just going over the top of the TARDIS as it appeared in the bubble.

'Oliver came to see me with a couple of A3 sheets of paper on which he'd sketched his own visualisation of the titles,' recalled Edwards in 1992. 'The sequence amounted to two main things: there was the end logo, which he'd already prepared, and he wanted something that felt like it was a switchback ride on a roller coaster. He wanted that kind of feeling, particularly at the beginning when we're coming down onto the galaxy, which, incidentally, was based on a faithful model of the Milky Way, with all the little detailed globular clusters.

'The idea for the bubble with the gas around it developed as we worked together, as did many of the sequences' effects. All the stars originally started off white, but Oliver wanted some of them to be different – either a bluey, purplish or an orangey colour. So, we looked at it as it stood, which was basically a large white starfield with a large white blob and an occasional dot of colour! Then he said, "Let's see what it looks like the other way round." Now, when designers say things like that to me, I know that what they really mean is that they want a kind of negative. So, basically, I swapped all the colours: where they were white, I made them blue and so on. That's why the star background has that colour. Another example is on the TARDIS itself. If you look, you'll notice that the "POLICE – PUBLIC

Urak (Richard Gauntlett) mistakes his mistress, the Rani (Kate O'Mara), for Mel. *Time and the Rani.*

CALL – BOX" signs in the sequence are white lettering on a black background, but on the original TARDIS prop, the background is blue. Well, the reference they gave me had a black insert, so I created a black insert on the computer model.'

The most problematic aspect of the sequence was getting McCoy's face laid in.

'The idea originally was to create a skull-like shape first which then developed into the head,' said Elmes in 1992, 'which was a bit more sinister than what we eventually ended up with. But we had limited funds, and CAL Video actually did quite a lot for us within the £20,000 budget we had. In the end, the producer wasn't too happy with the original head, which was rather less detailed than the one that

The Tetraps leave their lair beneath the citadel. *Time and the Rani.*

STOCK FOOTAGE

Time and the Rani part four featured ten seconds of film from Dennis Film Services called 'The Life of the Stars'.

A section of the travelogue sequence seen at the start of **Paradise Towers** was taken from an eight-part series called **The Shock of the New** originally transmitted in 1980. The sequences intended to be used came from programmes four: 'Trouble in Utopia', seven: 'Culture as Nature' and eight: 'The Future that Was'. Because of difficulties experienced in satisfactorily clearing copyright on some of the images, the final travelogue used only a one-and-a-half second clip from programme four. The remaining scenes in the travelogue were all recorded while on location at Elmswell House for the swimming pool sequences.

Episode three of **Delta and the Bannermen** featured fourteen seconds of film of locusts from the NHU Film Library to create the attack by bees.

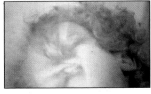

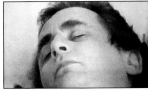

▲ The Doctor regenerates on the TARDIS floor after crashing on Lakertya. *Time and the Rani.*

◀ The Rani (Kate O'Mara) creates a giant super brain by kidnapping geniuses from across the galaxy. *Time and the Rani.*

NOTES

Different Title

A different version of the title sequence was transmitted by mistake at the beginning of part four of **Time and the Rani***. This was the version originally created by Elmes and Edwards featuring the more subtle skull-like face for the seventh Doctor.*

Casting Ideas

The part of the Deputy Chief Caretaker in **Paradise Towers** *was originally offered to Edward Hardwicke, but he was already working on a film at the time so it went instead to Clive Merrison.*

Different Director

The director of **Delta and the Bannermen** *was originally scheduled to be Bob Gabriel, who was due to move onto the production after completing work on* **EastEnders***. It is unknown why he did not eventually take the assignment.*

Different Ray

Lynn Gardner was originally cast as Ray in **Delta and the Bannermen***. However, she was injured in a minor crash during a driving lesson and unable to take part. The role therefore went to Chris Clough's second choice for the part, Sara Griffiths. Gardner was also cast by Clough as the Tannoy voice in* **Dragonfire***.*

Costume design for Mel and the Rani created by Ken Trew. Time and the Rani. ▼

The model of the Rani's citadel is taken on location so that the effects shots using the model will match with the live action recording. *Time and the Rani.*

appears in the final version of the sequence. It looked far more as though it had been formed from the galaxy, with the blue clouds swirling through it. But because he wanted a very hard image, and we'd run out of money, we had to go back and superimpose the head as he wanted it over the one we'd done.'

In developing the sequence, Edwards had been trying to hark back to the original titles from the early sixties.

'One of the ideas that Oliver had sketched out,' he recalled, 'was that after we'd met the TARDIS, we'd see the Doctor's face and stars swirling all around it. Now, when I created the blue clouds that flow around and through the face, I was consciously trying to produce something that had throwbacks to the original sequence. I really was determined to get that same kind of swirling effect, and if you look at it, you'll see that it's very similar.'

The sequence was developed and animated on a

Sun Workstation and IRIS terminal running CAL Video's in-house software. A Quantel Paintbox was used to add all the colours and touch up some of the images, while the Doctor's face, the main galaxy and the TARDIS were all created using photographs placed on a caption camera. To edit all the elements together, the HARRY digital editing system was used. The whole job took CAL Video about six or seven weeks spread over a three-and-a-half-month period.

CAL Video made one further contribution to the seventh Doctor's debut story. This formed part of the pre-credits sequence for the opening episode and showed the TARDIS being attacked while in flight – the incident that would lead to the Doctor's regeneration.

Along with the new title sequence came another new arrangement of the series' theme music. This was commissioned from freelance composer Keff McCulloch on the recommendation of his future wife, actress Tracey Wilson, who had known Nathan-Turner since appearing in his 1982 *Cinderella* pantomime.

Recording for the story written by the Bakers to introduce the seventh Doctor started on location on 4 April 1987. It was renamed *Time and the Rani* for transmission, which commenced on 7 September 1987 – the series having now been given a weekly Monday evening slot starting around 7.35 pm, opposite ITV's enormously popular soap opera *Coronation Street*.

The Rani has taken control of the planet Lakertya and forced the peaceful Lakertyans to build a rocket silo-cum-refinery base into a cliff face. She is aided by the Tetraps, a race of bat-like creatures, and plans to fire a rocket loaded with loyhargil, a substance with the same properties as strange matter, at an asteroid completely composed of the latter. As a preliminary to this she has created a huge artificial brain and kidnapped a number of geniuses – including Pasteur and Einstein from Earth – to imbue it with the ability to calculate the correct way to create loyhargil for her in the refinery. The newly regenerated Doctor and Mel manage to stop her and the planet is saved. The Rani is captured by the Tetraps, who decide to take her as a prisoner back to their home world.

Morgan had first been approached to direct a *Doctor Who* story – season nineteen's *Time-Flight* – back in 1981. He had been unable to take on that assignment and was pleased to have another opportunity to work on the series for *Time and the Rani*.

The Chief Caretaker (Richard Briers), the overly officious controller of *Paradise Towers*.

The Doctor is questioned by the Deputy Chief Caretaker (Clive Merrison). *Paradise Towers*.

'Despite shooting in an awful quarry in Somerset, I must admit I enjoyed it very much,' he said in a 1993 interview. 'I did feel a bit bogged down with all the special effects technicalities and experts. I was a bit overawed by people telling me what I couldn't do. It was a bit like the tail wagging the dog.'

The sets for the story were constructed by Zircon, an external contractor based near Television Centre in Acton, and designer Geoff Powell had to keep a close eye on the work as it progressed.

'We're a bit behind,' he explained at the time, 'because the finished scripts were late coming in and there wasn't time to do fully detailed drawings as usual.'

Powell drafted some basic elevations of what was required in order to give Zircon something to work from, and his team liaised with them along the way to ensure that the finished sets matched the specifications of the scripts.

One of the most distinctive props built for the production was the giant brain. The set that housed this was raised some ten feet off the studio floor.

'As it's written,' explained Powell, 'a door has to slide up revealing a fourteen-foot-diameter brain in a rocky enclave. Visual Effects couldn't really build that, so what I've done is make the thing look bigger

by raising it up on an elevated gantry, which we can light from below and have effects beneath, which should make the whole thing look bigger.'

The brain itself was constructed in part by veteran effects designer Len Hutton using fibreglass with a latex 'skin' over the top. To achieve the effect of it pulsing, numerous condoms were taped under the skin and the effects assistants simply blew through air tubes to inflate and deflate them as required.

For the regeneration sequence at the start of the story McCoy was required to don the sixth Doctor's costume and – until the regeneration actually occurred – a curly blond wig so that, when shot from behind, he would resemble his predecessor. The seventh Doctor's regular costume was designed by Ken Trew of the BBC's Costume Department. It reflected McCoy's own preference, which was for an outfit that at first glance would appear quite ordinary and only on closer inspection would be seen to have the quality of eccentricity normally associated with the Doctor. The hat was McCoy's own, and had been worn by him at his first meeting with Nathan-Turner before he was offered the part.

With *Time and the Rani* established as the season opener, Cartmel's priority was to find stories to make up the remainder of the fourteen-episode run – and fast. A big fan of contemporary comics, he was keen to bring that influence to *Doctor Who*. Collections of

▲ Faroon (Wanda Ventham). *Time and the Rani*.

▲ Urak (Richard Gauntlett) hunts on the surface of Lakertya. *Time and the Rani*.

Tilda (Brenda Bruce), a ▲ cannibalistic resident of *Paradise Towers*.

The Doctor and Mel find ▲ themselves in the nightmare world of *Paradise Towers*.

Ray (Sara Griffiths) was ▲ considered as a possible companion for the Doctor, but the production team finally chose the character of Ace. *Delta and the Bannermen.*

Mel and the Doctor are held at gunpoint by the Red Kangs led by Fire Escape (Julie Brennon). *Paradise Towers.*

Alan Moore's *Halo Jones* stories from *2000 AD* consequently became virtually required reading for prospective *Doctor Who* writers.

'Alan Moore's *Halo Jones* showed me you didn't have to write comics in a stylised way,' he said in 1991. 'You could actually explore interesting aspects of a character's personality.'

Another suggestion Cartmel frequently made to writers unfamiliar with the series was that they read the 1983 media studies book *Doctor Who – The Unfolding Text* by John Tulloch and Manuel Alverado.

Amongst the writers contacted by Cartmel were several of his friends, including Malcolm Kohll and Ian Briggs, from his days at the BBC's Script Unit. Kohll and Briggs were each commissioned to provide a scene breakdown for a story, the former on 30 January 1987 and the latter (having previously had one idea rejected) on 9 March.

A writer named Stephen Wyatt sent in as an example of his work a script for a comedy-drama play called *Claws* about a power struggle in a cat club. Cartmel, liking the style of this, met him over the Christmas period to discuss possibilities for *Doctor Who*. As the script editor later recalled, Wyatt mentioned the J. G. Ballard novel *High Rise* and their discussions then turned to a story involving a skyscraper. The script for the first episode of *Paradise Towers* (called *Paradise Tower* on the commissioning documents) was formally commissioned on 30 January 1987 and those for the other three on 19 February, and this ultimately became the second story of the season.

The plot of *Paradise Towers* involves the Doctor and Mel making their way to the eponymous tower block as Mel has decided that she wants to go swimming and there is a fantastic pool there. When

The Bannerman leader Gavrok (Don Henderson) tracks the Chimeron Queen to Earth. *Delta and the Bannermen.*

Mel and the Doctor meet the Tollmaster (Ken Dodd). *Delta and the Bannermen.*

▲ **A Chimeron soldier.** *Delta and the Bannermen.*

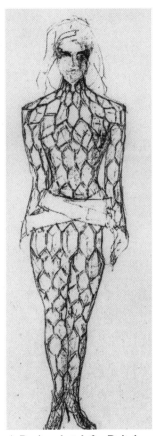

▲ **Design sketch for Delta's costume by Richard Croft.** *Delta and the Bannermen.*

▲ **Delta (Belinda Mayne).** *Delta and the Bannermen.*

they arrive they discover that the Towers are far from being the superb leisure resort they had expected. The whole place is run-down and dilapidated. The hallways are roamed by gangs of young girls known as Kangs; the apartments are inhabited by cannibalistic old ladies, the Rezzies; and the building is managed by a group of dictatorial caretakers, presided over by the Chief Caretaker. The latter is in thrall to the disembodied Great Architect Kroagnon, the building's creator, who is using giant cleaning machines systematically to kill all the occupants as he considers that they are spoiling his creation by living there. The Great Architect eventually manifests himself by taking over the Chief Caretaker's body, but the Doctor and Mel join forces with the Kangs, the Rezzies and Pex – the only young man left in the complex – to defeat his plans.

'We started with certain elements,' explained Cartmel in 1994. 'It's set in a high rise that's become a decaying urban maze. There's the hierarchy of the people who manage the building, and the fascistic girl gangs. But we needed a monster.'

Cartmel and Wyatt initially wanted something with tentacles, but this was vetoed by Nathan-Turner as being too complex to realise. In the end a compromise solution was found and, with the ingenuity of the BBC's Visual Effects Department, automated tentacles were featured on the cleaning machines.

The planet on which Paradise Towers was located was given no name on screen, although it had been referred to first as Kroagnon and then as Griophos with Pool in successive drafts of the scripts.

'I think *Paradise Towers* suffered by the fact that we didn't have a very clear idea of how Sylvester's Doctor was going to develop,' said Wyatt in 1989. 'I don't think Sylvester did either. The character of Mel – and this is actually no fault of Bonnie's – as far as I could see had no discernible characteristics whatsoever. It made it very difficult when I was writing *Paradise Towers* to find out exactly what it was that made the character tick. She was just a nice person who got involved in adventures, so there was not a lot to get your teeth into.'

The director of *Paradise Towers* was Nicholas Mallett. He too recalls that McCoy was initially uncertain in the role:

'He was quite nervous to start off with and needed a lot of reassurance – quite rightly taking over from Colin Baker, who was a different sort of actor. Not in a million years would Colin want to improvise something. Sylvester could quite easily. You could pitch a scene to Sylvester and say "We'll do something different with this," and he wouldn't be thrown by it. I think he almost preferred it because he found it quite difficult to learn such a lot of stuff quickly. In *Paradise Towers* he had a lot of heavy stuff

ANDREW CARTMEL
SCRIPT EDITOR

*After taking a post-graduate course in computer science, Andrew Cartmel started working for a computer company in Cambridge. He left that job to become script editor for **Doctor Who**. After leaving the show in 1989, Cartmel worked for a year as script editor on **Casualty** before leaving the industry and working in publishing on several computer magazines. He has also written comic stories for **2000 AD** and **Doctor Who Magazine** and has written several novels in Virgin Publishing's **Doctor Who – The New Adventures** range.*

MALCOLM KOHLL
WRITER

*Malcolm Kholl was born in South Africa and lived there for nine years before moving to Zimbabwe. He attended Rhodes University in Graemestown, South Africa, where he trained as a journalist. On completing his course he came to London and did a post-graduate in Film and Television, at Middlesex Polytechnic. He then tried to break into film and television, but found it harder than he had expected. **Delta and the Bannermen** was the first of his scripts to see production. After that he worked on several film comedies, and some serious historical/political work, including a potential mini-series and a pilot for a TV comedy series called **Chastity Brogan – US Marshal**. In 1995 he co-produced a film called **No Regrets**.*

Visual effects assitant Mike Tucker's design sketch for Glitz's ship, The Nosferatu. Dragonfire. ▼

On Svartos Mel and the Doctor meet Ace (Sophie Aldred) a teenage girl from Earth. *Dragonfire.*

to do, but really got it under his belt.'

At the time of its transmission, *Paradise Towers* was quite strongly criticised in sections of the fan press as a further move towards what some saw as a 'pantomime' style of drama in *Doctor Who*. Particular concerns were expressed about the highly stylised portrayal of the Chief Caretaker by Richard Briers (a distinguished character actor at that time perhaps best known for his starring role in the BBC sitcom *The Good Life*).

'Well, the Chief Caretaker was mad,' commented

Briers in 1995. 'I'd played escapist characters before, certainly, but he was completely outrageous – a manic fascist, a sort of Hitler. Those roles are difficult to turn down as they're actually very nice to play. They're also very exhausting.'

Cartmel rejects the suggestion that *Doctor Who* at this time veered towards a pantomime style.

'If we could have just brought the lighting right down, and got really imaginative, moody lighting, I think the whole pantomime thing would have evaporated. That bright artificial lighting gives a brashness and a lack of depth. That's what made it look like a pantomime. Shooting on video really doesn't help.

'A lot of the problem with *Doctor Who* is that people will say that they don't like a story, the writing is crap, when what they actually mean is that the studio lighting is bad. Frequently the reasons that stories didn't work related to the costumes or the lighting, but fans don't analyse it that way.'

Bonnie Langford had told Nathan-Turner at the start of 1987 that she would probably want to bow out of the series at some point during the course of the season. The production team decided in view of this to keep their options open by ensuring that the season's last two stories – the ones written by Kohll and Briggs – each featured a character who could if necessary succeed Mel as the Doctor's companion. There were practical considerations to this as well, as initially it was uncertain in which order the two stories would be transmitted. To ease matters, it was decided that both should be handled by the same director and production crew.

The potential companion character in Kohll's story was Ray (short for Rachel), played by Sara Griffiths, and that in Briggs's was Ace, played by Sophie Aldred (who had originally auditioned for the part of Ray). Ace was in fact a refined version of a potential companion character called Alf, for whom Nathan-Turner and Cartmel had drafted the following rough description dated 26 January 1987:

Alf is a teenage London girl who used to work on the till in a supermarket, until she was swept away from Earth by a time storm. The Doctor finds her in a distant galaxy … working on the till in a supermarket. Fed up with her routine job, determined to see the sights of the universe, Alf pours a drink into her talking till, quits and joins the Doctor on his adventures in the TARDIS.

Alf is uneducated but sharp, nobody's fool. She has a sense of wonder about their travels through time and space. She is smart and tough but protective of the Doctor. Can also

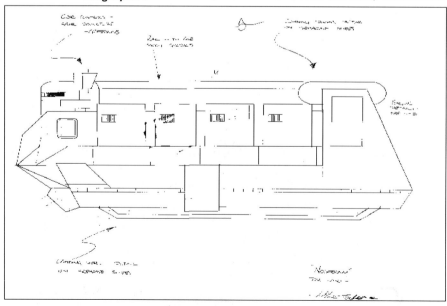

be stroppy and sullen. She approaches her cosmic adventuring with a down-to-earth pragmatism and a somewhat off-beat sense of humour.

Cartmel was particularly keen to ensure that the new companion would be strong and independent.

'We were going for that sort of sisters-are-doing-it-for-themselves kind of thing, which was not Bonnie,' he said in 1994. 'We wanted a post-*Alien* teenage girl.'

Kohll's story, *Delta and the Bannermen* (working title: *The Flight of the Chimeron*), turned out to be the third of the season both in production and in transmission. The writer had been asked to come up with a three-parter set in the recognisable past and featuring lots of location work. Nathan-Turner had been keen to use somewhere other than the south of England and suggested South Wales instead, so Kohll had taken this literally and set a large portion of the action in a South Wales holiday camp. The production team eventually decided that this story should be made entirely on location, and Briggs's entirely in the studio.

The plot revolves around a Chimeron Queen called Delta, the last surviving member of her race. She is being pursued by the evil Gavrok and his Bannermen, who are intent on completely wiping out the Chimeron people. Delta finds herself on board a space bus of tourists *en route* to Earth when it is knocked off course by an American satellite and ends up at a Welsh holiday camp in 1959. The Doctor and Mel, having won a holiday with the tourists, help Delta to evade the rampaging Bannermen long enough to allow her child to hatch from its egg and grow to maturity. She, her daughter and the human Billy – who sacrifices his humanity to be with her – then escape to start a new life and ensure the continuation of the Chimeron race.

The director assigned to *Delta and the Bannermen* was Chris Clough, who was faced with the difficult task both of capturing the feel of the 1950s and of realising convincingly the alien Chimeron and Bannermen.

'As with all aliens in *Doctor Who*,' he later explained, 'the writer gives clues as to the type of character that he has in mind and it is then up to me and the costume designer to come up with something that looks good, is logical, is easy to get in and out of and is not too expensive. We felt that black would be a good colour and overriding image for the Bannermen and, in view of their name, I thought we might as well incorporate that into a red coloured flag that they permanently wore on their

A melting wax mask over a moulded skull was used for the horrific scene where Kane is exposed to sunlight and begins to melt. *Dragonfire.*

IAN BRIGGS
WRITER

Ian Briggs studied drama at Manchester University and after that worked in the theatre on lighting and design, including on some jazz shows. Following that he worked at the BBC's Script Unit reading unsolicited scripts and also freelanced for the Royal Court and some film companies. He was commissioned by Andrew Cartmel first to write **Dragonfire** *and then season twenty-six's* **The Curse of Fenric**. *He was also commissioned by the BBC to write a pilot for a new series and has written some plays for the theatre as well as working on* **Casualty**. *In 1994 he returned to acting and appeared in* **The Derniers** *on television.*

▲ Design for Kane's costume by Richard Croft. *Dragonfire.*

◀ The Doctor dangles over an ice-cliff. *Dragonfire.*

The Dragon (Leslie ▶ Meadows) rescues Stellar (Miranda Borman) from the chaos on Svartos. Dragonfire.

MUSIC

Story	Composer
Time and the Rani	
	Keff McCulloch
Paradise Towers	
	Keff McCulloch
Delta and the Bannermen	
	Keff McCulloch
Dragonfire	*Dominic Glynn*

*The incidental music for **Paradise Towers** was originally composed by David Snell, but director Nicholas Mallett felt that his work was unsuitable. After discussion with John Nathan-Turner, Snell's score was abandoned and Keff McCulloch contracted to provide a replacement at very short notice.*

*The songs recorded by Keff McCulloch and The Lorells (Robin Aspland, Justin Myers, Ralph Salmins, Tracey Wilson and Jodie Wilson), with David Kinder singing the vocals, for **Delta and the Bannermen** were: 'Calling All Workers' by Eric Coates; 'Rock Around The Clock' by Max Freedman and Jimmy de Night; 'Children's Favourites' by White; 'The Parade Of The Tin Soldiers' by Jessell; 'In Party Mood' by Jack Strachey; 'Singing The Blues' by Melvin Endsley; 'Why Do Fools Fall In Love' by Frank Lyman and George Goldner; 'Mr. Sandman' by Pat Ballard; 'That'll Be The Day' by Buddy Holly and Norman Petty; 'Only You' by Buck Ram and Ande Rand; 'Lollipop, Lollipop, Oh Lollipop' by Beverley Ross and Julius Dixon; 'Who's Sorry Now' by Bert Kalmer, Harry Ruby and Ted Snyder; 'Happy Days Are Here Again' by Jack Yellen and Milton Ager; and 'Goodnight Sweetheart' by Noble.*

*A version of 'The Devil's Gallop' by Charles Williams was used for chase sequences in **Delta and the Bannermen**. This music is perhaps better known as the theme for the popular 1940s/1950s radio series **Dick Barton**.*

*Dick Mills from the BBC's Radiophonic Workshop composed some music for the sequences of **Dragonfire** set in the 'Singing Trees' area of Iceworld's underground caverns.*

backs (I admit it was borrowed directly from Kurosawa), which gave a good flash of colour.'

Kohll's original scripts had linked the story into the launch of the Sputnik in 1957. It had subsequently been realised that the story was overrunning, so this element had been removed and a time frame of 1958-1959 introduced instead. This enabled Clough and McCulloch, who had been commissioned to provide the story's incidental music, to research and use many popular songs from that period.

'Billy was in a band, it was a holiday atmosphere, so it seemed like a good idea to use as much of the music as we could,' explained Clough.

McCulloch re-recorded the songs to avoid copyright problems and David Kinder, who played Billy, performed the lead vocals.

The Chimeron baby was made by freelance effects specialists Susan Moore and Stephen Mansfield.

'We received a drawing from the effects designer,

Andy McVean, of a baby,' explained Moore. 'It was based on an elephant shark, which has leech-like tendrils hanging down around the mouth. We were told that this creature was going to be born with loads of loose-fitting sacs of skin that would contract and get tighter as it grew older, which it was going to do very quickly. The Costume Department would take over after the baby's first stage and it would end up in a leotard-type costume with honeycomb-like scales over the surface.'

Two versions of the baby were constructed. One, seen hatching out of the egg, was operated like a hand puppet. The other, seen cradled in Delta's arms, was rigged up with cables so that the arms and legs moved, the head swivelled around, veins on the forehead pulsated and the mouth opened and shut.

Another sequence requiring significant effects work was that of the holiday-makers' bus being hit in space by the satellite and subsequently stabilised by the Doctor in the TARDIS. A two-foot-long model coach was created and 'flown' on wires alongside a similarly scaled model police box, which had been built by effects assistant Mike Tucker for the previous season.

Delta and the Bannermen marked the debut appearance of the seventh Doctor's trademark umbrella with its question mark handle. This had been designed by effects contractor Stan Mitchell as a replacement for the standard brolly used in the earlier stories of the season.

Briggs's story – the season finale – had the working title *The Pyramid's Treasure*, but was retitled *Dragonfire* for production (reportedly after the alternatives *Pyramid in Space* and *Absolute Zero* had been considered and rejected). According to the writer's later recollection, it was initially to have featured a disgusting fourteen-year-old financial genius running a business empire with a sidekick called Mr Spewey. None of these ideas appears in the original scene breakdown, however, and it is possible that Briggs was in fact referring to his first, rejected submission.

The scene breakdown, dated 17 March 1987 and bearing the title *The Pyramid's Treasure*, told a story involving a villain called Hess running a frozen goods trading centre from a planet-sized pyramid in orbit around a larger planet. The Doctor and Mel arrive looking for refreshment and meet up with an intergalactic bounty hunter-cum-pirate called Razorback who tells them about a treasure hidden in the pyramid. The Doctor and Razorback go off to find the treasure, which turns out to be a lens that will focus the pyramid's energy and give Hess

Mel, Ace (Sophie Aldred) and Sabalom Glitz (Tony Selby) ponder the secrets of Iceworld. *Dragonfire*.

immense power. The Doctor realises that Hess's plans for galactic domination will be his downfall. This indeed proves to be the case as, when the pyramid moves out of the shadow of the larger planet, the heat causes Hess to melt away. At the end of the story, Ace – introduced as a human waitress at the trading centre – goes off with Razorback while Mel continues her travels with the Doctor.

The final scripts, the first of which was commissioned on 2 April 1987 and the other two on 13 April, stuck quite closely to this breakdown. One of the few significant changes arose from Langford deciding during the course of production to make this her last *Doctor Who* story. On 3 August 1987 Briggs submitted a new closing scene in which Mel is the one who goes off with the pirate – previously changed from Razorback to Glitz, the intergalactic rogue first seen in *The Trial of a Time Lord* – and Ace who leaves with the Doctor to become the new companion. Other, more minor changes from the scene breakdown included the amendment of the villain's name from Hess to Kane and the alteration of the concept of the trading centre – called Iceworld in the final version – from a planet to a city-like spacecraft on the dark side of another planet.

A new character outline for Ace was prepared in August 1987 in view of her confirmed status as a companion. It read as follows:

ACE is a volatile street-suss teenager from 1980s Perivale, West London. An expert chemist and a dab hand at brewing up home-made explosives, she was once suspended from school for accidentally blowing up the Art Room.

A more detailed set of notes on the girl's character and background would be prepared in October 1987 for inclusion in the guide supplied to prospective writers for the series.

The story was also notable for featuring numerous aliens and monsters. Most important was the Dragon – a legendary beast hunted by the Doctor and Glitz. Tucker, who again worked on the story, later recalled how this had been created:

'Andy McVean came up with some initial design drawings for the head, and effects assistant Lindsay McGowan prepared a small plasticine model of the creature for approval. Then McGowan sculpted a full-size version, which consisted of a latex and polyurethane foam suit and a fibreglass head. There was also a separate mechanical head that opened up to reveal the Dragon's treasure. The suit was then painted up by Lindsay and Paul McGuinness, another effects assistant. The head was sat on a helmet arrangement on top of the actor's own head, and the actor looked out through the neck.'

STEPHEN WYATT
WRITER

*Stephen Wyatt initially worked in education and in community and children's theatre before moving to a career as a freelance writer. The first piece he wrote for television was a play called **Claws**, which led to his being commissioned to write **Paradise Towers** and then **The Greatest Show in the Galaxy** for Doctor Who. He has since enjoyed a prolific career in radio, writing scripts for productions including **Fairest Isle** (1995), **The Amazons** (1995) and **Dead Souls** (1995), and for BBC TV, writing for **Casualty**.*

ANDREW MORGAN
DIRECTOR

*Andrew Morgan was born in Somerset in 1942 and started out wanting to be an actor, spending two years at RADA. He then decided to move into directing and got a job at the BBC as a holiday relief/assistant floor manager. After completing the director's course his first work was on **Sutherland's Law**. After that he worked on, amongst others, **Everyday Maths**, **Secret Army**, **Blake's 7**, **Squadron**, **The Knights of God** and **Swallows and Amazons**, in which he directed Colin Baker. After the two **Doctor Who** stories **Time and the Rani** and **Remembrance of the Daleks** he worked on **Casualty**, **Rides** and **EastEnders** amongst many other productions. He directed **Little Lord Fauntleroy** in 1994 and a new series of **The Famous Five** in 1995.*

▲ Actress Sophie Aldred at the press call to introduce the character of Ace.

SOPHIE ALDRED
ACE

Sophie Aldred was born in 1962 and brought up in Blackheath, South East London. After leaving school, she attended Manchester University, where she took a degree in drama. From University she sang in working men's clubs to obtain her Equity card, then worked in children's theatre, appeared in a fringe show, **Underground Man**, *at a pub theatre in London to get an agent, followed by more children's theatre. She was appearing in* **Fiddler on the Roof** *with Topol in Manchester when she landed the part of Ace. At the same time as appearing in* **Doctor Who**, *she presented a series for young children called* **Corners** *and later* **Melvin and Maureen's Music-a-grams**, *which combined her acting and music skills. She has appeared in a number of theatre productions, including a tour of* **Daisy Pulls it Off** *in which she played the lead, and she played Marjorie Pinchwife in the 1993 West End production of* **Lust**, *a version of* **The Country Wife**. *In 1995 she worked for the Children's Channel on satellite and also* **Love Call Live** *for Anglia television with David 'Kid' Jensen. In 1996 she co-authored with effects designer Mike Tucker a book looking at her time in* **Doctor Who** *called* **Ace!**.

Mel decides to leave the TARDIS and travel with Glitz in Iceworld, now renamed *The Nosferatu II*. *Dragonfire*. ▼

Other creatures were required for sequences set in Iceworld's refreshment bar, where Ace was seen working as a waitress. The intention was that these sequences should be reminiscent of *Star Wars'* famous cantina scene, with examples of a great many different alien life forms gathered together in one place.

'The make-up designer asked us if we had any off-the-peg masks that had not been used in any other TV or film production,' recalled Susan Moore. 'We had a number of bits and pieces and they chose a selection and used them on extras in the background. The director spotted a half-mask I'd made for a party, and thought that it would be perfect for a scene where a child wears a mask to frighten Mel. He also spotted Eric the puppet. For some obscure reason, every creature we make seems to end up being dubbed Eric! Eric was originally going to be in the background, but then they decided to start a scene with Eric, along with a fish creature that we provided, at a table in the foreground. They finished the scene off with Eric snapping at the Doctor.'

One aspect of the production that generated protests from a small number of viewers on transmission was the horrific final sequence in which Kane's face melts away in the light of the sun – another effect achieved by Moore and Mansfield. As Edward Peel, the actor cast as Kane, was reluctant to have a face cast made, the pair worked from Polaroid photographs to mould a bust that would be the basis for the effect.

'There were two major stipulations,' recalled Mansfield. 'As the effect had to be done on a live recording day, the face had to melt very quickly.

In addition, there were to be no red colours on the under-skull or any liquid resembling blood.'

The head was sculpted in water-based clay from which a multi-piece plaster mould was taken. From this mould six wax outer-skins were made.

'Using the teeth and the top of the head as registering points,' explained Moore, 'we started cutting away at the face, taking it back to what it would be if it had melted back to the bone. A silicone mould was then taken of this new sculpture, and two fibreglass skulls were cast. The skulls and the wax skins were then painted with an airbrush.

'As the melting had to be done very quickly, the wax skins had to be very thin. Therefore when they melted, they tended to give off only a very thin dribble of wax and not much else. To overcome this problem we fitted the under-skulls with various pipes – in the mouth, in the nose and under the helmet – and through these pumped a liquid coloured to match the molten wax, thus creating a more authentic, head-sized volume of wastage.

'Selected areas of the glass-fibre skull were cast in latex and acted as bladders. These sections, when inflated, helped to distort the face, and generally accelerated the degeneration process by pushing wax away from the skull. The whole lot – six skins, two under-skulls, liquid and so on – was finally completed with hours to spare, at about 4 am on the studio day, 29 July 1987.'

In studio, the fake head was mounted on a post and fitted with a dummy collar section and cap. Then Moore, Mansfield, Tucker and another effects assistant named Paul Mann directed hot-air guns at it, operated the bladders and pumped the liquid gunge. The melting effect took about ten minutes to complete, but was achieved in one take. For the final transmission, video effects designer Dave Chapman mixed in a shot of Peel screaming, so that the effigy appeared to scream as it melted. The recording was played back at about thirty times normal speed, and also slightly curtailed in editing to remove a section considered too gruesome for transmission. This was the first time that an effect of this type had been attempted on British television.

Studio recording for *Dragonfire* was completed on 13 August 1987 and the story's final episode transmitted on 7 December 1987, bringing the series' twenty-fourth season to a close.

CHAPTER SEVENTEEN

Season Twenty-Five: A Return to Mystery

T he urgency with which stories had been required to be commissioned for the twenty-fourth season had left new script editor Andrew Cartmel with little time for reflection. In preparing for the twenty-fifth, however, he was able to take a more considered approach. After viewing a number of highly regarded stories from *Doctor Who*'s past, including season thirteen's *The Seeds of Doom* and season fourteen's *The Talons of Weng-Chiang*, he formed the view that the essentially serious and dramatic approach of earlier eras had been rather more effective than the relatively light-hearted and comedic one that had prevailed during Sylvester McCoy's first season. He discussed this with John Nathan-Turner and they decided that the departure of the somewhat lightweight character of Mel and the arrival of the strong, streetwise Ace should mark the start of a more general shift of emphasis back towards that more serious and dramatic style.

Another move that Cartmel was keen to make was to introduce a greater degree of mystery into the Doctor's character. He felt that over the years there

SEASON TWENTY-FIVE	
CODE	TITLE
7H	Remembrance of the Daleks
7L	The Happiness Patrol
7K	Silver Nemesis
7J	The Greatest Show in the Galaxy

RATINGS

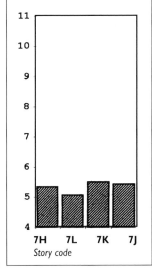

Story code

◀ The Doctor explains to Gilmore (Simon Williams) and Rachel (Pamela Salem) that they are facing an enemy that, 'Isn't even remotely human!' *Remembrance of the Daleks.*

Keith Murrell was hired on 9 June to sing 'Return to Sender' by Otis Blackwell and Winfield Scott for episode one of **Remembrance of the Daleks**. The recording was arranged by Keff McCulloch. For episode two, McCulloch used 'Children's Favourites' by White as a part of the incidental music and in episode three he used 'Apache' by Jerry Lordan.

The sound montage heard in the opening sequence for **Remembrance of the Daleks** featured the voices of the following people: John F. Kennedy, General de Gaulle, The Duke of Edinburgh and Martin Luther King.

The following tracks were heard playing in **Remembrance of the Daleks**: 'Do You Want To Know A Secret' by McCartney-Lennon, played by The Beatles; 'Lollipop' by Dixon and Ross, played by The Mudlarks; and 'A Taste of Honey' by Scott-Marlow, played by The Beatles.

Adam Burney was hired to play the harmonica out of vision in **The Happiness Patrol**.

A version of Hermann Hupfeld's 'As Time Goes By' was performed by Sylvester McCoy (vocal) and Richard D. Sharp (harmonica) in episode three of **The Happiness Patrol**.

Keff McCulloch hired a jazz quartet to provide the music for episode one of **Silver Nemesis**. The tracks were composed by Courtney Pine and called 'Pe Pi Po', 'Adrian's Affair' and 'Frank's Quest'. These were recorded at Lime Grove Music Studio on 12 June 1988 by Courtney Pine (saxophone), Adrian Reid (piano), Ernest Mothle (double bass) and Frank Tontoh (drums).

Also heard in **Silver Nemesis** was 'The Ride of the Valkyries' (Act III) from 'Die Walkure' by Wagner.

Part four of **The Greatest Show in the Galaxy** featured an excerpt from 'Narcissus', Opus 13 Number 4 by Ethelbert Nevil from 'Water Scenes' played by Alfredo Camoli and his Salon Orchestra.

Fascist sympathisers Mike (Dursley McLinden) and Ratcliffe (George Sewell) aid the Black Dalek and its forces. *Remembrance of the Daleks.*

Long time Dalek operator John Scott Martin (centre) clambers into a Dalek casing on location near Waterloo. *Remembrance of the Daleks.*

The Imperial Dalek scoutship requires a little mechanical aid from a crane, whilst recording the scenes where it lands in the school playground. *Remembrance of the Daleks.*

had been too much revealed about the initially enigmatic time traveller's background, and that this had considerably lessened the appeal of the character. With Nathan-Turner's approval, he therefore briefed the writers of the twenty-fifth season to include in their stories some elements casting doubt on aspects of the Doctor's established history and on the true nature of his character.

This was very much in line with McCoy's own thinking about the role. His initial instincts had

been to interpret it in a humorous way – most of his previous acting experience having been in comedy – but as he had settled in he had realised that it would be better if he played it much straighter.

'The first season I did was just written for any old Doctor,' he said in 1989, 'and I happened to come along. In between the first and second seasons I suddenly realised how it should be played, because I hadn't really seen it for years – I didn't really know. John, Andrew Cartmel and I then sat down and chatted about how we saw the Doctor. We were all agreed that we wanted to make him darker, harder, bringing in more anger, but at the same time keeping the humour.'

Cartmel continued for this season pursuing a policy of commissioning enthusiastic young writers who were new to the series and who had little or no previous TV experience; something in which he again had Nathan-Turner's full support.

'No matter if they had no track record,' recalled Cartmel in 1994, 'if John believed in them he'd give them the go-ahead. If I really believed in a writer, and I could convey that feeling to John, then he'd go with it.

'Having worked with other producers now, I realise how lucky I was then.'

One of the newcomers for season twenty-five was Ben Aaronovitch, who had come to Cartmel's attention when fellow BBC script editor Caroline Oulton had passed on to him a script that he had written. Aaronovitch's initial submission – an idea for a three-part sword-and-sorcery adventure with the working title *Nightfall* – was rejected as being not quite right for this season, although Cartmel was happy for him to continue to develop it for possible use in the future. To the writer's surprise and delight, however, he was then invited on the strength of this to contribute a four-part Dalek story that would launch the season on air. This idea had come about as Nathan-Turner was keen that the silver anniversary season should include stories pitting McCoy's Doctor for the first time against *Doctor Who*'s two most famous monster races: the Daleks and the Cybermen.

The story that Aaronovitch came up with was initially called *Nemesis of the Doctor* (under which title the script for the first episode was commissioned on 30 October 1987) but eventually went out as *Remembrance of the Daleks*. In keeping with the anniversary theme, it gave viewers a nostalgic reminder of the series' roots by tying together the events of the Doctor's first televised adventure, *100,000 BC*, with the on-going development of the

The Imperial Dalek faction land their scoutship at Coal Hill School. *Remembrance of the Daleks*.

The Imperial Daleks use a special weapons Dalek to help them defeat the faction led by the Black Dalek. *Remembrance of the Daleks*.

▲ Allison (Karen Gledhill) is sent to investigate the Dalek in I. M. Forman's junk yard. *Remembrance of the Daleks*.

▲ Group Captain Gilmore (Simon Williams). *Remembrance of the Daleks*.

A design drawing showing the construction and size of the Dalek scoutship prop. ▼ *Remembrance of the Daleks*.

Daleks' history that had begun with the introduction of Davros in season twelve's *Genesis of the Daleks*.

The TARDIS arrives in London in November 1963, where the Doctor and Ace discover that two rival factions of Daleks – one loyal to the Dalek Emperor and one to the Black Dalek Supreme – are searching for the Hand of Omega, an awesomely powerful Time Lord device that the first Doctor hid there just before the events of *100,000 BC: An Unearthly Child*. The Daleks are concentrating their search around Coal Hill School – the school that the Doctor's granddaughter Susan was seen attending in

An Unearthly Child – while a special military unit led by Group Captain Gilmore is attempting to resist their incursions.

The Doctor tries to keep Gilmore and his team out of harm's way while the two Dalek factions battle each other for control of the Hand. The imperial Dalek faction eventually overpowers the one led by

The Black Dalek and its forces use Ratcliffe (George Sewell) and a young girl (Jasmine Breaks) to try to seize the Hand of Omega. *Remembrance of the Daleks*.

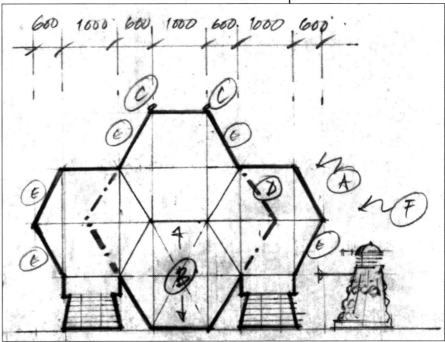

Make-up designer Dorka ▲ Nieradzik's design sketch for the Kandyman. *The Happiness Patrol.*

The Kandyman (David John ▶ Pope). *The Happiness Patrol.*

STOCK FOOTAGE

Silver Nemesis part one featured eleven seconds of footage from a BBC Outside Broadcast Entertainments and Events tape of Windsor Castle.

NOTES

Casting Happiness

The following artistes were considered for roles in The Happiness Patrol. The artiste actually cast in each case is given in square brackets.

Helen A   Patricia Routledge,
          Jill Bennett
          [Sheila Hancock]
Susan Q   Prunella Ransome,
          Rosalind Ayres
          [Leslie Dunlop]

Guest Appearance

The tourists being shown around Windsor Castle in Silver Nemesis when the Doctor and Ace arrive included some familiar faces and names: Ian Fraser (PA), Fiona Cumming (director), Andrew Morgan (director), Peter Moffatt (director), Nicholas Courtney ('the Brigadier') and Graeme Curry (writer).

Single Suggestion

Following completion of his work on **The Greatest Show in the Galaxy,** *composer Mark Ayres produced a demo of a song entitled 'The Psychic Circus'. This was written by Christopher Guard (who played Bell Boy in the story) and featured Ayres and Guard as well as Jessica Martin and other cast members. Ayres wrote to the head of BBC Records on 18 July 1988 to investigate the possibility of the record being released to tie in with transmission of the story. Nothing, however, came of this approach.*

the Dalek Supreme and captures the device. As the story reaches its climax, the true identity of the Dalek Emperor is revealed to be Davros, now with only the last vestiges of his humanoid form remaining. The Doctor begs him not to use the Hand, but is ignored. However, this is just the final ruse in a complex trap laid by the Time Lord to defeat his old adversaries. The Hand vaporises the creatures' home planet, Skaro, by turning its sun into a supernova and then returns to destroy their forces orbiting the Earth. The Doctor finally confronts the Dalek Supreme and causes it to self-destruct by convincing it that it is the sole surviving member of its race.

As usual for stories involving the Daleks, approval had to be obtained from their creator Terry Nation. The storyline was sent to him by Nathan-Turner on 21 December 1987. On this occasion Nation was apparently unhappy with certain aspects of the plot, and especially with the way in which Davros was used within it, and insisted on changes being made.

Davros had been included in the storyline at a relatively late stage on the suggestion of visual effects assistant Mike Tucker. Aaronovitch had taken his inspiration for the Emperor Dalek from the '60s Dalek comic strips featured in *TV Century 21*, which had depicted it as a golden, dome-headed variant of a normal Dalek. Tucker had then put forward the idea that the dome could conceal what remained of Davros's humanoid body, and Aaronovitch had been

happy to incorporate this into his story.

The first location recording for *Remembrance of the Daleks*, and thus for the season as a whole, began on 4 April 1988. The studio session took place from 27 to 29 April in TC8.

The guest cast for the story included Simon Williams, best known for his role as Captain Bellamy in *Upstairs, Downstairs*, as Group Captain (originally Colonel in Aaronovitch's storyline) 'Chunky' Gilmore; George Sewell, from *UFO* and *Special Branch*, as fascist Dalek collaborator Ratcliffe (originally Gummer); and Pamela Salem, who had appeared as Toos in the season fourteen story *Robots of Death*, as Rachel (originally Racheal), a scientist in Gilmore's team.

In Aaronovitch's storyline and scripts, the imperial Daleks had been described as 'Red Daleks' and the renegades loyal to the Dalek Supreme (or 'Black Dalek') as 'Blue Daleks'. On screen, however, the two factions retained the same colour schemes as in season twenty-two's *Revelation of the Daleks* — cream and gold for the former, grey and black for the latter.

Before production had got under way, Nathan-Turner had sent a memo dated 22 February 1988 to the three visual effects designers assigned to the season to stress the importance of keeping a tight rein on costs. This had been backed up by Peter Pegrum, the Head of the Visual Effects Department, in a memo dated 8 March 1988 in which he had emphasised that they should under no circumstances exceed their agreed budgets. It was therefore a source of considerable alarm to all concerned when it became apparent after the completion of work on *Remembrance of the Daleks* that there had been an overspend of as much as £12,788 on the effects. Stuart Brisdon, the effects designer for the story, was later called upon to account for this.

Remembrance of the Daleks provided the first evidence of the shift in direction that the production team had agreed upon for the series. The Doctor was presented as a somewhat more serious and mysterious character than in the previous season, shrewdly manipulating events in order to achieve his final aim. One consequence of this move towards a more enigmatic role for the Doctor was that an unusually high degree of emphasis was placed on his companion, Ace. In the past it had often been the case that the companion characters had suffered from a lack of development after their initial introduction, but the changes introduced by Cartmel and Nathan-Turner meant that Ace would be generally considered to have escaped this fate.

The opening episode of *Remembrance of the Daleks* was transmitted on 5 October 1988, the series having now been moved to a regular Wednesday evening slot starting at around 7.35 pm – again opposite ITV's flagship soap opera *Coronation Street*.

The second story of the season on transmission, although the last to be made, was an all studio-recorded three-parter written by another newcomer, Graeme Curry.

'It came about,' recalled Cartmel, 'because I'd read a radio play by Graeme called *Over the Moon*. The play was about football, of all things, but I could tell from it that the guy could write. I got him in and asked for story ideas. It was painful at first; he'd keep coming up with stories but we couldn't get one to click. He'd just about given up hope of ever doing one. Finally he came in one day, slumped in a chair in the office, and said, "What about a planet where everybody has to be happy, and if they're not, they're executed." Bingo! He'd done it! There were torments and rewrites to come, but the story was on.'

The script for the story's first episode was commissioned on 3 September 1987 and those for the other two on 30 September. The story had initially been referred to as *The Happiness Patrol*, but both Curry and Cartmel had intended to change this before transmission and so the scripts were commissioned under the working title *The Crooked Smile*. Nathan-Turner, however, preferred the original title and asked that it be reinstated. *The Crooked Smile* did make an appearance in the story, as the title of a local news-sheet read by some of the characters.

Arriving on the planet Terra Alpha, the Doctor and Ace discover a society in which sadness is against the law – a law enforced with considerable zeal by the garishly-attired Happiness Patrol. The planet is ruled over by Helen A with the aid of her companion Joseph C and her carnivorous pet Stigorax named Fifi (whose growl was the modulated sound of director Chris Clough's own voice). The penalty for those found guilty of unhappiness is to die in a stream of molten candy prepared by Helen A's executioner, the robotic Kandyman, and his associate Gilbert M. The time travellers help to foment rebellion amongst the downtrodden population and the subterranean Pipe People – the planet's original inhabitants – and Helen A is overthrown. Joseph C and Gilbert M escape in a shuttle, while the Kandyman is destroyed and Fifi killed. Helen A finally realises that happiness is nothing without the contrast of sadness.

Curry wrote *The Happiness Patrol* as a Kafkaesque satire of 1980s Britain under Prime Minister Margaret Thatcher (from whom actress Sheila Hancock drew inspiration in her performance as Helen A). Its serious underlying message was however carefully wrapped up in fantasy trappings so that it would not be immediately apparent to the casual viewer.

One of the most unusual features of the story was the Kandyman. The on-screen appearance of the robot differed considerably from the description given in Curry's original scripts, which had read as follows:

Humanoid but not human. He is actually composed of sweet substances and a robotic skeleton completely unseen deep inside his synthetic body. He is chubby and jolly looking but at the same time elegant and sinister. The colour of his skin, lips, etc, suggests sweets and sugar confections rather than human flesh. He is tall and powerful. He wears a white lab coat, a bow tie and red-framed movie-star glasses. These and his other items of apparel, the pens in his pocket, etc, are all made of candy.

Responsibility for realising the Kandyman was assigned – unusually – to the story's make-up designer, Dorka Nieradzik, rather than to the costume designer. According to Nieradzik's later recollection, however, there was never any question of it being done entirely with make-up: Nathan-Turner and Clough had always thought in terms of a costume being constructed as they wanted the character's robotic nature to be readily apparent to viewers. Nieradzik conceived of the Kandyman as being literally a robot made of sweets. The idea of dressing him in a lab coat was dropped as she felt that it would obscure too much of the body. Freelance model maker Robert Allsopp was

Making a Werewolf

The transformation of Jessica Martin, playing the part of the werewolf Mags in **The Greatest Show in the Galaxy**, *was achieved by make-up designer Dee Baron in four stages.*

STAGE ONE: Yellow contact lenses, cheek plumpers, start to change colour
STAGE TWO: Small fangs top and bottom, more colour, yellow slime from mouth
STAGE THREE: Add more coloured hair, start colour on hands, more slime from mouth, fur gloves, fur chest, fur earrings
STAGE FOUR: Large top-set fangs, add talons, complete colour change to face and hands, more slime, fur skirt.

▲ The Pipe People Wences (Philip Neve) and Wulfric (Ryan Freedman), Susan Q (Lesley Dunlop), the Doctor and Ace in the tunnels under Terra Alpha. *The Happiness Patrol.*

Helen A (Sheila Hancock) and Joseph C (Ronald Fraser). ▼ *The Happiness Patrol.*

Sylvester McCoy with ▲ American actress Delores Gray who played the part of an American tourist. *Silver Nemesis*.

The Cybermen line up for a ▶ photo call to publicise the twenty-fifth anniversary story *Silver Nemesis*.

commissioned to construct the costume from her designs. In doing so he had to be careful to leave room for all the electrical parts, which were provided by an outside effects company called Artem. The dental firm of Haynes and Kulp was called upon to make the metal teeth, which had to fit perfectly over actor David John Pope's own teeth so that he could speak his dialogue 'live' in the studio.

During the story's on-air run, Nathan-Turner received a letter dated 10 November 1988 from H. B. Stokes, Chairman and Chief Executive of Bassett Foods plc, who complained that the Kandyman bore a distinct resemblance to their Bertie Bassett character and that its unsavoury nature could damage sales of their products. Nathan-Turner discussed this with Nieradzik, who on 18 November sent him a letter drawing attention to numerous differences between the 'robotic' Kandyman and the 'cute' Bertie Bassett and denying that there were any similarities between the two. Brian Turner of the BBC's Copyright Department subsequently sent Stokes a reply dated 25 November stating that, having fully investigated the matter, he was satisfied that there was no direct connection between the Kandyman and Bertie Bassett. He concluded:

We are of course sorry if the portrayal of the KANDYMAN should lead to a negative effect on the sale of your products or have any detrimental effect on the perception of BERTIE BASSETT in the minds of the public but I am afraid I can find no evidence of copyright infringement and have little evidence to suggest any cause for confusion in the minds of the public except the fact that both characters are made out of sweets. I hope that in any case your concern will be eased by the fact that the KANDYMAN will no longer appear in our series.

The guest cast for *The Happiness Patrol* again included a number of prestigious actors, including not only Sheila Hancock as Helen A but also Harold

Innocent as Gilbert M; Ronald Fraser, famous from many British war films, as Joseph C; John Normington, who had played Morgus in season twenty-one's *The Caves of Androzani*, as Trevor Sigma; Georgina Hale as Daisy K; and Lesley Dunlop, who had played colonist Norna in another season twenty-one story, *Frontios*, as Susan Q.

The third story of the season, both in production and on transmission, was the all location-recorded three-parter *Silver Nemesis* (working titles: *The Harbinger* and *Nemesis*), the scripts for which had been commissioned on 20 January 1988. Writer Kevin Clarke – another newcomer – had been invited to come up with a special celebratory story to mark *Doctor Who*'s silver anniversary and it was decided that the most appropriate monsters to feature in it would be the silver Cybermen. *Silver Nemesis* also had the distinction of being the 150th *Doctor Who* story to be transmitted (although the previous season's *Dragonfire* had been promoted as such by the BBC as the production team had decided to count the four segments of *The Trial of a Time Lord* as four separate stories).

Set mainly in contemporary England, *Silver Nemesis* concerns the efforts of three rival factions – the Cybermen, a group of Nazis and a seventeenth-century sorceress named Lady Peinforte – to gain control of a statue made of a living metal, validium (amended from makarianite in Clarke's original scripts), that was created by Rassilon as the ultimate defence for Gallifrey. The statute has three components – a bow, an arrow and the figure itself – that must be brought together in order for it to be activated. They have been separated since 1638, when, in order to foil the first attempt by Peinforte to seize it, the Doctor launched the figure into orbit in a powered asteroid. This asteroid has been approaching the Earth at twenty-five-yearly intervals ever since, leaving a succession of disasters in its wake, and now in 1988 has crash-landed near Windsor Castle. The Doctor plays the three factions off against one other and eventually appears to concede defeat to the Cyber Leader. Like his scheme to vanquish the Daleks in *Remembrance of the Daleks*, however, this is just part of a carefully laid trap, and the Cybermen's fleet is totally wiped out by the statue.

Despite channelling their request through the story's lighting designer Ian Dow, who had worked as an outside broadcast manager on programmes covering state occasions and was consequently well known to royal officials, the production team were unable to gain permission to record the Windsor Castle scenes at the Castle itself. They consequently shot them at Arundel Castle instead. A clip of the

Production manager Gary Downie looks on as jazz saxophonist Courtney Pine makes a guest appearance in *Silver Nemesis*.

◀ Lady Peinforte (Fiona Walker) and her manservant Richard (Gerard Murphy) encounter two skinheads (Chris Chering, Symond Lawes) in 1988. *Silver Nemesis*.

▲ The Cybermen underwent yet another re-design for their appearance in *Silver Nemesis*. The new elements included chromed helmets and new bodysuits, which had a tendency to lose paint at the crotch area.

real Windsor Castle was however obtained from stock and edited into the first episode as an establishing shot.

A number of recorded scenes – including one set inside the Castle where Ace sees an antique painting of herself on the wall – had to be dropped in editing as the story would otherwise have run considerably over length. This was in part a consequence of rescheduling necessitated by problems that had arisen earlier in the year when routine refurbishment work at Television Centre had uncovered large quantities of dangerous white asbestos in the rafters. The story's rehearsal period had been considerably curtailed and this had made it much more difficult for the production team to form an accurate impression of the likely final timing of scenes.

The guest stars for *Silver Nemesis* were as distinguished as those for the previous stories of the season. Anton Diffring, famous for his many portrayals of Germans in war films, agreed to play the Nazis' leader de Flores – reportedly because it gave him the opportunity to come to Britain to see the Wimbledon tennis tournament – and Hollywood film star Delores Gray made a cameo appearance as an American tourist named Mrs Remington (amended from Mrs Hackensack and before that Milton P. Remington in earlier drafts of the scripts). Fiona Walker, who had made an early TV appearance as Kala in season one's *The Keys of Marinus*, played Lady Peinforte, while David Banks once more reprised his role as the Cyber Leader. There was even a cameo appearance by saxophonist Courtney Pine and his jazz quartet.

Production of *Silver Nemesis* was covered by a small crew from an American Public Broadcasting Service (PBS) station, the New Jersey Network, for the last of three documentaries that they had gained approval to make about the series. Produced and written by

Eric Luskin, this would be transmitted – in America only – as *The Making of Doctor Who – Silver Nemesis* (although it would eventually be made available in the UK on the 1993 BBC Video release of *Silver Nemesis*, which included some of the material edited out of the transmitted version).

The production team decided, in view of the Doctor's very similar schemes to destroy the Daleks in *Remembrance of the Daleks* and the Cybermen in *Silver Nemesis*, to promote the season as having an overall theme of 'unfinished business'. This phrase was used prominently in BBC press releases at the time as well as in a special video trailer put together to launch the season to the press. In the latter the Doctor tells Ace that 1988 marks the twenty-fifth anniversary of his first visit to Earth and that since

BEN AARONOVITCH
WRITER

Remembrance of the Daleks was Ben Aaronovitch's first work for television. He had been put in touch with Andrew Cartmel by a BBC script editor, Caroline Oulton, and he produced a story idea called *Nightfall* on spec before being commissioned for the Dalek story. Aaronovitch also scripted *Battlefield* for the twenty-sixth season. Aaronovitch has gone on to write for *Casualty* and also wrote with Andrew Cartmel an initial script for the 1989 *Doctor Who* stage play *The Ultimate Adventure*. More recently he scripted thirteen episodes of the BSB series *Jupiter Moon* and has written several novels in Virgin Publishing's *Doctor Who: The New Adventures* range.

◀ The Nemesis statue (Fiona Walker) in Lady Peinforte's mausoleum. *Silver Nemesis*.

GRAEME CURRY
WRITER

After leaving university, Graeme Curry progressed interests in journalism and writing as well as being a professional singer and actor. He won the **Cosmopolitan** *Young Journalist of the Year award in 1982 and won a screenplay competition with a play called* **Over the Moon***, which was later adapted for broadcast on Radio 4. It was on the strength of this that it was suggested he contact Andrew Cartmel regarding work for* **Doctor Who***.* **The Happiness Patrol** *was his first television commission and he has gone on to write for* **EastEnders** *as well as* **The Bill** *and the Radio 4 drama* **Citizens***.*

KEVIN CLARKE
WRITER

Kevin Clarke had written two plays and had managed to get one performed in New York and another he put on himself in order to gain some attention from the television companies. The gamble paid off and he was commissioned and paid to write for three series, none of which ultimately made it to production. Eventually he wrote an episode for a series called **Wish Me Luck***, on the strength of which he was contacted by Andrew Cartmel about working on* **Doctor Who***. He ended up writing* **Silver Nemesis***, the show's twenty-fifth anniversary story.*

ALAN WAREING
DIRECTOR

Alan Wareing became interested in directing through amateur theatre. After directing several plays he started working in television, first as an assistant floor manager and then as a production assistant before taking the BBC's director's course. Among the BBC shows he worked on were **The Onedin Line, Blake's 7, Juliet Bravo, EastEnders** *and* **Casualty***. He had worked on* **Doctor Who** *as a PA on* **The Keeper of Traken** *and* **Timelash** *before returning to the show as a freelance director to handle* **The Greatest Show In The Galaxy, Ghost Light** *and* **Survival***. Since then he has continued to direct, including* **Ghoul-Lashed!** *for Sky TV.*

Costume design for Mags ▶ (Jessica Martin) by Rosalind Ebbutt. The Greatest Show in the Galaxy.

Director Chris Clough works through a scene with Sophie Aldred and Sylvester McCoy on location for *Silver Nemesis*.

that time he has made a lot of enemies and built up a lot of 'unfinished business'.

The next story to be transmitted was a four-parter written by Stephen Wyatt and entitled *The Greatest Show in the Galaxy*, the first episode of which had been commissioned on 8 May 1987 and the other three on 29 September. Wyatt was the only one of the season's four writers to have worked on *Doctor Who* before, having contributed *Paradise Towers* the previous year.

The running order originally planned for the season had been *Remembrance of the Daleks*, *The Greatest Show in the Galaxy*, *The Happiness Patrol* and *Silver Nemesis*. In August 1988, however, Nathan-Turner was informed that, due to changes in BBC1's autumn schedules arising from coverage of the Seoul Olympic Games, the start of the season would have to be put back by several weeks. This threatened to throw out his plan for the first episode of *Silver Nemesis* to be transmitted on 23 November – the anniversary date itself – and so, in order to preserve the position, he hastily changed the order. *The Greatest Show in the Galaxy*, although made between *Remembrance of the Daleks* and *Silver Nemesis*, thus became the last story of the season to air, its closing episode going out on 4 January 1989.

The only drawback to this was that it created a small number of minor continuity glitches, the most obvious being that a distinctive earring acquired by Ace in *The Greatest Show in the Galaxy* could already be seen pinned to her jacket in *Silver Nemesis*. This led the producer to decide that in future all the series' stories should be completely self-contained so that they could be transmitted in whatever order might eventually be desired.

The action of *The Greatest Show in the Galaxy* centres around the Psychic Circus on the planet Segonax, where the Doctor and Ace meet a strange assortment of fellow visitors, including a pompous explorer named Captain Cook, a fan of the Circus referred to as the Whizzkid, a biker known as Nord and a punk werewolf called Mags. The Circus itself is dominated by the sinister Chief Clown and his deadly troupe of robot clowns, who organise a talent contest in which all visitors take part. The audience consists of just a single strange family – mother, father and daughter – seated at the ringside. Although hindered by the treacherous Cook, the Doctor eventually discovers that the Circus hides a terrible secret: the family are the Gods of Ragnarok, powerful creatures with an insatiable craving for entertainment who invariably destroy those who fail to please them. With Ace's help, the Doctor ends the Gods' influence here and returns the Circus to the control of its original hippie owners.

The Greatest Show in the Galaxy was the story most seriously affected by the discovery of asbestos at Television Centre, which led to the temporary closure of a number of the studios and threw production of many of the BBC's programmes into chaos. The story actually came close to being abandoned altogether – something that had happened only once before, with season seventeen's *Shada* – but the crisis was averted when Nathan-Turner and director Alan Wareing (making his

The Chief Clown (Ian Reddington), a macabre character from the Psychic Circus. *The Greatest Show in the Galaxy*.

▲ **Whizzkid (Gian Sammarco), a parody of the series' more obsessive fans. *The Greatest Show in the Galaxy*.**

◄ **The Captain (T. P. McKenna) and Mags (Jessica Martin). *The Greatest Show in the Galaxy*.**

Doctor Who debut in that capacity) arranged for the remainder of the recording to be carried out inside a huge tent erected in the car park of the BBC's Elstree Studios. This still presented a number of problems – including extraneous noise from passers-by and from low-flying private aircraft offering sightseers a glimpse of the nearby *EastEnders* set – but as a welcome bonus it meant that the scenes set within the Psychic Circus tent had a particularly realistic look.

The destruction of the Circus was achieved on location with the aid of a model built by the Visual Effects Department. Forced perspective was used to fool viewers into believing that a massive explosion had completely destroyed the tent. The live-action scene matching up with this involved McCoy walking coolly out of the tent and the entrance then exploding behind him. McCoy had been told during rehearsals that this explosion would be faked with air mortars – devices using compressed air to shoot out debris – and that an appropriate sound effect would be dubbed on later. When it came to shoot the scene, however, the Visual Effects team discovered that the air mortars had been supplied without the correct hoses, and so they decided to achieve the effect using real pyrotechnics instead. Unfortunately no one had thought to inform McCoy of the change, so it can be considered a great tribute to his acting skills that he showed absolutely no reaction when he felt the heat and heard the noise of a sizeable explosion taking place behind him.

A high-calibre guest cast was again secured for this story. Distinguished character actor T. P. McKenna took the role of the Captain; impressionist Jessica Martin played Mags; veteran actress Peggy

Mount had a cameo role as a stall holder; and Ian Reddington, later to find fame in *EastEnders*, was the eerie Chief Clown.

Responsibility for creating the look of the Psychic Circus clowns was shared between costume designer Ros Ebbutt and make-up designer Dee Baron. Ebbutt, with her assistant Sara Jane Ellis, carried out extensive research into the history of clowns and discovered that there were essentially three different types, two of which – a white-faced type and a red-nosed type – she decided to make the basis of the ones seen in *The Greatest Show in the Galaxy*.

'When we had pooled all our ideas together,' she recalled in a 1989 interview, 'I started to think through the Chief Clown, who was indicated in the script as being a white-faced clown. We did a lot of research into what fabrics were available, mainly because there wasn't going to be time to have the fabric made specially. I found two different sorts, both based on designs of black and silver. One, a sort of silver pebble design, was appliquéd onto the other, which was a predominantly black fabric with a spidery silver pattern, when we made the costume.

'For the other clowns, we found examples of different fabrics and, having decided which I wanted to use, I went away and designed using all the samples as reference. We were very lucky finding the colourful material for the basic costumes, and I appliquéd onto it some glittery metallic organzas that I found in an Indian shop in Southall. Overall the effect was just what I had hoped for.'

There were four basic designs for the red-nosed clowns and three for the white-faced. Over their heads the actors had to wear a balaclava affair so that, once they had put on their masks, there would be no

Nord (Daniel Peacock) ▶
arrives on Segonax to take part
in the Psychic Circus. *The
Greatest Show in the Galaxy.*

Ros Ebbutt's design sketch for
Nord's costume. *The Greatest
Show in the Galaxy.* ▼

Ros Ebbutt's design sketch for
the Chief Clown. *The Greatest
Show in the Galaxy.* ▼

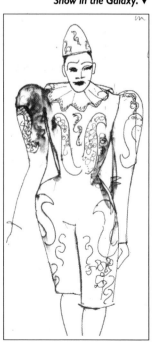

risk of their own skin being visible to the viewer. The masks themselves were created by Baron.

'For the white-faced clowns,' explained Baron in 1989, 'I cast Ian Reddington's face, then modelled up slightly bigger than that. Then I took another cast from *that* – a long process! – and then finally I vac-formed them over at Visual Effects, with the help of one of their assistants. So they all had Ian's basic face shape.'

After all the masks had been made, the next stage was to add the actual designs to the faces.

'I got each of my assistants to paint some of them up, because I thought "The only way they're going to look different is if we all do two or three clowns each."

'Although you saw only one mask per clown on screen, each one actually had ten masks. So something like a hundred masks were made altogether. We had to allow for them breaking, we had to allow for actors doubling up, we had to allow for it raining, for some getting lost … My one brief to my assistants before they started was, "Just remember, you've got to paint ten exactly the same." So we kept them quite basic and simple.'

Baron wanted the clowns' eyes to have an eerie,

metallic look, so she covered them with a foil-like material obtained from Visual Effects, which had properties similar to those of a two-way mirror.

Also realised as a collaboration between Ebbutt and Baron was Mags's transformation into a werewolf.

'Alan Wareing and I talked about it a lot,' recalled Baron, 'and he was very sympathetic to my ideas. I definitely didn't want someone disappearing behind a sofa, or whatever, and coming up wearing a mask! That would have looked ridiculous. So, because of the nature of *Doctor Who* and how it's shot, I thought it was better to go for something simpler; and, as Mags was a sort of punky character, I suggested extending the "punkiness" when she changed – making more hair shoot out of her, changing her eye colour and so on.

'These were cosmetic changes that could be done quickly, for example using contact lenses for the eyes – although poor Jessica Martin, the actress, had to have them three weeks beforehand to get used to them. We had originally intended to go for full, cat-like eyes, taking up the whole eye-ball, and Jessica was brilliant when we tried them out – she had no problems when these great big lenses were put in her eyes. But they were painful to wear, and we would have needed an optician standing by in the studio to put them in, so in the end we decided to do something a bit simpler.'

Martin also had to pay several visits to dental specialists Haynes and Kulp to have three sets of false teeth made for use in the different stages of the transformation, as well as a set of 'plumpers' – dental appliances designed to puff the cheeks out and give the face a more rounded look.

The Greatest Show in the Galaxy continued the depiction of the Doctor as an enigmatic manipulator of events with a distinctly mysterious past. Having guessed that the Circus is a cover for the Gods of Ragnarok, he describes them as old enemies – despite the fact that they have never before been mentioned in the series. Ace is again left to do much of the detective work and to handle most of the action scenes, including a fight with a robotic bus conductor and a number of deadly clowns.

These trends would be continued in the following season, when the Doctor – and the series as a whole – would become even darker in tone and an even greater emphasis would be placed on Ace. What no one at the time could have known was that, after more than a quarter of a century of adventures, the series would soon be facing a very uncertain future.

CHAPTER EIGHTEEN

Season Twenty-Six: The Journey Ends?

Johne Nathan-Turner had been content to remain as *Doctor Who*'s producer for the twenty-fifth anniversary season but had again asked his BBC superiors to make this his last year on the series. Paul Stone, another BBC staff producer, who had previously been responsible for the popular fantasy productions *Moondial*, *Aliens in the Family* and *The Box of Delights*, was reportedly asked if he would be willing to take over from him. Stone declined, and shortly afterwards left the BBC to pursue a freelance career. In the end, Nathan-Turner was once more persuaded to stay on with *Doctor Who* for a further season.

Andrew Cartmel also remained on the series for a third year as script editor. He had a number of writers in mind to contribute stories and on 16 September 1988 commissioned Ben Aaronovitch, who had been responsible for the previous season's *Remembrance of the Daleks*, to script a four-parter with the working title *Storm Over Avallion*. This was a revised version of *Nightfall*, the earliest idea the writer had submitted to the series, and had originally been envisaged as a three-parter. Aaronovitch would in fact work closely with Cartmel on the development of the whole of the twenty-sixth season, acting almost as an unofficial assistant.

This season would continue to show the Doctor acting in an increasingly enigmatic light, manipulating events from the background rather

SEASON TWENTY-SIX	
CODE	TITLE
7N	*Battlefield*
7Q	*Ghost Light*
7M	*The Curse of Fenric*
7P	*Survival*

RATINGS

Story code	Rating
7N	~4.1
7Q	~4.1
7M	~4.1
7P	~4.9

◀ The cast of *Battlefield* pose for publicity photos on Bessie: (from left) Christopher Bowen (Mordred), Jean Marsh (Morgaine), Sylvester McCoy, Nicholas Courtney (the Brigadier), Sophie Aldred, James Ellis (Peter Warmsley).

MUSIC

Story	Composer
Battlefield	Keff McCulloch
Ghost Light	Mark Ayres
The Curse of Fenric	
	Mark Ayres
Survival	Dominic Glynn

Pianist Alasdair Nicolson was hired to play the piano out of vision for Gwendolyn's song in **Ghost Light***. The song was called 'That's The Way To The Zoo', composed by J. F. Mitchell c. 1883.*

*   **The Curse of Fenric** *featured a 20-second excerpt from 'Requiem' Opus 48 by Fauré played by the Dresden State Orchestra conducted by Colin Davis.*

*   *Guitarist David Hardington was hired to work with composer Dominic Glynn in a session on 7 October 1989 to realise the music for* **Survival***.*

The two Brigadiers, ▲ **Bambera (Angela Bruce) and Lethbridge-Stewart (Nicholas Courtney).** *Battlefield.*

Sylvester McCoy and Sophie Aldred rehearse a scene on location for *Battlefield.* ▼

Morgaine (Jean Marsh) with Arthur's sword Excalibur. *Battlefield.*

than taking centre stage, while Ace gained an ever greater share of the action. The Doctor's companion would in fact turn out to be effectively the pivotal character in three of the season's four stories, which the behind-the-scenes team would come to refer to as 'the Ace trilogy', and Sophie Aldred was given an opportunity to talk to the writers about the development of the part during the early stages of production.

Aaronovitch's story, retitled *Battlefield* by Cartmel, was the second of the four to be made but the first to be transmitted. Its opening episode went out on Wednesday 6 September 1989, the season having been consigned to the same time slot as for the previous year.

Battlefield marked the return to *Doctor Who* of UNIT and Brigadier Lethbridge-Stewart, played as ever by Nicholas Courtney, who had last been seen in the twentieth anniversary special *The Five Doctors*. Aaronovitch's original storyline had had Lethbridge-Stewart promoted to General, and serious consideration was also given to the possibility of killing the character off at the end of the final episode, but in the event neither of these ideas was taken forward.

The story sees the Doctor and Ace arriving in the English village of Carbury, where a nuclear missile convoy under the command of UNIT's Brigadier Winifred Bambera has run into difficulties. Lying on the bed of the nearby Lake Vortigern is a spaceship from another dimension containing the body of King Arthur, supposedly held in suspended animation, and his sword Excalibur. Ancelyn, a knight from the other dimension, arrives on Earth to aid the King but is followed by his rival Mordred and the latter's mother, a powerful sorceress named Morgaine. They all recognise the Doctor as Merlin – a fact that the Time Lord attributes to events in his own future. A battle breaks out between UNIT and Morgaine's men. Brigadier Lethbridge-Stewart has come out of retirement to assist in the crisis and ends up using silver bullets to kill the Destroyer – an awesomely powerful creature unshackled by Morgaine to devour the world – although he himself is almost killed in the process. Morgaine tries to fire the nuclear missile but is overcome by shock when the Doctor tells her that Arthur is in fact dead. She and her son are then taken prisoner by UNIT.

The role of the evil Morgaine was taken by Jean Marsh, who had previously played Princess Joanna in season two's *The Crusade* and the short-lived companion Sara Kingdom in season three's *The Daleks' Master Plan*. The story's guest cast also included *Z Cars'* James Ellis as Peter Warmsly, head of an archaeological dig at Carbury, and Angela Bruce as Brigadier Bambera – a female successor to Lethbridge-Stewart.

A number of Aaronovitch's original ideas for the story ultimately proved too expensive to realise. For example, he had envisaged the knights as wearing sleek, futuristic combat suits engraved with alien designs and resembling armour, but in the event their costumes were just stock suits of armour with minimal alterations made to the visors and helmets.

Another change related to the Destroyer.

'In the original script,' recalled freelance effects specialist Stephen Mansfield in 1989, 'the Destroyer started out as an ordinary guy who transformed into a demon. Marek Anton had already been cast in the part because he had the ability to sort of scrunch himself up and then expand himself again as he transformed – that was the original idea.'

At a meeting involving Mansfield, his partner Susan Moore and designers from the Visual Effects, Costume and Make-up Departments – all of whom would be involved in realising the creature – it was decided that limitations of time, money and facilities would make such a complex effect impracticable.

'About half-way through the meeting,' continued Mansfield, 'they decided to lose the idea of the transformation and make him appear as a demon from the outset. The only remaining nod to the original concept is that he pulls a section of his chest armour off at one point.'

Moore and Mansfield had been contracted by the story's director, Michael Kerrigan, to make a mask for the Destroyer based on a maquette of a demon-like figure that they had created some time earlier and shown to Nathan-Turner as an advertisement for their work.

'We had to change the teeth,' noted Mansfield, 'as the Destroyer had dialogue and the actor wouldn't have been able to talk if the teeth had been as they were on the maquette.'

'What we tried to do was to give the Destroyer a bit more character than most run-of-the-mill monsters. It was supposed to be a very distinguished, proud-looking creature.

'The head was modelled in clay, to get the proportions correct, then split up into sections – the horns, the ears and so on – for moulding. The mould was made by a chap called Mick Hockney. Then foam latex was pumped into it to make the mask.

'Because the mask was quite a way from the actor's head, we had to work out a method to get a proper alignment of the eyes and the jaw, which are probably the most important areas. We used a fibreglass underskull for the mask and then another underskull to fit on the actor's head. These were put one on top of the other, aligned and then stuck together with a fibreglass paste. This made it comfortable to wear and also provided a strong base

for the two main horns.'

Owing to pressure of time, Mansfield called upon the services of freelance model maker Robert Allsopp actually to construct the horns.

Location recording of *Battlefield* was disrupted by

▲ The maquette model used as the basis for the Destroyer's head. *Battlefield*.

◄ The Destroyer (Marek Anton) as he appeared on screen. *Battlefield*.

▲ Brigadier Bambera (Angela Bruce) and Ancelyn (Marcus Gilbert). *Battlefield*.

◄ Director Michael Kerrigan discusses a scene on location with Nicholas Courtney and Jean Marsh. *Battlefield*.

Robert Jezek (Sergeant Zbrigniev), Sophie Aldred and writer Ben Aaronovitch indulge in a spot of horse play during a tea break on location.
▼ *Battlefield*.

Light (John Hallam) confronts the Doctor, Control (Sharon Duce), Inspector Mackenzie (Frank Windsor) and Ace. Ghost Light.

industrial action within the BBC, causing considerable difficulties for the cast and crew. It was during the studio recording that Aldred was involved in a potentially serious accident with a water tank – something that later became the subject of a rather sensationalised report under the headline Dr Who Girl Cheats Death in the tabloid newspaper *News of the World*. The accident occurred during recording of a scene in which Ace is trapped in an airlock that is rapidly filling with water. A loud crack was suddenly heard around the studio as the glass front of the tank cracked. Sylvester McCoy shouted to the effects crew stationed above the tank and they pulled Aldred clear just before the glass gave way and gallons of water flooded out over the studio floor and its many electrical cables. Aldred was unharmed apart from a few glass splinters in her hands.

Cartmel's preference was for working closely with

a small team of writers, so although unsuccessful preliminary discussions were held with a number of potential contributors to the series – including Alan Moore, Glenn Chandler, Chris Russell, Charles Vincent and David A. McIntee (who put forward an idea for a Lovecraftian tale set in 1927 and entitled *Avatar*) – there were only two stories during his time as script editor that were seriously considered for production but ultimately failed to make it to the screen. One of these was *Alixion* by Robin Mukherjee (who had had a number of earlier ideas rejected by Cartmel before this was commissioned), the other was *Lungbarrow* by Marc Platt.

Platt had been a fan of *Doctor Who* since it first began and had been submitting ideas to the production office since the mid-seventies. He had received encouraging feedback from successive script editors, including Robert Holmes, Christopher H. Bidmead and Eric Saward, and had more recently had discussions with Cartmel about a number of possible stories, including *Cat's Cradle* (which was set entirely within the TARDIS and would later see print as one of Virgin Publishing's original *Doctor Who* novels) and *Shrine* (set in nineteenth-century Russia and featuring stone-headed aliens). *Lungbarrow* however was the first to come close to being commissioned.

'*Lungbarrow* was the first thing by Marc that I groomed to show to John,' noted Cartmel in 1994. 'The Doctor goes home and faces his family. It was very *Gormenghast*, full of Mervyn Peake intricacies,

John Hallam rehearses the ▶ scene where Light kills one of the maids at Gabriel Chase. Ghost Light.

dark and Gothic.

'Lungbarrow was the name of the Doctor's home, and it was actually a sentient being. Marc had worked out all this stuff about the history of the Time Lords. In contrast to most of the stories set on Gallifrey – people in spangly togas and a brightly lit place – this would have been sort of *The Addams Family* on acid. There were a lot of great things about it, mostly the mood.

'When John was presented with it, he felt it was too way out for a lot of reasons. In retrospect I have to say I'm kind of glad, because we then came up with another Earth-based story and I'm very glad to have recognisable settings. *Lungbarrow* was the antithesis of that – the Doctor doing weird things in an extremely weird setting, even by the standards of *Doctor Who*.

'The Victorian cobwebbiness of *Lungbarrow* was one of the best things about it, so we stole that mood, that feel, and a few other elements and came up with *Ghost Light*.'

Ghost Light, an all studio-recorded three-parter, was commissioned from Platt on 16 November 1988 under the working title *Life-Cycle*, an earlier suggestion of *The Bestiary* having been vetoed by Nathan-Turner. It was the last of the season's four stories to be made – its recording being completed on 3 August 1989 – and, although originally planned as the third in transmission order, ultimately went out second.

The Doctor brings Ace to a house called Gabriel Chase in her home town of Perivale. The year is 1883 and the house is presided over by one Josiah Samuel Smith (whom Platt at one point considered renaming Josiah *Solomon* Smith in order to avoid any possible confusion with the Samuel Smith brewery company). Smith turns out to be the evolved form of an alien brought to Earth in a stone spaceship that is now in the basement beneath the house. Other occupants of the house include the explorer Redvers Fenn-Cooper, who has been driven mad by what he has witnessed there, and Nimrod, Smith's Neanderthal man servant. Smith intends to use Fenn-Cooper's unwitting help in a plot to kill Queen Victoria and restore the British Empire to its former glory. His plans are hampered by Control, a female alien whose life-cycle is in symbiotic balance with his own.

Ace inadvertently causes the release of the spaceship's true owner – a powerful alien being known as Light. Light originally came to Earth to compile a catalogue of its species but, on discovering

that his catalogue has now been made obsolete by evolution, he decides to destroy all life on the planet. He disintegrates when the Doctor convinces him that evolution is irresistible and that he himself is constantly changing. Control has meanwhile evolved into a lady and Smith has reverted to an earlier, primitive form. They leave in the spaceship, along with Nimrod and Fenn-Cooper, heading for new adventures.

Nathan-Turner's original intention for *Ghost Light*'s incidental music had been to commission a score played on conventional orchestral instruments – reviving a practice he had discontinued in favour of

▲ Sylvia Syms (Mrs Pritchard) rehearses out of costume on the set of *Ghost Light*.

MICHAEL KERRIGAN
DIRECTOR

Michael Kerrigan worked on a number of projects for TVS, including *The Knights of God* (1985) and *Mr Majeika*. In 1995 he was at the helm of a new series based on the *Famous Five* books of Enid Blyton.

◀ Light (John Hallam). *Ghost Light*.

Ken Trew's costume design sketch for Light.
▼ *Ghost Light*.

Reverend Wainwright ▶
(Nicholas Parsons), the vicar
of St Jude's church.
The Curse of Fenric.

MARC PLATT
WRITER

Born in Wimbledon in the early 1950s, Marcus Platt attended technical college to learn catering before working with Trust House Forte. He later joined the BBC on the administrative side, involved in the cataloguing of data regarding the BBC's radio output. He had long been a fan of **Doctor Who** *and* **Ghost Light** *was the first of many ideas submitted that was finally accepted. Platt also novelised the story for Virgin Publishing and provided background notes for Titan Books' script book of the story. He has also contributed to Virgin Publishing's* **Doctor Who: The New Adventures** *series of original novels.*

Josiah Samuel Smith (Ian ▲ Hogg) with Gwendoline (Katherine Schlesinger). *Ghost Light.*

Ace dons an evening suit for an evening at Gabriel Chase. *Ghost Light.* ▼

Ace struggles with two Haemovores whilst escaping from St Jude's church. *The Curse of Fenric.*

human would dissect a rat.'

Director Alan Wareing took an active interest in the character's realisation.

'I remember that Light was much more a physical character originally,' he recalled. 'I wanted him to be more a presence than a being. I wanted him to be an untouchable. There was a lot of physical contact in the earlier drafts of the scripts, not just with Light but with Control as well, and I felt this was wrong. The most important thing about Light for me was that he was an energy mass that had just taken on a temporary human form. Light was the source of power and it was Light that Nimrod worshipped, not a being or a person but an entity, and that was how I wanted him to appear … That was my starting point for the character.

'The two main qualities I wanted Light to have were to be tall and thin. Did you ever see *Poltergeist II*? It featured, as the chief ghost, a character like a Victorian preacher. He had the look that I wanted: sort of gaunt and predatory.'

Another important element in the character's realisation was the costume, designed by Ken Trew and made by Allsopp.

'I did find it very difficult to crack the character of Light,' admitted Trew. 'Then suddenly it hit me: the house had a stained glass window, and Light could be something almost pre-Raphaelite. I then thought of working in something about the idea of beetles coming to life and moving around the house. I realised that if I gave him a cloak like the shell of a beetle this would tie in with a line in the script, where he comes in through a window and folds his wings. There was a comma left out of the description so that it read "… Light settles and folds his cloak like wings" instead of "… Light settles and folds his

radiophonic tracks when he took over as producer. This turned out to be beyond the series' budget, so Mark Ayres – a *Doctor Who* fan who had also composed for two previous stories, *The Greatest Show in the Galaxy* and *The Curse of Fenric* – was engaged to provide a synthesiser-based score in the usual way. His first idea was to create something in the style of a chamber quartet, but this proved unsuccessful. He then adopted a range of different sounds, including a deep bass motif to emphasise the sinister atmosphere of Gabriel Chase, an African pipe theme, and some powerful organ chords.

One of the key elements of *Ghost Light* was the character of Light.

'I wanted something that was incredibly awesome and frightening, with god-like powers, and that was elemental,' explained Platt in 1989. 'Something incredibly archaic, that had been around for centuries and centuries. I initially wanted to give him a lot more background but in the end I decided not to, and I think that improved the mystery. Very early in the concept I don't think he actually spoke, but Andrew Cartmel thought that, as all the rest of the characters were so strong, he should have a more recognisable and identifiable character, and that helped in shaping the ideas.

'In essence, Light evolved as a *deus ex machina* but, rather than descending in glory at the end, he was there all along and turned out to be a rather amoral being. The fundamental concept was of a cosmic version of a Victorian naturalist, who would dissect a human just as quickly as a

A Haemovore in the graveyard of St Jude's church.
The Curse of Fenric.

◄ The cast of *The Curse of Fenric*: (from left) Sylvester McCoy, Sophie Aldred, Anne Reid (Nurse Crane), Tomek Bork (Sorin), Dinsdale Landen (Dr Judson), Alfred Lynch (Commander Millington).

Ken Trew's design sketches for the Ancient Haemovore's head.
▼ *The Curse of Fenric.*

cloak, like wings". That gave me another idea, and so the cloak got really big and I added metal feathers to the arms as a further pre-Raphaelite reference, like one of the great Rosetti angels.

'The colours I used in the costume came from the concept of Light as having no corporeal existence. I used a lot of gold and silver, and ultimately, seeing the finished programme with all the video effects added, I wish that I had used more of the gold that was on the neck piece, as that was more reflective. I did design it to be reflective as Henry Barber, the lighting designer, wanted to hit it with a lot of light from behind.'

Next in transmission order was a story by Ian Briggs, whose sole previous contribution to the series had been season twenty-four's *Dragonfire*. Briggs had originally planned to set his second story in the 1970s, but Cartmel felt that this era was too recent and so they jointly decided on the 1940s as a suitable alternative. The scripts were commissioned on 9 November 1988 and had the working titles *Wolf-Time* and *The Wolves of Fenric*. The final title, *The Curse of Fenric*, was thought up by Briggs at a relatively late stage when Nathan-Turner realised during rehearsals that the '*Wolves*' element – which was explained only at the very end of the story – might be confusing to viewers.

The TARDIS's latest port of call is a secret naval base off the coast of Northumberland towards the end of the Second World War. There, Dr Judson has built the Ultima Machine, an early computer designed to break German codes. The base's

Commander Millington plans to let a Russian commando unit led by Captain Sorin steal the Machine's core, which he has booby-trapped with deadly toxin. Judson uses the Machine to translate some ancient runes from the crypt of the nearby St Jude's church and this leads to the release of Fenric, an evil entity from the dawn of time whom the Doctor trapped seventeen centuries earlier in a Chinese flask by defeating it at chess. The flask was later stolen and buried at the church by Vikings.

The base and church are attacked by Haemovores. These are humans who have been transformed into hideous vampiric creatures by the Ancient Haemovore – the last survivor of a pollution-ravaged future Earth, who has been brought back in time by Fenric. Fenric takes over Judson's body to challenge the Doctor to a rematch at chess, and Ace unwittingly helps it to win. Fenric, now in Sorin's body, reveals that Ace, Judson, Millington, Sorin and Wainwright, the vicar of St Jude's, are all 'Wolves of Fenric' – pawns in its battle against the Doctor. It now plans to release the deadly toxin, but the Doctor succeeds in turning the Ancient Haemovore against it and its host body is killed by the gas. The baby of a young woman whom Ace helped to escape from the Haemovores is revealed to be her future mother.

Briggs conceived *The Curse of Fenric* as a retelling of vampire mythology in a Second World War setting, and also as a warning about mankind's

The Haemovores rise from ▶ the sea and invade the graveyard of St Jude's church. *The Curse of Fenric.*

Dr Who weaves its spell of success

Why is it that so many of the participants in *Dr Who* speak in these slack, vague, lazy London accents which one associates with such a large number of children's morning shows?

It is that, for sure, combined with consistently dreadful acting, which makes this programme's apparent magic so difficult to understand.

The doctor's assistant, Ace, seized by some dark force, suddenly shouted to her companion this week: "Listen 'ere you toe-rag – just you shut up or I'll knock your teeth out."

The whole show always makes me think that an unspeakably ropy North London amateur dramatic society has teamed up with a combination of low-budget special effects experts and a disaffected, camp Shakespeare wardrobe master who has escaped with the costume hamper.

The whole lot, one imagines, have gone off to some Essex gravel pits with a Dixon's video recorder.

It really is very, very bad indeed. But that, one suddenly sees in a flash that other more clever observers no doubt experienced many years ago, is probably the very essence of its huge success.

Peter Tory writing in the Daily Express, 23 September 1989

pollution of the Earth. He took the character of Fenric and the story's central Viking themes from an ancient Norse story about a wolf called Fenris that was chained by one of the gods. When the gods fell at Ragnarok, Fenris was freed to take vengeance on the god who had chained it. Briggs supplied the production team with detailed information about the Runic alphabets to be used for the crypt scenes, as well as instructions for building the flip-flop logic puzzle found by Ace in Judman's office.

This story was the first of the season to be made, and was recorded entirely on location over the period 4 to 20 April 1989. Its director Nicholas Mallett had originally been due to handle *Battlefield* but, owing to a rearrangement of the production schedule, swapped assignments with Kerrigan.

The guest cast engaged by Mallett brought several additions to the long list of household names that had graced the series over the previous few seasons. Nicholas Parsons, best known for presenting the Anglia TV quiz show *Sale of the Century* and for his work as a comedy straight man, played Wainwright; Alfred Lynch took the role of Commander Millington; and Dinsdale Landen played the wheelchair-using genius Doctor Judson.

Many problems were caused to the production by bad weather encountered on location. Recording

took place in near freezing temperatures, with heavy rain, hail and snow adding to the crew's headaches. This led to delays – as a consequence of which Mallett asked Nathan-Turner to direct some underwater sequences while he continued working on the main action scenes ashore – and also meant that Briggs was called upon to rewrite some lines of dialogue that had suggested stifling heat.

The overall concept for the appearance of the Haemovores evolved in discussions between Trew, make-up designer Dee Baron and the three freelancers Moore, Mansfield and Allsopp. The Ancient Haemovore was actually the first to be designed, and this fell largely to Trew after an earlier attempt by the Visual Effects Department – whose concept had been of a white, leech-like creature that would have been operated as a puppet – was judged unsuitable.

'I had meetings with John Nathan-Turner and Nick Mallett to work out what he, she or it should look like,' recalled Trew. 'As there were a lot of Viking influences in the story, I initially tried doing something like the prow of a dragonship; then I started looking at Viking armour. Neither of these ideas seemed to work. Finally, I thought about vampires and blood and, without being obvious and using the Hammer vampire fangs, I wondered how you could get blood out of a person. I immediately thought of a leech. Then I considered that a leech has only one sucker: so what about using something like an octopus arm? The concept developed from there.

'I drew the head, working out how big it should be and what parts ought to be movable. I put in the gills and the suckers around the mouth and, because the Ancient One was more developed than the other Haemovores, I put suckers all over the place. Then I considered how this mutated human figure would support its head and came up with the idea of the

Phyllis (Joanne Bell), a ▶ young evacuee, is transformed into a Haemovore. *The Curse of Fenric.*

Ace adopts period dress for an adventure set during the Second World War. *The Curse of Fenric.*

Costume designer Ken Trew is surrounded by his creations. *The Curse of Fenric.*

◀ Sylvester McCoy watches as Nicholas Parsons (Wainwright), Joanne Bell (Phyllis) and Joann Kenny (Jean) record a scene on location for *The Curse of Fenric.*

▲ Sylvester McCoy and Sophie Aldred keep warm on location. *The Curse of Fenric.*

▲ Nurse Crane (Anne Reid) and Dr Judson (Dinsdale Landen). *The Curse of Fenric.*

Commander Millington (Alfred ▼ Lynch). *The Curse of Fenric.*

spine coming up out through the back of it.

'The basic idea for the costume was of all the old rubbish he'd collected from the bottom of the sea, all encrusted on him with barnacles. There were pieces that went over the shoulders and came out of the chest, like extensions of the lungs, which actually went into a man-made bit at the back. There was a tube at the back and the rib cage was built out. The effect I hope we achieved was that this creature had almost built itself a breathing apparatus that was incorporated into its own flesh, and that the body had actually been stripped of skin. By the time I'd finished it I thought, "You've got a very nasty mind, Ken Trew!".'

Once Trew had completed his designs he passed them to Moore, Mansfield and Allsopp, who were responsible for making the creature.

When the time came to record a scene in which the Haemovores rise up from the sea and walk to the beach it was discovered that all the air trapped in their masks and costumes made it difficult for the actors to submerge themselves. The production crew were forced to hunt all over the beach to find rocks and stones with which to weigh them down until the cue for action was given.

The Doctor's costume was changed for this production to reflect the darker mood of the new season. His previous light coloured jacket was replaced by an identical dark brown one, and his tie and hat band were similarly exchanged for darker versions. McCoy decided to wear a duffel coat for the early scenes of the story so that the change of costume would come as more of a surprise to viewers when he removed it. The impact of this was lost however when *The Curse of Fenric* was moved from first to third place in transmission order, as the costume had already been seen in *Battlefield* and *Ghost Light*.

The story ran significantly over length when it came to be edited, so a number of scenes were shortened or cut out altogether. (Much of this deleted material would later be made available to the public in a special extended version of the story released by BBC Video in 1991.) Other sequences intended as part of the climactic finale were irretrievably lost when a tape of the original recorded material was accidentally wiped before editing took place.

'It is very difficult to time a *Doctor Who* episode,' noted Nathan-Turner in 1989. 'You can read a script from front to back endlessly and get fifty-three *different* timings. For example, it might depend on how long you are going to hold on a battle: are you going to hold on it forever, or are you going to make it very tight? Because of the way we shoot the programme, those sort of things are quite often not decided until it's on the bench and we're cutting it. Then you suddenly realise that, even though you conceived it as a two-minute battle, all you want are the first two gun shots. Also, because so many scenes in *Doctor Who* have no dialogue, it's very difficult to time how long they are going to take, even in the rehearsal room. When we do cut it together, it is simply with regard to pace and not to time. Then we try to detach ourselves from it and make the trims afterwards.'

The third story of the season to be made and the last to be transmitted was the three-parter *Survival* (working titles: *Blood-Hunt* and *Cat Flap*), also recorded entirely on location. It was written by newcomer Rona Munro, from whom the script for the first episode was commissioned by Cartmel on 16 November 1988 and those for the other two on 11 January 1989.

'BBC Scotland sent me on a training course,' recalled Munro in 1992, 'and Andrew was one of a number of script writers brought in to talk to us. I just sort of went up to him and told him that I adored the show, had watched it since I was about two and would love to write for it. He advised me to send in some examples of my work, which I did, and from there I was asked to submit a story.

'I started off by producing a treatment – a detailed

**Two Cheetah People go ▶
hunting for food on
horseback.** *Survival.*

RONA MUNRO
WRITER

*As with many other writers introduced
in the final years of the series, Rona
Munro's first television work was her
contribution to* **Doctor Who**. *She
had met Andrew Cartmel at a BBC
writer's training course and this had
led to her being commissioned to
write* **Survival**. *Since then she has
gone on to write for* **Casualty** *and
has won: the Susan Smith-Blackburn
Award for her play* **Old Girls**; *the
Evening Standard Most Promising
Playwright; and the Critics Circle Plays
and Players Award. 1995 saw her
play* **The Maiden Shore** *in
production.*

**Anthony Ainley as the ▲
Master in his new costume
and yellow contact lenses.**
Survival.

**Midge (Will Barton), becomes
infected by the Cheetahs'
planet.** *Survival.* ▼

synopsis – which Andrew worked on with me, to
develop what he called a *Who* concept. Basically, this
is where the writer comes up with the story and then
the production team make it fit into the world of
Doctor Who. Once the treatment was agreed I went
ahead and wrote the script.'

Survival sees the Doctor taking Ace to present-day
Perivale so that she can revisit her old friends. It
transpires that most of them have been transported
by cat-like Kitlings to the planet of the Cheetah
People, an ancient race with the power to teleport
through space. Ace is also transported and joins
forces with two of her friends, Midge and Shreela,
and a boy named Derek. The Doctor follows close
behind and encounters the Master, who has drawn
him into a trap to try to gain his help. The Master
explains that this planet gradually transforms its
inhabitants into Cheetah People – an influence to
which he himself has fallen victim – while they in
turn, through the savagery of their actions, cause the
planet to move ever closer to total destruction.

Midge is overcome by the planet's influence, and
this enables the Master to use him to teleport to
Perivale. Ace, who has developed an affinity for a
Cheetah woman called Karra, gains the same ability
and takes the Doctor and the others back there as
well. The Master first uses Midge to go after the
Doctor and then kills him. He also kills Karra, who
has followed them all to Earth, at which point she
reverts to human form. The Master, succumbing to
the influence of the now-disintegrating Cheetah
planet, drags the Doctor back there. The Doctor

refuses to fight him, however, and is transported
back to Earth. He rejoins Ace, and they head off for
new adventures.

Survival saw the introduction of a new costume for
the Master. This was designed by Trew at the request
of Nathan-Turner, who thought that after virtually a
decade a new look was in order for the character.
Made entirely of silk, the costume was much cooler
and more comfortable for Anthony Ainley to wear
than his original, predominantly velvet one.

'It's stylish,' commented Ainley during the
making of the story. 'I like the idea of the silver collar
of the waistcoat coming out over the collarless black
jacket. I've never seen that before.'

The look of the Cheetah People was the joint
responsibility of Trew and make-up designer Joan
Stribling.

'There were eight Cheetah People,' noted
Stribling, 'and we had to take face casts of each of the
eight actors and actresses that were playing them.
The Cheetah faces were then sculpted and casts made
of them. The main part of the prosthetic was made
out of airbrushed cold-foam with hair attached. From
the nose back, they were overhead masks, but for the
part above the lip we used a hot-foam prosthetic
piece to enable them to open their mouths and snarl.'

Hair was stuck onto the actors' cheek bones to
give their faces a triangular look, and special contact
lenses and teeth completed the transformation.

One problem with these costumes was that they
were extremely hot to wear – particularly as
recording of the scenes set on the Cheetah planet (the
location for which was a quarry in Warmwell,
Dorset) happened to take place during a heat wave.
This resulted in one of the actresses who had been
cast to play a Cheetah extra quitting before recording
had been completed.

Munro considered that the realisation of the
Cheetah People was just one of a number of areas in
which, owing to budgetary constraints, the
production failed to do full justice to her scripts.

'The Cheetah People were not as sinister as I
would have liked,' she noted. 'They *never* looked real.
What I wanted was for them to be very human with
perhaps just fangs and a feline look about the cheeks
and strange cat-like eyes. My original idea – way,
way back – was to have them hunting, shooting,
fishing and charging around on horses, hunting
humans. That would have been much more
frightening.

Sylvester McCoy and Sophie Aldred look on as Julian Holloway (Sergeant Paterson) rehearses a scene in the youth centre. *Survival.*

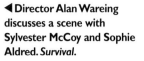

◄ Director Alan Wareing discusses a scene with Sylvester McCoy and Sophie Aldred. *Survival.*

▲ The Master (Anthony Ainley) on his chair of bones. *Survival.*

'If you have something that looks human until it bares its teeth, then that is scary. Alan Wareing, Andrew Cartmel and I all sat around talking about what these Cheetah People would look like, and Alan kept saying, "As long as we don't get *Puss in Boots*". Unfortunately, I think that's exactly what we did get.'

Munro was however generally happy with the realisation of her story, given the limited resources that were available.

The resolution of the story was originally intended to be somewhat different from that seen on transmission. In Munro's script, the Doctor and the Master returned to Earth together after their confrontation on the Cheetah planet, and the following exchange then took place:

THE MASTER: The planet …?

THE DOCTOR: It isn't there any more. It's … destroyed.

THE MASTER: How?

THE DOCTOR: It was too old … too dangerous. And I said we were an explosive combination.

(The Master stares at the Doctor with growing realisation)

▲ Ace becomes infected by the planet and starts to change. *Survival.*

◄ The Cheetah People. *Survival.*

Effects assistant Paul ▲
McGuiness prepares the
animatronic Kitling. *Survival.*

Sergeant Paterson (Julian ▲
Holloway). *Survival.*

Sylvester McCoy and ▲
Sophie Aldred clown around
at the end of a day on
location for *Survival.*

The Doctor and the Master ▶
fight for their lives on the
Cheetah's Planet. *Survival.*

Effects assistant Mike Tucker operates the animatronic Kitling on location at the youth centre. *Survival.*

THE MASTER: Yes, but how did it happen? How did we get back here? Who are you?

(The Doctor looks at him quizzically)

THE MASTER: <u>What</u> are you?

THE DOCTOR: (GRINS) We were at university together. Remember?

(The Master shakes his head)

THE MASTER: You're not a Time Lord!

(The Doctor winces. He doesn't want to get into this)

THE DOCTOR: Well strictly speaking … that is to say… well not <u>just</u> a Time Lord. We all have to evolve a bit, as the years go by.

(He looks at the Master, murmurs)

THE DOCTOR: Evolve or become extinct.

THE MASTER: <u>What are you?</u>

(The Doctor draws himself up. He grins wickedly)

THE DOCTOR: Shall we just say I'm multi-talented?

The Master was then to have used a Kitling to escape to fight another day. Nathan-Turner, however, thought this scene went too far in undermining the Doctor's established history and decided that it should not be included.

The final episode of *Survival* was transmitted on 6 December 1989, bringing eighties *Doctor Who* to a close. Unlike in the past, however, there was no announcement made at the end of the episode to reassure viewers that the series would be back for a further season of stories the following year.

It seemed that this might prove to be the end of an era in more ways than one.

CHAPTER NINETEEN

K-9 And Company: A Girl's Best Friend

K-9 and Company: A Girl's Best Friend, the first bona fide TV spin off from *Doctor Who*, was transmitted on Monday 28 December 1981 as part of the Christmas season on BBC1.

The approximately fifty-minute programme, production of which had been prompted by the public outcry following John Nathan-Turner's decision to drop K-9 from *Doctor Who* itself, saw actress Elisabeth Sladen reprising her popular role as Sarah Jane Smith – something she had previously resisted doing when invited first by Graham Williams and then by Nathan-Turner himself to return as a regular in the parent series. John Leeson again provided the robot dog's voice.

The initial outline for the story was written by Nathan-Turner under the working title *One Girl and Her Dog* and dated 29 April 1981. It read as follows:

Our story starts in South Croydon. Sarah Jane Smith is supervising two removal men who are packing Sarah Jane's belongings – packing cases, some furniture, etc – into a small furniture van. Sarah is moving to the country to her Aunt Lavinia's home in a small village, Morton Harward, where she is to continue writing cookery books, tend her Aunt's small local produce shop and look after her Aunt's ward, Brendan, a thirteen-year-old youth. The removal men depart leaving behind one tea chest. Perplexed, Sarah Jane takes it indoors to her now almost empty house, deciding to contact the removal firm's head office. Whilst in the process of making the phone call, she notices the chest is labelled 'for the attention of S.J.S.'. She hangs up, and unpacks the chest.

ELISABETH SLADEN
SARAH JANE SMITH

Elisabeth Sladen attended drama school for two years before joining the local repertory theatre in her home town of Liverpool. She met actor Brian Miller during her first production there and they were later married after meeting again in Manchester three years later. Early television work included appearances in **Coronation Street** *(1970),* **Doomwatch** *(1972),* **Some Mothers Do 'Ave 'Em** *(1973),* **Public Eye** *and* **Z Cars**. *Between 1974 and 1976 she had a regular role in* **Doctor Who** *as Sarah Jane Smith, a part she has since reprised in* **K-9 and Company** *(1981),* **The Five Doctors** *(1983), the* **Doctor Who** *radio serials* **The Paradise of Death** *(1993) and* **Doctor Who and the Ghosts of N-Space** *(1996), the* **Children In Need** *skit* **Dimensions In Time** *(1993) and the spin-off video drama* **Downtime** *(1995). Other work on television has included* **Stepping Stones** *(1977-78),* **Send in the Girls** *(1978),* **Take My Wife** *(1979),* **Gulliver in Lilliput** *(1982),* **Alice in Wonderland** *(1985) and* **Dempsey and Makepeace** *(1985). In 1980 Sladen appeared in the cinema film* **Silver Dream Racer**. *Since the birth of her daughter Sadie in 1985, she has spent most of her time being a mother and housewife, but has made occasional television appearances, including in* **The Bill** *(1989) and* **Peak Practice** *(1996).*

◄ **Sarah Jane Smith (Elisabeth Sladen) and her present from the Doctor, K-9.** *K-9 And Company: A Girl's Best Friend.*

SARAH JANE SMITH

There had never been a formal character outline drawn up for Sarah during her years as the Doctor's companion. The following was specially prepared by John Nathan-Turner and Antony Root for the purposes of K-9 and Company:

Established history

Sarah Jane Smith was born in Liverpool's dockland in 1949.

Her father worked in a local newspaper office, but both he and his wife died while Sarah Jane was still young.

The orphaned girl travelled south to live with her aunt, the well-known scientist Lavinia Smith, author of *Teleological Response of the Virus*.

It was the royalties from this work, a major medical advance of the sixties, that enabled Lavinia to pay for Sarah Jane's education through school and university.

It was at university that Sarah Jane developed her interest in writing and journalism. She achieved a First Class degree and in her final year edited her college magazine. She was also a campaigner for the Equal Opportunities Bill that was passing through Parliament at the time.

Straight out of university Sarah Jane joined a newly founded magazine*. She wrote some acclaimed articles before becoming a freelance contributor with the right to choose her own assignments.

During this period she built up an impressive list of contacts. Among those she interviewed were Lady Collingford, the novelist Nigel Carter, and the Olympic Gold Medallist John Crichton.

But after a while Sarah Jane became bored with writing women's interest pieces. She wanted to write a strong scientifically-based story.

While Lavinia was away on a lecture tour in America, an invitation arrived for her to visit a top-secret government research establishment. Sarah Jane impersonated her aunt and entered the complex. Here she met the physicist Joseph Rubeish and one Dr. John Smith, scientific adviser to UNIT.

Dr. Smith turned out to be a Time Lord, the Doctor in disguise, and after inadvertently stowing away on board the TARDIS, Sarah Jane spent three years travelling in space and time. (15.12.73-23.10.76.)

Summoned to Gallifrey in 1976, the Doctor was forced to drop Sarah Jane back on Earth. They said goodbye on a bright autumn day somewhere in England, perhaps South Croydon.

* *Metropolitan*

Character

Sarah Jane has always displayed a tough independence, but not without the warmth and wit of her native Liverpool. She believes in women's liberation but is not a forceful feminist. She has both a woman's and a journalist's intuition: a formidable combination.

A section from the storyboards for the title sequence of *K-9 And Company: A Girl's Best Friend*.

Inside is K-9. Sarah Jane has never met K-9 before. K-9 informs her that he has been sent by the Doctor. {The audience will almost certainly remember that K-9 Mk 1 was left on Gallifrey with Leela and K-9 Mk 2 was left in E-Space with Romana.}

Sarah Jane does not comprehend why K-9 has been sent – but expects little else, remembering her experiences with the Doctor! Their conversation is halted by a toot of a car horn. It is Aunt Lavinia, on her way in a chauffeur-driven car to London Airport, en route for a fact-finding scientific mission to America. She has arrived to bid farewell to Sarah Jane and deliver Brendan to her charge. Brendan is a keen scholar, especially keen in Chemistry and Physics. Aunt Lavinia departs, leaving last-minute instructions. Brendan discovers K-9, and Sarah Jane takes him into her confidence. The trio of Sarah Jane, Brendan and K-9 set off in Sarah Jane's open-top MGB for the country. On their arrival, Sarah Jane remeets Captain Pollock, head of the local hunt, a crotchety man of 50, who must never discover K-9's presence – Pollock does not approve of computers or pets.

From this point our three heroes become embroiled in a black magic yarn – a web of intrigue, pentagrams, goats of Mendies, etc, during which K-9's original evil

intentions are discovered (he was in fact built and despatched to Sarah Jane by the Master, who we never meet) and Brendan is able to reconfigure the dog's circuits and return K-9 to the benevolent animal we have come to love.

The story should concentrate on 'Avengerish' action rather than Doctor Who-type effects and should conclude with the possibility of a full spin-off series.

The reference to 'Avengerish' action reflected Nathan-Turner's intention that the programme should be more in the style of *The Avengers* – the famous ABC TV espionage thriller show of the sixties – than of *Doctor Who*. The suggestion that a full spin-off series could result was also Nathan-Turner's idea, and not something that had at this point been seriously considered by BBC management.

Nathan-Turner and script editor Antony Root quickly produced a fuller format document for the programme. This was entitled *A Girl's Best Friend* and dated 1 May 1981. It contained a refined synopsis of the proposed story – with no mention this time of the idea of K-9 being under the Master's control – and also character outlines for

Sarah Jane Smith (Elisabeth Sladen) with canines both artificial and flesh and blood. *K-9 And Company: A Girl's Best Friend.*

K-9 on location during the recording of the title sequence for his own spin-off series. *K-9 And Company: A Girl's Best Friend.*

LIFE AFTER THE DOCTOR

The notes prepared by John Nathan-Turner and Antony Root when planning **K-9 and Company** *included the following speculative description of a possible history of Sarah's life after her travels with the Doctor:*

Sarah Jane Smith left the Doctor in October 1976.

On being returned to Earth and Earth-time she went back to live with her aunt. She fabricated an explanation for her three-year absence, thinking that Lavinia would never believe the truth. The missing three years are now only referred to by Lavinia as 'the time you were away'.

Sarah Jane quickly picked up her career as a journalist and after a time as a feature writer on a national paper became Diary Editor of a London Evening. In this job she continued to meet the famous and spend most of her evenings at parties, receptions, theatres and concerts.

In 1979 Lavinia moved to the country and took her fourteen-year-old ward Brendan with her. She bought an old manor house at Moreton Harwood in the Cotswolds and left Sarah Jane to live in the Croydon house alone.

Three separate things have now combined to change the direction of Sarah Jane's life. First, she has been made redundant following a newspaper merger. Second, she has had interest from a publisher for a novel. Third, Lavinia has decided to spend at least a year in America lecturing and researching. Someone, therefore, is needed to look after Brendan, the manor and the market garden business that Lavinia has been running.

Sarah Jane will move to the manor, taking some of her things with her, and hopes to start her novel. Sarah is something of a judo expert.

Sarah and K-9. The document concluded by maintaining that 'this self-contained story *may* be continued as a series' and noting that it would 'almost certainly have a later transmission time than *Doctor Who*' – a suggestion that proved correct as the programme eventually went out at a quarter to six in the evening, whereas *Doctor Who* had most recently been transmitted in a ten past five time slot.

It was shortly after this, on 12 May 1981, that Nathan-Turner first contacted Sladen to see if she would be willing to appear in the special. To his delight, she readily agreed. Terence Dudley was then approached to write the script.

Dudley began work on the project by preparing a detailed scene breakdown, and then – after discussions with the production team – wrote a full draft script, still under the title *A Girl's Best Friend*. This stuck quite closely to the ideas developed by Nathan-Turner and Root, but fleshed them out accordingly.

Root's successor, Eric Saward, made a number of amendments to Dudley's script during September 1981 – by which time the special had acquired its final title of *K-9 and Company* (BBC executives having requested that it refer explicitly to K-9), with *A Girl's Best Friend* relegated to a subtitle. This rewriting led to an increasingly heated exchange of correspondence during the early part of the following month as Dudley objected to some of the changes that had been made and Saward took offence at the disparaging terms in which he did so.

Head of Series and Serials David Reid had some concerns of his own about Dudley's script and conveyed these to Nathan-Turner in a memo dated 5 October 1981. He observed that the inclusion of witchcraft rituals was likely to provoke complaints

from some quarters and identified a number of religious dialogue references, including 'Act of God' and 'Keep the faith alive', that he considered should be either cut or handled extremely carefully. He also urged that the programme's designers be kept away from 'inverted crosses or other anti-Christ suggestions' and noted with regard to a scene involving Brendan being held prostrate on a sacrificial altar that, as he obviously could not be shown naked, a ceremonial robe would have to be created for him. Nathan-Turner responded to these comments in a memo dated 3 November 1981:

I note your comments on K-9 and Company *and will certainly be very careful with the 'anti-Christ' aspects of the script and production thereof.*

However, I would like to retain 'Act of God' ... as this is, in this instance, purely insurance jargon but is necessary for the narrative line. We haven't yet decided about Brendan on the altar. Obviously if he <u>were</u> naked, once again, we'd be very careful in the way the sequence was shot.

The production team film the robot dog on location for *K-9 And Company: A Girl's Best Friend.*

K-9

*The following was the character outline for K-9 prepared by John Nathan-Turner and Antony Root for **K-9 and Company**:*

K-9 is a real-time data analyser robot, which is in the form of a mechanical dog.

The new K-9 is Mark III (Mark I was left on Gallifrey with Leela, Mark II was left in E-Space with Romana II).

Unless K-9 is immobilised, his eyes are always on and the panel on his back shows flashing lights. Around his neck is a dog collar with dog-tag attached (blank).

When K-9 is asked to consult his data banks, analyse objects, etc, his ears (or 'crisps') waggle.

From K-9's mouth is a ticker tape, used, for example, when K-9 is left alone to do a detailed analysis of something. The ticker tape does not discharge on cue.

Set into K-9's head between his eyes is a probe. This will extend to enable K-9 to reach areas out of his immediate range.

In K-9's snout area there is a blaster which will extend on cue. The blaster can kill or stun – the red ray from the blaster is achieved during the Gallery Only session.

K-9's head can move up and down in order to direct his blaster towards a particular area or person. In the past K-9's blaster ray has appeared to emanate at any required angle. In future please position the dog and his head to avoid this anomaly.

K-9's tail can move up and down and from side to side – this is usually a display of his feelings!

K-9 is fitted with tank-type tracks to facilitate his movement on uneven surfaces.

The voice of K-9 is JOHN LEESON (engaged by producer).

There is a duplicate light-weight non-practical version of K-9, should any actor have to carry K-9 at any time and be unable to manage the real model.

K-9 OR K9?

Opinions differ as to the correct spelling of the name of the Doctor's robot dog. Is it 'K-9' or 'K9'? Scripts and other official paperwork are inconsistent on this point. However, since there is a dot positioned between the 'K' and the '9' on the side of the prop itself, and also in the title of the 1981 spin-off programme, we have chosen to adopt the 'K-9' spelling throughout our books (even, for the sake of consistency, when quoting from original documentation which uses the alternative spelling).

Brendan Richards (Ian Sears) and Sarah Jane Smith investigate black magic in the village of Moreton Harwood, where they meet George Tracey (Colin Jeavons) and Commander Pollock (Bill Fraser). *K-9 And Company: A Girl's Best Friend.*

As the black magic aspects of the story are eclectic, I don't feel we could in any way be accused of indicating that this is representative of witchcraft today.

The programme's title sequence – which Nathan-Turner decided should be in the same style as those for the US series *Hart to Hart* and *Hawaii Five-0* – was shot on 9 November 1981. The main location sequences were then filmed between 12 and 17 November. The chosen locations were all near Cirencester in the Gloucestershire countryside. Moreton Harwood was represented by Miserden village, and other scenes were shot in and around North Woodchester and Barnsley village. A two-day studio session subsequently took place over 29 and 30 November in Studio A at the BBC's Pebble Mill facility in Birmingham, when the remainder of the required scenes were committed to tape. (This was just days after the recording of the season nineteen *Doctor Who* story *Earthshock* had been completed at Television Centre in London.)

In the story as transmitted, Sarah pays a Christmas visit to her Aunt Lavinia's house in the village of Moreton Harwood. She discovers that Lavinia, a noted scientist, has yet to return from a lecture tour of the USA. She does however meet Brendan – Lavinia's ward – and Commander Bill Pollock – her partner in a small market garden business. Also in the house, in a box sent to her by the Doctor, she finds K-9. Brendan is kidnapped by a local coven of witches who want to sacrifice him to the goddess Hecate. Sarah, with K-9's assistance, foils their plan and unmasks their leaders – Commander Pollock and local postmistress Lily Gregson.

K-9 and Company won a quite respectable viewing figure of 8.4 million and would no doubt have done even better had it not been for the fact that the Winter Hill transmitter in the North West region suffered a power blackout at the time. The option of a full series was never pursued, however, probably due in part to changes that had taken place in BBC management since its inception. The programme had just a single repeat screening, on 24 December 1982 on BBC2, where it understandably pulled a much lower audience of 2.1 million.

'I do think that, with Lis Sladen in the show, it worked very well,' reflected Nathan-Turner in 1993. 'Our only mistake was that we focused a little bit too much on black magic. I think if it had been something a little less potentially sinister, we might be getting *K-9 and Company* now. I take full responsibility for that focus, but we should have done something a bit different.'

CHAPTER TWENTY

The Ultimate Adventure

Theatrical producer Mark Furness approached the BBC in the spring of 1988 with a proposal to put on an original *Doctor Who* stage play. He discussed the idea with John Nathan-Turner and Andrew Cartmel, and – although he had previously contacted Terrance Dicks to see if he would be interested in providing the script, as he had for the 1974 stage play *Doctor Who and the Daleks in Seven Keys to Doomsday* – the suggestion emerged that Nathan-Turner should direct a script written by Cartmel and Ben Aaronovitch.

The story devised by Cartmel and Aaronovitch was unfavourably received and ultimately rejected by Furness.

'The plot was the first problem,' recalled Aaronovitch in a 1993 interview. 'Basically it went like this: the Doctor bops around bits of the universe setting up a very elaborate trap for the next generation of Daleks. He has to pull together lots of different elements.

'It turns out the Doctor created Stonehenge. The Doctor arrives at a rock festival near Stonehenge in 1968, and you can hear stuff like Tangerine Dream in the distance. He meets a hippie who tells him this weird theory about a dome-shaped formation of rocks which is actually a parabolic antenna and the Doctor says "Yeah, it took me ages to get them here." Stonehenge was built to send a signal to a star which was so far away the Doctor had to build it all that

WHO ON STAGE
Doctor Who – The Ultimate Adventure was the third major stage production of **Doctor Who** to be presented in the UK. The first **Doctor Who** stage play was mounted in 1965 when David Whitaker's **Curse of the Daleks** played at the Wyndham's Theatre in London. The next production was in 1974 when Terrance Dicks' **Doctor Who and the Daleks in Seven Keys to Doomsday** appeared at the Adelphi Theatre, again in London. Both of these productions closed after their initial runs and never toured, although a different production of **Doctor Who and the Daleks in Seven Keys to Doomsday** was mounted by the Buxton Drama League late in 1981. There had also been several other **Doctor Who**-related theatre productions, most notably Richard Franklin's 1984 Edinburgh Fringe production **Recall UNIT or, The Great T-Bag Mystery** and also John Ostrander's **The Inheritors of Time**, which was staged at American conventions during the eighties.

▲ The poster for *Doctor Who – The Ultimate Adventure*.

◀ The Doctor (Jon Pertwee) and Jason (Graeme Smith) meets the Prime Minister (Judith Hibbert). *Doctor Who – The Ultimate Adventure*.

LOCATIONS AND TOUR DATES

All dates are in 1989.

Jon Pertwee

Wimbledon Theatre, London
23/03 – 01/04

Her Majesty's Theatre, Aberdeen
03/04 – 08/04

Empire Theatre, Liverpool
10/04 – 15/04

Theatre Clwyd, Mold
17/04 – 22/04

Alexandra Theatre, Birmingham
24/04 – 29/04

The Bristol Hippodrome
01/05 – 06/05

Towngate Theatre, Basildon
08/05 – 13/05

Theatre Royal, Glasgow
15/05 – 20/05

Manchester Opera House
22/05 – 27/05

Apollo Theatre, Oxford
29/05 – 03/06

Colin Baker

Theatre Royal, Newcastle
05/06 – 10/06

Theatre Royal, Nottingham
12/06 – 17/06

Grand Theatre, Leeds
19/06 – 24/06

Theatre Royal, Brighton
26/06 – 01/07

The Edinburgh Playhouse
03/07 – 08/07

Grand Theatre, Wolverhampton
10/07 – 15/07

Derngate, Northampton
17/07 – 22/07

Marlowe Theatre, Canterbury
24/07 – 29/07

King's Theatre, Southsea
31/07 – 05/08

Congress Theatre, Eastbourne
07/08 – 19/08

Doctor Who – The Ultimate Adventure **featured an impressive array of laser effects supplied by Laser Grafix Ltd. and designed by Steve Playford.**

time ago so the signal would reach the star at the right time.

'We invented an alien race called the Metatraxi who turned out to be really funny. They were Samurai insect creatures who loved to fight and found the idea of taking prisoners faintly immoral, in much the same way we find making toilet jokes faintly immoral.

'They don't like to fight people who are unarmed so they have a moral quandary with the Doctor who hasn't got any weapons. There's a running joke where they keep trying to lend the characters weapons so they can fight them.

'The Doctor meets a woman who's a torch singer, science fiction magazine fan and gun runner from

1958 Algiers and he takes her to a planet which she changes to her vision of what the future should be like. She turns it into a pirate base. There's a scene set in a stolen Metatraxi battle-cruiser where the Doctor gives a long economical and sociological lecture about why piracy is impossible in deep space and the next thing of course they're boarded by pirates and this woman.

'The planet they end up on turns out to be the lair of the data vampire – a vampire which eats data by sucking up the inane nucleoids from people's blood. It had a lot of typical Andrew touches; he has this thing about scaring people, reassuring them and then revealing that they were right the first time! We built up the vampire, then said it was OK because it ate data, and then revealed it ate data by drinking your blood!'

Aaronovitch admitted that the script was really too demanding.

'It was a case of me and Andrew being totally over-ambitious as to what could be done and what people wanted from us. It's a perfectly good story but it should be filmed.'

A change of plan was required not only in relation to the script but also in relation to the direction after it transpired that the play would be in rehearsal at the same time that production of the TV series' twenty-sixth season was getting under way and that consequently Nathan-Turner would be unavailable.

'I would dearly have loved to direct it, as I do love the theatre,' Nathan-Turner explained in an interview at the time, 'but they put the dates back to

Rebecca Thornhill (Crystal) ▲ struggles with a Cyberman at a press call to promote the play Doctor Who: The Ultimate Adventure.

The occupants of the ▶ TARDIS rest while the Cybermen, Karl (David Banks) and the Emperor Dalek make their plans. Doctor Who – The Ultimate Adventure.

when we were just about to begin rehearsals for the new television series. Mark Furness then asked me if I would be creative consultant for the play, which was a role I thoroughly enjoyed. It was rather marvellous *not* to direct it, and just to be consulted.'

Furness brought in Carole Todd, a director and choreographer recently returned from an Australian run of Andrew Lloyd-Webber's *Starlight Express*, to direct a new script commissioned from Dicks.

Dicks, working to a very tight deadline, completed his initial synopsis on 19 December 1988. It was sent to Nathan-Turner for his approval at the start of 1989 – by which time Jon Pertwee had been secured to star in the production. The synopsis was acceptable to all concerned, and Dicks stuck closely to it in preparing the first draft of his script. Minor departures included a change of name, from Miranda to Crystal, for the Doctor's female companion. Other features not present in the synopsis but added to the script at Furness's suggestion were: sequences of 'moonwalking' when the Doctor's companions first arrive on an alien planet; a magical illusion (termed 'net illusion' by Furness); the joining of the human crew by an alien creature ('looking like an ugly E.T. ... v. loveable' noted Furness); a pantomime routine of dodging meteorites in space; the setting of a French Revolution sequence in Paris and not in a field as suggested by Dicks; and finally an illusion where the TARDIS blows up.

The second draft of Dicks's script was completed on 22 February 1989, and it was this version that went forward to rehearsal and initial performance. One advantage that a stage play has over a videotape or film production is that the script can be constantly tailored and amended as the weeks pass. This is exactly what happened on *The Ultimate Adventure*; as the tour progressed, numerous alterations were made to the dialogue and action, and whole scenes were even dropped altogether. It is probably true to say that no two nights' performances were ever the same. Someone who saw the play on the opening night could thus enjoy a significantly different one – albeit still with the same plot – several months later.

To try to recover part of his production costs – estimated to be around £184,000 for the initial tour at a weekly rate of around £23,750 – Furness invited participants to invest in the production, monetary units of £8,000 each being available in down to one-eighth (£1,000) units. This strategy proved successful and, with finance secured, rehearsals took place in the weeks leading up to the opening night at London's Wimbledon Theatre on Thursday 23 March 1989.

Alongside Pertwee as the Doctor were Graeme Smith as his companion Jason and Rebecca Thornhill as the night-club singer Crystal, who joins them on their travels.

'I love singing,' stated Thornhill at the play's press launch on 23 February 1989, 'so I'm looking forward to the songs. I don't want to be a screamer or a thick dolly bird – I want to get away from that.'

Furness had negotiated English speaking rights for the play (with certain restrictions in the USA) and it was initially hoped that it might tour Australia following its UK launch. To this end, enquiries were made as to the availability of Australian artistes Kylie Minogue and Jason Donovan for the parts of Crystal and Jason respectively. Both had appeared in the popular Australian soap opera *Neighbours* and subsequently launched successful singing careers. In the event, however, these plans came to nothing.

Dicks's script featured not only the Daleks (which were especially built for the production based on plans drawn up by BBC visual effects designer Peter

◀ Jon Pertwee hands over the role of the Doctor on stage to Colin Baker. *Doctor Who – The Ultimate Adventure.*

REBECCA THORNHILL
CRYSTAL

Rebecca Thornhill was born in Dartford and trained at the Arts Educational School until 1988. While still a student she appeared in cabaret at the Royal Albert Hall, the Waldorf Hotel and Maxims de Paris in London. Her first professional engagement was at a Dougie Squires Spectacular in Cannes. She appeared in the TV film **Eye on L.A!** *as well as a cinema advertisement for Levi Jeans. In 1994 she toured in a production of* **Me and My Girl.**

GRAEME SMITH
JASON

Born and bred in Australia, Graeme Smith studied classical piano at the Sydney Conservatorium of Music, and drama at Sydney's Theatre of Youth. His professional debut came in an Australian tour of Lionel Bart's **Oliver** *which was followed by leading roles in* **Pal Joey** *and* **Butterflies are Free.** *Soon after arriving in London, he appeared in* **Peter Pan – The Musical, My Fair Lady, Hello Dolly** *and playing Brad in a national tour of* **The Rocky Horror Show.** *On television he has appeared in* **The Young Doctors, Prisoner** *and* **Kings.**

SCENERY PROBLEMS

'There was one bit of scenery that I hated. It was the planet scene in the second half – it was changed later on to a laser beam. Originally there was this large lump in the middle of the stage, and the audience just knew that when Graeme and I sat down we were launching into a song. It was awful and much better after it got changed. There has been a lot of criticism of the songs, but I think they worked for the benefit of the play, "Sky High" probably being the best of the three. Although, I must say, I was also a big fan of the Bay City Rollers in my youth.'
Rebecca Thornhill interviewed by Darren Floyd for the DWAS Reference Department's Index-File Special on The Ultimate Adventure, 1994.

◀ The Doctor and his companions find themselves in the Bar Galactica. *Doctor Who: The Ultimate Adventure.*

ULTIMATE SONGS

The Ultimate Adventure featured three songs: 'Strange Attractor', sung by Crystal in the night club at the start of the show and then again at the end; 'Business Is Business' sung by Madame Delilah and the patrons of her Bar Galactica; and 'Sky High' sung by Crystal and Jason as they start to fall in love as the story progresses. The lyrics to the latter two songs were by Carole Todd and it is unknown who wrote 'Strange Attractor'.

This is a show that has almost everything, certainly it has something to appeal to practically everybody.

For the dedicated believer the Daleks and Cybermen are out in force. For the cynics there is a script written so deliciously tongue in cheek it can carve a smile on a face made of stone. And for those among us who crave nothing more than two hours of escapism it contains an array of high-tech effects, including lasers, that ensure our interest never wavers.

It is a production difficult to categorise. With only three songs it cannot be described as a musical. It certainly isn't a pantomime – even if one of the song cues does appear to have blatantly stepped out of one. It is, indeed, just a fast-moving adventure suitable for all the family.
Ray Jones-Davies writing in an unknown newspaper

During the tour David Banks understudied the role of the Doctor, and played the role twice during Jon Pertwee's run. Doctor Who – The Ultimate Adventure. ▼

The Doctor's alien friend Zog (Stephanie Colburn). Doctor Who – The Ultimate Adventure.

Logan for the 1979 TV story *Destiny of the Daleks*) and the Cybermen (which were hired in from freelance costumier Derek Handley) but also a humanoid villain in the person of Karl the mercenary, played by David Banks (who had appeared as the Cyber Leader in a number of *Doctor Who* stories on TV). The remainder of the cast each played numerous roles ranging from Daleks and Cybermen to winged ant-creatures, bodyguards and the cute alien Zog (Stephanie Colburn). During a scene set in an outer space bar, the Bar Galactica, two other familiar *Doctor Who* monsters – a Draconian (Wolf Christian) and a Vervoid (David Bingham 23/03/89-15/07/89 and Gavin Warwick 17/07/89-19/08/89) – were evident (again courtesy of Handley).

The plot revolves around a scheme by the Daleks, the Cybermen and Karl to kidnap a peace envoy (Chris Beaumont) prior to a world peace conference and then to destroy the conference by returning him to it with a bomb. The Doctor is asked to help by Mrs T (Judith Hibbert), the Prime Minister of England at the time, and he and Jason meet Crystal at their first port of call. After many adventures in space and time, including visits to the infamous Bar Galactica run by Madame Delilah (Hibbert), they manage to defeat the plans of the rogue aliens and finish up having tea with Mrs T.

Pertwee was contracted for only the initial ten venues of the play's run. When demand extended beyond that, a new actor was needed to take over. Colin Baker, who had attended the first night at Wimbledon Theatre, was asked if he would be willing to step in. He agreed, and played the Doctor for a further ten venues.

Banks understudied the part of the Doctor for the entire run, and actually played it for two performances in Birmingham on 29 April when, due to exhaustion, Pertwee had to bow out just five minutes into the first performance. Graeme Smith fell ill between shows on 21 April and the role of Jason was played by Bingham for the second performance on that day and for both shows the next. Smith later left the company and Bingham took over the role on a permanent basis from 17 July until the end of the show's run.

The Ultimate Adventure was a resounding success and gained many good reviews. Maureen Paton, writing in the *Stage and TV Today* on 13 April said: 'This first-ever national tour restores the guts to a character that has become a disembowelled travesty on TV in recent years. Jon Pertwee travels back in time to reassume the air of authority and foppish sense of style he brought to the role of the good Doctor in the seventies ... Director Carole Todd achieves a happy medium between stage and screen by employing such devices as 3-D screens and conjuring tricks to deceive the eye. The laser beam technology is sophisticated enough to excite the most demanding adult fan and the pace only flags in the somewhat unnecessary musical interludes.'

It was initially hoped that the play might extend its run into the Christmas season in London's West End, with overseas tours in America and Australia to follow. In the event, however, the final performance was given at the Congress Theatre in Eastbourne on 19 August 1989 and the play was not subsequently restaged. Shortly after it closed, Mark Furness Ltd suffered financial problems and the company was wound down.

CHAPTER TWENTY-ONE

Exhibitions: On Display

1974 had seen the setting up by BBC Enterprises of two permanent *Doctor Who* exhibitions – one at Longleat House in Warminster, Wiltshire, and the other on the Golden Mile in Blackpool, Lancashire. These were still going strong in 1980, by which time their format had become well established. Visitors entered through an enlarged version of a police box and made their way along a winding passageway lined with exhibits of costumes and props from the series until they came to a larger display area centred around a simplified replica of the TARDIS control console. They then exited via a shop offering a wide range of spin-off merchandise. The props and costumes on display were generally drawn from recently transmitted stories, although a few older ones – including a Yeti from season five's *The Web of Fear* – were occasionally in evidence. Items were regularly swapped between the two exhibitions to ensure a good variety.

The Longleat exhibition continued throughout the 1980s and into the 1990s, but the Blackpool one closed its doors for the last time at the end of October 1985, mainly because the lease on the building in which it was housed had expired. Both exhibitions were overseen for most of the decade by BBC Enterprises' Julie Jones. In 1988, however, Jones left the BBC and joined forces with designers Lorne Martin and Martin Wilkie in an independent firm, M & J Media Ventures, which was then subcontracted to organise the Longleat exhibition from the following year onwards.

Aside from those at Longleat and Blackpool, there were two other semi-permanent exhibitions of note in the UK during the eighties, both of them in central London. The first was mounted at the famous Madame Tussaud's waxworks in 1980 and the second at a venue called Space Adventure in 1988.

The Madame Tussaud's display, called *The Doctor Who Experience*, opened on 29 August 1980 and was designed by a team from Tussaud's headed by Michael Wright. It featured waxwork reproductions of the Doctor and Romana along with a model of K-9 and replicas of several alien creatures – specifically Davros, a Dalek, a Sontaran, a Nimon from *The Horns of Nimon*, a Foamasi from *The Leisure Hive*, Meglos from the story of the same name (making Tom Baker the only person ever to have been portrayed twice in the same exhibition at Tussaud's) and a Marshman from *Full Circle*. The wax likenesses of Baker were sculpted by Judith Craig. Although originally due to close on 31 March 1981, the exhibition proved so popular that it was extended well beyond that date.

The exhibition at Space Adventure – which was launched on 15 November 1988 with a press event

▲ A Sontaran warrior on display at Madame Tussaud's. 1980.

▲ A Nimon on display at Madame Tussaud's. 1980.

▲ Fans queuing outside the Blackpool exhibition before it closed its doors for the last time in 1985.

▲ The central console on display inside the Blackpool exhibition.

◄ Tom Baker became the first person to have two waxworks on display at the same time, once as the Doctor and once as Meglos, at Madame Tussaud's *Doctor Who* Exhibition in 1980.

A Cyberman, Colin Baker, ▲
Janet Fielding, a Cryon, Nicola
Bryant and Bessie appear at
the press launch of the
Doctor Who US travelling
exhibition.

The logo for the US ▲
travelling tour.

Setting up the exhibits ▲
inside the US exhibition
trailer.

Tom Baker on stage at the
Twenty Years of a Time Lord
celebration held at Longleat
in 1983. ▼

marking (a few days prematurely) *Doctor Who's* twenty-fifth anniversary – complemented the sophisticated space shuttle simulation ride that was the venue's main attraction. It consisted of a display of props and costumes, mostly from recent stories, grouped around a replica of the TARDIS console. All the monster exhibits – including a Sontaran, the Special Weapons Dalek from *Remembrance of the Daleks* and the Kandyman from *The Happiness Patrol* – were animated in some way, and maximum use was made of the relatively small area available. 1989 saw some new items added, including the Emperor Dalek and one of its minions from season twenty-five's *Remembrance of the Daleks*, and publicity for the exhibition was given a boost when Sylvester McCoy and John Nathan-Turner took part in a four-hour signing session there on 2 September. The following year, however, saw the company behind Space Adventure running into financial difficulties and the venue was ultimately closed down.

In the autumn of 1985, plans were laid by BBC Enterprises in collaboration with its US distributor Lionheart Television International and its US exhibitions and promotions agent Monarch International for a major new *Doctor Who* exhibition to tour the USA housed in a forty-eight-foot-long trailer (too large to be driven legally on Britain's roads). The trailer was made by a firm called Vanplan in Warrington, and after numerous delays was unveiled to the British press at an event at Elstree attended by Colin Baker, Nicola Bryant, Janet Fielding, Nathan-Turner and artist Andrew Skilleter. It was then shipped over from Liverpool to New York, where the tour was launched on 9 May 1986 by Peter Davison and Controller of BBC1 Michael Grade.

The interior display area, designed by BBC designer Tony Burrough, was entered through a mock-up police box and featured amongst other exhibits a Dalek, a Silurian, a Sea Devil, a Sontaran, K-9, a Tractator from *Frontios* and the Ergon from *Arc of Infinity*. The huge murals for the exterior, the responsibility of Skilleter, featured the Dark Tower on Gallifrey (as seen in *The Five Doctors*) and acted as a backdrop to the exhibition shop.

Although it encountered numerous problems (caused in part by extensive damage incurred when it was accidentally dropped while being loaded for shipping at Liverpool docks), the exhibition ran for some months and was joined at various points along its route by stars from the series, including Tom Baker and Colin Baker.

In addition to the permanent and semi-permanent exhibitions already mentioned, there was also a very notable one-off event held in 1983. Entitled *The Doctor Who Celebration: Twenty Years of a Time Lord*, this took place at Longleat over the Easter bank holiday weekend, Sunday 3 April and Monday 4 April, and featured guest appearances by all four surviving Doctors – Patrick Troughton, Jon Pertwee, Tom Baker and Peter Davison – along with William Hartnell's widow Heather and daughter Anne and many of the actors and actresses who had played the Doctor's companions.

The main event area was behind the House, where marquees housed: displays by the BBC's Costume, Make-up, Design and Visual Effects Departments and Radiophonic Workshop; a forum in which panel discussions and guest interviews were presented; a cinema in which the complete stories *The Dalek Invasion of Earth* (Hartnell), *The Dominators* (Troughton), *Terror of the Autons* (Pertwee), *Terror of the Zygons* (Baker) and *The Visitation* (Davison) were shown; and a sales area where large quantities of spin-off merchandise were on offer and an auction of *Doctor Who* props and costumes took place – the first time such items had ever been made available to the public to buy. A large conservatory adjoining the House was meanwhile called into service as an autograph room.

This event was, if anything, a victim of its own success, as it drew much bigger crowds than expected and queues stretched into the distance as every marquee was filled to capacity. The organisers had apparently anticipated around 50,000 people spread over the two days, but over 35,000 came on the Sunday alone, and many disappointed families who had not pre-booked had to be turned away at the gate.

The success and proliferation of *Doctor Who* exhibitions during the 1980s provided ample evidence of the series' enduring popular appeal, and would continue well into the 1990s.

CHAPTER TWENTY-TWO

Fandom Comes of Age

The main hub of *Doctor Who* fan activity for much of the 1980s was the United States of America. Episodes – particularly those from the fourth Doctor's era – were shown on an almost daily basis on PBS stations all over the country, generating an enormous cult following for the series.

It seemed that barely a weekend went by without a *Doctor Who* convention taking place somewhere in the States. The show's stars, both past and present, were in constant demand to attend these celebrations, with high fees and travel expenses being offered to entice them from UK shores. John Nathan-Turner even began to act as a semi-official guest liaison officer for the organisers of these events. The biggest convention of all, attended by an estimated 20,000 people, was billed as –

appropriately enough – the Ultimate Celebration. This took place in Chicago over the series' twentieth anniversary weekend in 1983 and achieved the unique feat of bringing all four surviving Doctors – Patrick Troughton, Jon Pertwee, Tom Baker and Peter Davison – on stage together, along with many of their companions from the series.

The North American *Doctor Who* Appreciation Society (NADWAS), which like its UK forebear had been essentially non-profit-making, now gave way to professional operations. Barbara Elder, who ran NADWAS, went over to working on a commercial basis, and competition came from organisations including Spirit of Light – who staged the Ultimate Celebration amongst many other conventions – and the *Doctor Who* Fan Club of America. The latter was set up by two commercially minded fans, Ron Katz and Chad Roark, after they met Nathan-Turner at

FANZINE ROOTS

The eighties saw a huge number of independent, non-profit-making **Doctor Who** *fanzines being published by eager devotees of the series. Non-DWAS produced* **Doctor Who** *fanzines had however first started to appear in the mid to late seventies. Notable titles from that era had included* **Gallifrey** *(edited by Geraint Jones and Tim Dollin),* **The Doctor Who Review** *(edited by Gary Hopkins, Tim Robins and Paul Mount) and* **Oracle** *(edited by David J. Howe and later by Chris Dunk). Their readership had still consisted mainly of DWAS members, but these fanzines had paved the way for the eighties trend towards diversification within fandom.*

▲ The *Whovian Times*, the newsletter of the *Doctor Who* Fan Club of America. 1987.

◀ Fans gathered at Imperial College in London for the DWAS's PanoptiCon VII convention in 1986.

ON THE FRINGES

*Doctor Who fandom became more and more decentralised during the eighties. The first signs of this had however become apparent during the closing years of the seventies when, in addition to the **Doctor Who** Fan Club (DWFC) and the **Doctor Who** Appreciation Society (DWAS), a number of other **Doctor Who**-related organisations had sprung up on the fringes of fandom.*

*In 1974 Stuart Money (who had earlier been prevented by the BBC from setting up a rival to the DWFC) had formed a Jon Pertwee Fan Club with the assistance of fellow Pertwee devotees John Hudson, Peter Capaldi and Brian Smith (the latter of whom had also acted as the DWFC's photographer). Members received a duplicated monthly newsletter giving all the latest news of Pertwee's many activities, with quite a heavy emphasis on **Doctor Who**. The Club wound down in 1976 but was relaunched just a few months later with a new, more expensive magazine and two new assistants, Leonora Rich and Gordon Roxburgh, supporting Money.*

*Soon after Tom Baker had taken over from Pertwee as the Doctor, he too found himself the subject of his own fan club, the Friends of Tom Baker. Run by Linda Williams, this produced some relatively high-quality fanzines, including the fiction-based **Timelord**, but focused mainly on organising social events and gatherings for the many fans of the new Doctor.*

*Actor-orientated clubs enjoyed their heyday during this period, and fans also had an opportunity to join the Patrick Troughton Preservation Society, run by Chris Marton and Martin Wiggins through their fanzine **The Wheel in Space**, and the Elisabeth Sladen Friendship League, organised by Bev Manton.*

*A British-based club intended to cater for fans worldwide was the DWIFC – the **Doctor Who** International Fan Club. This was launched by Smith in early 1976. Its newsletter was well printed by 1976 standards, but Smith was forced to discontinue it after only two issues as he had discovered that he was running at a considerable loss. Subsequently the DWIFC was absorbed into the DWAS.*

*Following in this tradition, the late eighties saw the establishment of the Midlands-based Whonatics organisation, the main aim of which was to act as an alternative to the DWAS's Local Group network. Headed by fan Simon Horton, it produced a newsletter entitled **Celestial Farmyard** and a fanzine called **Second Dimension**.*

Members of the *Doctor Who* Appreciation Society's Executive commitee and helpers mail out the Society's newsletter *Celestial Toyroom* in 1983: (From left) David Saunders, David J. Howe, Paul Zeus, Robert Moubert, Rosemary Fowler and Dominic May.

Nicola Bryant and Peter Davison sign autographs for the fans at PanoptiCon VI in Brighton in 1985.

BBC Enterprises' Longleat event in 1983. Its members, who came to number some 30,000 by the middle of the decade, received a regular newspaper entitled *The Whovian Times* (*Doctor Who* fans being commonly referred to as Whovians in the States). This featured interviews and news items – including columns by Nathan-Turner and prominent British fan Jeremy Bentham – and also numerous adverts for a wide range of merchandise items produced in the States during this period. Readers were even given regular invitations to join a group called the Gallifrey Beach and Body Club!

It was during Colin Baker's time as the Doctor that the series arguably hit the peak of its eighties popularity in the States. Like Davison before him, Baker made his first convention appearance at an American event (PanoptiCon West in Ohio in July 1984). Sylvester McCoy followed suit, but his tenure in the role coincided with a slight downturn in the series' fortunes. This was due largely to the fact that, with the reduction to fourteen episodes per season, it was now being produced at too slow a rate to satisfy the scheduling needs of the PBS stations, leaving them with the choice of either continuing to rerun old episodes over and over again or else dropping the

The fifth Doctor and his companions on stage at PanoptiCon VII: (From left) Gerald Flood, Sarah Sutton, Peter Davison, Janet Fielding and Mark Strickson.

series altogether. As the BBC's American agents, Lionheart, were also charging higher and higher fees for the rerunning of old episodes, an increasing number decided on the latter course. Interest in the series nevertheless remained strong at the end of the decade, with a new organisation called the Friends of *Doctor Who* emerging to take the lead in US fandom.

Elsewhere on the North American continent, considerable fan support had developed for *Doctor Who* in Canada. This revolved mainly around a group known as the *Doctor Who* Information Network, which in 1984 began publishing a regular fanzine entitled *Enlightenment*.

Doctor Who also remained very popular 'down under' during the eighties. The Australasian *Doctor Who* Fan Club continued to publish issues of its high-quality fanzine *Zerinza*, as well as a more basic newsletter, and attracted a large influx of new members. A number of '*Doctor Who* Parties' and other events were held, with guests including former companion, actress Katy Manning, who now lived in Australia. Other groups, such as the *Doctor Who* Club of Victoria, produced fanzines and carried out activities on a more local basis. In New Zealand, too, the series had won an enthusiastic band of loyal followers. Of particular note were the activities of the New Zealand *Doctor Who* Fan Club, which in 1987 launched its fanzine *Time/Space Visualiser* (or *TSV* for short).

In the UK, meanwhile, the *Doctor Who* Appreciation Society remained at the forefront of organised fandom throughout the eighties, although its dominance was now being challenged by other fan groups and, in the publication field, by independent fanzines.

After its original organisers bowed out in mid-1980, the Society was effectively saved from collapse by David Saunders, who became co-ordinator, David J. Howe, who had the previous year taken over from

Bentham as head of the Reference Department, and Chris Dunk, the editor of the *Celestial Toyroom* newsletter.

Over the next couple of years, the Society's organising body took steps to put its organisation and finances on a sounder footing. Dunk was succeeded on *Celestial Toyroom* by Gordon Blows and David Auger (1981), Gary Russell (1981-1982), Gordon Roxburgh (1983-1984), Dominic May (1984-1985) and Ian Bresman (1985-86). The Society's other main publications during the first half of the decade were the fanzine *TARDIS*, edited by Richard Walter (1980-84) and Ann O'Neil (1985), and the fan fiction periodical *Cosmic Masque*, edited initially by John Peel and then, from 1981 onwards, by Ian K. McLachlan.

The Society's membership was boosted considerably by a strong presence at the Longleat event and subsequent advertising in Marvel Comics' official *Doctor Who Magazine*, and topped the 3,000 mark for the first time.

The Society meanwhile continued to stage its own events, initially under the aegis of Convention Department organiser Paul Zeus. In addition to the major PanoptiCon each year, a number of smaller and more informal Inter-Face and DWASocial gatherings were held. It was a constant source of irritation to the Society's executive that the PanoptiCons had to be scheduled so as not to clash with major American events, as the latter would always be more successful in attracting guests.

One example of this occurred in 1984, when PanoptiCon VI, planned for the last weekend in November, had to be postponed as many of the potential guests were going to be at a huge Spirit of Light convention in America, which had been unexpectedly rescheduled from October. The British event was eventually moved to the last weekend in July 1985. It took place in Brighton, Sussex, and was notable not only for featuring the first and only British fan convention appearance by Troughton but also for leaving the Society with a hefty bill to pay and insufficient funds to do so. *Celestial Toyroom* later reported that the convention's finances had been mismanaged by its organisers.

New co-ordinator Tony Jordan, who formally succeeded Saunders at the beginning of September 1985, had to lead the executive in recovering the Society from the brink of bankruptcy while continuing to provide its members with a reasonable service. To this end, 1986 saw *TARDIS* being incorporated into *Celestial Toyroom* – now edited by Neil Hutchings after Roxburgh and Mark Stammers

Gordon Roxburgh interviews Patrick Troughton and Michael Craze at PanoptiCon VI. The event was Troughton's only UK fan convention.

had filled in with a few issues at the beginning of the year – and the membership fee increased. Another big convention, PanoptiCon VII, was held – this time with an edict to put the Society back on a sound financial footing and with a new team, headed by Roxburgh, in charge. The event was judged by some to be the best the Society had ever organised, and an added bonus for attendees was that they were able to watch the transmission of the first episode of *The Trial of a Time Lord* on a big convention screen along with some 500 of their fellow devotees.

By the end of 1986 the Society was again financially stable. Jordan was succeeded as co-ordinator by Andrew Beech, while Howe, who during his time at the Reference Department had amongst other things launched the Plotlines series of story synopsis dossiers, bowed out to be replaced by Julian Knott (1986-1989).

The beginning of 1988 saw the Society suffering another financial crisis when the discovery was made that substantial back-payments of Value Added Tax were owing. This resulted in *Celestial Toyroom* being given a reduced page-count and lower standard of production than in the recent past and in other economy measures being taken. Brian J. Robb became editor of the newsletter around the middle of

Jon Pertwee at an early DWAS convention.

NEWS MANAGEMENT

When John Nathan-Turner took over as **Doctor Who**'s *producer at the end of 1979 he was like Graham Williams before him, concerned to prevent too much news about forthcoming stories leaking out via the fan 'grapevine'. Amongst the steps he took towards this end were: withholding specific information from the DWAS and fanzine editors; closing the public viewing gallery overlooking the studio whenever a particularly newsworthy episode was being recorded; stepping up studio security; logging in and out all copies of the scripts issued each day during recording; and even putting about disinformation.* **Logopolis** *was the first story for which the public viewing gallery was closed, in an attempt to keep the circumstances of the Doctor's regeneration a secret. Later instances occurred on, amongst others,* **Earthshock, The Five Doctors** *and* **The Caves of Androzani**.

▲ *Dimension 4*, one of many American *Doctor Who* fanzines produced in the 1980s.

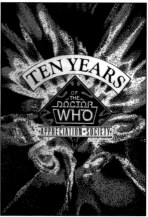

▲ The *Doctor Who* Appreciation Society reached its tenth anniversary in 1986 and celebrated by publishing a special magazine, edited and designed by Mark Stammers, for the anniversary.

WE WERE FRAMED

David J. Howe and Stephen James Walker had both been involved in **Doctor Who** fandom for many years – the former running the **Doctor Who** Appreciation Society's Reference Department and the latter editing the fan-produced reference work **An Adventure in Space and Time** – when they decided to edit and publish a new **Doctor Who** fanzine together in late 1986. Joining them in this venture was Mark Stammers, who had been running the DWAS's Graphics Department and who had got to know Howe through his work for the Society. The fanzine that they published from February 1987 until spring 1993 was called **The Frame** and from the start was unlike most others available in that it was well printed, featured numerous never-before-seen photographs, concentrated on the background of **Doctor Who** and generally avoided negative criticism. The publication was a major success and during its 24-issue run, won the DWAS''Best Fanzine' award every year. It was also voted the best **Doctor Who**-only fanzine by readers of **Doctor Who Magazine**. It was through research for **The Frame** that the editors found themselves in contact with the various publishers and manufacturers of **Doctor Who** products and this led to them acting as advisers for a number of commercial companies, including W. H. Allen and Fine Art Castings. In 1989 they started discussions with Virgin Publishing as to a book-project that would showcase their writing and research and, after much discussion, two series of books were finalised: a range of paperback **Doctor Who Handbooks**, one per Doctor, and also a series of hardbacked illustrated volumes covering the history of **Doctor Who** decade by decade. The book you are holding is the third in the series, having been preceded by **The Sixties** and **The Seventies**.

Nicola Bryant, Patrick ▶ Troughton, Colin Baker, Janet Fielding and Mark Strickson take part in a sponsored walk in aid of Banardo's in 1984.

1988, and would remain in that post for just over a year. At the beginning of 1989 Craig Hinton took over the co-ordinator's role from Beech, who in turn replaced Roxburgh's successor, Andrew Hair (1988-89), as convention organiser. *TARDIS* meanwhile re-emerged as a separate publication, now in A4 rather than the traditional A5 format, with quarterly issues edited by Mark Wyman. Andrew Martin and Andy Lane saw out the last three months of the eighties as editors of *Celestial Toyroom*, standing in until a permanent replacement for Robb could be found.

The eighties saw the DWAS losing its previous monopoly on the staging of UK *Doctor Who* conventions as, particularly during the second half of the decade, other fan groups became increasingly active in this area. Phoenix Promotions, a body set up and headed by Zeus after his departure from the DWAS, held events in Manchester in 1985 and 1986 and in London in 1987; Graeme Wood of the DWAS's Merseyside Local Group (MLG) organised a series of popular conventions in Liverpool, starting with Monstercon in 1986; the Falcon team made Bath the venue for their three gatherings mounted in 1986, 1987 and 1988; and there were many other examples ranging from small-scale local group meetings to major · events with hundreds of attendees.

In the field of reference publications, too, the DWAS found itself facing competition as, following his departure from the executive, Bentham formed his own CyberMark Services organisation. The flagship CMS publication was *Doctor Who – An Adventure in Space and Time*. Devised by Tim Robins and Gary Hopkins, this had a loose-leaf format and was intended to build up, in monthly instalments, into a complete history of the series. The first release, covering the series' opening episode *An Unearthly Child*, was issued in May 1980. The publication was edited initially by Robins, then by Hopkins and finally, from 1983 to 1987, by Stephen James Walker, who in 1982 had launched another loose-

leaf CMS publication, the Data-File story synopsis series (co-operating with the DWAS to ensure that its coverage differed from that of their Plotlines series).

Robins decided to bring *Doctor Who – An Adventure in Space and Time* to an end once it had completed its coverage of the third Doctor's era, but Bentham subsequently launched a successor publication entitled *In-Vision* to document the remainder of the series' history. This had an A4 magazine format and was edited initially by Justin Richards and Peter Anghelides.

Apart from *Celestial Toyroom* and Marvel's *Doctor Who Magazine*, in which news was generally scant and consisted mainly of brief details about forthcoming stories, the other main source of current *Doctor Who* information during the eighties was a monthly fanzine entitled *Doctor Who Bulletin* – referred to as *DWB* for short and renamed *Dreamwatch Bulletin* in 1989. This was launched in 1983 by editor and publisher Gary Levy (who later changed his surname to Leigh) and went on to become highly successful. In contrast to *Celestial Toyroom* and *Doctor Who Magazine*, which tended to report news and current events without comment, *DWB* was noted as having a highly outspoken and controversial editorial style. It started out with a fairly positive attitude towards *Doctor Who* and its producer but then, following the cancellation of the original season twenty-three, took on a far more negative stance.

DWB was at the forefront of a more general trend in fanzines towards the airing of strongly negative criticism of the series – something that on occasion even degenerated into vitriolic personal attacks on members of the cast and production team, particularly Nathan-Turner. The closing years of the decade saw a reaction against this as a number of new fanzines emerged that took a more balanced and positive attitude towards the appreciation of *Doctor Who*. These titles – foremost amongst which were *Private Who*, edited by Guy Daniels (1985-1988), John Ingleton (1985-1986), John B. McLay (1988-1989) and Rod Ulm (1989), and *The Frame*, produced and edited by Howe, Stammers and Walker (all from 1987 onwards) – typically had an A4 format, boasted a high standard of production and featured in-depth factual and analytical articles illustrated with numerous rare and previously unpublished photographs.

Doctor Who fandom had continued to grow in strength, sophistication and diversity during the eighties and was in very healthy shape as it moved forward into the nineties.

CHAPTER TWENTY-THREE

Welcome to the Toyshop

By the start of the eighties, the BBC had already effectively split into two separate organisations: BBC Television, which made and transmitted programmes; and BBC Enterprises, which exploited the programmes commercially.

Roy Williams had been joined in the licensing division of BBC Enterprises by Chris Crouch and between them they looked after this side of the organisation through the eighties. *Doctor Who* formed a large part of their workload as there was ever more interest in the production of spin-off items.

Whereas in the sixties and seventies, the interest had been primarily from large, established book publishers and toy manufactures, in the eighties, it was the small fan-led concerns which dominated. Organisations like Whomobilia, BCP Promotions, Sevans Models, Who Dares Publishing, Reeltime Pictures and Mediaband had all come into existence through a fan demand for product, and in many cases were set up and run by fans. There were numerous demands for licences for small, one-off projects which the BBC were generally reluctant to grant, feeling that their royalty would not be worth the cost of issuing a licence.

Along with the swell of demand for *Doctor Who* products came the establishment of a second key line, which, along with W. H. Allen's range of novelisations and factual hardback books, would go on to dominate *Doctor Who* merchandise into the nineties. This was BBC Video's range of *Doctor Who* releases. There were also some casualties with World International Publishing's *Doctor Who* Annual, up to that point the longest running range of *Doctor Who* merchandise, ceasing publication following the 1985 release of an Annual for 1986. Fine Art Castings also underwent a boom and a subsequent decline during the decade, producing the most comprehensive and accurate range of *Doctor Who* models up to that time.

Another factor in the eighties were the great technological strides that placed the ability to create basic merchandisable items like T-shirts and badges into the price range of just about anyone. Because of this, it is almost impossible to document accurately all the items issued during the decade in question. A large number of unofficial and unlicensed items appeared, often being produced in small numbers and sold exclusively at *Doctor Who* conventions both in the UK and in America. Some of these are documented in this chapter, but others no doubt existed.

Generally, merchandise produced by fans and fan clubs on a non-commercial basis – and there was an

▲ *Doctor Who* bathroom tiles.

A selection of activity books
▼ released during the eighties.

incredible amount of it, ranging from calendars and diaries to badges, pens, magazines, mugs and videos – has for reasons of space been omitted from this chapter. Some of it is however mentioned in Chapter Twenty-Two.

ACTIVITY BOOKS

The activity publications in the eighties were split between two publishers: W. H. Allen and Methuen Children's Books.

In 1981 W. H. Allen published **The Doctor Who Quiz Book** by Nigel Robinson. This contained some very taxing questions requiring a fairly in-depth knowledge of *Doctor Who* to answer. Robinson followed this up with **The Doctor Who Crossword Book** in 1982, a second Quiz Book in 1983 and a third in 1985.

By 1983, it was obvious that *Doctor Who* was big business, so the number of tangential *Doctor Who* books published by W. H. Allen started to increase. **The Doctor Who Cookbook** was by Gary Downie, a production assistant at the BBC and a great friend of John Nathan-Turner's. This collected together recipes from a large number of the cast and crew of *Doctor Who* both past and present. **The Doctor Who Pattern Book** was by Joy Gammon, a well-known knitter and clothes designer. **Brain-Teasers and Mind-Benders** was a book compiled by 16-year-old fan Adrian Heath. Mark Harris meanwhile created **Build the TARDIS**, a large format book containing press-out components. Both these latter titles had initial print runs of 20,000 copies.

Methuen Children's Books' titles were all written by

Michael Holt. The **Doctor Who Quiz Books** were published in paperback form during 1982 and 1983. They contained stories, information, games, quizzes and puzzles where the fifth Doctor and his companions explored the worlds of Dinosaurs, Science, Magic and Space respectively. The initial proof cover for the *Quiz Book of Dinosaurs* was changed at Nathan-Turner's request after he pointed out on 28 July 1982 that the photograph of Peter Davison they had used made him look as though he had no eyes. He also requested a change to the back cover text, to use the words 'the Doctor' rather than 'Doctor Who' when talking about the character. In 1985, Holt created a **Doctor Who Puzzle Book** from the same publishers while his *Quiz Book of Space* and *Quiz Book of Science* were picked up as a hardcover edition by Severn House.

ANNUALS

By 1980 the format of the **Doctor Who Annual** from World International had changed little. It still consisted of a mixture of text and comic strip stories, punctuated with factual features about space travel. Although the Annuals featured no credits for authors or artists, Paul Crompton handled the artwork for the 1980 Annual with Glenn Rix taking over from 1981 to 1983. Mel Powell (who had handled the strip stories from 1981) took over for the final two Annuals. All the Annuals in the eighties had photographic covers.

For the 1982 Annual (published in September 1981), although Peter Davison had been cast as the Doctor, there were no photographs available of him in costume, necessitating the use of a photograph of his head only on the cover. This Annual also saw editor Brenda Apsley taking an active role in managing the content and a factual piece about the TARDIS appeared along with the space related features.

For the 1983 Annual (September 1982), Apsley requested that World be allowed to include more factual material and Nathan-Turner agreed, despite his reservations about the general quality of the books. When the 1983 Annual appeared, it contained, along with the fiction, factual pieces on the Visual Effects Department, the costume design for the fifth Doctor, set design and costumes and on Nathan-Turner himself. Nathan-Turner was not at all happy with the final product and in a memo dated 21 July 1982 to BBC Enterprises he suggested taking the Annual away from World and offering it elsewhere. Eventually he agreed to meet with a representative from World and on 20 September 1982 agreed to them keeping the license.

The BBC initially withdrew the offer for a 1985

The *Doctor Who* annuals released during the eighties. ▼

Annual (September 1984), although the content had been agreed with Nathan-Turner, apparently because World had published an Annual for *Top of the Pops* without fully gaining BBC consent. This was a temporary delay and the BBC eventually agreed to the Annual going ahead on 4 January 1984. This time Apsley's factual material covered the designers and visual effects and was illustrated with colour photographs and designs.

Early in 1984 Janet Fielding expressed concern that photographs of her had been used without proper clearance and payment. This resulted in Equity and the BBC agreeing a new deal for all artistes appearing in BBC copyright *Doctor Who* photographs and artwork used in commercial publications. More details of this can be found in the section on Novelisations. At the start of 1985, the BBC made a claim for back-payment of copyright from World on photographs used in the 1983, 1984 and 1985 Annuals.

It seems that the cumulative effect of all these problems was that World dropped the *Doctor Who* Annual following the 1986 edition (September 1985). In a letter to the BBC, they explained that the 1985 Annual had not been successful for them, and that with the absence of *Doctor Who* from television – this was during the break between seasons twenty-two and twenty-three – they had decided not to proceed with the license.

There are few sales figures available for the *Doctor Who* Annuals, but it is known that the 1981 Annual sold around 61,800 units, the 1982 Annual around 44,500 units and the 1983 Annual around 46,000 units.

Also published in 1982 was a 1983 **K-9 Annual** inspired by the *K-9 And Company* spin off show. Nathan-Turner was approached about this on 8 June 1981 and had no objections to the title being published.

The K-9 and 'Make Your Own Adventure' books.

Two other titles should be noted. The first was published in 1981 by World and was called **Doctor Who – Adventures In Time and Space**. This collected together material from past *Doctor Who* books published by World including the 1976 Ty-Phoo Tea promotional book. In 1985, the Galley Press, an imprint of the booksellers W. H. Smith, published **Doctor Who Special**, another similar compilation of stories from past *Doctor Who* Annuals. This had an initial print run of 20,000 copies. The publishers were reprimanded by the BBC for using the BBC's own logo on the cover, which they were not permitted to do. This title was available in an American edition called **Doctor Who: Journey Through Time** published by Crescent Books in 1986.

BOOKS

With the continued success of K-9 in the TV series, David Martin, who with Bob Baker had created the character, wrote a series of four **K-9 picture books** published by Sparrow Books in 1980 for a very young market. Each title featured a story revolving around K-9, told through simple language and full-page artwork pictures by R.C.S. Graphics Ltd. The four titles were 1: *K9 and the Time Trap*, 2: *K9 and the Beasts of Vega*, 3: *K9 and the Zeta Rescue* and 4: *K9 and the Missing Planet*.

In *K9 and the Time Trap*, K-9 enters a time trap in space wherein the betrayed Time Lord Omegon resides. Omegon was once a great engineer who created the system that gave the Time Lords time travel. He was betrayed and marooned in the time trap. This was based on the story of Omega from season ten's *The Three Doctors*, also written by Baker and Martin. The other titles did not feature any material inspired by the TV series, and, indeed, departed from established continuity by giving K-9 a spacecraft of his own called K-NEL.

'Make Your Own Adventure' type books had become very popular in the early eighties and on 8 May 1984, an approach was made to BBC Enterprises by Clare Dannatt to produce what she described as a Plot-As-You-Go book called *Save the Doctor*. BBC Enterprises were enthusiastic but discovered that, unknown to them, Nathan-Turner had already given an unofficial go-ahead to publishers Severn House to produce a series of books with the same basis. This unofficial agreement was formalised on 26 June 1984 and Severn House eventually published in 1986 a series of *Doctor Who* related titles under the generic title **Make Your Own Adventure With Doctor Who**.

Aside from *Crisis In Space* by Michael Holt, these

PROMOTIONS

The only major promotion of note came in 1986 when **Golden Wonder** joined forces with Marvel Comics and gave away a small comic book with each of their multi-packs. There were six comic books to collect, featuring abridged colour artwork stories from **Doctor Who Magazine**, although Peri had been removed from all the frames. The crisp and snack packets were also emblazoned with the **Doctor Who** logo for the period of the promotion and advertised copies of the 1987 **Doctor Who** Calendar, a special edition of which was printed up for this purpose.

In 1987 Marvel Comics joined forces with the Berni Inn chain of restaurants and gave away special editions of issue 122 of **Doctor Who Magazine** to children who dined at the restaurant for the duration of the promotion. The issue was the same as the standard issue 122, except that the cover featured a 'Berni Funtime' flash on the bottom corner, and the price was amended to 'free'.

When **Doctor Who** faced cancellation in 1985, both the **Daily Star** and the **Sun** ran campaigns to re-instate it to the screen. As a part of the campaign, readers could send off for **stickers** proclaiming loyalty to the cause, and each newspaper produced its own design of sticker.

JIGSAWS

Titan's Script books, the Doctor Who diary and Quinn & Howitt's Doctor Who fun books.

books were all by writers who had worked on the TV series: David Martin (*Garden of Evil* and *Search for the Doctor*), Philip Martin (*Invasion of the Ormazoids*), Pip and Jane Baker (*Race Against Time*) and William Emms (*Mission to Venus*). Emms' title was actually based on an unused TV story, *The Imps*, that had at one point been considered for inclusion in the series' fourth season in 1966.

The idea behind the books was that readers were asked to make decisions at certain points in the plot which took them to different parts of the book, guiding the Doctor and his companions through the events to emerge unscathed at the end. Events were shaped in David Martin's two titles by the rolling of dice and in the other books by simply making a decision about where to go next.

In Martin's *Search for the Doctor*, the characters of Omega (from *The Three Doctors*) and Drax (from season sixteen's *The Armageddon Factor*) appeared and in the Bakers' *Race Against Time*, the Rani (from season twenty-two's *The Mark of the Rani*) was the main villainess. The books' covers and internal illustrations were by American fan Gail Bennett. They were also available in packs, each containing two titles, and the individual titles were released in America by Ballantine/Young under the umbrella title *Find Your Fate*.

W. H. Allen's *Doctor Who Classics*.

Alongside their ongoing programme of new novelisations, W. H. Allen also released eight *Doctor Who* Gift Sets which each collected together four of the novelisations in a boxed set. The first two gift sets were released in 1982 and they were then issued at the rate of two a year until the end of 1985.

A *Doctor Who* diary was proposed by an unknown company in October 1983 but nothing came of it. However, in 1985, a **pocket diary** was released by International Scripts. This featured a wrap-around cover of Andrew Skilleter's artwork for the Target novelisation of *The Web of Fear*. Inside there was a brief article on the show and listings of the Target books available; where in the world *Doctor Who* has been shown; fan club addresses; and the Doctor's companions.

During a 1988 stock take, W. H. Allen discovered that, despite their huge sales figures, they had almost one million copies of the *Doctor Who* Target paperbacks in their warehouse. Therefore, in an attempt to convert some of that stock into cash, on 19 May 1988 they proposed starting up a *Doctor Who* **Classics** series of books which would allow them to repackage the already printed stock.

There were seven books released in the *Doctor Who Classics* series and they were published under W. H. Allen's Star imprint, rather than the Target imprint. Two recovered novels were featured in each book and the collections were: *The Dalek Invasion of Earth / The Crusaders*, *The Dominators / The Krotons* (which replaced the proposed teaming of *The Krotons* with *The Seeds of Death*), *The Myth Makers / The Gunfighters*, *The Dæmons / The Time Monster*, *The Face of Evil / The Sunmakers*, *The Mind of Evil / The Claws of Axos* and *The Seeds of Doom / The Deadly Assassin*.

The idea of *Doctor Who* scripts being published, rather than novelisations of them, had been around for some time. In June 1985 the BBC had suggested the publishing of scripts but nothing came of this. In 1988, however, Titan Books picked up a licence to produce a range of *Doctor Who Script Books*, edited by John McElroy. McElroy had been an active member of the *Doctor Who* Appreciation Society for several years, and ran the DWAS' overseas membership department before leaving to set up his own company, Whomobilia, selling licensed *Doctor Who* photographs.

The first script book was of the first *Doctor Who* adventure, *100,000 BC*, and was published under the title *The Tribe of Gum*. The book featured a cover by Dave McKean, a factual section written by Jan Vincent-Rudzki (who had helped in the setting up of the *Doctor Who* Appreciation Society in the seventies), covering a little of the behind the scenes making of the story, cast and credits lists and the scripts themselves. It had originally been planned to include as an added bonus the script for the untransmitted pilot episode, but this was dropped apparently at the insistence of Nathan-Turner. McElroy also chose to edit the scripts so that they reflected what had actually been transmitted rather than what the original script contained.

There were a further three script books published in the eighties, and they followed the same format as the first. The books released were *The Daleks* (cover by Tony Clark), *The Talons of Weng-Chiang* (cover by Duncan Fegredo) and *The Tomb of the Cybermen* (cover by Tony Clark).

Looking for ways to supplement the schedule of Target paperbacks published, W. H. Allen commissioned novelisations of some of the unused scripts for the abandoned twenty-third season (see Chapter Fourteen). In the latter part of 1989, novelisations of **The Nightmare Fair** and **The Ultimate Evil** were published.

Another W. H. Allen initiative was a series of books called **The Companions of Doctor Who** which was launched in 1986 with Tony Attwood's **Turlough and the Earthlink Dilemma**. This novel was subsequently the subject of a dispute when writer Peter Grimwade claimed that Turlough was his copyright character and that the BBC had no right to license a book which featured him in a dramatic context without seeking permission. After a protracted series of negotiations between Grimwade's agent and the BBC's lawyers which involved both former script editor Eric Saward and the Writer's Guild, the BBC ended up paying compensation to Grimwade while W. H. Allen escaped any form of formal retribution as they were seen as innocent parties – the novel had, after all, been licensed by the BBC. This action resulted in the *Doctor Who* production office being ever more careful about who ended up owning the copyright on regular characters in the TV series. As a gesture of good faith, Peter Grimwade was offered a publishing contract by W. H. Allen for an original novel of his own. The novel was called *Robot* and allegedly featured many characters and situations which reflected life behind the scenes on *Doctor Who*.

There were two further books in *The Companions of Doctor Who* series. The first, **Harry Sullivan's War** (original title: *Harry Sullivan and the War of Nerves*), was also published in 1986 and was written by actor Ian Marter. It featured Harry Sullivan, the character he had portrayed on TV in seasons twelve and thirteen, becoming involved in espionage. There was

an intention for Marter to pen a sequel, a project which was under discussion at the time of his death in 1986. Also at this time, Janet Fielding, who played Tegan in the TV series, was involved in discussions about a book project and Richard Franklin, who had played Captain Mike Yates during the Pertwee era, also submitted a proposal for a novel featuring the character of Yates. Nothing came of these discussions. The third and final title in the series was a novelisation, **K9 and Company**, by Terence Dudley, based on the *Doctor Who* spin off, *K-9 and Company: A Girl's Best Friend* (see Chapter Nineteen), published in 1987. In October 1981, W. H. Allen had been interested in novelising the stories in the projected *K-9 and Company* series but this had come to nothing when the series was not made.

Tim Quinn and Dicky Howett, who had been providing the regular humorous *Doctor Who?* comic strip in *Doctor Who Magazine* (see Magazines) for several years, put together two all-new collections of their work. The first was called **The Doctor Who Fun Book** and was published in 1987 by W. H. Allen with an initial print run of 30,000 copies. This was followed in 1988 by **It's Bigger on the Inside**, published by Marvel Comics.

Finally, in 1984, W. H. Allen published **Doctor Who – Dalek Omnibus**, a hardback edition collecting together Terrance Dicks' novelisations of *The Daleks Invasion of Earth*, *Day of the Daleks* and *Planet of the Daleks*.

Of tangential interest was a book called *The BBC Radiophonic Workshop – The First 25 Years*. Published in 1983 by the BBC and written by Desmond Briscoe and Roy Curtis-Bramwell, this was an illustrated history of the BBC's Radiophonic Workshop. An entire chapter was given over to *Doctor Who*, and also

▲ The *Companions of Doctor Who* series, together with the novelisations of two unused stories for the abandoned twenty-third season.

GREETINGS

Two mass-market greetings cards are known to have been released in the eighties which featured **Doctor Who**. The first was issued by Athena International in their Recycled World series and featured a woman being chased by three giant cans of hair spray chanting 'Exterminate … Exterminate'. The other was from Camden Graphics numbered BG134 and called **Hector's House**. The front depicted some popular TV shows – **Hector's House**, **Thunderbirds**, **Daleks** (not **Doctor Who** itself) and **Basil Brush** – and went on to imply that recipients of the card were old if they remembered them.

detailed in the book were the careers of such *Doctor Who* stalwarts as Dick Mills and Brian Hodgson (special sounds devisers) and many other composers and musicians who worked on the series.

Other proposed titles for one reason or other failed to reach fruition during this period. An illustrated hard-cover book on 15 years of *Doctor Who* was suggested in May 1979 by Denis Segrue of Denis Alan Print; and a *Doctor Who* pop-up book suggested by David Booth Publishing in November 1983. In 1984 novels of an American stage play and Richard Franklin's *Recall UNIT* play were suggested, but both were rejected by the BBC. A *Doctor Who Comic Book* was suggested in February 1985, the idea being to reprint comic strips which had appeared in *TV Comic*, *Countdown* and *TV Action* in the seventies. The BBC was unable to grant a licence as it conflicted with existing contractual commitments. In February 1986, Saward suggested an 'official' biography of the Doctor be produced but, although Nathan-Turner supported the project, nothing came of it. A novelisation of the Argo record *Doctor Who and the Pescatons* was proposed in February 1987 and a

Peshawear's *Doctor Who* ▲ gloves.

Mothercare's *Doctor Who* ▲ slippers.

novelisation of the stage play *The Ultimate Adventure* in March 1989.

CLOTHING

1980 saw the release of the most unlikely piece of *Doctor Who* merchandise ever. It was British Home Stores' **Doctor Who underpants**. Perhaps because of the novelty value, they did quite well with a total of around 46,000 units sold.

A company called Deanem Ltd produced a **Dalek Hat** in 1985. This was a baseball cap headpiece with a Dalek eye-stalk mounted on the front and attached to the top of the hat by a length of 'invisible' plastic cotton so that it bounced as the wearer moved. The eye-stalk was made from felt filled with an expanded foam material.

In 1985 a range of **Doctor Who gloves** was produced by Peshawear UK Ltd in a number of sizes. These black and silver items were adorned on the back of the hand area with a blue neon *Doctor Who* logo.

Dapol produced a complete **Doctor Who outfit** in 1988 based on the seventh Doctor's costume. It included a fawn jacket, green checked trousers, a question-mark pullover and paisley scarf. To go with this, they brought out a **Mel outfit** based on that worn by the character in *Time and the Rani*: a pink and white top and a pair of white trousers. In 1989 Dapol also produced a larger-sized **Doctor Who pullover** with the question-mark motif.

In 1989 Mothercare brought out a pair of child's **pyjamas** in blue and white with black collar and cuffs, featuring an image of the TARDIS and a Dalek and the words 'The Time Lord Doctor Who' on the front. There was also a matching pair of **slippers** available.

The eighties saw a phenomenal array of T-shirts and sweat shirts being produced featuring *Doctor Who* logos, Daleks, Cybermen, K-9, the Doctor and assorted combinations of these together with other images from the programme. There were also several baseball caps available.

One item that didn't make it was a *Doctor Who* scarf which Luke Eyres Ltd wanted to produce in 1980. The idea was dropped after the company's contact with the BBC was killed in a car crash.

FACTUAL BOOKS

Although there had been a few factual books and publications about *Doctor Who* made available in the seventies, it was in the eighties that these became more prevalent.

Wardrobe of a fan: *Doctor Who* items from the eighties, including the TARDIS Tent from D. Dekker.

The first title to see print was one of a series of semi-educational books looking at different jobs. **A Day With A TV Producer** took as its subject Nathan-Turner, who at the time was just starting as *Doctor Who*'s producer. Author Graham Rickard followed Nathan-Turner on what the book claimed was a 'typical day' in the life of the producer, taking in all the aspects which go to make up the job. In fact the book compressed the entire production process of *The Leisure Hive* into one day, with meetings with designers, rehearsals, location filming, studio recording and many other activities all taking place. In total there were 54 subjects covered, all with accompanying photographs.

Probably the most successful factual book yet published about *Doctor Who* first saw print in 1981. Frenchman Jean-Marc Lofficier had been writing about science fiction and fantasy for many years for the French magazine *L'Ecran Fantastique*, and, in the course of writing a dossier on *Doctor Who* – eventually published in issues 23 and 24 – had corresponded with Terrance Dicks. On seeing the final dossier, Dicks felt that it was worth bringing to a wider audience and spoke to W. H. Allen. Editor Christine Donougher liked the idea and the updated dossier was split by W. H. Allen into a two-volume guide collectively called **The Doctor Who Programme Guide**. The first volume was a story-by-story look at the series, with cast lists, synopses and transmission dates. The second volume was an encyclopaedic view of the characters, places, monsters and other things mentioned in the context of *Doctor Who*'s fictional history. The books sold well and, although containing some errors and some editorial material linking together dates and events which had not been taken from the television series, provided for the first time an extensive guide to *Doctor Who* (prior to this the only material available had been the 1973 *Radio Times'* tenth anniversary special and Terrance Dicks and Malcolm Hulke's 1972 book *The Making of Doctor Who,* which had been revised and re-issued in 1976). The first volume of *The Doctor Who Programme Guide* was updated and corrected in 1989, maintaining the title's status as the definitive reference work about the series to that date.

1982 saw publication of **Doctor Who – The Making of a Television Series** by Alan Road with photographs by Richard Farley. This followed the production of *The Visitation* and covered all the different stages that the story went through before it reached the screen. Although the text was in places somewhat simplistic, the book contained many photographs showing all the facets of the TV production.

It was in 1983 that W. H. Allen entered the world

of the large-format illustrated book. They wanted a publication to celebrate the twentieth anniversary of the show, and in November 1982 Donougher suggested an Art Book which would contain 96 pages and 40 full colour illustrations. This idea fell through and instead the idea of doing a history of the programme was born. W. H. Allen's Managing Director, Bob Tanner, brought in Peter Haining to write the book, which had the working title *Two Decades Through Time and Space.*

Doctor Who – A Celebration, as it was retitled for publication, covered the twenty-year history through text and pictures. Fan historian Jeremy Bentham, who had run the *Doctor Who* Appreciation Society's Reference Department in the seventies and who had been the primary writer on the early issues of *Doctor Who Weekly* (see Magazines) in 1979 and 1980, was asked to provide the factual history of the TV series in an extensive chapter detailing the stories, while Haining brought together a fairly concise history of the development of the show. Although it contained a few factual errors and some material that was apocryphal, the book sold phenomenally well, even reaching the number one best-seller slot in the Chicago *Tribune*, and W. H. Allen realised that there was a large market for this sort of publication.

Haining followed up this book with a further four titles, each taking a slightly different view of the TV programme. 1984's **The Key To Time** was a diary of *Doctor Who*'s production from 1963 to what was then the present day. In fact some of the dates were wrong, and the book was, by and large, less accurate than the

▲ The Peter Haining collection.

The leather-bound edition ▲
of Haining's *The Key to Time*.

UNPUBLISHED

Titles mooted but not produced included a collection of **Doctor Who** *Target cover artwork proposed in August 1985. Although the BBC had no objections, the idea was eventually dropped by W. H. Allen in June 1986. A large-format paperback book looking at the making of* **The Mark of the Rani** *was proposed by W. H. Allen in September 1985, but this was vetoed by Nathan-Turner as he felt that the production was not typical of* **Doctor Who**. **The Lost Stories** *was proposed to W. H. Allen in August 1988 by Adrian Rigelsford. Nathan-Turner rejected this proposal partly due to the fact that stories that had been rejected by the production team – the book's intended focus – were not strictly 'lost' and that the proposal was misleading in that respect.*

Another publication proposed late in 1989 was **Daleks**. *The concept was originated by David J. Howe, Stephen James Walker, Mark Stammers and Tony Clark partly as a potential follow-up to the* **Cybermen** *book. Howe and Stammers had been involved with the* **Doctor Who** *Appreciation Society, in running the Reference and Graphics Departments respectively; Walker had, amongst other things, been involved in editing the reference work* **Doctor Who – An Adventure in Space and Time**; *and Clark was a popular fan artist. Ultimately the project fell through in February 1990 as Terry Nation's agents refused to license the book, stating that it would 'breach the competitive clause in the agreement for* **The Official Doctor Who & the Daleks Book** *published by St Martin's Press'. The clause stated that the author would not publish or cause to be published a work that competed with the book in question. Nation's agents felt that granting permission for a book to be published in England would compete with a book that was licensed only for America.*

other Haining volumes. It was illustrated by fan artists who had been requested to send work in by W. H. Allen for a 'mystery project'. This was a cheap way of illustrating the book as fewer photographs were used as a result. The initial print run on this title was 15,000 copies. This was followed in 1985 by **The Doctor Who File**, which took as its basis interviews with key figures in *Doctor Who*'s history and included a number of profiles constructed by Haining from quotes given in other publications. 1986 saw publication of **The Time-Traveller's Guide**, which contained a background article on time travel, a history of the Time Lords and alphabetical listings of Villainous Humanoids, Dangerous Robots, Evil Monsters, Alien Worlds and Spacecraft. The book was rounded off with an update on events since publication of *Doctor Who – A Celebration*, again partly written by Bentham. It had an initial print run of 10,000 copies. The last of Haining's books was **Doctor Who – 25 Glorious Years** in 1988, which covered similar ground to *Doctor Who – A Celebration*. Nathan-Turner, who wanted something special to mark the anniversary, had been concerned that this latest book should not be a re-hash of the previous works. It had an initial print run of 12,000 copies. Almost the entire number went to America, and consequently only the reprinted edition (in November 1988) was available in the UK.

There was one other large format hardback published by W. H. Allen in the eighties. This was Bentham's own **Doctor Who – The Early Years**, published in 1986 with an initial print run of 15,000 copies. During 1983, Bentham had been in contact with Raymond P. Cusick, one of the original BBC designers to have worked on *Doctor Who*, and the man who originally designed the Daleks. Cusick had a wealth of photographic and other material from his work on the series and in March 1984 Bentham proposed a book that would showcase all this while

effectively covering the entire history of the William Hartnell era. *Doctor Who – The Early Years* was hailed by fans as the best factual *Doctor Who* book published up to that point, despite the fact that W. H. Allen's designers had decided to crop and cut out from their backgrounds many of the photographic images. The publication of *Doctor Who – The Early Years* established an important precedent in the use of private photographic material within commercially produced *Doctor Who* books as, after a dispute over this issue, it was established that the photographs within it were Cusick's copyright and that permission for their use need not be obtained from any other party.

Three other titles were published by W. H. Allen in this period. **The Doctor Who Illustrated A–Z** by artist Lesley Standring was a 1985 publication that did not pretend to be definitive and simply took its listing from the paintings completed by Standring. The initial print run was 12,000 copies. Terrance Dicks' **The Doctor Who Monster Book** was re-issued by Target in 1985. **Travel Without the TARDIS** by American fans Jean Airey and Laurie Haldeman was a 1986 paperback guide, inaccurate in places, to *Doctor Who* locations from the point of view of a visiting American.

Severn House published Mark Harris's **The Doctor Who Technical Manual** in 1983. This contained diagrams and plans of many *Doctor Who* monsters, robots and gadgets.

In March 1984, Brenda Gardner, ex-editor at W. H. Allen, wrote to Nathan-Turner asking if he would be willing to write a book for Piccadilly Press for whom she now worked. Nathan-Turner was interested and the result was **The TARDIS Inside Out**, published in 1985. With text by Nathan-Turner and illustrations by Andrew Skilleter, the

A selection of factual books published in the eighties.

book looked at each of the incarnations of the Doctor from the producer's point of view. Although slim on text, the book was very successful and inspired a sequel, **Doctor Who: The Companions**, the following year. This time artist Stuart Hughes was contracted to provide the artwork. Nathan-Turner's text was biased towards those companions with whom he had worked. Nathan-Turner credited both Christopher H. Bidmead and Johnny Byrne in the front of the book, thanking them for co-operating, but Bidmead claimed at the time of publication that he had done no such thing and demanded that publication be suspended until the matter was cleared up. This dispute was not resolved and publication went ahead regardless.

Because sales of the *Doctor Who* titles were good, Piccadilly Press picked up on a proposal from David Saunders, ex-Co-ordinator of the *Doctor Who* Appreciation Society, for a multi-volume encyclopedia of *Doctor Who*. Illustrated by Tony Clark, the first volume of **The Encyclopedia of The Worlds of Doctor Who** appeared in 1987 and covered the letters A to D. The publication of hardback volumes by Piccadilly Press was dependent on a paperback sale to make it commercially viable. Knight Books, the children's imprint of Hodder and Stoughton, picked up the option to the paperbacks. By the end of the eighties, the first two hardbacks had been published, and both had appeared in paperback. Subsequently Knight books, whose operation had been scaled down due to the economic recession, declined to take up the option for future paperbacks, leaving Piccadilly Press with little option but to suspend the series after the third hardback, covering L to R, was eventually published in 1990.

Artist Andrew Skilleter had set up his Who Dares Publishing company to handle his own projects and in 1985 he published **Timeview – The Complete Doctor Who Illustrations of Frank Bellamy**. Written by Bellamy's son, David, this book collected together all the *Doctor Who* artwork that the artist had completed for the *Radio Times* in the seventies. This included covers and small graphics that accompanied programme listings. The second *Doctor Who* book published by the company was 1988's **Cybermen**, a project started back in 1985 by Skilleter and actor-turned-writer David Banks, who had played the Cyber Leader in the eighties Cyberman stories on TV. The book looked at the Cybermen in all their different stories and attempted to weave their history together into a seamless whole. It also contained a factual section written by fan Adrian Rigelsford and was illustrated with Skilleter's artwork, graphics by artist Tony Clark and a selection of photographs. This title was acclaimed by fans as superseding Bentham's *Doctor Who – The Early Years* as the best factual *Doctor Who*

book yet published.

It also became the most expensive *Doctor Who* book yet published when a specialist collectors' limited edition was released. Only seventy-five of these were made available, although the actual number sold fell considerably short of this. Each was individually bound and finished by hand by French artist Cathy Robert with two initials (specified by the purchaser) incorporated into an embossed Cybermark design on the front cover. The book was bound in a silver material, developed by NASA, as thin as cellophane but immensely strong and durable. It came in a black slipcase with a limited edition certificate pasted in, was signed and numbered by Banks, Skilleter and Robert, and had a black satin marker and silvered graphite page edges. The price of this special edition was £95.00 (plus £5.00 postage and packing) and the books were created as they were ordered.

There were four other factual publications of note during this period. First was John Tulloch and Manuel Alvorado's media studies book **Doctor Who – The Unfolding Text** which, as an academic work, was complex and hard-going for the lay-person to read. The book included interviews with the crew on *Kinda* and Bentham advised the authors on aspects of *Doctor Who* history. Second was the **Doctor Who Master Index** to the first 142 issues of *Doctor Who Magazine*. This had been put together by a fan named Murray Easedale and was published in 1989. As Easedale had used a version of the *Doctor Who* logo on the cover, the BBC insisted on payment of a fee with the further condition that more money would be payable on any future editions of the book. Thirdly, author John Peel and Terry Nation, creator of the Daleks, collaborated on a book published only in America by St. Martin's Press. **The Official Doctor Who & the Daleks Book** looked at all the stories in different media in which the Daleks had featured. It also included a history tying all the material together and featured Nation's original synopsis – called *The Survivors* – for the creatures' first ever TV appearance and the original synopsis for a pilot called *The Destroyers* for an unmade American TV series. Finally, visual effects designer Mat Irvine wrote *Doctor Who* **Special Effects** for Hutchinson in 1986. This looked in detail at how some of *Doctor Who*'s many effects had been achieved.

MAGAZINES

Doctor Who Weekly became a monthly magazine from issue 44 onwards and changed its name accordingly to **Doctor Who Monthly**. The magazine's name was to change several times during the eighties as the publication changed editors and

One of the limited edition ▲
busts released by Fine Art
Castings.

styles. Dez Skinn, who had originated the title, stayed as editor until issue 23 when Paul Neary took over. Alan McKenzie was at the helm from issue 49 until issue 97, when Sheila Cranna took over for one issue. Cefn Ridout was in charge from issue 98 until issue 107 when Cranna became editor on a permanent basis. Finally John Freeman took over as editor from issue 137 and saw the magazine through to the end of the eighties. In 1981 the publication won the Eagle Award for Best Comic Magazine.

Although the monthly publication still retained its comic strip, the move was very much away from the somewhat childish approach of the weekly issues and towards a more adult and analytical approach spearheaded by McKenzie and Bentham, the title's regular writer. There were more factual interviews and features, the archives section became steadily more comprehensive and the number of photographs printed also increased. There were features on merchandise and on those who produced it, a regular question/answer column and numerous other features and fillers. The emphasis on factual material was continued following Bentham's departure by Richard Landen, Gary Russell, Richard Marson, David J. Howe and Andrew Pixley, all of whom contributed to the magazine and acted as consultants during the eighties.

Generally the comic strip followed the same Doctor/companion teaming as the TV series and no attempt was made to explain how or why the Doctor changed after each regeneration. The strips were written and drawn by an increasingly diverse range of people as individuals were commissioned for individual stories rather than the approach taken through the sixties and seventies where a single artist was responsible for a run of stories. In 1985 the magazine hit its one hundredth issue and in 1989 it celebrated ten years of publication, no mean feat in a marketplace renowned for short-lived and one-off publications.

Marvel also published numerous **Specials**. Generally each year saw both a Summer and a Winter Special being published, usually themed around different aspects of the series. Another special magazine was published by the *Radio Times* to celebrate the programme's twentieth anniversary in 1983. The idea was suggested to Brian Gearing, the editor of the *Radio Times*, by Nathan-Turner. The structure and content of the special were mapped out over several meetings between Gearing and Nathan-Turner. In charge of the writing was journalist Gay Search and the contents were to cover the making of the show through features on all the different BBC departments that contributed to it.

The **Radio Times Doctor Who 20th Anniversary Special** was received very well indeed and sales were nothing short of phenomenal. In a memo dated 7 November 1983, the Head of Rights and Exports at the BBC noted that Pitman in Australia had ordered 25,000 copies and might order more depending on how the screening of *The Five Doctors* was received. 5000 copies went to New Zealand, the same number to Canada, and even Singapore ordered 200 copies. The American market was catered for by Starlog Communications, who signed a contract to print and distribute copies themselves. Their initial print run was 25,000 copies and they hoped that they would need to reprint. In fact the only slight problem was when copies of the UK edition found their way into America which contravened the contract with Starlog. These copies were hastily brought back to the UK.

A free **magazine/wall chart** was published by the BBC's Information and Education Departments in 1987 as a supplement to the educational series *Zig Zag*. This one-sided fold-out publication featured *The Trial of a Time Lord* and contained photographs and other material on all aspects of the production from planning through design and special effects to editing and publicity. This publication was not commercially available although copies could be obtained at the time by writing to the appropriate BBC department.

MODELS

Stuart Evans had been a fan of *Doctor Who* for many years and was also interested in building models. He therefore worked out the dimensions and constructed a foot-high Dalek which he took up to show Chris Crouch at BBC Enterprises. To his amazement he walked away with a licence to manufacture and produce the kits commercially. Sevans Models, as his company was known, first released the **Dalek kit** in 1984. It was the most accurate model of a Dalek ever to be released. The kit was not simple to put together, however, and contained a great many parts. Evans ensured that sufficient parts were included to enable every type of Dalek up to that point in the series' history to be built.

There was a lengthy delay before the next kits from Sevans were made available. These were an Ice Warrior kit in 1987 and an *Earthshock*-style Cyberman kit in 1988. A Davros kit and a new TV and Movie Dalek kit were announced in 1989, although they were not generally available until 1990.

Fine Art Castings, well known at the time for their range of military pewter models, entered the *Doctor Who* market in 1984 with a range of very accurate and well-crafted **white pewter figures** of the Doctors, companions and enemies. This range expanded through 1985 and 1986 and eventually over 80 different models were issued. Shortly after launching the range with a fourth Doctor figure, a Cyberman and a Dalek, Fine Art Castings started liaising with fan historians Howe and Stammers. This resulted in far greater accuracy in the models – for example, they were to correct an error in the original cast of the 80mm Sea Devil which featured the creature as seen in the 1972 story *The Sea Devils* holding a gun from the later story *Warriors of the Deep* – and also an expanded production schedule of monsters old and new from the series' history.

Fine Art Castings also brought out in 1985 a 'limited edition' set of **metal busts** featuring all six Doctors. Each bust retailed for £9.44, bringing the total for the set to £56.64. Also supplied was a wooden peg-stand on which to display the busts and a certificate of authenticity. The set was limited to 2000 copies. A set of six 'villain' busts was issued in 1986, again in an edition of 2000. The enemies featured were the Celestial Toymaker, an Ice Warrior, the Master, a Voc Robot, a Cyberman and Sil. A Dalek was considered but dropped as it was considered too tricky to produce a bust of something with no obvious head. The villains were chosen to give one well-known enemy from each Doctor's era. Each bust cost £12.30 (total set cost: £73.80) and the set again came with a certificate.

A final range of **metal figures** was produced by Citadel Miniatures in 1985 to tie in with the Fasa

Corporation's *Doctor Who* role-playing game (see Toys). These small 25mm metal figures were far cruder than the Fine Art Castings ones, and in the case of the human characters were barely recognisable. Several different sets were issued, both in the UK and in America.

In 1987, Citadel Miniatures released a set of **plastic Daleks and Cybermen**, again for the gaming market. The box contained 20 Daleks and 20 Cybermen, ideal for staging battles between the two foes.

BCP Promotions was set up by fan Barry Payne to produce and market a **Cybermat kit**, which, once constructed, could be animated using a simple radio-

▲ **A Sevans Dalek. One of the most complex and accurate commercial Dalek model kits ever produced.**

◄ **One of Susan Moore's *Doctor Who* sculptures.**

A selection of Fine Art Castings figures. Over ninety figures and packs of figures were released in three different sizes: 80mm, 40mm and 25mm.

COVER ARTWORK

Numerous different artists were commissioned to work on the Target novelisation covers during the eighties. The main contributors to the range were, however, Andrew Skilleter, Tony Masero, David McAllister and Alister Pearson. A number of commissioned pieces were not ultimately used. The cover for **The Enemy of the World** *was originally commissioned from artist Steve Kyte, but was rejected by W. H. Allen and a new one obtained from Bill Donohoe.* **The Visitation** *was to have sported a painting by David McAllister but Peter Davison's agent objected to the likeness of his client and it was not used. Because Davison's agent was very concerned about artwork depictions of the actor, a decision was taken to use photographs on the covers of the novels for the first time. Therefore no first edition novelisation of a fifth Doctor story featured an artwork image of Davison's face, with the sole exception of* **The Five Doctors.** *The novel of* **Mawdryn Undead** *was originally to*

continued on page 161

The original painting and the final cover for The
▼ **Ambassadors of Death.**

Citadel Miniatures' *Doctor Who* **range.**

control system found in many toy cars. Retailing at £10, the kit sold around 350 units in the two months following its launch in April 1985.

Susan Moore was another fan of the series and had been producing a range of resin figures for the fan market during 1982 and 1983. She was asked by the BBC to apply for a licence to sell the figures on a wider basis, but she instead decided not to progress with the range. Her initial range consisted of three small **resin badges** of an Ice Warrior head, a Robot of Death head (which came in silver, green or black) and a Cybermat as well as small four-and-a-half-inch-high **resin figures** of the fourth Doctor and the Master. Eventually Moore had two different Master figures (one in a cloak and one in a Nehru suit), a Menoptera with thin and fragile clear resin wings, a Robot of Death (which again came in the three colours), a Sontaran and a Time Lord in full ceremonial regalia from *The Deadly Assassin*. She also produced a resin facsimile of the small metal Dinky police box model first released in the fifties, various designs of 'Cyber-logo' as seen on the door of the Cybercontroller's tomb in *The Tomb of the Cybermen* and a range of photographic stickers and keyrings.

NOVELISATIONS

At the end of 1979, a potential threat to the continuation of the **Target Doctor Who novelisations** came when Nick Webb, Editorial Director of New English Library, contacted the BBC. He informed them that he 'would like to write a series of *Doctor Who* paperbacks with rather more substance, both in length and in detail than at presently published by W. H. Allen' and indicated that he had several skilled writers in mind who 'would combine to produce publications on a number of topics'. The BBC's response to this approach was that Webb should be asked to provide some sample chapters. After looking further into the practicalities of publishing *Doctor Who* novels, Webb reluctantly decided that the project would take more time than could be afforded. Another factor was that the

LISTING OF *DOCTOR WHO* NOVELISATIONS 1980-1989

TITLE: Doctor Who °	PUB DATE	PRICE FORMAT
Junior Doctor Who and the Giant Robot	1980	75p p/b
Junior Doctor Who and the Brain of Morbius	1980	£2.95 h/b 85p p/b
and the Underworld	01/80	£3.75 h/b 75p p/b
and the Invasion of Time	02/80	£3.75 h/b 75p p/b
and the Stones of Blood	03/80	£3.75 h/b 75p p/b
and the Androids of Tara	04/80	£3.95 h/b 75p p/b
and the Power of Kroll	05/80	£3.95 h/b 85p p/b
and the Armageddon Factor	06/80	£3.95 h/b 85p p/b
and the Curse of Peladon	07/80	£3.95 h/b
and the Keys of Marinus	08/80	£3.95 h/b 85p p/b
and the Nightmare of Eden	09/80	£3.95 h/b 85p p/b
and the Horns of Nimon	10/80	£3.95 h/b 85p p/b
and the Monster of Peladon	12/80	£3.95 h/b 85p p/b
and the Creature from the Pit	01/81	£4.25 h/b 90p p/b
and the Terror of the Autons	02/81	£4.25 h/b
and the Enemy of the World	03/81	£4.25 h/b 95p p/b (04/81)
and the Green Death	04/81	£4.25 h/b
and the Sea Devils	06/81	£4.25 h/b
and the Cybermen	07/81	£4.50 h/b
and the Day of the Daleks	08/81	£4.50 h/b
and the State of Decay	09/81	£4.50 h/b £1.00 p/b (01/82)
and An Unearthly Child	10/81	£4.95 h/b £1.25 p/b
and the Auton Invasion	11/81	£4.25 h/b
Doctor Who and the Dæmons *	01/82	£4.95 h/b
and the Doomsday Weapon	03/82	£4.95 h/b
and Warriors' Gate	04/82	£4.95 h/b £1.25 p/b
and the Keeper of Traken	05/82	£4.95 h/b £1.25 p/b
and the Leisure Hive	07/82	£4.95 h/b £1.25 p/b
and the Visitation	08/82	£4.95 h/b £1.25 p/b
Full Circle	09/82	£5.25 h/b £1.25 p/b
Logopolis	10/82	£5.25 h/b £1.25 p/b
and the Sunmakers	11/82	£5.25 h/b £1.25 p/b
Time-Flight	01/83	£5.25 h/b £1.35 p/b (04/83)
Meglos	02/83	£5.25 h/b £1.35 p/b (05/83)
Castrovalva	03/83	£5.25 h/b £1.35 p/b (06/83)
Four to Doomsday	04/83	£5.25 h/b £1.35 p/b (07/83)
Earthshock	05/83	£5.25 h/b £1.35 p/b (08/83)
Terminus	06/83	£5.50 h/b £1.50 p/b (09/83)
Arc of Infinity	07/83	£5.50 h/b £1.35 p/b (10/83)
Mawdryn Undead	08/83	£5.50 h/b £1.35 p/b (01/84)
The Five Doctors	11/83	£5.95 h/b £1.50 p/b
Kinda	12/83	£5.95 h/b £1.35 p/b (03/84)
Snakedance	01/84	£5.95 h/b £1.35 p/b (04/84)
Enlightenment	02/84	£5.95 h/b £1.35 p/b (05/84)
The Dominators	04/84	£5.95 h/b £1.50 p/b (07/84)
Warriors of the Deep	05/84	£5.95 h/b £1.50 p/b (08/84)
The Aztecs	06/84	£5.95 h/b £1.50 p/b (09/84)
Inferno	07/84	£5.95 h/b £1.50 p/b (10/84)
The Highlanders	08/84	£5.95 h/b £1.50 p/b (11/84)
Frontios	09/84	£5.95 h/b £1.50 p/b (12/84)
Planet of Fire	10/84	£5.95 h/b £1.50 p/b (01/85)
The Caves of Androzani	11/84	£5.95 h/b £1.50 p/b (02/85)
Marco Polo	12/84	£5.95 h/b £1.50 p/b (04/85)
and the Crusaders	01/85	£5.95 h/b
and the Abominable Snowmen	01/85	£5.95 h/b
The Awakening	02/85	£5.95 h/b £1.50 p/b (06/85)
The Mind of Evil	03/85	£5.95 h/b £1.50 p/b (07/85)
The Myth Makers	04/85	£6.25 h/b £1.50 p/b (09/85)
The Invasion	05/85	£6.25 h/b £1.50 p/b (10/85)
The Krotons	06/85	£6.25 h/b £1.50 p/b (11/85)
The Gunfighters	07/85	£6.25 h/b £1.60 p/b (01/86)
The Two Doctors	08/85	£6.95 h/b £1.75 p/b (12/85)
The Time Monster	09/85	£6.25 h/b £1.60 p/b (02/86)
The Twin Dilemma	10/85	£6.25 h/b £1.60 p/b (03/86)
Galaxy Four	11/85	£6.50 h/b £1.60 p/b (04/86)
Timelash	12/85	£6.50 h/b £1.60 p/b (05/86)
Mark of the Rani	01/86	£6.50 h/b £1.60 p/b (06/86)
The King's Demons	02/86	£6.50 h/b £1.60 p/b (07/86)
The Savages	03/86	£6.95 h/b £1.60 p/b (09/86)
The Giant Robot	04/86	£6.95 h/b
Fury from the Deep	05/86	£7.95 h/b £1.95 p/b (10/86)
The Celestial Toymaker	06/86	£6.95 h/b £1.60 p/b (11/86)
The Seeds of Death	07/86	£6.95 h/b £1.60 p/b (12/86)
Slipback	08/86	£6.95 h/b £1.75 p/b (01/87)
Black Orchid	09/86	£6.95 h/b £1.75 p/b (02/87)
The Ark	10/86	£7.25 h/b £1.75 p/b (03/87)
The Mind Robber	11/86	£7.25 h/b £1.75 p/b (04/87)
The Faceless Ones	12/86	£7.25 h/b £1.75 p/b (05/87)
The Space Museum	01/87	£7.25 h/b £1.80 p/b (06/87)
The Sensorites	02/87	£7.50 h/b £1.95 p/b (07/87)
The Reign of Terror	03/87	£7.50 h/b £1.95 p/b (08/87)
The Romans	04/87	£7.50 h/b £1.95 p/b (09/87)
The Ambassadors of Death	05/87	£7.50 h/b £1.95 p/b (10/87)
The Massacre	06/87	£7.50 h/b £1.95 p/b (11/87)
The Macra Terror	07/87	£7.95 h/b £1.95 p/b (12/87)
The Rescue	08/87	£7.95 h/b £1.95 p/b (01/88)
Terror of the Vervoids	09/87	£7.95 h/b £1.95 p/b (02/88)
The Time Meddler	10/87	£7.95 h/b £1.99 p/b (03/88)
The MysterioUSA Planet	11/87	£7.95 h/b £1.99 p/b (04/88)
Time and the Rani	12/87	£7.95 h/b £1.99 p/b (05/88)
Vengeance on Varos	01/88	£7.95 h/b £1.99 p/b (06/88)
The Underwater Menace	02/88	£7.95 h/b £1.99 p/b (07/88)
The Wheel in Space	03/88	£7.95 h/b £1.99 p/b (08/88)
The Ultimate Foe	04/88	£7.95 h/b £1.99 p/b (09/88)
The Edge of Destruction	05/88	£7.95 h/b £1.99 p/b (10/88)
The Smugglers	06/88	£7.95 h/b £1.99 p/b (11/88)
Paradise Towers	12/88	£1.99 p/b
Delta and the Bannermen	01/89	£1.99 p/b
The War Machines	02/89	£1.99 p/b
Dragonfire	03/89	£1.99 p/b
Attack of the Cybermen	04/89	£1.99 p/b
Mindwarp	06/89	£1.99 p/b
The Chase	07/89	£1.99 p/b
Mission to the Unknown	09/89	£1.99 p/b
The Mutation of Time	10/89	£1.99 p/b
Silver Nemesis	11/89	£1.99 p/b
The Greatest Show in the Galaxy	12/89	£1.99 p/b

NB: *Where a hardback edition is indicated, the publisher was W. H. Allen & Co. Ltd. From Snakedance onwards, the hardback publisher was W. H. Allen & Co. PLC.*
All paperback editions were in the Target imprint of the hardback publisher.
No hardback editions were published from Paradise Towers onwards.
The year shown is the date of the first edition. The publication date of the paperback is shown alongside the paperback price.
*The hardback edition of The Dæmons really did feature the words Doctor Who twice.

number of clearances that had to be obtained to do the novels was prohibitive. He therefore dropped the idea.

W. H. Allen continued their series of novelisations of the *Doctor Who* stories in 1980 but, as with Graham Williams before him, Nathan-Turner was less than happy with the quality of the artwork that was presented for the covers. On 25 February 1980, he singled out the artwork for *The Armageddon Factor* and *The Power of Kroll* as being very poor and later, on 9 June, he commented upon seeing the original artwork for the cover of *The Keys of Marinus* that the TARDIS should be blue and not grey and that the light on the top should be white and not red. These comments were not taken on board by W. H. Allen.

One of the biggest problems to hit the range of books since the paper shortages of 1974 came in 1981, when members of the Writers' Guild went on strike, resulting in many Guild authors not delivering manuscripts to publishers. This had the result of throwing the *Doctor Who* schedule into complete disarray for most of 1981, and only four new novelisations were published as a result. W. H. Allen took the opportunity to publish hardback editions of titles previously unavailable in that format.

Brenda Gardner had left W. H. Allen as editor of the *Doctor Who* range late in 1979 and her place had been taken by Christine Donougher. The relationship between Donougher and Nathan-Turner was not helped by the publication of *The Doctor Who Programme Guide* in 1981. The two-volume work contained some errors but Nathan-Turner was pleased that an erratum slip was included with the hardback volumes. When the next factual book, Nigel Robinson's *Quiz Book*, was pitched by Donougher, Nathan-Turner suggested that Ian Levine, a knowledgeable fan, check the manuscript. This was done, but a few errors still crept through and Levine was unable to get them corrected at proof stage. Donougher told him at the time that the errors would be corrected in any re-print of the book.

One of the innovations introduced by Donougher was to number all the books in the Target range. This was an attempt to rationalise the titles for retailers and was done by numbering the already published books in alphabetical order up to that point, and then numbering them in publication order thereafter. The only problem with this system was where a book was delayed and had to slip in the schedule, resulting in the numbers changing around. This happened to *The Twin Dilemma* and *Vengeance on Varos*.

Around the end of 1982, Nathan-Turner asked that all material relating to the books be passed through his office for clearance. He requested that an epilogue contained within Andrew Smith's novelisation of *Full Circle* be deleted and that material relating to *The Five Doctors* contained in Peter Haining's *Doctor Who – A Celebration* be removed as the book was being published two months before transmission of the story.

After suggesting that a novelisation of the first ever *Doctor Who* story, *100,000 BC,* be published to tie in with the forthcoming *The Five Faces of Doctor Who* repeat season, and also suggesting that the novelisation of *Mawdryn Undead* be tied in with the first transmission (which didn't ultimately happen), Nathan-Turner was enthusiastic when the novelisation of *The Five Doctors* in 1983 was set to appear at the same time as the transmission. He nevertheless made it very clear to the publishers that the book should not go on sale before the publication date of 26 November, and was greatly annoyed when he was told that copies had been on sale as early as two weeks prior to transmission. As a result of this, in a memo dated on the anniversary itself, 23 November, Nathan-Turner requested a meeting with BBC Enterprises to discuss the merchandising of *Doctor Who* in general. He also suggested that Brian Gearing, editor of the *Radio Times*, might be interested in discussing the possibility of editing and publishing the novels through the BBC's own imprint. Ultimately the growing unease between W. H. Allen and *Doctor Who's* producer was smoothed over and the licence to publish the novelisations stayed where it was.

The novelisations were doing phenomenal business. In the four-year period up to the end of 1983, over half a million copies of the books had been sold. In 1983, the royalty gained by the BBC on the W. H. Allen titles was over £35,000, and in the second six-month period of 1984 it was over £23,000.

The next major problem came about when, in October 1984, following months of discussion with Equity, apparently after complaints from Janet Fielding, the BBC decided that clearance was needed by any actor or actress whose likeness was featured on the cover artwork used on the novels. Furthermore, if the artwork had been copied from a photograph, clearance from the owner of the photograph's copyright was also required. This decision affected many *Doctor Who* licence holders and the BBC claimed back-payment of copyright fees from both Marvel Comics and World International for the use of BBC photographs. The BBC later revised their guidelines over the use of artwork. Legally it was all right to use likenesses, they now said, and the copyright clearance aspect was more a courtesy to the artistes involved than a legal requirement.

have featured a different photographic montage of the Doctor and the Brigadier. As **The Twin Dilemma** was the debut adventure for the sixth Doctor, Andrew Skilleter was asked to provide a cover for the novelisation which featured that Doctor. The final cover was printed up in proof form, but Colin Baker's agent, when asked to approve the likeness, suggested that he would like to discuss some form of payment for the use of the image. It seems that W. H. Allen decided not to pursue this line of negotiation and instead hastily commissioned Skilleter to paint another cover for the book, this time without Baker's likeness on. When asked about this later, Baker replied that he was mystified as to why W. H. Allen never even responded to his agent's letter as they would have been quite satisfied with a nominal courtesy payment. For the cover of **Time and the Rani**, W. H. Allen first commissioned a painting from Tony Masero. When the cover was first proofed, however, the designer had not realised that these creatures were hanging from the roof and had placed the image upside down. Masero's painting was then rejected in favour of a special photograph taken by Chris Capstick of the bat-like Tetraps hanging in a cave. An original cover for **The Ultimate Foe** by Alister Pearson featuring the Valeyard and the Inquisitor was rejected due to objections from the artistes concerned and another, featuring Mr Popplewick, commissioned to replace it. The original painting for **The Ambassadors of Death** featured the Doctor with dark hair. Artist Tony Masero was asked to alter it to depict the Doctor with white hair which was closer to the character as seen on television.

▲ Tony Masero's original artwork cover for *Time and the Rani.*

FOREIGN BOOKS

Several foreign language editions of W. H. Allen's Doctor Who novelisations were released in the eighties.

In 1980 Hayakawa Publishing Inc of Japan released at least three of the novels: **The Cave Monsters, The Auton Invasion** *and* **The Day of the Daleks.** *The books featured original cover and internal paintings and were translated into Japanese by Yukio Sekiguchi.*

In 1986 Presença published a series of Portuguese editions, translated by Eduardo Nogueira and Conceição Jardim. The titles in the series were: **Doutor Who e a Invaso Dos Autones** *(The Auton Invasion),* **Doutor Who e os Monstros Das Cavernas** *(The Cave Monsters),* **Doutor Who e os Demonios** *(The Dæmons),* **Doutor Who e a Arma Total** *(The Doomsday Weapon),* **Doutor Who e os Demonios Marinhos** *(The Sea Devils),* **Doutor Who e o Dia Dos Daleks** *(The Day of the Daleks),* **Doutor Who e os Daleks** *(The Daleks),* **Doutor Who e os Cruzados** *(The Crusaders),* **Doutor Who e os Abominaveis Das Neves** *(The Abominable Snowmen)* and **Doutor Who e os Zarbi** *(The Zarbi). All the covers were by Rui Ligeiro with the exception of those for* **The Doomsday Weapon** *and* **The Crusaders,** *which were by an artist called Shanti.*

Also in 1986, a set of eight French adaptations was published by Garancière. The books were 'introduced' by Igor and Grichka Bogdanoff – the hosts of a French children's SF TV show. The titles released were: **Docteur Who – Entre En Scene** *(An Unearthly Child, translated by Jean-Daniel Breque),* **Les Croises** *(The Crusaders, t. André Ruaud),* **Les Daleks** *(The Daleks, t. Gilles Bergal, adapted by Corine Derblum),* **Les Daleks Envahissent la Terre** *(The Dalek Invasion of Earth, t. Roland C. Wagner, a. Corine Derblum),* **Le Cerveau de Morbius** *(The Brain of Morbius, t. Francine Mondolini, a. Corine Derblum),* **Le Masque de Mandragore** *(The Masque of Mandragora, t. Richard D. Nolane, a. Corine Derbulm),* **L'Abominable Hommes des Neiges** *(The Abominable Snowmen, t. Corine Derblum)* and **Meglos** *(Meglos, t. Corine Derbulm). The covers for the French books were painted by an artist called Penichoux.*

Finally, in 1989, three German adaptations were published by Goldmann. Translated by Peter Tuscher (first title) and Bettina Zeller (others), the books utilised cover artwork from the Target novels. The following were released: **Doctor Who und die Invasion der Daleks** *(The Daleks, with cover artwork from* Destiny of the Daleks),* **Doctor Who und das Klompott der Daleks** *(The Dalek Invasion of Earth, with correct cover artwork)* and **Doctor Who und der Planet der Daleks** *(Planet of the Daleks, with correct cover artwork).*

Christine Donougher stopped editing the *Doctor Who* range in 1984. Editorship was then taken on by Nigel Robinson, who stayed with the company for 3 years and oversaw a major schedule of novelising all the older stories, which had not up to that point been done. Many of the authors of the original scripts came to pen the novelisations, with Terrance Dicks and Ian Marter picking up those stories for which the original author declined or was unavailable to do so.

With the novelisations now being produced at the rate of around 12 a year, Robinson realised that before long every televised story would be in print. He therefore approached the BBC on 18 October 1985 about the possibility of commissioning some original *Doctor Who* novels. Nathan-Turner replied that he was not happy to consider this at the time, and suggested deferring the decision to January 1987.

Robinson moved on in April 1987 and editorship of the Target range passed to Sara Barnes for a short while before briefly being taken on by Tim Byrne before finally being taken over by Jo Thurm.

With the programme of novelisations rapidly reaching its end, Thurm approached the BBC on 6 February 1989 to ask again if W. H. Allen could commission original *Doctor Who* adventures to publish as novels. This was one of the final acts performed by Thurm as she then moved on from the range, handing over the reins to Peter Darvill-Evans, who had joined the company as a part-time freelance editor to look after the *Doctor Who* publishing schedule.

Darvill-Evans needed no convincing that there should be some original fiction to complement the novelisations and, following several telephone calls, meetings and a lengthy letter dated 7 July 1989 arguing the case, Nathan-Turner finally agreed on 30 August the same year. All that remained was to work out the format for these new novels, which was done in the latter half of 1989.

The eventual launch of **Doctor Who – The New Adventures** was not to happen for a further two years as, following agreement of the format early in 1990, writers had to be found and commissioned and the books themselves written.

By the end of 1989, the majority of *Doctor Who* stories had been novelised, and those that remained were scheduled for the future – with the notable exception of David Whitaker's two Dalek stories, *The Power of the Daleks* and *The Evil of the Daleks*; Douglas Adams' *Doctor Who* work, *The Pirate Planet, City of Death* and *Shada*; and Eric Saward's Dalek stories

Resurrection of the Daleks and *Remembrance of the Daleks*. The Dalek stories were held up because Terry Nation and his agents were in dispute with W. H. Allen and Saward over the royalty for allowing these stories to be novelised. Adams, who had by now found fame and fortune with his *Hitch-Hiker's Guide to the Galaxy* series, also proved unwilling to allow novelisation of his stories. However, he later used plot elements from both *Shada* and *City of Death* as the basis for his 1987 novel *Dirk Gently's Holistic Detective Agency*.

Other titles suggested in this period included a Braille edition of *An Unearthly Child* which was proposed in March 1984. It is not known if such an edition was ever produced.

RECORDS AND RECORDINGS

The original **Doctor Who theme** had been available on BBC Records right up to 1980. When the TV theme was updated for the eighteenth season by Peter Howell, BBC Records released an updated record with a photograph of Tom Baker on the sleeve. The same record was then re-released each time a new Doctor took over, with the sleeve suitably updated with a new photograph. When Dominic Glynn updated the theme in 1986, the BBC decided to release three versions: an ordinary single; a 12-inch single packaged in a sleeve with a hologram on the cover and a piece of artwork of the TARDIS console; and a cassette tape packaged in the same way. This was to be the last version of the theme released by BBC Records and Tapes in the eighties as the Keff McCulloch version (used for all Sylvester McCoy's stories) was never released as a single.

A selection of Doctor Who recordings on cassette.

It was in 1983, to coincide with the programme's twentieth anniversary, that Dick Mills, who had worked on *Doctor Who* providing special sound effects since 1972, finally persuaded the BBC that a compilation of incidental music was a good idea, and **Doctor Who – The Music** was released. This was a collection of music and sound effects primarily from the eighteenth and nineteenth seasons, but a bonus was the inclusion of some of Malcolm Clarke's score for *The Sea Devils*. In 1985 **Doctor Who – The Music II** was released, a further compilation, this time without sound effects and covering the twentieth and twenty-first seasons. For this collection the composers went back to their original tapes and compiled sequences of music together, giving a sort of symphonic tour through the moods and feelings of a particular story.

In 1988 for the twenty-fifth anniversary, McCulloch compiled some of his incidental music tracks onto **The Doctor Who 25th Anniversary Album**. It featured material from *Delta and the Bannermen*, *Remembrance of the Daleks*, *Paradise Towers* and *Time and the Rani*.

The theme music to the *Doctor Who* spin-off programme **K-9 and Company** was released as a single in two versions; the first released in 1982 by Solid Gold Records with a plain sleeve and an unrelated 'B' side; and the second issued by BBC Records in 1983 for the American market with a picture sleeve and Peter Howell's suite of music for *The Leisure Hive* taken from '*Doctor Who* – The Music II' on the 'B' side.

There were several novelty records released during the eighties that were either about or inspired by *Doctor Who*. In 1980 a group called Blood Donor released a single called 'Doctor …?'. This was later re-released in 1984 as a 'B' side to a re-release of the 1972 Jon Pertwee single 'Who Is The Doctor?'. The Pertwee track was also released by the BBC for the American market in 1983 with Malcolm Clarke's *The Sea Devils* suite from '*Doctor Who* – The Music' on the 'B' side. 1981 saw the group The Human League include a track called simply 'Tom Baker' on the 'B' side of their single 'Boys and Girls' (Virgin VS 395). In 1983 an Australian group, Bullamakanka, released a single called 'Dr. Who is Gonna Fix It' and in 1985 a combination of recording artists and *Doctor Who* stars got together for the first ever *Doctor Who* charity record, 'Doctor In Distress'. The latter record was organised by fan Paul Mark Tamms and Jeff Weston, Managing Director of Record Shack Records, and written and produced by Ian Levine and Fiachra Trench, to draw attention to the fact that the BBC had 'rested' the programme for 18 months. Eighties pop bands whose names were – or may have been –

inspired by *Doctor Who* included Dalek I Love You, The K9s, The Cybermen, The Daleks, The Dalex and The Brains of Morbius. The records released by these bands had nothing to do with *Doctor Who*, with the possible exception of Dalek I Love You's track 'Dalek I Love You' (Back Door Records 1980).

In 1988 The Timelords (an early incarnation of the KLF who were to enjoy major chart success in the late eighties) released a single called 'Doctorin' The Tardis'. This mixing of Gary Glitter's 'Rock and Roll Part II' with the *Doctor Who* theme eventually reached the top of the charts for one week in June of the same year. A number of remix versions of this single, a CD single version, and a vinyl 45 picture disc in the cutout shape of Ford Timelord were also released, and for promotional purposes there was a humorous video showing Ford Timelord (an American-style police car) battling Dalek-like robots constructed from packing crates.

In 1989 Metro Music International released the 'Variations on a Theme' EP. This brought together *Doctor Who* composers Mark Ayres, Glynn and McCulloch, each of whom presented a different arrangement of Ron Grainer's *Doctor Who* theme.

As well as the various presentations on vinyl and CD, there were several recordings released on cassette tape only.

The first 'official' talking book related to *Doctor Who* was released in 1981 by Pickwick and was a 55-minute reading by Tom Baker of an abridged version of the Target novelisation of **State of Decay**. This was re-issued by Ditto in 1985 as a boxed two-tape set, and then simply as two cassette tapes held together with sticky tape. The RNIB also had available a tape cartridge featuring Gabriel Woolf reading from the novelisations *Carnival of Monsters*, *The Three Doctors* and *The Loch Ness Monster* and also from Alan Road's 1982 book *Doctor Who – The Making of a Television Series*.

▲ *Doctor Who* LP's and 12" singles.

▲ *Doctor Who* meets Gary Glitter in The Timelords' number one hit single 'Doctorin' the Tardis'.

ASSOCIATED RECORDS

*The Radiophonic Workshop's twenty-fifth anniversary release 'Soundhouse' (1983 BBC REC 467) contained Malcolm Clarke's 'The Milonga' which was composed for **Borges at 80**, but also used in the **Doctor Who** story **Enlightenment**. 'Sci-Fi – Sound Effects No. 26' (1981 BBC REC 420) featured numerous sound effects from **Doctor Who**, primarily from the eighteenth season.*

Doctor Who singles. Two ▲
versions of Blood Donor's
single 'Doctor ... ?' are shown.
The original 1980 release and
the 1984 re-issue.

Two related cassette releases featured the work of composer Mark Ayres, who had at the time yet to work on *Doctor Who* directly. In 1987 he released **Timeflight**, a cassette of music from a video which followed a group of *Doctor Who* fans and professionals – including Colin Baker – as they trained for and performed a charity parachute jump. In the same year Ayres released **Myth Makers – The Music** which contained some of the original music composed for Reeltime Pictures' video interview series.

Following the publication of *Cybermen* in 1988, David Banks recorded and released a number of cassette readings from the book. **Origins of the Cybermen** and **The Early Cybermen** appeared in 1989. Banks also released **The Ultimate Interview** where actor Colin Baker spoke about his life in an interview conducted during his run in *The Ultimate Adventure* stage play in 1989.

The 1976 LP **Doctor Who and the Pescatons**, an original adventure featuring the fourth Doctor and Sarah, was re-issued on LP and cassette in 1985, and the radio play **Slipback** was paired with the 1979 LP release of 'Genesis of the Daleks' and released in a double-cassette pack as a part of the BBC Audio Collection in 1988.

In 1987 the Reference Department of the *Doctor Who* Appreciation Society released a cassette tape of stock music which had been used in many of the black and white *Doctor Who* stories. The tape was called **Space Adventures** and featured twenty tracks ranging from *Three Guitars Mood 2* (the music heard by Susan in the first episode of *100,000 BC* as she listens to the radio) to several tracks from the 1968 adventure *The Web of Fear*. This tape was followed in 1988 by a second collection called **Black Light**. This featured the work of Dominic Glynn and contained music from *The Trial of a Time Lord* and *Dragonfire*.

A series of fan-produced audio *Doctor Who* adventures were also released on cassette in the eighties. Twenty-three different titles were available by the end of 1989. The tapes had been the brainchild of fan Bill Baggs and were edited and produced to a professional standard. Baggs moved on to other ventures part-way through the series and the task of producing the releases was taken on by John Ainsworth and Gary Russell. The tapes featured occasional guest appearances by professional actors and actresses, including Michael Wisher, Peter Miles and Nabil Shaban, all of whom had appeared in *Doctor Who*. The Doctor was played for the majority of the tapes by actor and journalist Nick Briggs.

STATIONERY

In 1980 A. B. & Sons apparently released a **Doctor Who telephone pad**. This item came in two sizes but no other information is available. Another telephone pad was released by Anker International in 1988. This again came in two sizes and the larger included a jotter pad and pencil.

1982 saw the Interwainer Handbag company release a **TARDIS pencil case**. A similar item was issued by Hummingbird Products Ltd the same year. The Interwainer case was dark blue with black windows and the front doors were on the same side as the zipper while the Hummingbird case was slightly larger, a lighter blue, had white slashes on the windows and the doors were on the opposite side from the zipper. In 1983 A. B. & Sons released a white **Doctor Who eraser** with a blue or red *Doctor Who* logo which was sold alongside the plethora of stationery items produced by BBC Enterprises for the

A selection of *Doctor Who*
stationery. TARDIS and Dalek
pencil cases, TARDIS
telephone pads, erasers,
rulers, pens and pencils. ▼

two permanent *Doctor Who* exhibitions.

A **Dalek pencil case** was released by the Interwainer Handbag Company in 1984 along with a flat version of their **TARDIS pencil case**. In 1987, Light Fantastic, a specialist hologram shop based in the Trocadero at London's Piccadilly Circus, released a set of seven **hologram cards**. The holograms were all images of Fine Art Castings' metal miniatures and featured a Dalek, Davros, a Cyberman, Sil, a Sontaran and a Sea Devil. The TARDIS also appeared on a card although this was artwork against a hologrammatic background. The cards could be purchased at £1.95 each or mounted on stands at £3.45 each.

Space Adventure released a white **pencil** with an eraser on the end and a white **plastic 12" ruler** with the words: 'I've journeyed through the World of *Doctor Who* exhibition' printed in black to tie in with their 1989 *Doctor Who* exhibition.

TOYS

1980 saw Games Workshop release **The Game of Time and Space**, a sort of role-playing game involving the hunt for the Key of Time across a board depicting the universe. Along similar lines but without the restriction of a set plot and mission to follow was **The Doctor Who Role Playing Game** from the Fasa Corporation. This was produced primarily for the American market but was also generally available in the UK. Numerous supplement books could also be bought for the game.

Finally, in 1989, The Games Team brought out **Battle for the Universe**, another role-playing game involving a board and attribute cards for a large number of enemies and companions.

Viewmaster was a stereoscopic viewer toy through which two separate images could be viewed as one single image in 3D. There were numerous packs of circular slides available. In 1980 a set for the Tom Baker story *Full Circle* was issued, and in 1982 a set for the Peter Davison story *Castrovalva*. Each contained three reels and featured 21 pictures from the story. A **Viewmaster Gift Set** was also released in 1982 which contained a viewer as well as a set of the *Full Circle Doctor Who* slides.

Avon Tin produced a series of **metal tins** printed with the TARDIS exterior with the Doctor standing in the doorway. In 1980 they issued a fourth Doctor version and then in 1982 a fifth Doctor one. The tins were available in two basic designs: the lid was hinged, or lifted straight off. These tins have, over the years, been sold as money boxes, tea-caddies, pencil boxes and storage tins.

In 1982 D. Dekker Ltd released a **TARDIS Tent**. This featured a plastic tubular frame with a printed plastic outer shell that fitted over the basic framework. The inside of the outer layer had a TARDIS console printed on it. The box featured children dressed as the fifth Doctor, Nyssa and Tegan, but their costumes were not available to buy.

Computer games were in their infancy during the

▲ Lee Sullivan's seventh Doctor painting.

The *Doctor Who* playmat together with a selection of eighties *Doctor Who* toys.

The first ever *Doctor Who* ▶
computer game, *The First
Adventure*.

Front and rear of the ▲
boxed *Doctor Who*
Viewmaster set.

eighties, and BBC Software released two games to tie
in with *Doctor Who*. The first was appropriately called
The First Adventure and was a very basic four-
game package. The first game, 'The Labyrinth of
Death', involved moving a cart around a mine,
avoiding dangerous snakes along the way. The
second, 'The Prison', was a variation on the game
'frogger', where the TARDIS must be moved across
three hazard areas by either hopping onto or avoiding
objects that moved into the player's path. The third,
'The Terrordactyls', involved moving up to the
TARDIS while avoiding flying beasts. The fourth,
'The Box of Tantalus', was a form of electronic
'Battleships'. The whole package was loaded from
cassette tape and the graphics and game play were
somewhat rudimentary.

Doctor Who and the Warlord was the second
release from the BBC. This was a two-part text-only
game and the idea was, in the first part, to locate the
Doctor on a strange planet in the distant future, and
in the second part to try to stop the Warlord from
interfering with history at the Battle of Waterloo.
There were several rather devious puzzles and 250
locations in each part.

A selection of Dapol toys
released in the late eighties. In
the centre is the twenty-fifth
anniversary playset.▼

The final computer game to be released in the
eighties was **Doctor Who and the Mines of Terror**
from Micropower. This came in a number of formats

– Commodore 64, Spectrum, Amstrad and BBC
Micro – and was available on cassette, disk or 16K
ROM and disk formats. The accompanying
documentation was obscurely worded and the game,
a sophisticated platform adventure, gave few hints as
to how it should be played.

Imagineering Ltd, who had provided many of the
visual effects props and monster costumes for the
Davison era, developed a marketing leg called Image
Screencraft to exploit their new designs – in
particular the Cyberman – onto T-shirts, sweat shirts
and badges. They also released a flat cardboard
Cyberman mask in 1983. In 1987 Imagineering
released, under their own name and in conjunction
with one specific *Doctor Who* dealership, a range of
full-head **latex masks** of *Doctor Who* characters. The
range consisted of two versions of Davros (*Genesis of
the Daleks* and *Resurrection of the Daleks*), two versions
of Silurian (*Doctor Who and the Silurians* and *Warriors
of the Deep*), a Draconian (*Frontier in Space*) and a
Sontaran (*The Two Doctors*).

Another mask was released in 1988 by Sevans
Models. In response to perceived demand, Stuart
Evans produced a limited run of *Earthshock*-style
Cyberman helmets that came in matt black.

Sport and Playbase Ltd brought out a **Doctor
Who playmat** in 1984 which featured an artwork
rendition of the sixth Doctor and Peri in the middle
of a battle between Daleks and Cybermen. The same
company also issued for the American market a mat
featuring images of the fourth Doctor and Leela in
place of the sixth Doctor and Peri.

In 1988 Dapol released small **plastic jointed
models** of the seventh Doctor and Mel, along with a
Dalek, a green coloured K-9 and a Tetrap (*Time and
the Rani*). They also released a **25th Anniversary
Playset**. This included a **TARDIS exterior** (with
flashing light) which could be disassembled to form
the inner TARDIS walls for a diorama which
included a five-sided version of the standard **control
console** with a central column that rose and fell. The
set also included one of each of the Dapol figures
except the Dalek. The elements within the playset
were also later available to buy separately.

Towards the end of the decade Dapol planned a
range of models, several of which didn't actually reach
the shops until the start of the nineties. This consisted
of a range of Daleks in different colour combinations
(standard were: white/gold, black/gold, black/silver,
grey/blue and red/black), a Cyberman, Davros (which
was initially produced with two arms, one of which
was hastily removed) and an Ice Warrior. A six-sided
console and a grey K-9 were also promised.

VIDEO

By the close of the seventies home video had become more affordable than in the past and, although the price of blank tapes was still very high in the UK (around £18 for a single 180-minute tape), many homes were equipping themselves with video recorders. The first pre-recorded videos released relevant to *Doctor Who* were the two sixties **Dalek films**, released by Thorn EMI in 1982 for £39.95 each. They were re-released in 1988 by Warner Home Video for £9.99, which had become by then the established cost of a sell-through tape.

The first *Doctor Who* **TV story** released by the BBC was an edited version of season twelve's *Revenge of the Cybermen*. The tape was released towards the end of 1983, and the choice of story had been made following a poll conducted at the massive Longleat *Doctor Who* convention earlier that year. Questionnaires had been distributed asking which stories fans would most like to see, and the Patrick Troughton story *The Tomb of the Cybermen* had come out top. As this story did not at that time exist in the BBC archives, the selectors theorised that any Cyberman adventure would do as well.

The second release was *The Brain of Morbius* in 1984. This was a one-hour-long edited version, and sold for £19.95. Both these initial releases were available as video disks for £9.99 each.

The Five Doctors was the next story to be issued on video, followed in 1985 by *Pyramids of Mars*, *The Seeds of Death* and *Day of the Daleks* and in 1986 by *The Robots of Death*. All these releases retailed at £24.95 and were available in both the VHS and Betamax formats. They were also all edited in one way or another, with the opening and closing title sequences missing between episodes and seemingly random cuts made throughout the stories. The tapes were eventually re-released at the lower budget price; however the re-issued versions were identical in content to the original.

Perhaps due to the negative response from fan magazines to the editing of the stories, and perhaps due to the difficulty in obtaining clearance from all the cast members featured (for example, *Pyramids of Mars* was held up because Bernard Archard's agents initially refused to accept the fee the BBC were offering), further additions to the range were brought out very infrequently up to the end of the decade. In several cases commercial tapes had been released overseas years before they were released in England (*Terror of the Zygons* and *Talons of Weng-Chiang* were released in Australia in 1987 while their UK release wasn't until 1988 and *The Deadly Assassin* was

A selection of *Doctor Who* video and laser disc titles from the eighties.

released in America in 1985 while the UK release did not occur until 1991). Eventually the tapes were available only in the VHS format.

With the BBC tapes appearing at a slow rate, another company set about releasing more material into a market by now desperate for this type of product. Keith Barnfather had worked for the BBC and helped set up Channel 4 before leaving to start Reeltime Pictures, an independent video production company which specialised in corporate videos. As a sideline, and because Barnfather had been a fan of *Doctor Who* since the early days (he had organised the first ever *Doctor Who* convention in 1977), Reeltime also released a series of video interviews with people connected with the series. These were professionally produced and featured the companions, the Doctors, the production personnel, and even Marvel Comics. By the end of the eighties, Reeltime Pictures had released eighteen of these **Myth Makers** tapes. Other tapes released by the company were **PanoptiCon VII**, a behind-the-scenes look at one of the *Doctor Who* Appreciation Society's annual conventions, including interviews with the attending celebrities, and **Myth Runner**, a collection of out-takes and specially recorded material from the 'Myth Makers' series.

Doctor Who confectionery.

CONFECTIONERY

Doctor Who candy favourites *had originally arrived in the shops in 1979. These white chocolate shapes could be bought in 1980 as a boxed set for 60p. The shapes available were the TARDIS, K-9, a Dalek and a Cyberman. This selection of images also turned up in 1982 as* **milk chocolate novelties** *and again, in a slightly different form, as oval, foil-wrapped* **Christmas tree decorations** *in 1981. These decorations cost 7p each, whereas the milk chocolate shapes were 4p each. All were produced by Goodies.*

1982 also saw Famous Names/Goodies produce a range of **Doctor Who Favourites bars.** *These retailed at 3p each and were available in three flavours: apple, raspberry and orange. These were re-issued in 1983 as tubs of* **Christmas Candy.** *The tubs each included one of the 1965 Cadet Sweet Cigarette cards, re-printed by Goodies, but these were hastily withdrawn when the manufacturers realised that the Doctor was no longer played by William Hartnell.*

Easter 1982 saw Suchard produce their first **Doctor Who** *Easter egg. This was a* **TARDIS Egg,** *and featured a cut-out of Peter Davison behind the movable front doors. It also contained a small book entitled* **Doctor Who's Little Book Of Villains** *and an accompanying set of rub-down transfers. This was a very popular item, with around 33,000 units being sold. The following year saw the release of a second egg by Suchard, this time with the title* **Invasion of the Daleks,** *featuring a board game on the box. This time the sales were around 50,000 units.*

In 1981, Streets confectionery in Australia released a vanilla and chocolate flavour **Doctor Who ice lolly.** *This product was marketed only in that country.*

One item that didn't quite make it to the shops was a range of **Doctor Who** *soft drinks proposed and developed in 1981 by Strantons Hartlepool Ltd. A licence was issued by BBC Enterprises for the production of Lemonade, Cola and Orangeade, but, due to a price war in the drinks industry at the time, they were delayed. Ultimately they were not released at all due to the company being taken over in 1984.*

MISCELLANEOUS

*Of interest to **Doctor Who** collectors in the eighties were a series of **Police Box** models released by Langley Model Miniatures in 1984. These were kits of two sizes comprising thin, pre-cut sections of brass which could be assembled and painted to create the models. They were intended for railway enthusiasts to complete realistic scenes for the trains to run through.*

*Peter Davison lent his name to two collections of short science fiction stories published by Arrow in 1982. **Peter Davison's Book of Alien Monsters** and **Peter Davison's Book of Alien Planets** each also featured a photograph of the actor on the front cover.*

*In 1982 Nathan-Turner directed a **Cinderella** pantomime over the Christmas period and a souvenir programme was released which contained much **Doctor Who** material. The cast included Peter Davison, his wife Sandra Dickinson and Anthony Ainley as well as sisters Jody Wilson and Tracey Howard, who went on to appear in **Delta and the Bannermen** as part of The Lorells singing group.*

*Another souvenir programme was released by the British Film Institute in 1983 to accompany a short season of **Doctor Who** episodes being shown at the National Film Theatre on London's South Bank. The programme was written by Jeremy Bentham and featured a cover by fan artists Stuart Glazebrook and Gordon Lengden and internal illustrations by Phil Bevan.*

continued on page 169

Another production from Reeltime Pictures was the first ever independent, professionally produced *Doctor Who* spin-off drama, **War Time**. Directed by Barnfather, scripted by Andrew Lane and his wife Helen Stirling, starring John Levene as Sergeant Benton and featuring Michael Wisher as his father, the 1988 video told of a moment in Benton's life when he was forced to face and defeat his childhood nightmares.

SUNDRIES

This section describes all those items which cannot be easily placed in any other category.

The Larkfield Printing Co. were responsible for most of the *Doctor Who* promotional **postcards** produced for the BBC in the eighties. Prior to 1981 the cards were printed via a letterpress process on copper plates and thereafter the printers switched to a litho method. Cards were produced for all the various Doctors and companions featured in the series, and there were additional cards for *The Five Doctors*. The initial cards released for Susan and Sarah Jane Smith from the latter story were withdrawn after the artistes concerned expressed dislike for the images featured. Some of the characters had two different cards released: Tegan, Nyssa and Ace among them.

The only toiletry item to be released in the eighties was a boxed **TARDIS Bubble Bath** released by DMS Toiletries in 1988. Along with this item, fans could decorate their bathroom with a set of nine **ceramic tiles** released by Pictiles Ltd. These showed an image of Tom Baker and the Daleks, which was supplied by an American *Doctor Who* fan organisation.

Doctor Who **wallpaper.**

Royal Doulton brought out a set of *Doctor Who* collectable **plates** in 1985. There were five 21cm diameter plates issued in all, respectively featuring the first three Doctors, the Master (Roger Delgado) and Davros with a Dalek. The plates featured black outline sketches of the characters against the white porcelain of the plate and an eight-carat gold rim and sold for £9.95 each. Gladstone Pottery, the location used by the BBC for the recording of the final segment of the twenty-third season, also suggested producing a *Doctor Who* plate in 1987, but the idea was not progressed. To mark the occasion of Patrick Troughton's death in 1987, a company called Seabridge Ceramics produced in 1988 a **commemorative plate**.

Doctor Who Wallpaper was released in 1982. Available from Coloroll it featured a repeating image consisting of a photograph of Peter Davison, and artwork of three Daleks firing their guns, the TARDIS and a Cyberman head against a star-scape background.

Andrew Skilleter's Who Dares Publishing company started in 1983 with the launch at the BBC's Longleat convention of a series of art prints.

Miscellaneous items: the NFT brochure, Cinderella programme, Longleat programme, Peter Davison's Book of Alien Monsters, cat badge, resin TARDIS and Langley police box miniature.

Collectively called **Profile Prints,** these poster-sized images featured specially commissioned artwork by Skilleter and text by *Doctor Who Magazine* writer Richard Landen. They could be obtained either laminated (sealed in a clear protective coating) or un-laminated. The launch titles were *The Cybermen* and *Omega.* They were a great success and Skilleter followed them with a further four Profile Prints and four other prints in the same format, but not in the Profile Print series: K-9, the sixth Doctor, the fourth Doctor and a print celebrating *The Five Doctors.*

Who Dares Publishing also launched several other items which made use of Skilleter's *Doctor Who* artwork. There were **calendars** for 1986, 1987, 1988 and 1989 (the 1988 calendar also contained artwork by Stuart Hughes, who had illustrated Nathan-Turner's book *Doctor Who: The Companions*). Each featured a mixture of artwork re-printed from other projects and original pieces. **Bookmarks** and small **artcards** were also released using re-printed images. In 1987 Who Dares Publishing released a small blue and white *Doctor Who* **pennant**. Images from the 1986 calendar turned up as **print paks** in 1987. These were pages from the calendar cut down to leave just the artwork image.

Artist Chris Achilleos in 1986 released through Titan Books an **art portfolio** of his *Doctor Who* work. This was intended as the first in a series of art portfolios but the idea never got beyond the first edition which featured large reproductions of Achilleos's Target cover art for *Invasion of the Dinosaurs, Genesis of the Daleks, The Web of Fear, The Three Doctors* and *The Making of Doctor Who.*

In 1987, Who Dares Publishing released 300 of a set of **Frank Bellamy art prints** for £36.50 per set. The set comprised full colour A2 reproductions of: the *Radio Times* cover art for *Day of the Daleks*; an internal *Radio Times* illustration for *Terror of the Zygons*; and a black and white illustration of *Jon Pertwee and the Daleks* originally used as part of *Radio Times'* *Doctor Who* competition promotion.

In 1988, Holdcourt Ltd brought out a **TARDIS telephone** for £99.95. The item consisted of a lightweight plywood TARDIS with a telephone handset inside.

In 1980 the BBC's photographic department decided to make available to readers of the *Radio Times* some pictures from their favourite shows. The first programmes to be featured were *The Onedin Line* and *Doctor Who.* Five pictures were issued featuring: K-9 (from *The Invisible Enemy*); the fourth Doctor and Romana (one from *The Leisure Hive* and another from a publicity shoot for *Destiny of the Daleks*); the fourth Doctor (publicity); and the fourth Doctor in the TARDIS control room (publicity).

Two companies produced 'official' **first-day covers** to mark *Doctor Who*'s twenty-fifth anniversary in 1988. Covercraft's cover featured a full-colour image of the *Doctor Who* logo and the TARDIS and presented a special 'Gallifrey' postmark over postage stamps from the Post Office's 'Space' collection. Copies were obtainable either in a pristine state or signed by one of the Doctors. The second first-day cover may have been produced some time later than the actual anniversary. Available from Arlington Supplies Ltd it again featured the distinctive Gallifrey postmark, but the envelope was smaller and was stamped with a blue image of the TARDIS and the words 'Special Postmark 25th Anniversary Dr. Who' in either blue or red. Once again, the covers could be obtained either in pristine form or signed by one of the Doctors. A company called Acorn Marketing wanted to issue a *Doctor Who* postage stamp in 1983 to celebrate the twentieth anniversary, but the product did not appear.

Seeing that there was a demand for **photographs** from *Doctor Who,* several individuals stepped in to try to fill the gap in the market. The BBC had decided that they could not fulfil the demand themselves and so John

When Colin Baker took over as the Doctor it was decided to feature a **cat badge** on the lapel of his coat. Costume designer Pat Godfrey therefore went out and bought several designs of badge to use for this purpose. One of the designs – that used in **The Twin Dilemma** – was created by a lady called Suzie Trevor, who made copies available in a jewellery store in London's Earlham Street, as well as by mail order. Two subsequent designs were created especially for Baker by Maggie Howard of Maggie's Moggies, and were based on Baker's own cats, 'Eric' and 'Weeble'. Copies of these badges were made available for sale by Howard for £3.25 each.

Finally, the computer games manufacturer Lumpsoft released a game called **The Key to Time** which featured a plot not dissimilar to that of **Doctor Who**'s sixteenth season. No other details are known about this game.

▲ **DMS Toiletries' TARDIS bubble bath.**

Sundry items: *Doctor Who* tiles along with mugs, bubble bath, hologram card, bookmark, pennant, keyfob and patch.

A selection of *Doctor Who* ▲ badges released in the eighties.

The American cover for *The Seeds of Doom*, published in the eighties. ▼

McElroy was licensed to sell prints of BBC photographs through his Whomobilia company. From 1984 to the end of the eighties, McElroy released 14 different series of black and white and colour pictures covering over 500 BBC photographs as well as 36 pictures from the collection of ex-BBC designer Raymond P. Cusick. Other non-BBC photographs were commercially released by several individuals with access to their own shots taken on location. In late 1989 a company called Mediaband announced the release of some specially taken photographs of Sophie Aldred and Sylvester McCoy. Whilst these items had nothing to do with *Doctor Who*, as such, they were sold and marketed to *Doctor Who* fans.

Other sundry items included mugs, balloons, carrier bags, binders for *Doctor Who Magazine*, bookmarks, a *Doctor Who* umbrella, key rings, a police box fairground ride and a Dalek clock. *The Ultimate Adventure* stage play also generated several items of merchandise, including a souvenir magazine (of which there were two versions available – one for each Doctor), posters, photographs, baseball caps and a clock.

AMERICAN MERCHANDISE

The American market for *Doctor Who* ephemera has always been difficult to document and categorise mainly because it covers such a wide area, but also because a great many unlicensed products have been produced over the years.

There was little in the way of home-grown American product up until the eighties. What had been produced was mainly to tie in with the release of the two Dalek films in the sixties, But American editions of some of the Target novelisations were also published by Pinnacle in 1979 and 1980.

The boom in *Doctor Who* merchandise in the United States came in 1982, when Tom Baker's stories went into syndication across the country and many Americans discovered that they liked this quirky English programme with its charismatic and larger-than-life hero. Fan clubs sprang up everywhere and along with the unofficial concerns came two much larger organisations: Spirit of Light, which was the commercial arm of the massive *Doctor Who* Fan Club of America, and The Barbara Elder Corporation (which also traded as Nightstar Inc.).

Between them these two organisations were responsible for producing and marketing the vast majority of *Doctor Who* items released in the eighties.

Product could be found in all the main categories and, unfortunately, space dictates that we are unable to print a full listing in this book.

There were many badges of different types (heat sensitive, plastic, enamel, round, square, oblong and diamond shaped), all featuring slogans, familiar faces and title logos from the series; there were American editions of UK-originated books, including the final two novelisations from Pinnacle Books (*The Seeds of Doom* and *The Android Invasion*) and editions of the Severn House 'Make Your Own Adventure' books were re-issued by Ballantine/Young under the title 'Find Your Fate'; T-Shirts, sweat-shirts, caps and polo shirts were released in many different colours and featuring designs, artwork and logos connected with *Doctor Who*; there were several magazines, in particular a series generically known as 'Files Magazine'. This was published by PsiFi Movie Press and was written by John Peel. Each issue concentrated on different eras of the show and attempted to document the series for an American audience.

Posters were popular and several were released; there were re-issues of a few UK-originated records, including some collector's edition picture-discs; in the stationary category there were pens, pencils and notepads, the latter produced by fan Gail Bennett; there were many sundry items ranging from cheque book covers and passports to bumper stickers, calendars, key fobs, Frisbees, mugs, wallets, bags, towels, binoculars, a digital watch, an easel clock, sunglasses and even a stained glass window of the diamond logo (which retailed for $125) and a limited edition Hirschfeld lithograph sold through the Margo Field Galleries in New York for $595.

For fans of role-playing games, the FASA corporation released a *Doctor Who* variant together with collectible game pieces and supplement booklets.

Finally, several items could be bought on video in addition to the BBC Video releases. These included a tape called *The Home Whovian* released by Lionheart, the BBC's American distributor and two tapes from Scorpio International, one featuring Tom Baker, and the other looking at *Doctor Who* in America.

For assistance in tracking down the American merchandise we are indebted to Chris daLuca for his time, enthusiasm and unstinting efforts.

CHAPTER TWENTY-FOUR

The End of an Era

Towards the end of recording on *Doctor Who*'s twenty-sixth season it became apparent to the production team that the series was again in danger of being cancelled by their BBC superiors, or at least of being rested for a significant period of time.

'We were told to wait and see about another season,' recounted Andrew Cartmel in 1994, 'but there was definitely a flavour of "you'll have to wait a very long time".'

John Nathan-Turner consequently decided that the Doctor should be given a poignant new speech to deliver at the close of *Survival* to allow for the fact that this could actually turn out to be the end of the entire series.

'I ended up writing that speech,' noted Cartmel, 'because we weren't sure the show was ever coming back. There was a great responsibility to leave the series open for continuation or to put in some final words that would echo honestly. That was quite a sad moment. What a shame.'

The location work for *Survival* had already been completed by this point, so the new speech was post-recorded by Sylvester McCoy on 23 November 1989 – the series' twenty-sixth anniversary – and dubbed onto the soundtrack during editing:

DOCTOR: There are worlds out there where the sky is burning, where the sea's asleep and the rivers dream. People made of smoke and cities made of song. Somewhere there's danger, somewhere there's injustice and somewhere else the tea is getting cold. Come on, Ace, we've got work to do.

As rumours of the series' possible demise began to spread, concerned fans sought reassurances from the BBC. Peter Cregeen, the new Head of Serials (the Series and Serials Department having at this point been split back into two), attempted to allay their fears. Responding to readers' letters in the 25 November – 1 December 1989 edition of the *Radio Times*, he wrote:

'I would like to reassure *Doctor Who* devotees that there are no plans to axe *Doctor Who*. There may be a little longer between this series and the next than usual, but I very much hope that it will continue to be as successful in the '90s as it has been for the last twenty-six years.'

While welcoming this statement, and others of a similarly encouraging nature, many fans remained doubtful that the BBC had been completely frank about its intentions. These fears would ultimately appear to have been justified, as it would be over six years before *Doctor Who* would again return to production – and then in a very different form from that it had taken in the past.

If a twenty-seventh season had gone ahead as originally planned, it is probable that Nathan-Turner would have remained as producer. Whether or not Cartmel would have continued as script editor is less certain, but the likelihood is that he would not. (In the event, he was 'head-hunted' to work in a similar capacity on the BBC's hospital drama series *Casualty*.) If he had stayed on, writers in the running to contribute stories to the season would have included Ben Aaronovitch, Marc Platt, Robin Mukherjee (possibly with a revised version of his earlier commission *Alixion*), Charles Vincent and Cartmel himself. If he had not, then Aaronovitch and Platt would have been at the top of the shortlist of candidates to take over from him.

The intention was that McCoy would remain as the Doctor throughout the fourteen-episode season, but that Sophie Aldred would bow out as Ace after the first seven episodes (although she was under contract for eight) to be replaced by a new companion character.

The season was to have opened with a three-part, studio-bound story written by Aaronovitch and featuring as its principal villains the Metatraxi (the war-like insectoid race previously used by Aaronovitch and Cartmel in their abortive script for the new *Doctor Who* stage play – see Chapter Twenty).

FILM PROPOSALS

The most serious proposal for a **Doctor Who** feature film during the seventies had been developed by Tom Baker, Ian Marter and producer James Hill under the working titles **Doctor Who and the Big Game** and **Doctor Who Meets Scratchman**. After much negotiation, BBC Enterprises granted Hill, with effect from 1 November 1978, a one-year option to make the film, with no commitment on their part to renew. The project eventually fell through due to difficulties in raising the necessary finance. The eighties saw a number of other approaches being made to BBC Enterprises by parties interested in acquiring the rights to produce a spin-off film. One came in May 1980 from Brian Eastman of Paramount; another in August 1982 from Anthony Williams of Sandfire Productions, based at Pinewood Studios; and another in May 1984 from producer Norman Rubenstein. These all came to nothing. Milton Subotsky, co-producer of the two sixties **Doctor Who** films, contacted Head of Series and Serials Jonathan Powell in April 1984 to indicate that he would like to do a third. This had the working title **Doctor Who's Greatest Adventure** and would have involved two Doctors teaming up to combat some giant monsters. Powell turned the idea down, and confirmed with Head of Copyright Brian Turner that there was nothing in Subotsky's original contracts from the sixties with the BBC that gave him any rights in this regard. A proposal that progressed a little further was put forward in October 1984 by Edward Joffe of Multivision Communications Ltd. The BBC stipulated as conditions for granting the film rights to Multivision that John Nathan-Turner would have to be involved in the project; that one of the actors who had played the Doctor on TV would have to be given the lead role; and that a fee of around £50,000 would have to be paid. Peter Davison was subsequently contacted to see if he would be interested in starring in the film, and Christopher H. Bidmead was earmarked as a possible writer. In the end however this also fell through. In May 1985 Nathan-Turner suggested that **Doctor Who**'s first producer Verity Lambert might be a good candidate to make a film based on the series. Then, the following month, producer Michael Bond proposed a film entitled **The Crossroads in Time**. This too came to nothing, as did an approach on 18 June 1986 from an American company called Batfilms Productions Inc. It would in fact be another two years before the film rights would be finally awarded to a company, namely Coast-to-Coast Productions Ltd, in a deal that would extend well into the 1990s.

ARCHIVES

During the seventies, much DoctorWho material was purged from the BBC archives and in 1978 the process was halted. The BBC appointed an official Archive Selector, a post initally held by Sue Malden, and the task of trying to catalogue and 're-discover' material that had been destroyed began. The first task was to bring together all the material known to be held. Thus material from BBC Enterprises and the British Film Insitute was obtained and catalogued alongside that which the BBC Film and Video library already held. Other gaps were plugged with material returned from Canada and from off-air NTSC U-Matic domestic video recordings made in the USA. Between 1980 and 1989, there were several items returned to the BBC from private film collectors, overseas television stations and from being found in unlikely places in England:

*1982: **The Abominable Snowmen** 2, **The Reign of Terror** 6*
*1983: **Invasion of the Dinosaurs** 1 (black and white copy), **Colony In Space**, **The Sea Devils**, **The Daleks' Master Plan** 5 and 10*
*1984: **The Celestial Toymaker** 4, **The Wheel In Space** 3, **The Time Meddler**, **The War Machines** and a complete print of **The Web Planet***
*1985: **The Reign of Terror** 1, 2 and 3, **Inferno**, **Frontier in Space***
*1987: **The Faceless Ones** 3, **The Evil of the Daleks** 2, **The Time Monster** 6 (black and white copy)*
*1988: **The Ice Warriors** 1, 4, 5 and 6*

Philip Segal, the executive producer of the American co-production of Doctor Who. ▼

'The story was to have been set on a large space cruiser,' wrote Aldred and visual effects man Mike Tucker in 1995, 'and would have opened with the camera panning around all the duty stations — navigation, engineering, communications and so on. The camera would have come to rest on the captain's chair, containing a uniformed Ace. She announces that she is going to her ready room and leaves the bridge. Her ready room contains the TARDIS and the Doctor, and as he looks up at her she says, "Professor, this isn't going to work!" '

Ace's swansong, a four-parter, was to have been written by Platt and set either on Mars or in London in 1968. The former setting was mooted as Platt had decided that his story should feature the Ice Warriors and he was considering a plot involving the terraforming of their home planet. The latter – which would almost certainly have been the one ultimately chosen – was thought of as Platt, Aaronvitch and Cartmel considered the sixties to be an era that the BBC's designers were particularly adept at re-creating, as demonstrated on season twenty-five's *Remembrance of the Daleks*.

'The idea that had evolved for Ace's departure,' explained Aldred and Tucker, 'was that she was to be left on Gallifrey, the Doctor enrolling her in the Academy, determined to rock the Time Lords' cosy existence to its very foundations. The Time Lords agree and send a delegation of business suited agents with a mission for Ace to test her suitability – in the process having a problem solved that they don't want to involve themselves in. The Doctor is furious but can't interfere without spoiling her chances of being accepted.'

Further to this, Platt had formulated some links that might lead into the next story and the introduction of a new companion. Platt's story would have featured a young hippie couple living on a house-boat. The man would have had dubious underworld connections and his girlfriend was to have been pregnant. At the end of the final episode the woman would have given birth to a baby daughter. The Doctor names the baby and promises to return to see her at some later date.

The third story was to have been set in eighties London. It would have reintroduced the hippie man and revealed that he had recently 'gone straight' after a period spent as a gangland boss. This was envisaged as paving the way for him to become a new semi-regular ally for the Doctor in Earth-based stories. His daughter, now grown up, was to have become the new companion.

'Ben and I had a great sequence that we'd cobbled together for introducing the new companion,' recalled Cartmel. 'There's this big mansion house, a big party going on … full of debutantes, a costume ball, a big upper-class kind of party, people dripping with diamonds.

'And there's this girl, this beautiful girl in a dress. She goes up a sweeping staircase, down a long corridor and then into a room. She takes off her gloves and sweeps back the black curtains on one wall to reveal a huge safe. She kneels by the safe – she's a safecracker! – and spins the dial and cracks the safe. She opens the door and there's Sylvester jammed inside. He says: "What kept you?" Bang, and straight into the opening titles. And the safecracker would have been our new companion.

'We wanted a companion who was street level like Ace, but more like Emma Peel from *The Avengers*, an aristo character, who could be quite intriguing. I think we would have gone for a girl companion; that always seemed the best option. I love the idea of her being a safecracker. Although there's a rough edge, she's always kind of a goodie. A darker companion would've been nice …'

'We needed someone who was going to be street-wise but not the same as Ace,' explained Aaronovitch in 1993. 'If we'd had another street urchin it would just have been Ace II and it would have been so transparent. We wanted that edge of criminality, so we decided she was in fact the daughter of a former gangland boss who's gone legitimate and sent her to public schools and finishing schools in Switzerland in order to make her an upper class young lady. Except she doesn't want to mix with aristocracy as she's spent most of her free time hanging around with his former associates, learning how to crack safes, learning how to break into buildings and doing that sort of thing.'

The *Doctor Who* production office remained open for some months after season twenty-six had been completed and transmitted but was then closed down as, with no new production in prospect, its continued existence was no longer justified.

The demise of *Doctor Who* as a traditional BBC production was disappointing to the series' fans, but not entirely surprising. Many commentators, both within the BBC and elsewhere, had apparently overlooked the scheduling of seasons twenty-four to twenty-six opposite the hugely popular *Coronation Street* – the toughest competition possible – and had consequently misinterpreted their relatively low ratings as a sign of indifference or downright displeasure amongst the viewing public. In any case, the series had over the previous few years found itself increasingly disdained by BBC management, its principal critics having included the then Controller of BBC1 Michael Grade and Head of Series and Serials (later Grade's successor as Controller) Jonathan Powell. Cregeen was also reportedly less than well disposed towards the series and his superior, Head of Drama Mark Shivas, was similarly unreceptive to viewers' requests for a new season, his interest apparently lying more with made-for-TV films than with series and serials.

The personal preferences of BBC executives were, however, by no means the only factor that contributed towards the series' downfall; arguably more significant were wider developments within the BBC, and contemporary trends in British broadcasting in general.

The BBC, although it remained committed to the highly successful *EastEnders*, was increasingly moving away from making long-running, multi-episodic drama series such as *Doctor Who*. So too were the ITV companies. British-produced television drama in the early 1990s would consist largely of films, self-contained mini-series and – often seemingly aimed as much at the lucrative US market as at the domestic one – a few short seasons of 'quality' productions such as *Inspector Morse, Miss Marple, The House of Eliott* and *Casualty*. For a British drama other than a soap opera to have a run of more than six episodes in any one year would become exceptional, whereas during the 1960s and 1970s, and even the early 1980s, it had been commonplace. This trend had already impacted on *Doctor Who* prior to its demise, with the reduction to only fourteen episodes per season for each of the last four seasons – a development that had made it much harder for the series to create an impact and build up viewer loyalty.

Science fiction was particularly out of favour at this time. Not only had *Doctor Who* disappeared, but there was also nothing to match other 70s and 80s successes such as the BBC's *Doomwatch, Survivors* and *Blake's 7* or ITV's *UFO, Space: 1999* and *Sapphire & Steel*. The genre was represented only by the *Red Dwarf* comedy series (produced by the BBC's Light Entertainment Department); by imported products such as *Star Trek: The Next Generation*; and by occasional children's drama series such as *Dark Season*. Again this was due both to the personal preferences of TV executives and to a number of other factors, including in particular the relatively high cost of this type of production.

Within the BBC, an increased emphasis on cost-cutting coupled with the introduction of Producer Choice – a scheme requiring in-house departments

to compete with outside suppliers to sell their services to producers – resulted in dozens of highly experienced designers and technical staff becoming redundant, leaving a much diminished skills base and a correspondingly reduced capacity to mount productions of the complexity of *Doctor Who*. In tandem with this, and under pressure from the Government, the BBC was buying in more and more of its programmes directly from independent production companies rather than making them itself. There had indeed been rumours throughout the seventh Doctor's era that consideration was being given to the idea of farming *Doctor Who* out to be made by an independent company, although ultimately – despite interest being expressed by a number of parties, including some former members of the series' production team – nothing had come of this.

The early 1990s was in fact a period during which the whole of the British TV industry was in a state of almost unprecedented upheaval and disarray. The four terrestrial channels were finding themselves up against increasingly stiff competition from the satellite stations, from cable TV and from pre-recorded video; the impact of the first ITV franchise auction was starting to be fully felt; Channel 4 was having to fight for its own advertising revenue, whereas previously it had been treated as part of the ITV network for this purpose; a new Channel 5 was mooted; and, perhaps most significantly of all where *Doctor Who* was concerned, the whole future of the BBC was under wide-ranging review in the run-up to the expiry – and, it was hoped, renewal – of its Royal Charter.

All these considerations militated against *Doctor Who* remaining in production at this time, but its absence from the nation's screens (barring repeats – both terrestrial and satellite – and the 1993 charity production *Dimensions in Time*) seemed to have very little impact on fan and merchandising activity. On the contrary, the series' public profile had rarely been higher. Aside from the aforementioned repeats, there were numerous videos – not only BBC releases of stories from the series' past but also independent fan productions – CDs, toys, books – including the *New Adventures* and *Missing Adventures* series of original novels from Virgin – magazines and, inevitably, numerous different fanzines.

All this activity would eventually culminate in *Doctor Who* returning to production in 1996 for the first of a possible series of TV movies, made in Canada and the USA as a joint venture between the BBC and an American production company.

That, though, is another story…

COAST-TO-COAST

*It was in March 1985 that Coast-to-Coast Productions Ltd – run by co-directors Peter Litten, George Dugdale and John Humphreys – first entered into negotiations with BBC Enterprises with a view to acquiring the rights to make a **Doctor Who** feature film. In November of the same year, Litten wrote to BBC Enterprises' Director of Business Administration John Keeble setting out the company's latest proposals for the film. He stated that: actors Denholm Elliott, Steven Berkoff, Caroline Munro, Tim Curry and Laurence Olivier had all agreed to be involved; composer Mike Oldfield had been approached to adapt the series' theme tune and provide the incidental music; make-up artist Christopher Tucker would be creating the monsters; John Stears would be in charge of visual effects; Rodney Matthews and Anton Furst would be teaming up to design the sets and costumes; Douglas Adams would be acting as script consultant; Robert Holmes would be providing the screenplay; and Richard Lester was being considered as director. He also stated that Sun Alliance had undertaken to provide financial backing for the film, and that only the BBC's agreement was now required. Head of Series and Serials Jonathan Powell, when shown Litten's letter, expressed considerable scepticism, indicating that it struck him as being 'slightly full of baloney' and suggesting that the BBC itself should retain the film rights to **Doctor Who**. Negotiations with Coast-to-Coast continued, however, and were eventually concluded around July 1987, when the company was finally granted the rights in return for a substantial fee. The summer of 1988 was at one stage announced as the likely filming period, with Johnny Byrne now earmarked to provide the script and Munro – who would later marry Dugdale – said to be in the running to play either the Doctor's companion or, possibly, a villain. By the close of the decade, however, filming had still to get under way – and in the 1990s (when Coast-to-Coast would transform first into Green Light Productions and then into Daltenreys) the wait would ultimately prove to be in vain as the project foundered.*

LISTING OF *DOCTOR WHO* MERCHANDISE RELEASED 1980-1989

NAME	PUBLISHER/MANUFACTURER	YEAR	PRICE	CATEGORY
'Doctor Who Rules the Universe' ruler	BBC Enterprises	1982	£1.25	Stationery
'I'm On Target with Doctor Who' Badge	W. H. Allen & Co. PLC	1985	free	Badges
'I've Journeyed through the World of *Doctor Who* exhibition' Ruler	Space Adventure	1989		Stationery
'I am A Doctor Who Reader' Badge	W. H. Allen & Co. Ltd.	1983	free	Badges
'The How, Why and Where of Doctor Who' Badge	André Deutsch Ltd.	1982	free	Badges
1985 Summer Special Classic Doctor Who (The Iron Legion)	Marvel Comics	1985	£1.20	Graphic Novels
25th Anniversary First Day Cover	Arlington Supplies Ltd.	1988	£5.95	Sundries
25th Anniversary First Day Cover	CoverCraft	1988	£2.50	Sundries
25th Anniversary Playset	Dapol	1988	£39.95	Toys
4th Doctor Print	Who Dares Publishing	1986	£1.95	Sundries
6th Doctor Poster	John G. McElroy	1986	£2.00	Posters
6th Doctor Print	Who Dares Publishing	1984	£1.95	Sundries
A Day With A TV Producer (Graham Rickard)	Wayland Publishers Ltd.	1980	£3.25 h/b	Factual Books
Ace Postcard (from *Dragonfire*)	JCS Printers Ltd.	1987	15p	Sundries
Ace Postcard (Publicity shot)	JCS Printers Ltd.	1988	15p	Sundries
Adric Postcard (From *Full Circle*)	Larkfield Printing Co. Ltd.	1980	15p	Sundries
Art Cards (9 different)	Who Dares Publishing	1985	50p each, £3.50 set	Sundries
Art Portfolio No 1 by Chris Achilleos	Titan Books Ltd.	1986	£3.99	Sundries
Badges – Assorted Cyberman (day-glo, blue/green, prismatic, black/blue)	Image Screencraft	1983	50p each	Badges
Badges – Assorted Doctor Who (day-glo, blue/green, prismatic, black/blue)	Image Screencraft	1983	50p each	Badges
Badges – Assorted Photographic (7 diff)	Denis Alan Print	1980	35p each	Badges
Ballpoint Pen in gold card box	BBC Enterprises	1985	£1.20	Stationery
Ballpoint Pen in plastic box	BBC Enterprises	1985	95p	Stationery
Battle for the Universe	The Games Team	1989	£14.99	Toys
BBC Photographs (500+, Ray Cusick Collection 1-36)	Whomobilia	1984 – 1989	60p, £1.50, £2.50, £5.00	Sundries
BBC Picture Pack (5 B/W photographs)	BBC Picture Publicity	1980	£3.99	Sundries
BFI Doctor Who – *The Developing Art* programme	British Film Institute	1983		Miscellaneous
Black Light (RDMP 2)	Dominitemporal Services Ltd.	1988	£4.99 (cass)	Records
Bookmarks (two sets of 9)	Who Dares Publishing	1985	40p each, £1.99 set	Sundries
Canvas Bag	Peter Black (KLY) Ltd.	1985	£5.95	Sundries
Cap		1985		Clothing
Carrier Bags (Blackpool, Longleat, neon Logo)	BBC Enterprises	1983	10p each	Sundries
Cat Badges	Susie Trevor	1985	£3.50 each	Miscellaneous
Cat Badges	Maggy's Moggies	1987	£3.25 each	Miscellaneous
Christmas Tree Decorations (Dalek/Cyberman, TARDIS/K-9)	Goodies	1981	7p each	Confectionery
Cinderella Pantomime Programme	Lovett Bickford Ltd.	1982	75p	Miscellaneous
Cloth Patch	John Fitton	1988	£4.24	Sundries
Cotton Scarf	Aristocrat Textiles Ltd.	1981		Clothing
Cyberman	Dapol	1989	£2.99	Toys
Cyberman Helmets	Sevans Models	1988	£42.50	Toys
Cyberman kit	Sevans Models	1988	£17.95	Models
Cyberman mask	Image Screencraft	1983		Toys
Cybermat kit	BCP Promotions	1985	£9.80	Models
Cybermen Figures (3) (DW4)	Citadel Miniatures	1985	£1.95	Models
Dalek (grey/blue, red/black)	Dapol	1989	£3.99	Toys
Dalek (white/gold, black/gold, black/silver,)	Dapol	1988	£3.99	Toys
Dalek Clock	K.B.W.	1988	£26.50	Sundries
Dalek Construction kit	Sevans Models	1984	£11.95	Models
Dalek Figures (2) (DW3)	Citadel Miniatures	1985	£1.95	Models
Dalek Hat, The	Deanem Ltd.	1985	£6.99	Clothing
Dalek Pencil Case	Interwainer Handbag Co.	1984	£3.30	Stationery
Dalek Postcard	BBC Enterprises	1986	65p	Sundries
Daleks & Cybermen Plastic Figures	Citadel Miniatures	1987	£4.95	Models
Daleks Postcard (From *Day of the Daleks*)	Larkfield Printing Co. Ltd.	1980	15p	Sundries
Daleks Postcard (From *Resurrection of the Daleks*) Large Format	Larkfield Printing Co. Ltd.	1985	35p	Sundries
Davros	Dapol	1989 / 90	£4.99	Toys
Davros kit	Sevans Models	1989	£19.95	Models
Davros, Dalek & K9 Figures (DW8)	Citadel Miniatures	1985	£1.95	Models
Day-Glo Stickers (Peter Davison, Cyberman)	Image Screencraft	1983	75p each	Sundries
Doctor ...? By Blood Donor (SAFE 29)	Safari Records	1980		Records
Doctor In Distress by Who Cares (DOC 1 / DOCT 1)	Record Shack Records	1985	£1.75 (7") £3.50 (12")	Records
Doctor Who – 25 Glorious Years (Peter Haining)	W. H. Allen & Co. PLC	1988	£14.95 h/b	Factual Books
Doctor Who – 25 Years Badge	BBC Enterprises	1988	50p	Badges
Doctor Who – A Celebration (Peter Haining)	W. H. Allen & Co. Ltd.	1983	£30 l/b £10.95 h/b	Factual Books
Doctor Who – A Marvel Winter Special	Marvel Comics	1981	45p	Magazines
Doctor Who – A Summer Special (JunkYard Demon/Absalom Daak)	Marvel Comics	1983	60p	Magazines
Doctor Who – Adventures in Time and Space	World International Publishing Ltd.	1981	£2.25 h/b	Annuals
Doctor Who – Brain-Teasers and Mind-Benders (Adrian Heath)	W. H. Allen & Co. PLC (Target)	1984	£1.50 p/b	Activity Books
Doctor Who – Build the TARDIS (Mark Harris)	W. H. Allen & Co. PLC (Target)	1987	£3.95 lfp/b	Activity Books
Doctor Who – Cybermen (David Banks)	Who Dares Publishing / Silver Fist	1988	£100 special edition £14.95 h/b	Factual Books
Doctor Who – The Calendar (1986)	Who Dares Publishing	1985	£5.50	Sundries
Doctor Who – The Calendar (1987)	Who Dares Publishing	1986	£5.95	Sundries
Doctor Who – The Calendar (1988)	Who Dares Publishing	1987	£5.95	Sundries
Doctor Who – The Calendar 1989	Who Dares Publishing	1988	£5.95	Sundries
Doctor Who – The Companions (John Nathan-Turner)	Piccadilly Press Ltd.	1986	£7.95 h/b £4.95 lfp/b	Factual Books
Doctor Who – The Early Years (Jeremy Bentham)	W. H. Allen & Co. PLC	1986	£75 l/b £13.50 h/b	Factual Books
Doctor Who – The Early Years (Jeremy Bentham)	W. H. Allen & Co. PLC/Comet	1988	£6.95 lfp/b	Factual Books
Doctor Who – The Game of Time and Space	Games Workshop	1980	£6.75	Toys
Doctor Who – The Key to Time (Peter Haining)	W. H. Allen & Co. Ltd.	1984	£50 l/b £12.50 h/b	Factual Books
Doctor Who – The Key to Time (Peter Haining)	W. H. Allen & Co. PLC/Comet	1987	£5.95 lfp/b	Factual Books
Doctor Who – The Making of a Television Series (Alan Road)	André Deutsch Ltd.	1982	£4.95 h/b	Factual Books
Doctor Who – The Making of a Television Series (Alan Road)	Puffin	1983	£1.95 p/b	Factual Books
Doctor Who – The Music II (REH 552 / ZCR 552)	BBC Records and Tapes	1985	£4.75 (LP) £4.25 (Cass)	Records
Doctor Who – The Nightmare Fair (Graham Williams)	W. H. Allen & Co. PLC (Target)	1989	£1.99 p/b	Books
Doctor Who – The Sequel by Mankind (MTR001)	Motor Records	1984	7", 12"	Records
Doctor Who – The TARDIS Inside Out (John Nathan-Turner)	Piccadilly Press Ltd.	1985	£7.50 h/b £4.95 lfp/b	Factual Books
Doctor Who – The Ultimate Evil (Wally K. Daly)	W. H. Allen & Co. PLC (Target)	1989	£1.99 p/b	Books
Doctor Who – The Unfolding Text (Tulloch & Alvarado)	Macmillan Books	1983	£20.00 h/b £6.95 p/b	Factual Books
Doctor Who – Time-Traveller's Guide, The (Peter Haining)	W. H. Allen & Co. PLC	1987	£14.95 h/b	Factual Books
Doctor Who – Travel Without the TARDIS (Jean Airey & Laurie Haldeman)	W. H. Allen & Co. PLC (Target)	1986	£1.60 p/b	Factual Books
Doctor Who –Dalek Omnibus	W. H. Allen & Co. Ltd.	1983	£8.95 h/b	Books
Doctor Who 20th Anniversary carrier bag	BBC Enterprises	1983	10p each	Sundries
Doctor Who 25th Anniversary Special	Marvel Comics	1988	£2.25	Magazines
Doctor Who A Marvel Monthly (Issue 44 – 60)	Marvel Comics	1980 – 1982	30p – 40p each	Magazines
Doctor Who and the Mines of Terror (Computer Game)	Micro Power Ltd.	1985	£18.95 (BBC Cass), £19.95 (BBC Disk), £18.95 (Amst Disk), £11.95 (Amst Cass), £13.95 (CBM Disk), £11.95 (CBM Cass), £unknown (Spectrum)	Toys
Doctor Who and the Pescatons re-issue (414 4591 LP, 414 4594 cass)	London Records	1985	£4.50 (LP & Cass)	Recordings
Doctor Who Annual	World International Publishing Ltd.	1981	£2.25 h/b	Annuals
Doctor Who Annual	World International Publishing Ltd.	1982	£2.50 h/b	Annuals
Doctor Who Annual	World International Publishing Ltd.	1983	£2.75 h/b	Annuals
Doctor Who Annual 1981	World International Publishing Ltd.	1980	£1.95 h/b	Annuals
Doctor Who Annual 1985	World International Publishing Ltd.	1984	£2.99 h/b	Annuals
Doctor Who Annual 1986	World International Publishing Ltd.	1985	£3.25 h/b	Annuals
Doctor Who Balloons	BBC Enterprises	1981		Sundries

Doctor Who Bonanza Competition	W. H. Allen & Co. PLC	1985	free	Promotions
Doctor Who Bust Set	Fine Art Castings	1985	£9.44 each bust	Models
Doctor Who Celebration Longleat Badge	BBC Enterprises	1983		Badges
Doctor Who Classics – *The Dalek Invasion of Earth / The Crusaders*	W. H. Allen & Co. PLC (Star)	1988	£2.95 p/b	Books
Doctor Who Classics – *The Dæmons / The Time Monster*	W. H. Allen & Co. PLC (Star)	1989	£2.95 p/b	Books
Doctor Who Classics – *The Dominators / The Krotons*	W. H. Allen & Co. PLC (Star)	1988	£2.95 p/b	Books
Doctor Who Classics – *The Face of Evil / The Sunmakers*	W. H. Allen & Co. PLC (Star)	1989	£2.95 p/b	Books
Doctor Who Classics – *The Mind of Evil / The Claws of Axos*	W. H. Allen & Co. PLC (Star)	1989	£2.95 p/b	Books
Doctor Who Classics – *The Myth Makers / The Gunfighters*	W. H. Allen & Co. PLC (Star)	1988	£2.95 p/b	Books
Doctor Who Classics – *The Seeds of Doom / The Deadly Assassin*	W. H. Allen & Co. PLC (Star)	1989	£2.95 p/b	Books
Doctor Who Collected Comics	Marvel Comics	1986	£1.75	Graphic Novels
Doctor Who Cookbook, The (Gary Downie)	W. H. Allen & Co. PLC	1985	£6.95 h/b £3.50 lfp/b (1986)	Activity Books
Doctor Who Crossword Book (Nigel Robinson)	W. H. Allen & Co. Ltd. (Target)	1982	£1.25 p/b	Activity Books
Doctor Who Diary 1986	International Scripts	1985	£2.95	Books
Doctor Who Eraser	Space Adventure	1989		Stationery
Doctor Who Exhibition Badge	BBC Enterprises	1983	30p	Badges
Doctor Who Exhibition Car Sticker	BBC Enterprises	1984	25p	Sundries
Doctor Who Exhibition/TARDIS Key Ring	BBC Enterprises	1982		Sundries
Doctor Who Figure (see separate listing)	Dapol	1988	£2.99	Toys
Doctor Who Figures (see separate listing)	Fine Art Castings	1984 – 1987	various	Models
Doctor Who File, The (Peter Haining)	W. H. Allen & Co. PLC	1986	£75 l/b £14.95 h/b	Factual Books
Doctor Who File, The (Peter Haining)	W. H. Allen & Co. PLC	1989	£9.99 lfp/b	Factual Books
Doctor Who Foil Balloons	Marlow Engineering Ltd.	1985		Sundries
Doctor Who Fun Book, The (Tim Quinn & Dicky Howett)	W. H. Allen & Co. PLC (Target)	1987	£1.95 p/b	Books
Doctor Who Illustrated A – Z, The (Lesley Standring)	W. H. Allen & Co. PLC	1985	£8.95 h/b	Factual Books
Doctor Who Illustrated A – Z, The (Lesley Standring)	W. H. Allen & Co. PLC	1987	£3.50 lfp/b	Factual Books
Doctor Who Jigsaws (set of two – series 5333.20/21)	Arrow	1984	£1.99 each	Jigsaws
Doctor Who Leather Key Rings (green, black, blue, red, brown)	BBC Enterprises	1980	35p each	Sundries
Doctor Who Magazine (Issue 107 – 155)	Marvel Comics	1985 – 1989	75p – £1.50 each	Magazines
Doctor Who Magazine 1979–1989 (10th Anniversary Special)	Marvel Comics	1989	£2.50	Magazines
Doctor Who Magazine Autumn Special (Designers)	Marvel Comics	1987	£1.95	Magazines
Doctor Who Magazine Binder	Napier & Son Ltd.	1983	£3.50	Sundries
Doctor Who Magazine Binder	John Fitton	1988	£5.95	Sundries
Doctor Who Magazine Master Index	Asquith Publishing	1989	£7.50 p/b	Factual Books
Doctor Who Magazine Summer Special (Historical Stories)	Marvel Comics	1986	£1.10	Magazines
Doctor Who Magazine Winter Special (T.Baker Years)	Marvel Comics	1986	£1.10	Magazines
Doctor Who Magazine Winter Special, The (Pertwee Special)	Marvel Comics	1985	£1.00	Magazines
Doctor Who Magazine, The (Issue 99 – 106)	Marvel Comics	1985	65p – 75p each	Magazines
Doctor Who Monster Book, The (Terrance Dicks) reissue	W. H. Allen & Co. PLC (Target)	1985	£1.95 p/b	Factual Books
Doctor Who Monthly (Issue 61 – 84)	Marvel Comics	1982 – 1984	45p – 60p each	Magazines
Doctor Who Mug (block logo & TARDIS on white china)	A. B. & Son	1987		Sundries
Doctor Who Mug (diamond logo & TARDIS on white china) two diff.	A. B. & Son	1980	£1.50	Sundries
Doctor Who Mug (neon logo & star pattern on white china)	A. B. & Son	1983	£1.25	Sundries
Doctor Who Mug (neon logo on blue china)	BBC Enterprises	1984		Sundries
Doctor Who Outfit (fawn jkt, green check trs, pullover, scarf)	Dapol	1988	£19.99	Clothing
Doctor Who Pattern Book, The (Joy Gammon)	W. H. Allen & Co. PLC	1984	£7.95 h/b £3.50 lfp/b (1986)	Activity Books
Doctor Who Pencil	Space Adventure	1989		Stationery
Doctor Who Photograph Album (red, brown, tan)	Whomobilia	1985	£4.99	Sundries
Doctor Who Poster	Marvel Comics	1988	£3.50	Posters
Doctor Who Programme Guide Vols 1 & 2, The (Jean-Marc Lofficier)	W. H. Allen & Co. Ltd.	1981	£4.50 h/b £1.25 p/b (Target)	Factual Books
Doctor Who Pullover	Dapol	1989	£32.50 (30") £34.50 (36"–46")	Clothing
Doctor Who Puzzle Book (Michael Holt)	Methuen Children's Books (Magnet)	1985	95p p/b	Activity Books
Doctor Who Quiz Book of Dinosaurs (Michael Holt)	Methuen Children's Books (Magnet)	1982	95p p/b	Activity Books
Doctor Who Quiz Book of Magic (Michael Holt)	Methuen Children's Books (Magnet)	1983	95p p/b	Activity Books
Doctor Who Quiz Book of Science (Michael Holt)	Methuen Children's Books (Magnet)	1982	95p p/b	Activity Books
Doctor Who Quiz Book of Space (Michael Holt)	Methuen Children's Books (Magnet)	1983	95p p/b	Activity Books
Doctor Who Quiz Book of Space (Michael Holt)	Severn House Publishers Ltd.	1985	£5.95 h/b	Activity Books
Doctor Who Quiz Book, The (Nigel Robinson)	W. H. Allen & Co. Ltd. (Target)	1981	£1.25 p/b	Activity Books
Doctor Who Special	W. H. Smith & Sons/Galley Press	1985	£7.95 h/b	Annuals
Doctor Who Special Effects (Mat Irvine)	Arrow Books Ltd. (Beaver Books)	1986	£5.95 lfp/b	Factual Books
Doctor Who Special Effects (Mat Irvine)	Hutchinson	1986	£8.95 h/b	Factual Books
Doctor Who Summer Special	Marvel Comics	1982	55p	Magazines
Doctor Who Summer Special (Merchandise)	Marvel Comics	1984	95p	Magazines
Doctor Who Summer Special (The Iron Legion)	Marvel Comics	1980	40p	Magazines
Doctor Who Technical Manual, The (Mark Harris)	Severn House Publishers Ltd.	1983	£4.95 h/b	Factual Books
Doctor Who Technical Manual, The (Mark Harris)	Sphere Books Ltd.	1983	£2.50 lfp/b	Factual Books
Doctor Who The Music (REH 462/ZCF 462)	BBC Records	1983	£3.75 (LP) £3.25 (Cass)	Records
Doctor Who The Programme Guide (Jean-Marc Lofficier) revised edition	W. H. Allen & Co. PLC (Target)	1989	£1.99 p/b	Factual Books
Doctor Who The Scripts – The Daleks (ed. John McElroy)	Titan Books Ltd.	1989	£3.95 p/b	Books
Doctor Who The Scripts – The Talons of Weng-Chiang (ed. John McElroy)	Titan Books Ltd.	1989	£3.95 p/b	Books
Doctor Who The Scripts – The Tomb of the Cybermen (ed. John McElroy)	Titan Books Ltd.	1989	£3.95 p/b	Books
Doctor Who The Scripts – The Tribe of Gum (ed. John McElroy)	Titan Books Ltd.	1988	£2.95 p/b	Books
Doctor Who Theme by Dominic Glynn (RESL 193 / ZRSL 193 / 12RXL 193)	BBC Records and Tapes	1986/7	£3.25 (12" & Cass) £1.75 (7")	Records
Doctor Who Theme by Peter Howell (RESL 80) C.Baker sleeve	BBC Records	1984	£1.65 (7")	Records
Doctor Who Theme by Peter Howell (RESL 80) P.Davison sleeve	BBC Records	1982	£1.30	Records
Doctor Who Theme by Peter Howell (RESL 80) T.Baker sleeve	BBC Records/PRT	1980	£1.15	Records
Doctor Who Viewmaster Gift Set	GAF Corporation	1982		Toys
Doctor Who Viewmaster: *Castrovalva*	View Master International	1983	£1.95	Toys
Doctor Who Viewmaster: *Full Circle*	GAF Corporation	1981	£1.95	Toys
Doctor Who Voyager	Marvel Comics	1989	£4.95	Graphic Novels
Doctor Who Weekly (Issue 12 – 43)	Marvel Comics	1980	12p each	Magazines
Doctor Who Winter Special	Marvel Comics	1982	60p	Magazines
Doctor Who Winter Special (Archives)	Marvel Comics	1984	95p	Magazines
Doctor Who Winter Special (Producers)	Marvel Comics	1983	95p	Magazines
Doctor Who: Timeview – The Complete Doctor Who Illustrations of Frank Bellamy (David Bellamy)	Who Dares Publishing	1985	£5.95 h/b £3.95 lfp/b	Factual Books
Doctor Who: Variations on a Theme (12 MMI 4, 12X MMI4)	Metro Music International	1989	£5.50 (12" std), £6.50 (12" lim)	Records
Doctorin' The TARDIS by The Timelords (KLF003 / KLF003T / KLF003R (12" Picturedisk) / KLTCD003 (Video CD))	KLF Communications	1988	12", 7", CD, Video CD	Records
Doctors 1, 2, 3 (DW1)	Citadel Miniatures	1985	£1.95	Models
Doctors 4, 5 and The Master Figures (DW2)	Citadel Miniatures	1985	£1.95	Models
Dr. Who and the Daleks Film Poster	MOMI	1989		Posters
Dr. Who is Gonna Fix It by Bullamakanka (RESL 132)	BBC Records	1982		Records
Eighth Doctor Who Gift Set (D, FFF, 6M, 6R)	W. H. Allen & Co. PLC (Target)	1985	p/b	Books
Encyclopedia of The Worlds of Doctor Who (A-D) (David Saunders)	Piccadilly Press Ltd.	1987	£5.95 h/b	Factual Books
Encyclopedia of The Worlds of Doctor Who (A-D) (David Saunders)	Hodder & Stoughton Ltd. (Knight Books)	1988	£2.99 p/b	Factual Books
Encyclopedia of The Worlds of Doctor Who (E-K) (David Saunders)	Piccadilly Press Ltd.	1989	£7.95 h/b	Factual Books
Encyclopedia of The Worlds of Doctor Who (E-K) (David Saunders)	Hodder & Stoughton Ltd. (Knight Books)	1989	£3.50 p/b	Factual Books
Eraser	BBC Enterprises			Stationery
Eraser (Blue, Red)	A. B. & Son	1983		Stationery
Favourites Bars (Orange/Apple/Raspberry)	FamoUSA Names	1982	3p each	Confectionery
Fifth Doctor Postcard (From *The Visitation*) (two diff)	Larkfield Printing Co. Ltd.	1981	15p	Sundries
Fifth Doctor Who Gift Set (5Y, 6E, 6D, 6L)	W. H. Allen & Co. PLC (Target)	1984	£6.50 p/b	Books
First Adventure, The (Computer Game)	BBC Software	1983	£10.00	Toys
First Doctor Postcard (From *The Five Doctors*)	Larkfield Printing Co. Ltd.	1984	15p	Sundries
First Doctor Who Gift Set (A, PP, 5P, 5S)	W. H. Allen & Co. Ltd. (Target)	1982	£5.25 p/b	Books
Fourth Doctor Postcard	Larkfield Printing Co. Ltd.	1980	15p	Sundries
Fourth Doctor Postcard (Publicity shot – Season 18 Costume)	Larkfield Printing Co. Ltd.	1984	15p	Sundries
Fourth Doctor Print	Who Dares Publishing	1987	£1.50 (plain) £1.95 (laminated)	Sundries
Fourth Doctor Who Gift Set (4A, 5P, 5V, 6C)	W. H. Allen & Co. Ltd. (Target)	1983	£5.75 p/b	Books
Frank Bellamy Art Prints	Who Dares Publishing	1987	£36.50	Sundries
Gloves	Peshawear UK Ltd.	1985	£4.99 (sizes 4,5,6) £6.99 (sizes 7-10)	Clothing
Golden Wonder Doctor Who Marvel Adventure Comics (1 – 6)	Golden Wonder / Marvel Comics	1986	free	Promotions
Harry Sullivan's War (Ian Marter)	W. H. Allen & Co. PLC (Target)	1986	£1.60 p/b	Books
Hologram Cards (7 diff)	Light Fantastic	1987	£1.95 unframed or £3.45 framed	Sundries

Item	Manufacturer	Year	Price	Category
Ice Warrior	Dapol	1989 / 90	£2.99	Toys
Ice Warrior kit	Sevans Models	1987	£15.95	Models
Ice Warror Figures (3) (DW5)	Citadel Miniatures	1985	£1.95	Models
Invasion of the Daleks Easter Egg	Tobler Suchard Ltd.	1983	£2.45	Confectionery
It's Bigger on the Inside (Tim Quinn and Dicky Howett)	Marvel Comics	1988	£1.95 lfp/b	Books
Jigsaws (Set of 4 – Series 051)	Waddingtons	1982	£1.50 each	Jigsaws
K-9 and Co. Theme by Fiachra Trench and Ian Levine (SGR 117)	Solid Gold Records Ltd.	1982	£1.15 (7")	Records
K-9 Annual 1983	World International Publishing Ltd.	1982	£2.50 h/b	Annuals
K-9 Postcard (from The Horns of Nimon)	Larkfield Printing Co. Ltd.	1982	15p	Sundries
K-9 Retractable pens (yellow, red, blue)	BBC Enterprises		60p each	Stationery
K9 and Company (Terence Dudley)	W. H. Allen & Co. PLC (Target)	1987	£1.95 p/b	Books
K9 Figure (Green, Grey)	Dapol	1988	£3.29	Toys
K9 Print	Who Dares Publishing	1983	£1.25	Sundries
Key Ring Pens	BBC Enterprises		60p each	Stationery
Key Rings	Susan Moore	1984	£1.00	Sundries
Key to Time (Computer Game)	Lumpsoft	1984	£5.99	Miscellaneous
Latex Masks (Davros (1), Davros (2), Draconian, Silurian (1), Silurian (2), Sontaran)	Imagineering Ltd.	1987	£39.95	Toys
Leather Bookmark (grey, orange, brown, green, light green)	BBC Enterprises	1983	£1.00	Sundries
Make Your Own Adventure With Doctor Who – Crisis in Space (Michael Holt)	Severn House Publishers Ltd.	1986	£1.95 p/b	Books
Make Your Own Adventure With Doctor Who – Invasion of the Ormazoids (Philip Martin)	Severn House Publishers Ltd.	1986	£1.95 p/b	Books
Make Your Own Adventure With Doctor Who – Mission to Venus (William Emms)	Severn House Publishers Ltd.	1986	£1.95 p/b	Books
Make Your Own Adventure With Doctor Who – Race Against Time (Pip and Jane Baker)	Severn House Publishers Ltd.	1986	£1.95 p/b	Books
Make Your Own Adventure With Doctor Who – Search for the Doctor (David Martin)	Severn House Publishers Ltd.	1986	£1.95 p/b	Books
Make Your Own Adventure With Doctor Who – The Garden of Evil (David Martin)	Severn House Publishers Ltd.	1986	£1.95 p/b	Books
Mel Postcard (from The Trial of a Time Lord 9–12)	Larkfield Printing Co. Ltd.	1986	15p	Sundries
Melanie Figure (pink jacket, blue jacket)	Dapol	1988	£2.99	Toys
Melanie Outfit (white trs, pink & white top)	Dapol	1988	£15.99	Clothing
Metal Logo Badge	John Fitton	1988	£4.24	Badges
Milk Chocolate Novelties (Dalek/Cyberman/TARDIS/K-9)	Goodies	1982	4p each	Confectionery
Monsters Bust Set	Fine Art Castings	1986	£12.30 each bust	Models
Mug		1987	£1.75	Sundries
Myth Makers The Music (MART-1)	Reeltime Pictures	1987		Records
Nyssa Postcard (From Logopolis)	Larkfield Printing Co. Ltd.	1980	15p	Sundries
Nyssa Postcard (Publicity shot – TerminUSA costume)	Larkfield Printing Co. Ltd.	1982	15p	Sundries
Official Doctor Who Magazine, The (Issue 85 – 98)	Marvel Comics	1984 – 1985	60p – 65p each	Magazines
Origins of the Cybermen Cassette (TC-DB1)	Silver Fox	1989	£5.99 (cass)	Recordings
Patrick Troughton Commemorative Plate	Seabridge Ceramics	1988	£16.00	Sundries
Pencils (blue, white, yellow)	BBC Enterprises		15p each	Stationery
Pennant	Who Dares Publishing	1987	£4.99	Sundries
Peri Postcard (Publicity shot – The Twin Dilemma Costume)	Larkfield Printing Co. Ltd.	1984	15p	Sundries
Peter Davison's Book of Alien Monsters	Arrow Books Ltd. (Sparrow)	1982	95p p/b	Miscellaneous
Peter Davison's Book of Alien Planets	Arrow Books Ltd. (Sparrow)	1982	95p p/b	Miscellaneous
Photograph Keyrings	Susan Moore	1983	£1.00	Sundries
Planet of the Daleks B/W Poster	MOMI	1988	£3.50	Posters
Plates (1st Dr, 2nd Dr, 3rd Dr, Master, Davros & Dalek)	Royal Doulton	1985	£9.95 each	Sundries
Playmat (Sixth Doctor & Peri)	S.P. Sport & Playbase Ltd.	1984	£8.99 (l)	Toys
Police Box Fridge Magnet		1987	£1.99	Miscellaneous
Police Box Models	Langley Model Miniatures	1984	£3.50 (4.5cm) £4.75 (7.5cm)	Miscellaneous
Police Box Phone Index (large – 400 entries)	Anker International PLC	1988		Stationery
Police Box Phone Index (small – 300 entries)	Anker International PLC	1988		Stationery
Police Box Telephone Pad	A. B. & Son	1980	£2.50 (two sizes)	Stationery
Portrait Poster – Jon Pertwee	Robbaz Illustrations	1984	85p	Posters
Portrait Poster – Patrick Troughton	Robbaz Illustrations	1983	85p	Posters
Portrait Poster – William Hartnell	Robbaz Illustrations	1983	85p	Posters
Posters (5 different) 27" x 19"	W. H. Allen & Co. PLC	1984	£1.50 each	Posters
Printpack (12 prints from 1986 Calendar)	Who Dares Publishing	1987	£2.50	Sundries
Profile Print – Cybermen (PP1)	Who Dares Publishing	1983	£1.25(plain) £1.99 (laminated)	Sundries
Profile Print – Davros and the Daleks (PP5)	Who Dares Publishing	1984	£1.95	Sundries
Profile Print – Omega (PP2)	Who Dares Publishing	1983	£1.25 (plain) £1.99 (laminated)	Sundries
Profile Print – Sontarans (PP3)	Who Dares Publishing	1983	£1.25 (plain) £1.95 (laminated)	Sundries
Profile Print – The Master (PP4)	Who Dares Publishing	1983	£1.25 (plain) £1.95 (laminated)	Sundries
Profile Print – The Sea Devils (PP6)	Who Dares Publishing	1984	£1.95	Sundries
Pyjamas	Mothercare	1989	£9.50 (l) £8.50 (s)	Clothing
Radio Times Doctor Who 20th Anniversary Special	Radio Times / BBC	1983	£1.50	Magazines
Resin badges (Ice Warrior head, Robot of Death head, Cybermat, Cyber-logo)	Susan Moore	1982	£1.00	Badges
Resin figures (Fourth Doctor, Master in cloak, Master in suit, Menoptra, Robot of Death, Sontaran, TARDIS, Time Lord)	Susan Moore	1983	£2.00 – £5.00 each	Models
Retractable Pens	BBC Enterprises		60p each	Stationery
Role Playing Game	FASA Corporation	1985	$15.00 (£14.95 import)	Toys
Romana, Jo & Turlough Figures (DW11)	Citadel Miniatures	1985	£1.95	Models
RPG Supplement: City of Gold	FASA Corporation	1986	£5.50 import	Toys
RPG Supplement: Countdown	FASA Corporation	1985	$7.00 (£4.95 import)	Toys
RPG Supplement: The Cybermen	FASA Corporation	1986	£4.95 import	Toys
RPG Supplement: The Daleks	FASA Corporation	1985	$10.00 (£9.95 import)	Toys
RPG Supplement: The Hartlewick Horror	FASA Corporation	1985	$7.00 (£4.95 import)	Toys
RPG Supplement: The Iytean Menace	FASA Corporation	1985	$7.00 (£4.95 import)	Toys
RPG Supplement: The Legions of Death	FASA Corporation	1986	£5.50 import	Toys
RPG Supplement: The Lords of Destiny	FASA Corporation	1985	$7.00 (£4.95 import)	Toys
RPG Supplement: The Master	FASA Corporation	1985	$7.00 (£9.95 import)	Toys
RPG Supplement: The Sontarans (**May not have been produced**)	FASA Corporation	1986		Toys
RPG Supplement: The Warrior's Code	FASA Corporation	1986	£5.50 import	Toys
Sarah Jane Smith Postcard (From K9 and Company)	Larkfield Printing Co. Ltd.	1984	15p	Sundries
Sarah Jane Smith Postcard (From The Five Doctors)	Acanthus Press Ltd.	1983	15p	Sundries
Sarah Jane, Leela & Adric Figures (DW7)	Citadel Miniatures	1985	£1.95	Models
Save Doctor Who Stickers	Sun/Star Newspapers	1985	free	Promotions
Sci-Fi Sound Effects (REC 470 LP, ZCM 470 Cass)	BBC Records	1981	£2.99 (LP & Cass)	Records
Sea Devil Figures (3) (DW10)	Citadel Miniatures	1985	£1.95	Models
Second Doctor Postcard (From The Five Doctors)	Larkfield Printing Co. Ltd.	1984	15p	Sundries
Second Doctor Who Gift Set (5N, 5R, 5T, 5X)	W. H. Allen & Co. Ltd. (Target)	1982	£5.25 p/b	Books
Second Doctor Who Quiz Book, The (Nigel Robinson)	W. H. Allen & Co. Ltd. (Target)	1983	£1.35 p/b	Activity Books
Seventh Doctor Postcard	JCS Printers Ltd.	1987	15p	Sundries
Seventh Doctor Who Gift Set (FF, DDD, 6N, 6Q)	W. H. Allen & Co. PLC (Target)	1985	p/b	Books
Sixth Doctor Postcard (Publicity shot)	Larkfield Printing Co. Ltd.	1984	15p	Sundries
Sixth Doctor Who Gift Set (TT, 6F, 6H, 6K)	W. H. Allen & Co. PLC (Target)	1984	£6.50 p/b	Books
Slipback/Genesis of the Daleks Cassette (ZBBC 1020)	BBC Records and Tapes	1988	£5.99	Recordings
Slippers	Mothercare	1989		Clothing
Snap Pen (blue, white, yellow, red)	BBC Enterprises	1987	£1.00	Stationery
Sophie Aldred Photographs	Mediaband	1989	various	Sundries
Space Adventures (RDMP 1)	DWAS Reference Department	1987	£3.99 (cass)	Records
State of Decay Talking Book (1 Cassette) (PTB 607)	Pickwick International	1981	£2.25	Recordings
State of Decay Talking Book (2 Cassettes) (DTO 10517)	Ditto	1985	£1.99	Recordings
Sun Visor		1987	£1.99	Clothing
Susan Postcard (From The Five Doctors)	Acanthus Press Ltd.	1983	15p	Sundries
Sweat Shirt – 20 Years – A Celebration	Image Screencraft	1983	£5.95 (s) £7.95 (l)	Clothing
Sweat Shirt – Cyberman	Image Screencraft	1982	£5.95 (s) £7.95 (l)	Clothing
Sweat Shirt – Doctor Who (colour on Black)	Image Merchandising Ltd.	1987	£9.99 (S,M,L) £10.99 (XL)	Clothing
Sweat Shirt – Doctor Who (Pocket Phosphor on Navy)	Image Screencraft	1982	£5.95 (s) £7.95 (l)	Clothing
Sweat Shirt – K-9	Miles Bros.	1980	£5.25 (s) £6.75 (l)	Clothing
Sweat Shirts	BBC Enterprises			Clothing
Sylvester McCoy Photographs	Mediaband	1989	various	Sundries
T1 Playset	Dapol	1988	£49.75	Toys
Talking Book (Carnival of Monsters, The Three Doctors, The Loch Ness Monster)	RNIB	1981	-	Recordings
TARDIS	Dapol	1988	£12.00	Toys
TARDIS 3D Pencil Case	Hummingbird Productions Ltd.	1982	£1.75	Stationery
TARDIS 3D Pencil Case	Interwainer Handbag Co.	1982	£2.99	Stationery

TARDIS Bubble Bath	DMS Toiletries	1988	59p	Sundries
TARDIS Clock	K.B.W.	1988	£26.50	Sundries
TARDIS Console	Dapol	1988	£15.00	Toys
TARDIS Console Postcard	Larkfield Printing Co. Ltd.	1985	15p	Sundries
TARDIS Easter Egg	Tobler Suchard Ltd.	1982		Confectionery
TARDIS Flat Pencil Case	Hummingbird Productions Ltd.	1984	£2.99	Stationery
TARDIS Telephone	Holdcourt Ltd.	1988	£99.95	Sundries
TARDIS Tent	D. Dekker Ltd.	1982	£15.99	Toys
TARDIS Tin – The Fifth Doctor	Avon Tin	1982	£1.75	Toys
TARDIS Tin – The Fourth Doctor	Avon Tin	1980	£1.65	Toys
Tee Shirt – Cyberman	Acme Ltd.	1988		Clothing
Tee Shirt – Cyberman	Levendis Enterprises Ltd.	1989		Clothing
Tee Shirt – Cyberman (Green & Black on White)	Image Screencraft	1982	£3.25 (s) £3.95 (l)	Clothing
Tee Shirt – Dalek	Levendis Enterprises Ltd.	1989		Clothing
Tee Shirt – Daleks	Acme Ltd.	1988		Clothing
Tee Shirt – Daleks (3 colour screenprint)	Image Merchandising Ltd.	1984	£3.25 (s) £3.95 (l)	Clothing
Tee Shirt – Doctor Who (limited hand-printed background)	Image Merchandising Ltd.	1986	£5.99	Clothing
Tee Shirt – Doctor Who (Red & Yellow on White or Phosphor on Navy)	Image Screencraft	1982	£3.25 (s) £3.95 (l)	Clothing
Tee Shirt – Doctor Who Across The Universe (4 colour screenprint)	Image Merchandising Ltd.	1986	£3.99	Clothing
Tee Shirt – K-9	Miles Bros.	1980	£2.50 (s) £2.75 (l)	Clothing
Tee Shirt – TARDIS and K9 (2 designs)	Levendis Enterprises Ltd.	1989		Clothing
Tee Shirt – The Fifth Doctor (Colour art on White)	Image Screencraft	1983	£3.25 (s) £3.95 (l)	Clothing
Tee Shirt – The Ultimate Adventure		1989	£5.00	Clothing
Tee Shirts	BBC Enterprises			Clothing
Tegan Postcard (From *Logopolis*)	Larkfield Printing Co. Ltd.	1980	15p	Sundries
Tegan Postcard (From *Mawdryn Undead*)	Larkfield Printing Co. Ltd.	1983	15p	Sundries
Tetrap Figure	Dapol	1988	£2.99	Toys
The Adventures of K9 – 1: K9 and the Time Trap (David Martin)	Arrow Books Ltd. (Sparrow)	1980	65p p/b	Books
The Adventures of K9 – 2: K9 and the Beasts of Vega (David Martin)	Arrow Books Ltd. (Sparrow)	1980	65p p/b	Books
The Adventures of K9 – 3: K9 and the Zeta Rescue (David Martin)	Arrow Books Ltd. (Sparrow)	1980	65p p/b	Books
The Adventures of K9 – 4: K9 and the Missing Planet (David Martin)	Arrow Books Ltd. (Sparrow)	1980	65p p/b	Books
The Brigadier Postcard (From *Mawdryn Undead*)	Larkfield Printing Co. Ltd.	1983	15p	Sundries
The Doctor Who 25th Anniversary Album (REB 707 / ZCF 707 / BBC CD 707)	BBC Records and Tapes	1988	£6.49 (LP) £11.99 (CD) £6.99 (cass)	Records
The Doctor Who Celebration (programme)	BBC Enterprises/The Warminster Press	1983	50p	Miscellaneous
The Early Cybermen Cassette (SF-AT2)	Silver Fist	1989	£5.99 (cass)	Recordings
The Five Doctors Print	Who Dares Publishing	1984	£1.95	Sundries
The Master Postcard (From *Logopolis*)	Larkfield Printing Co. Ltd.	1980	15p	Sundries
The Master Postcard (Publicity shot)	Larkfield Printing Co. Ltd.	1982	15p	Sundries
The Ultimate Adventure Badge		1989	60p	Badges
The Ultimate Adventure Baseball Hats		1989		Clothing
The Ultimate Adventure Clock		1989	£10.00	Sundries
The Ultimate Adventure Photographs (two colour prints)	Mark Furness Ltd.	1989		Sundries
The Ultimate Adventure Posters (two different)	Mark Furness Ltd.	1989	£1.00 (s) £1.50 (l)	Posters
The Ultimate Adventure souvenir brochure (2 versions)	Peter Griffiths Associates	1989	£2.00	Sundries
The Ultimate Interview Colin Baker talks with David Banks (SF-UI 1)	Silver Fist	1989	£5.99 (cass)	Recordings
Third Doctor Postcard (From *The Five Doctors*)	Larkfield Printing Co. Ltd.	1984	15p	Sundries
Third Doctor Who Gift Set (5Z, 5W, 6B, 6G)	W. H. Allen & Co. Ltd. (Target)	1983	£5.75 p/b	Books
Third Doctor Who Quiz Book, The (Nigel Robinson)	W. H. Allen & Co. PLC (Target)	1985	£1.50 p/b	Activity Books
Time Lord Figures (4) (DW9)	Citadel Miniatures	1985	£1.95	Models
Timeflight (MAC-1)	Metro Music International	1987		Records
Tom Baker and K-9 Poster	Madame Tussauds	1982	£1.99	Posters
Turlough and the Earthlink Dilemma (Tony Attwood)	W. H. Allen & Co. PLC (Target)	1986	£1.80 p/b	Books
Turlough Postcard (From *Mawdryn Undead*)	Larkfield Printing Co. Ltd.	1982	15p	Sundries
TV and Movie Type Daleks	Sevans Models	1989	£17.95	Models
Umbrella	BBC Enterprises	1983	£6.00 (s) £7.00 (l)	Sundries
Underpants	British Home Stores	1980	85p	Clothing
UNIT Figures (3) (DW6)	Citadel Miniatures	1985	£1.95	Models
Very Best of Doctor Who, The (Marvel Summer Special)	Marvel Comics	1981	45p	Magazines
Video Disk: *Revenge of the Cybermen*	BBC Video	1985	£9.99	Video
Video Disk: *The Brain of Morbius*	BBC Video	1985	£9.99	Video
Video: *Daleks Invasion Earth 2150 A.D.*	Thorn EMI	1982	£39.95 (Beta, VHS)	Video
Video: *Daleks Invasion Earth 2150 A.D.*	Warner Home Video	1988	£9.99 (VHS)	Video
Video: *Death to the Daleks*	BBC Video	1987	£9.99 (VHS)	Video
Video: *Dr. Who and the Daleks*	Thorn EMI	1982	£39.95 (Beta, VHS)	Video
Video: *Dr. Who and the Daleks*	Warner Home Video	1988	£9.99 (VHS)	Video
Video: *Myth Makers 1* – Michael Wisher	Reeltime Pictures	1984	£8.95 (VHS)	Video
Video: *Myth Makers 10* – Deborah Watling	Reeltime Pictures	1986	£9.99 (VHS)	Video
Video: *Myth Makers 12* – Ian Marter	Reeltime Pictures	1987	£9.99 (VHS)	Video
Video: *Myth Makers 13* – John Levene	Reeltime Pictures	1987	£9.99 (VHS)	Video
Video: *Myth Makers 14* – Peter Grimwade	Reeltime Pictures	1987	£9.99 (VHS)	Video
Video: *Myth Makers 15* – Jon Pertwee	Reeltime Pictures	1989	£15.00 (VHS)	Video
Video: *Myth Makers 16* – Richard Franklin	Reeltime Pictures	1989	£10.00 (VHS)	Video
Video: *Myth Makers 17* – Tom Baker	Reeltime Pictures	1989	£15.00 (VHS)	Video
Video: *Myth Makers 18* – Marvel Comics	Reeltime Pictures	1989	£10.00 (VHS)	Video
Video: *Myth Makers 2* – John Leeson	Reeltime Pictures	1984	£8.95 (VHS)	Video
Video: *Myth Makers 3* – Nicholas Courtney	Reeltime Pictures	1985	£8.95 (VHS)	Video
Video: *Myth Makers 4* – Carole Ann Ford	Reeltime Pictures	1985	£8.95 (VHS)	Video
Video: *Myth Makers 5* – Janet Fielding	Reeltime Pictures	1985	£8.95 (VHS)	Video
Video: *Myth Makers 6* – Nicola Bryant	Reeltime Pictures	1985	£9.99 (VHS)	Video
Video: *Myth Makers 7* – Wendy Padbury	Reeltime Pictures	1986	£9.99 (VHS)	Video
Video: *Myth Makers 8* – Michael Craze	Reeltime Pictures	1986	£9.99 (VHS)	Video
Video: *Myth Makers 9* – Sarah Sutton	Reeltime Pictures	1986	£9.99 (VHS)	Video
Video: *Myth Runner*	Reeltime Pictures	1987	£15.00 (VHS)	Video
Video: *Panopticon VII*	Reeltime Pictures	1986	£15.00 (VHS)	Video
Video: *Pyramids of Mars*	BBC Video	1985	£24.95 (VHS, Beta)	Video
Video: *Pyramids of Mars*	BBC Video	1987	£9.99 (VHS)	Video
Video: *Revenge of the Cybermen*	BBC Video	1984	£24.95 (VHS, Beta, V2000)	Video
Video: *Revenge of the Cybermen*	BBC Video	1986	£9.99 (VHS)	Video
Video: *Revenge of the Cybermen* (two covers)	BBC Video	1983	£39.95 (VHS, Beta, V2000)	Video
Video: *Spearhead from Space*	BBC Video	1988	£9.99 (VHS)	Video
Video: *Terror of the Zygons*	BBC Video	1988	£9.99 (VHS)	Video
Video: *The Ark in Space*	BBC Video	1989	£9.99 (VHS)	Video
Video: *The Brain of Morbius*	BBC Video	1984	£19.95 (VHS, Beta)	Video
Video: *The Daleks* (two tape set)	BBC Video	1989	£19.99 (VHS)	Video
Video: *The Day of the Daleks*	BBC Video	1986	£24.95 (VHS, Beta)	Video
Video: *The Day of the Daleks*	BBC Video	1988	£9.99 (VHS)	Video
Video: *The Five Doctors*	BBC Video	1985	£24.95 (VHS, Beta)	Video
Video: *The Robots of Death*	BBC Video	1986	£24.95 (VHS, Beta)	Video
Video: *The Robots of Death*	BBC Video	1988	£9.99 (VHS)	Video
Video: *The Seeds of Death*	BBC Video	1985	£24.95 (VHS, Beta)	Video
Video: *The Seeds of Death*	BBC Video	1987	£9.99 (VHS)	Video
Video: *The Talons of Weng-Chiang*	BBC Video	1988	£9.99 (VHS)	Video
Video: *The Time Warrior*	BBC Video	1989	£9.99 (VHS)	Video
Video: *War Time*	Reeltime Pictures	1988	£10.00 (VHS)	Video
Wall Tiles	Pictiles	1982	£18.00 set of 9	Sundries
Wallpaper	Colouroll	1982	£2.50 per roll	Sundries
Warlord (Computer Game)	BBC Software	1985	£7.95	Toys
Who Is The Doctor by Jon Pertwee/*Doctor ...?* By Blood Donor (DOCTOR 1)	Safari Records	1985	£2.00	Records
Zig Zag Poster Magazine	BBC Education/BBC Information	1986	free	Magazines

Authors' Note: We have made every effort to ensure that this merchandise listing is as complete as possible, but if you have any further information about any of the items mentioned, or know of any items which are not listed, please contact the authors at the publisher's address at the front of this book.